African Language Literatures

An Introduction to the Literary History of
Sub-Saharan Africa

African Language Literatures

An Introduction to the Literary History of Sub-Saharan Africa

Albert S. Gérard

THREE CONTINENTS

First Edition

©1981 by Albert S. Gérard

American Edition (Three Continents)

ISBN 0-914478-65-6
     0-914478-66-4 (pbk)

LC No 79-3103

Three Continents Press, Inc.
1346 Connecticut Avenue, N.W., Washington D.C. 20036, U.S.A.

CONTENTS

Regional/Political Maps

FOREWORD

> I would be quite satisfied if my novels did no more than teach
> my readers that their past was not one long night of savagery
> from which the first Europeans delivered them.
>
> Chinua Achebe

Until about a dozen years after the end of World War II, sub-Saharan Africa was universally regarded as the homeland of an oral art, of which little was known and less understood. During the period that saw the preparation and the achievement of independence in the greater part of the continent, however, African creative writing in European languages grew rapidly, and soon came to be recognized as a legitimate topic for serious critical discussion and scholarly research. This was acknowledged as nearly officially as can be in 1965 when the monumental *Annual Bibliography* issued by the Modern Literature Association of America set up a special section devoted to African literature; until then, such few African items as had been tracked down had been unmanageably dispersed under a variety of headings, including the conveniently vague "etc." in "Canada, Australia, etc." In 1965, this new section listed 181 items, many of which were really about linguistics and folklore. Ten years later, the number had risen to 660, nearly all of them dealing with creative writing. During the sixties, too, courses on African literature began to adorn the curriculum of a large number of universities all over the world.

Most of these efforts, however, were and still are, mainly concerned with African writing in English, French and Portuguese. And yet, as early as 1955, a Swiss scholar had produced a remarkable book that dealt with imaginative literature created in several of the languages of southern Africa. Unfortunately, Peter Sulzer's *Schwarze Intelligens Ein literarisch-politischer Streifzug durch Süd-Afrika* failed to make an impact, most probably because it was written in German.

Likewise, Xhosa scholar A.C. Jordan's pioneering research into the beginning of Xhosa writing, published all too quietly in the journal *Africa South* during the period of 1957 to 1960, passed almost unnoticed.

Then, Janheinz Jahn's *Gesamtbibliographie der neoafrikanischen Literatur* supplied for the first time the basic bibliographical data concerning an unexpectedly large number of African works written in some fifty vernacular languages. This work (translated into English in 1965) has now been superseded by his more extensive *Bibliography of Creative African Writing*, which appeared in 1971, a few years before Jahn's untimely death.

Herdeck's *African Authors: A Companion to Black African Writing 1300 –
1973* (1973) provided often detailed bio-bibliographical-critical information on some 233 authors who had been published in 37 African
languages, but the Jahn bibliography remains the best inventory to date
of the total corpus of African language writings.

While Ulli Beier's *Introduction to African Literature* (1967) could discuss
vernacular art under the heading "The Oral Traditions", with no serious allusion to *written* (published) African-language creative literature,
it was evident that a balanced view of African writing could only be
gained when due consideration was given to the output in African tongues. The past decade has steadily focused scholarly attention in this
new field, but chiefly in the form of books and articles of a mono-
graphic kind, often dealing piecemeal with single works, authors, or
language.

Accordingly, Jahn's *Geschichte* was symptomatic of a further need that
was beginning to be felt—a desire for a general overview, a systematic
survey, of the whole of African writing. And it was in response to this
need that three Czech scholars, Vladimir Klíma, Karel F. Růžička and
Petr Zima, co-operated to produce *Literatura Cerne Afriky* (1972), an
English version of which was later published as *Black Africa: Literature
and Language* (1976). It is to the same need that the present book is
intended to minister, the difference being I have been able to draw on
much more information than was available to them and to Jahn, but I
have tried to organize the material along strictly diachronic historical
lines, something the Czech scholars had chosen to ignore.

The reader should not be allowed to suffer from delusions which the
author himself does not entertain. African writing is in more than fifty
different languages—often as different one from the other as Russian
is from Spanish, or even English from Chinese. No single person can
be seriously expected to master all, or even a small proportion of these
languages. Only a scholarly group, and a substantial one at that, could
ever hope to produce a totally satisfactory survey of African vernacular
writing.

Needless to say, such a team would have to be made up of African
scholars, for they alone are both able and entitled to offer cogent critical
comment on the works that have been written in their own languages.
What I have tried to do in this volume is to embark upon the task of
gathering as many relevant historical facts within my scope of knowledge
in languages that are known to me and ordering them into some sort
of coherent pattern covering the fifteen-odd centuries that have elapsed
since written composition began in Ethiopia.

Indeed, important segments of subsaharan Africa had been introduced to writing and to written literature long before the first white

man reached her shores. In fact, at least one part of the continent had produced written works in its own languages even before the earliest literatures appeared in western Europe in Celtic and Germanic languages. This was Ethiopia which was invaded at the beginning of the Christian era by Semitic tribes from southern Arabia. They brought their own alphabet with them which was gradually adapted for the transcription of the local Ethiopic tongue. Known as Ge'ez, it remained for several centuries the sole medium for religious thought, culture and literary writing. Indeed, this sacred language is still used today by conservative writers, mainly for the composition of hymns, theological treatises and other devotional works. The whole of Ge'ez literature has always been essentially religious and didactic in inspiration.

By the fourteenth century, the spoken language was very different from Ge'ez which had become an esoteric idiom, no longer understood by the common people. There thus arose a vernacular literature in a language known as Old Amharic. Its main source of inspiration was no longer sacred, but secular. The most important works preserved from that period are the so-called "imperial songs", praise poems in honour of the rulers of the time. It was not, however, until the twentieth century that Amharic was to gain the upper hand over Ghe'ez. It is now the main literary language of Ethiopia and has produced an impressive amount of works, not only in poetry, but also in the main genres imported under European influence: stage drama and prose fiction.

While the written art was thus being securely established in Ethiopia, a second wave of literacy swept over vast areas of subsaharan Africa with the Muslim conquest during the first few centuries after *hijra*. The new religion brought its own language, Arabic, and the Arabic script. But the history of Islamic writing in black Africa shows two distinct patterns of development.

In East Africa, along the coast of the Indian Ocean and on the offshore islands such as Zanzibar, close integration of immigrants of Arab stock into the native society created a hybrid culture with its own, non-Arabic, language: Swahili. The earliest preserved monuments of Swahili literature date back from the early eighteenth century. The essential feature of Swahili writing resides in the predominance of narrative poetry. In the eighteenth century, those epics dealt mainly with the life of Muhammad and his wars against the Christians soon after *hijra*: they were based on popular Arabic accounts. But in the nineteenth century a process of secularization set in and side by side with religious epics of the traditional kind, there appeared other narrative poems recounting major contemporary events in the experience of the Swahili community, such as the antagonism between the Sultan of Zanzibar and the governors of coastal towns, and, later, the resistance offered by the inland tribes to the invasion of the Europeans.

Muslim writing in West Africa followed an entirely different pattern. Black West Africa was originally converted to Islam by the Berber dynasty of the Almoravids in the eleventh century, and Sudanic Islam inherited the strong fundamentalist trend which is central to Berber religion. Two stages can be traced in the historical evoluͺ ͺn of this West African literature. Until the late eighteenth century, the Arabic language remained the sole medium for the written art. This led to the ʼemergence of Timbuctoo as a renowned centre of Islamic learning in the fourteenth, fifteenth and sixteenth centuries, and to the compositionʼ there of a large number of manuscripts dealing, in Arabic verse, with the major disciplines of Muslim culture. But in the eighteenth century, the fundamentalist trend in West African Islam took on a more proselytizing posture and the need was felt to make Muslim learning available to people in their own tongues. There thus arose several literatures of a type known as *ajami*, that is, using the Arabic alphabet for non-Arabic languages. As far as I have been able to ascertain, the languages concerned were Fulani in various parts of West Africa, Hausa in Northern Nigeria, and Wolof in Senegal. But it must be emphasized that a number of black *literati* have kept on producing poetry in Arabic to this day.

The Muslim cultures of black Africa have shown a remarkable resilience to the impact of the West, in part because they are firmly grounded in one of the great religions of the world. Only two of these literatures—Swahili in the East and Hausa in the West—have submitted to various forms of modernization, turning to the roman script, availing themselves of the printing press, and adopting, although with great caution and even reluctance, such alien genres as prose fiction and stage drama. The reason for this special development seems to be that the territories where these literatures flourished were parts of the British empire, whose representatives, unlike those of France, Portugal or Spain, gave genuine attention to the native languages and to the spreading of literacy in the African vernaculars.

This takes us to the third wave of literacy, which started covering the whole of black Africa in the nineteenth and twentieth centuries as a result of the European conquest. As we survey diachronically the literary consequences of western colonialism, we observe that it occurred in two phases, each of which has its own characteristic features.

Throughout the nineteenth century and well into the twentieth, apart from a few scattered experiments which are interesting but of no great numerical significance, literary activity came into existence in British territories, especially in Southern Africa, and was almost entirely in the vernacular languages. French colonial policies had the effect of educating the colonized Africans to become as French as possible and had for the most part alienated them from the common people, their own languages, and their own background. In the British colonies, on the other hand, cultural activities, especially teaching, were in the hands of Protestant missionaries, who found it easier and more expeditious to translate the Bible into African languages, their goal being to spread the Christian message rather than to teach English. As a result, a pattern thus developed, first of all in South Africa, but later in other areas as well: the missionaries learned the indigenous languages, reduced them to writing, taught their early converts reading and writing, and then translated and printed scriptural material. Writing, however, was a skill that was capable of many applications. Besides reading the Scriptures and often helping with the work of translating them, at an early stage converts were encouraged to do some writing of their own, in their own languages.

Much of this missionary-sponsored literature in African languages was and still is primarily concerned with moral edification and the propagation of Christianity. Bunyan's *The Pilgrim's Progress* became the most widely translated piece of western fiction, and it was imitated by many African writers of moralizing allegorical novels. As the nineteenth century wore on, however, there appeared vernacular writers, especially in South Africa, who were better educated and who were more and more outspoken about the abuses of white power. With the increasing industrialization and urbanization of South Africa after the first World War, black writers began to practise realistic prose fiction, but in their diagnosis of the African's plight, they felt it advisable to lay the emphasis on the failures of individual morality rather than on the injustice and oppressiveness built into the system.

Side by side with the interest in the ideas introduced by the white man and in the situations created by his activities, a second type of inspiration was operative in vernacular writing from the very beginning. For, in British Africa at any rate, generation after generation of newly educated writers displayed immense respect for their ancient oral traditions. And as the Celtic and Germanic peoples of Western Europe had done in the early Middle Ages, they availed themselves of the technological improvement brought by the new medium to commit to writing important fragments of their oral legacy: proverbs, praise poems, tales, myths, legends and historical chronicles.

While black Africa, then, with its large (although decreasing) percentage of illiteracy, still has a predominantly oral culture, written art in the roman script has been in existence since the early decades of the nineteenth century. Inevitably, that output is little known outside the continent and even outside the linguistic groups which produced it, although quite a few of those works have genuine intrinsic value as works of art, and not as pieces of anthropological or linguistic evidence, and deserve to be translated into more popular world languages.

The reason for the comparative dearth of interest in these works to
date resides of course in the fact that any serious student of any particular body of vernacular creative writing ought to have a thorough
knowledge of its languages and of the society where it is spoken, at the
same time as genuine expertise in the methods of literary history and
criticism. By contrast, European-language writing is in full swing in Africa today, further eclipsing the work being done in vernacular languages. But we might ask outselves how long this phenomenon will last.
As long as the predominance of Latin in medieval Europe? As long as
the predominance of Greek in Byzantium?

The enormous growth of popular fiction in English suggests that
there exists a fairly large readership which is not composed of what Ali
Mazrui cleverly called Afro-saxons—that is, members of the privileged,
educated middle class, whose mother tongue is English—but of ordinary
people who have reached a sufficient degree of literacy in the English
language to enjoy reading books in it and to make publishing such books
a profitable business proposition. It is possible that this trend toward a
brash, popular literature in European language may become stronger
as time goes on. Nonetheless, we should not be blind to another possi-
bility, illustrated at present by two well-known individual cases which
seem to me worth pondering.

The first is that of Ousmane Sembène, who, like many francophone
authors of his generation, has practically given up writing since independence. This was not because he had become an ambassador, a minister, or a head of state like so many of his intellectual contemporaries.
He found that he could come close to the ordinary people of Senegal
only by turning to the cinema, and producing movies in the people's
language, a sophisticated, modernized variety of traditional oral art,
strengthened by modern technology.

The second case is that of Ngugi wa Thiong'o. In the late seventies,
with an enviable social status as a professor at the University of Nairobi
and with his literary reputation firmly established throughout the English-speaking world and beyond, he decided to write a play in his own
language and had it performed in a village not far from Nairobi. The
play was mildly critical of the social situation in Kenya, though not as
forcefully as had been much previous writing in English, including his
own. Nevertheless, it earned Ngugi a year in detention and the loss of
his academic position for a period whose duration is, at this writing, still
indefinite. The work obviously had an appeal no book could claim with
the popular audiences, and of course it was their own language they
were hearing in such a dramatic fashion. The Government duly took
note.

These two cases suggest that the problem of the survival of European-language writing in Africa is far more complex and has wider implications than we, mere literary scholars, are apt to imagine. It is true that the young countries of Africa and their governments have an extra-literary need for the European languages.

Their spreading has a double effect: first, in the administration they help cement the unity of those poly-ethnic, multilingual forces that threaten their very existence (or they block an over-enthusiastic reaction to vernacular expression). Second, they are the only means of communication with the modern world, its technology and its science.

On the other hand, it is also true that many producers of imaginative literature in European languages are not very happy writing mainly for a foreign readership or for a tiny privileged minority in their own societies. Indeed, this was the function and role of Latin in the European middle ages and we should not forget that even in areas such as Spain and France which had been part of the Roman empire for several hundred years, the absolute monopoly and literary supremacy of Latin did not last for more than some six centuries after the fall of the empire.

Whether Europe's languages are in Africa to stay, or whether they will go the way of Latin, to become dead languages there and making room for triumphant vernaculars, is a matter that is not likely to be known until a few centuries to come.

Albert S. Gérard

KEY TO MAP

COUNTRIES

1 Morocco
2 Algéria
3 Tunisia
4 Libya
5 Egypt
6 Western Sahara
7 Mauritania
8 Mali
9 Niger
10 Tchad
11 Sudan
12 Ethiopia
13 Somalia
14 Senegal
15 Gambia
16 Guinea-Bissau
17 Guinea
18 Sierra Leone
19 Liberia
20 Ivory Coast
21 Upper Volta
22 Ghana
23 Togo
24 Benin

25 Nigeria
26 Cameroon
27 Central African Republic
28 Equatorial Guinea
29 Gabon
30 Congo (Brazzaville)
31 Zaïre
32 Uganda
33 Kenya
34 Rwanda
35 Burundi
36 Tanzania
37 Angola
38 Zambia
39 Malawi
40 Mozambique
41 Madagascar
42 Zimbabwe
43 Botswana
44 Namibia
45 South Africa
46 Swaziland
47 Lesotho

KEY TO MAP

LANGUAGES[1]

Akan (Fante + Twi) 2.000.000 (3.000.000[xx]) 22b, 22d, 22f
Akuapem Twi 22c
Amharic 4–8.000.000 .... 1, 2, 3, 4, 5, 6, 7, 8,
Arabic 9, 10, 11, 14, 16, 22,
Asante Twi 1.000.000[x] 25
Bamum 75.000 .... 12a
Bemba 400.000[xx] 22f
Bulu 110.000 (220.000[x]) 26d
Duala 23.000 .... 38a
Efik-Ibibio 2.000.000 (+) 26c
Embu 204.000 .... 26b
Ewe 1.000.000 .... 25d
Fante 33f
Fula 4–5.000.000 .... 22e + 23
Ga-Adangme 250.000 .... 22b
Ganda 1–2.000.000 .... 14a, 17a, 25a, 26a
Ge'ez 22c
Harari 35.000 12
Hausa 25.000.000 (12.000.000[x]) 32a
Idoma 250.000 .... 12d
Igbo 8.000.000 (?) .... 25a + 22g
Kamba 612.000 (1.200.000[xx]) 25e
Kikuyu 1.000.000 (2.200.000[xx]) 25c
Kinyarwanda 2.300.000 .... 33c
Kongo 3.000.000[x] 33b
Krio 34
Lenje 32.600 .... 31a
Lozi 18a
Luo 800.000 (1.500.000[xx]) 38e
Luvale 1.000.000[x] 38c
Luyia 713.000 .... 32d, 33d
Malagasy 7.000.000[xx] 38f
Mende 586.000 .... 33h 41 18b

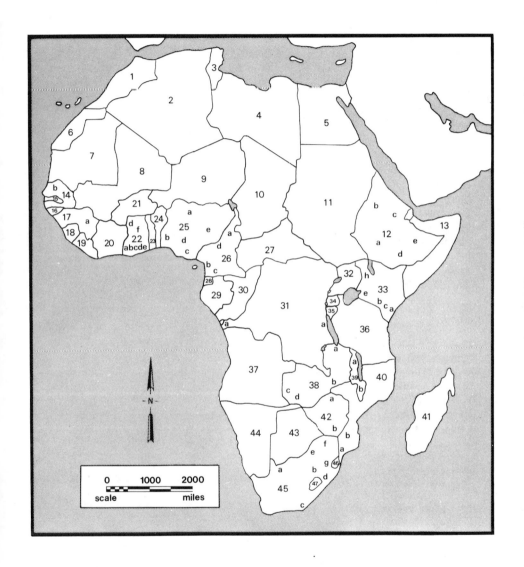

(1) Most figures are thoroughly unreliable. They are here given merely to provide the reader with an approximate idea of the relative importance of the languages concerned. Except when otherwise noted (see asterisks below), they are taken from Wm. E. Welmers, "Checklist of African Languages and Dialect Names", *Current Trends in Linguistics* VII (1971), 759–900.

(x) Figures from Bernd Heine, *Status and Use of African Lingua Francas* (Munich, 1970). Heine usually specifies his sources.

(xx) Figures from the *African Encyclopedia* published by the Oxford University Press (London, 1974). No sources given.

PART I

THE SABA INHERITANCE

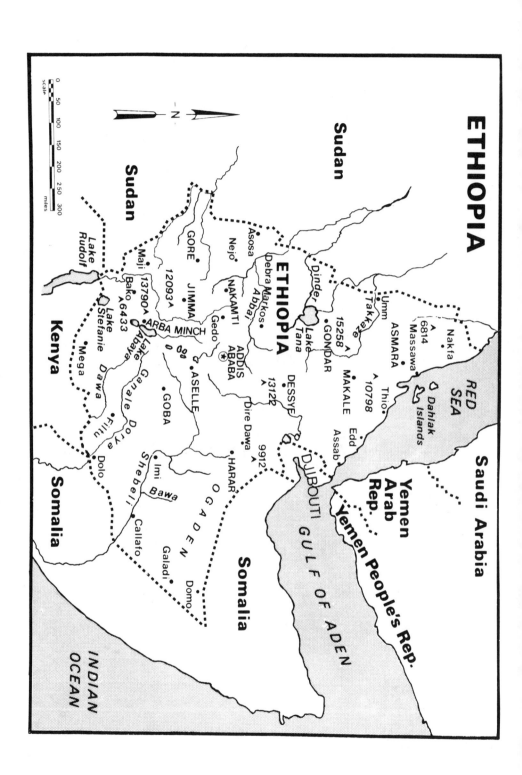

ETHIOPIA

Sudan

Sudan

Sudan

Kenya

Somalia

ETHIOPIA

RED SEA

Saudi Arabia

Yemen Arab Rep.

Yemen People's Rep.

GULF OF ADEN

DJIBOUTI

INDIAN OCEAN

scale
0
50
100
150
200
250
300
miles

N

Lake Rudolf

Lake Stefanie

Maji
Bako
13790
^6433
12093^

GORE

Nejo

Asosa

Debra Markos

Dinder

Lake Tana

Takkaze

Umm

ASMARA

Massawa

6814
Nakfa

Dahlak Islands

JIMMA

NAKAMTI

Abbai

Gedo

ARBA MINCH

ADDIS ABABA

ASELLE

GOBA

Mega

Filtu

Dolo

Genale Doria

Shebeli

Imi

Bawa

Callafo

Galadi

Domo

O G A D E N

HARAR

Dire Dawa

DESSYE

13122

15258

GONDAR

MAKALE

10798

Thio

Edd

Assab

9912

Mega

Dawa

CHAPTER ONE
THE LITERATURES OF ETHIOPIA[1]

1. The Axumite Period[2]

Except in a few uncommonly creative or peculiarly lucky societies, writing is imported, not invented. Centuries before Christ, Semitic tribes from South-Western Arabia began to settle on the African mainland, bringing over from Yemen their culture, the art of writing, and their Sabean dialects. They did not stay long on the inhospitable coastline of the Horn. At some unspecified date, they started moving to the mountainous area where the Blue Nile takes its source; there they mixed with the original African populations. Among the most powerful of those invaders or immigrants were the Habashat, who gave their name to Abyssinia, and the Agazi, whose language, Ge'ez, in the course of time, became the official language of Ethiopia. By the 3rd century B.C. their descendants had gained control of a vast territory stretching over present-day Eritrea and Northern Tigre, with Axum as its capital. Epigraphic evidence suggests that the Axumites first kept the Sabean language and alphabet, and later used the unvocalized Sabean script to transcribe their own language which, by then, had evolved considerably.

During the first half of the fourth century A.D., King Ezana (320–340) was converted to Christianity by an Alexandrian monk named Frumentius. This event had far-reaching consequences. For one thing, it made for fairly close relations with the eastern Roman Empire, where Constantine the Great had recently enthroned Christianity as the official religion. Further, a special relationship was established between Ethiopia and the Alexandrian church, whose patriarch enjoyed until recently the privilege of nominating the *Abuna*, the head of the Ethiopian church. During the fifth century, the Ethiopian church and a number of other Eastern churches embraced the Monophysite doctrine, which to this day has remained the central tenet of the Coptic Church. The Monophysite heresy holds that there is only one, divine, nature in the person of Christ: this denial of the human nature in Christ is probably responsible to a large extent for the almost manichean characteristics which Ethiopian culture has in common with Byzantine and other Middle Eastern Christian cultures: the rigid, authoritarian, dogmatic organization of church and society, the hieratic forms in the visual arts, the edifying and moralizing character of the written arts.

During the second half of the fifth century, the task of Christianizing the country was mostly pursued by Greek-speaking Monophysite monks from Syria. These early scholars were the real founders of Ethiopian literature, for they were responsible for completing the adaptation of the old Axumite script in such a way as to permit transcription of vowel sounds although rudimentary forms of this vocalized alphabet had already appeared on inscriptions dating from the reign of Ezana. Although no Ethiopian manuscript has survived from the period before the fourteenth century, it is known that by the end of the seventh century the whole of the Bible, including most of the Apocrypha, had been translated from the Greek into Ge'ez; indeed, the Ethiopian apocryphal book *Enoch* is the only complete version extant.

2. The Golden Age of Ge'ez

The spreading of Islam in the seventh century brought the Axumite kingdom to an end and ushered in a period of unrest and disorder which lasted until the late thirteenth century. Although Abyssinia was then surrounded by Muslim states which effectively severed its links with the outside world, it somehow managed to maintain the essentials of its independence and its basically Christian outlook. But the *political* centre of the country was forced southwards, into a region which had been settled in the earliest days of the Semitic invasions by the Amhara. The consequence of this was that by the tenth century Ge'ez had almost vanished from *spoken* usage, to be replaced by Amharic, though Ge'ez maintained its privileged position as the language of the liturgy, and of administration and culture, thus fulfilling the same functions as Latin enjoyed in Western Europe at the same time.

What has been called "the golden age of Ge'ez literature" began in 1270, when Yekuno Amlak (1270–1285) mounted the throne and founded a new dynasty which, over the next 250 years, managed to overcome the surrounding Muslim emirates and to strengthen Amhara supremacy. Several important literary developments occurred during this flourishing period. The reign of Amda Tseyon (1314–1344) saw the emergence of original Ethiopian writing, both religious and secular. Significantly, the earliest of these original works was the *Kabra Nagast* ("Glory of Kings"), still the most illustrious and widely venerated book in Ethiopia. It was written between 1314 and 1322 by members of the

Axumite clergy in order to vindicate the claims of the new dynasty. Its central part relates the journey of Makada, Queen of Sheba, to Solomon, and the birth of their son Menelik, whom the Hebrew Emperor himself installed as King of Ethiopia; the rest of the book is concocted of miscellaneous legends, some of which may well reflect earlier oral traditions or even historical truth. Their general purpose is to demonstrate the legitimacy of the new royal house on the basis of allegedly uninterrupted descent from Menelik and Solomon.

Under Amda Tseyon, major clashes occurred between Ethiopia and the chain of Muslim states to the East. The king's victories were duly recorded, in great detail and with uncommon freshness, by an anonymous priest who was also an eye-witness.[3] Thus began a form of writing which came to constitute a very important segment of Ethiopian literature, the royal chronicles; they were to be continued until the reign of Menelik II at the beginning of this century. According to Richard Pankhurst, they were:

> the work of court historians and as such are mainly concerned with court life. Their attention is centred on the sovereign's official life: his education, preparation for his high office, marriage and coronation, his wars and expeditions, appointments and dismissals of provincial governors and other officials, the issue of proclamations and decrees, the founding of towns and the building and endowment of churches, and the settlement of religious and other disputes and controversies, as well as various problems connected with the succession. Despite such emphasis on activity at court, the chronicles contain many passages of wider economic and social interest, affording us, for example, interesting descriptions of famine and epidemics, systems of taxation and the utilization of foreign craftsmen.
>
> The chronicles . . . were in most cases produced to perpetuate and glorify the memory of the ruler for whom they were written and who probably supervised their composition from time to time. Their authors tended inevitably to present the sovereign's character and actions in the best possible light rather than to attempt any impartial assessment. There were, however, cases in which the chroniclers wrote after the death of the sovereign whose reign they described. In such cases, the authors could write with greater freedom but might seek to blacken their subject's life in order to brighten the contrast with the rulers then in power. Despite such inevitable failings, the chronicles . . . are documents of immense historical value.[4]

Much of this, obviously, can also be said of the annals and chronicles compiled in Latin and in the vernaculars in fourteenth century Europe.

It is also from the times of Amda Tseyon that the earliest samples have been preserved of a secular poetic genre which had presumably

existed in oral form and which was to remain part of the creative tradition of Ethiopia to this very day. They are usually called "soldiers'
songs" or "imperial songs" or "war songs." Actually, they are praise
poems in honour of the reigning monarch. Their exceptional significance resides in the fact that they were written not in Ge'ez but in Old
Amharic, that is, in the vernacular tongue at the time of its differentiation from the official language of church and culture.[5]

However, the bulk of Ethiopian writing, during the fourteenth and
subsequent centuries, was of religious inspiration and still consisted
mainly of translations. Indeed, it is important to note that the biblical
translations from the times of Axum are still preserved while the original
manuscripts have long perished. Additionally, further ecclesiastical
works were made available in Ge'ez, including not only scriptural translations, but also liturgical, hagiographical and other devotional books.
The main agent of this literary breakthrough was an Egyptian Copt,
Abba Salama (d. 1387), who was appointed metropolitan of Ethiopia in
1350. By that time, the Egyptian Copts had adopted the Arabic language
and script, and Abba Salama had already translated a number of works,
and caused many others to be translated, not only from the Greek, but
from the Arabic as well.

Of special interest is Salama's version of the *Acts of the Martyrs*, still
one of the most popular books in Ethiopia : a holy man's life crowned
by martyrdom and salvation appeals greatly to the otherworldliness of
Ethiopian Christianity, and it was to remain a favourite topic for creative
writers well into the twentieth century.

Under King David (1382–1411), other monks produced the *Book of
the Miracles of Mary*, which has been traced back to a French collection
of the early thirteenth century through a slightly later Arabic version;
this, too, became highly popular, and became even more popular in the
middle of the fifteenth century.

It was also towards the end of the fourteenth century that the *Synaxarium*, the calendar of the Alexandrian saints, was translated from the
Arabic; the Ge'ez version being continuously enlarged during the next
two centuries.

Fruitful comparisons could be made between this derivative body of
hagiographical writing and the romances and saints' lives that had
formed the bulk of European literature in several languages one or two
centuries earlier. For example, the Ethiopian life of St. Alexis transfers
the story from Rome to Constantinople and makes the saint a son of
the Roman emperor Theodosius II, rather than of a Roman senator.
The original probably goes back to a Byzantine version, now lost. Even
more significant, the Ge'ez story of Alexander the Great is very unlike
the courtly romances which Alexander's life gave rise to in France and
other European countries. Nevertheless, like the many Western ver-

sions, it derives from the Pseudo-Callisthenes, but the Ethiopian tale descends from an Arabic version. In its emphasis on Alexander's chastity, however, it evinces a strong otherworldly character, not necessarily due to direct Manichean influence, but possibly the result of an organic adaptation to the ascetic dimension that is so central to Ethiopian Christianity.

Side by side with asceticism, the distinguishing feature of Ethiopian religiousness as it is reflected in literature is the taste for miraculous events and esoteric symbolism: this is clearly evident in the *Book of the Mysteries of Heaven and Earth*. This original work is a strange miscellany of legends and visions compiled by one Yeshaq, a monk who claims that those "revelations" were made by an angel to his master, Ba Haile Mikael. It is perhaps to the point to recall that in European literature the fourteenth century began with Dante's *Divine Comedy* and ended soon after Langland had produced the third version of *Piers the Plowman*.

While original composition of a devotional character had begun almost concurrently with secular writing, hagiographical writing reached its apogee under the son of David I, Zara Yaqob (1434–1468). It arose from the triple need to restore the unity of the Ethiopian Coptic church (threatened at the time by various heresies), to raise the educational level of the clergy, and, finally, to provide Christian substitutes for many pagan customs, legends and beliefs that were still widely held among the population. The king himself was a prolific producer of devotional compilations and treatises.

In order to counteract the popularity of magical incantations, persistent remnants from pagan times, Zara Yaqob encouraged the composition of Christian hymns, which were to become, under the name of *qenè*, the most important single poetic genre in Ethiopian literature. According to a tradition which no objective evidence has substantiated, original hymn-writing in Ge'ez goes back to an Axumite poet called Yared. What is sure is that the earliest hymns which have been preserved were composed in the fourteenth century, the best-known collection being the *The Praise of Mary*, compiled by Abba Salama. Two further collections were composed under Zara Yaqob: *God's Reign* and *The Harp of Mary*. But it was apparently under his successor Eksender (1478–1494) that hymn-writing received the distinctive features that were to make the genre, in the words of Donald Levine, "a key to the genius of Amhara culture and a highly distinctive Amhara contribution to Ethiopian culture." For, in Amhara society, most poetry, and indeed a considerable proportion of all verbal communication, is based on the wax and gold principle, a metaphorical form of expression in which the figurative meaning of the words is called "wax" and their hidden meaning "gold." As Levine further says,

The chief delight of Ethiopic poetry is to attain a maximum of thought with a minimum of words. This effect is reached . . . through subtle allusions and plays on words. The point may be a serious moral comment, the understanding of which requires one to decipher hidden references to biblical passages or sacred legends; or it may be a jest about love based on a pornographic pun. In any case, the more ingeniously compact and obscure the construction of the verse, the more pleased will be the poet and his audience. . . . The creation of the wax and gold figures was an integral part of the development of qenè, *the genre of verse composed to be sung at the conclusion of devotional services in the church. . . . Educated Amhara traditionalists extol wax and gold as a unique creation of their culture. . . . They further maintain that Ge'ez* qenè *contains a unique kind of wisdom, dark and deep. Instruction in this occult art of verse composition has traditionally been regarded as propaedeutic to the study of religious texts. Partly this is because Ge'ez grammar, which must be known in order to understand those texts, is normally taught only in the schools of* qenè. *The more philosophical reason given, however, is that by affording exercise in fathoming secrets it "opens the mind" and thereby enhances the student's ability to approach the divine mysteries.*[6]

Because of the vast amount of scriptural erudition required for its understanding, and because of its esoteric metaphorical system—which cannot but call the European scholar's mind to the *Kenningar* of Scaldic poetry—*qenè* composition has maintained an unparalleled prestige in the Amhara provinces of Ethiopia to this day, both in Ge'ez and in Amharic.

The last significant novelty, introduced in the fifteenth century, was the emergence of local hagiography. In a mood of religious nationalism, and self-reliance, Ethiopian monks whose piety had hitherto fed on the Alexandrian saints of the *Synaxarium,*began to celebrate the holy men of their own church : not only the saintly abbots of such renowned monasteries as Debra Libanos, or the thirteenth-century monk Takla Haymanot, who allegedly contributed to the advent of the Solomonian dynasty in 1270, but also earlier kings such as Lalibala (1190–1225), the builder of the famous monolithic churches.

3. The Decline of Ge'ez Writing

After two centuries of remarkable growth, Ge'ez literature began to wane in the sixteenth century, when Ethiopia was affected by the tremendous Turkish expansion that was leading, in Europe, to the annexation of the whole Balkan peninsula to the Ottoman empire. In 1529, the very year when the Turks reached Vienna, Imam Ahmed Grañ b. Ibrahim el Ghazi of Harar, supplied with Turkish arms, proclaimed a holy war (*jihad*) and defeated the army of Negus Lebna Dengel (1508–1540). The Ethiopians turned to the Portuguese (whose ships had first reached the eastern coast of Africa in 1494) to obtain support in the fight against the Muslims. Some 400 Portuguese soldiers reached Ethiopia in 1541. Ahmed's army was defeated and its leader killed in 1543. But the Amhara kingdom had been utterly exhausted by fifteen years of war, and was unable to prevent the inroads of the Galla, who conquered about a third of Abyssinia's territory between 1545 and 1570. At the same time, the Portuguese troops had been supplemented by Portuguese Jesuits who, in the wake of the Counter-Reformation, began proselytizing for the Catholic church.

The main centre of Muslim activity was Harar, which soon became a focus of Islamic literature as well. Part of this was written in Arabic, as exemplified in the *Story of the Conquest of Abyssinia,* whose author, Shihab ed-din Ahmed ibn Abd al-Kader, was nicknamed "the Arab lawyer" because he had studied Koranic law in Yemen. But there also emerged a literature in Harari, a Semitic language akin to Ge'ez and Amharic: this was writing of the *ajami* (foreign) type, in that it made use of the Arabic script for a non-Arabic language. One of those Harari works was the *Book of Duties,* a précis of the Moslem creed, partly couched in the form of aphoristic proverbs. Another was the *Lay of the Four Caliphs,* a long poem of about 5000 lines celebrating the four Caliphs of Sunnite Islam.

As many Ethiopian Christians had been more or less forcibly converted to Islam during the period of Ahmed Grañ's victories, a large proportion of Ge'ez writing of the sixteenth century was designed to encourage such apostates to recant. One of the most prolific authors was Embaqom,[7] himself once a Moslem merchant, probably of Iraqi origin, who was converted to Christianity and became prior of the monastery at Debre Libanos; it seems that he renounced his office in 1526 to devote himself to study and writing. Apart from his *The Gate of Faith,* written in refutation of Islam, he is chiefly remembered for providing, in 1553, a Ge'ez version of the legend of *Barlaam and Josaphat.* This was originally an Indian story relating how Siddharta, aged 29, had left his wife, his children and his riches, to lead a humble beggar's life; after seven years, as he was resting under a fig-tree, he received the light in a vision and was henceforth known as "Buddha" (the Enlightened One). Making its way through Persia, the tale became transposed into Christian terms, presumably in Afghanistan in the sixth century : Siddharta became Prince Josaphat, who left his pagan father and the luxury and temptations of this world to become converted to Christianity by a holy hermit named Barlaam. The story immediately appealed to the otherwordly characteristics in Oriental, and indeed in most medieval, Christianity : it was first translated into Syrian, Armenian and Hebrew;

a Greek version was composed in the eleventh century, apparently by St. John Damascenus; and this was soon made available in a Latin translation, a summary of which was included in the *Legenda Aurea*, which was itself the main source for the many versions in Western languages. Embaqom's Ge'ez rendering was based on a Christian Arabic version which had been composed well before the thirteenth century.

Ge'ez literature in the sixteenth century returned to the essentially derivative character of its beginnings. Because of the Ethiopian Church's association with Alexandria, sources used during the Axumite period had been Greek; for the same reason, Christian literature in Arabic became the main source for Ethiopian *literati* after the Arab conquest of Egypt. Direct Western influence, however, was not totally absent. A Portuguese trader, Francesco Alvarez, who visited Ethiopia in 1521–1525, reported the existence of a Ge'ez *Life of Saint Sebastian*, which was later shown to have been translated from a ninth-century Latin *vita* erroneously attributed to St. Ambrosius.

As no Old Amharic war songs were preserved after the reign of Zara Yaqob, original Ethiopian writing remained confined to the enlargement of hymn collections and to the continuation of the royal chronicles under Lebna Dengel (1508–1540), Galawdewos or Claudius (1540–1559) and Sartsa Dengel or Malak Sagad (1563–1597). To these writings should be added the *History of the Galla* composed *c.* 1595 by a court priest named Bahrey.

Yet the most dangerous threat to the autochthonous quality of Ethiopian culture came from the Jesuit missionaries who had been sedulously active since 1557. Their influence at court threatened to disrupt the religious and political unity of the country. King Sartsa Dengel, in fact, was killed by his Coptic vassals after his conversion to western Christianity, and one of his successors, Susenyos (1607–1632), was forced to abdicate after his unsuccessful attempt to turn Catholicism into the official religion of the country. Finally, Fasilidas (1632–1667) felt he had to expel the Jesuits from Ethiopia, and even made arrangements with the Muslim emirs of the coastal states to have all Catholic priests who attempted to reach Ethiopia put to death.

But ideas, too, were to be fought against. And less than three decades after Embaqom had composed *The Gate of Faith* in defence of Christianity against Islam, King Galawdewos himself wrote a *Confession of Faith* containing an apology of the Coptic faith and of Ethiopian church customs in refutation of Catholic criticisms. On the other hand, it seems that contact with and discussion of Catholic doctrines prompted a more extreme reassertion of Ethiopian transcendentalism in the form of a revival of the Michaelite heresy which had been successfully repressed in the fifteenth century by Zara Yaqob. The Michaelites proclaimed the absolute impotence of the human mind, and especially its inability to gain any knowledge of God. The doctrine was expounded in the six-teenth century in a treatise entitled *Interpretation of the Godhead,* whose convoluted, allusive style makes it almost impenetrable to lay minds. Further, Catholic missionaries, such as the Spanish Jesuit Pedro Paez (1564–1622), who had arrived in Ethiopia in 1604, were also keen stu-dents of the country's vernacular language, to which they resorted for missionary purposes. This "popular" attack from within compelled the Coptic clergy to retort in kind, and by the late sixteenth and early sev-enteenth centuries, a number of devotional works had been translated from Ge'ez into Amharic, including a Psalter and Abba Salama's *Praises of Mary.* Once the Jesuits had been expelled, however, and their books burnt, religious writers felt free to turn back to the sacred language, even though vernacular words and turns of speech would crop up with increasing frequency in the royal chronicles of the seventeenth and eighteenth centuries. The fact remains that vernacular (i.e. Amharic) writing of the period arose out of the need for the Coptic church to counteract the influence of European missionaries among the lower clergy and the illiterate population.

Until the first quarter of the seventeenth century, a modicum of po-litical unity and administrative efficiency in the kingdom had been en-sured by the fact that the monarchs did not have a fixed capital. Instead, they kept an itinerant court, a procedure which enabled them to control their vassals fairly regularly. But in 1636 Fasilidas established his capital in the city of Gondar. Court historiographers continued the royal chron-icles, and the vogue of *qenè* persisted unabated. Under Iyasu the Great (1862–1706), a few more Arabic works were translated and the *Fetha Nagast* ("Laws of the Kings")—a compilation of civil and canon law prepared for the Coptic church of Egypt in the thirteenth century—became the legal code of Ethiopia for nearly three hundred years. One of the last works to be translated into Ge'ez was *Spiritual Medicine,* a penitential manual, by Michael, Bishop of Atrib. In 1706, Iyasu the Great was assassinated by his son Takla Haymanot (1706–8), and the empire fell apart. A time of chaotic feudal division and unruliness set in, known as the era of the *masafint* (princes), which was not brought to an end until the middle of the nineteenth century.

4. The Emergence of Amharic[8]

Ethiopia, then, is the first country in subsaharan Africa to have pro-duced a written literature of its own, whose origins are practically con-temporary with those of the earliest literatures of Western Europe. Im-pressive though this achievement undoubtedly is, it is necessary to emphasize that Ge'ez literature could only be written and read by an

upper class minority of the population. Couched in a language which
had fallen into disuse for centuries, it had many features in common
with the Latin literature of the European Middle Ages. The product of
a theocentric society, it had also much in common with Byzantine literature. It was expressly designed to bolster the position of the Coptic
church which was, throughout the centuries, the pillar of Ethiopian
society. To the common people it was as unintelligible as Church Latin
was to Catholic congregations of the same period. We cannot doubt that
there was in existence a corpus of oral art in the vernacular, far more
lively and picturesque and original than the pious output of Coptic
clerics. But it is highly probable that vernacular folk art was held in
utter contempt by the *literati* in Ethiopia as it was, until the late eleventh
century at the earliest, in the areas which had been part of the Roman
Empire in Western Europe, and, until the fifteenth century, throughout
the Byzantine empire.

Two reasons account for the spasmodic and short-lived emergence of
vernacular writing prior to the nineteenth century. The "imperial
songs" were written down, in all probability, because it was in the
interest of the rulers to have such praise poems preserved and disseminated. And, towards the seventeenth century, as noted, religious Ge'ez
works were translated into Amharic in response to the threat presented
by Catholic priests who used the language of the people to spread their
own doctrine.

A similar combination of political and religious factors was powerfully
at work in the nineteenth century and ensured the ultimate triumph of
Amharic, even though some devotional literature and many *qenè* are still
produced in Ge'ez. The main agents of this portentous change were
King Tewodros II and the European, mainly Protestant, missionaries.

The Gondarine dynasty came to an end when an upstart adventurer
called Kassa vanquished the feudal lords of Gojjam, Gondar and Tigre,
and had himself crowned as Tewodros II at Axum in 1855. His ambition was to restore the unity of Ethiopia and the emperor's authority
over the feudal lords. In order to increase the efficiency of his army, he
welcomed Western missionaries in spite of their religious affiliations
because he hoped to exploit their supposed technological abilities to his
own benefit.

One of the two trends that thus converged towards the establishment
of Amharic as a literary language was Tewodros's determination to
gain popular support, by-passing the feudal lords and the clergy in
order to reach the common people, who could be read to in the latter
language. The results of this policy were of tremendous significance in
the development of Ethiopian literature. It is important to note that
both Dabtara Zareb and Alaqa Walda Maryam, the authors of the royal
chronicles dealing with Tewodros, used Amharic, even though they

were hostile to the king's policies. So did the chronicler of Tewodros's successor, Yohannes (1871–1889), who was a Tigrean. And Menelik II, who ruled as King of Shoa (1865–1889) before he was crowned emperor of Ethiopia (1889–1913) had his own chronicle written in Amharic by Gäbrä Sellasse, who became Minister of the Pen in 1907, when Menelik formed the first-western-type government of Ethiopia.

The second trend was due to the eagerness of the western missionaries likewise to address the people in the latter's own tongue in order to convert them to various brands of Western Christianity. Yet, in this respect, the earliest Amharic products of missionary enterprise in the mid-nineteenth century are curious freaks. Attributed to two seventeenth-century "Abyssinian philosophers", *The Quest of Zara Yaqob* and *The Quest of Walda Maryam*, two short treatises, exhibit a spirit of doubt and scepticism which is utterly alien to Ethiopian cultural tradition. Later research has shown them to be the work of a Capucin missionary, Giusto da Urbino (1814–1856), who wrote them at a time of spiritual crisis and despondency, and under the inspiration of *Les soirées de Carthage* (1847) by the third-rate French writer, François Bourgade (1806–1866).

The European contribution to Ethiopian writing began in earnest under Yohannes IV (1871–1889) when Protestant missionaries started composing didactic works in Amharic and in several other Ethiopian languages. Martin Flad produced an Amharic version of the Bible stories which Heinrich Barth, the German explorer, had originally arranged for missionary use in West Africa; this was later (1920) printed in Asmara. Charles William Isenberg wrote a treatise in Amharic, somewhat ambitiously entitled *History of God's Kingdom from the Creation of the World to Our Day,* which went through a second edition in 1893.

It must be remembered, however, that the early missionaries, Protestant as well as Catholic, were mainly based not in Amhara country but in Eritrea. There they enjoyed the protection of the Italian government which had secured a foothold on the Red Sea coast at Assab (1882) and Massawa (1885). The French had occupied Jibuti in 1885, and French Capucins were soon at work among the Galla in Dire Dawa. As a result, several peripheral, non-Amharic languages, such as Tigré, Tigrigna and Galla were reduced to writing. Indeed, some attempts were made to use the Arabic, rather than the Amharic, script for the Moslem Galla. Those initiatives did not lead to any literary activity worth mentioning, except in the case of Tigrigna, which is spoken in Northern Eritrea and the neighbouring areas.

Admittedly, Tigrigna had already been used, in the days of Tewodros, for writing poems, some of which have been preserved, but the main impulse came from the Swedish Evangelical Mission and, to a smaller extent, the Franciscan Catholic Mission, both based in Asmara. It was in response to this challenge that Ethiopian churchmen wrote a Tigrigna *Treasury of the Faith* which contains a restatement of and apology for, Monophysite doctrines. Conceivably, Teresa de Sanctis' Tigrigna version of *The Pilgrim's Progress*, which was published by the Swedish Mission in 1934, could have acted—as Bunyan's ubiquitous work did in many parts of subsaharan Africa—as an incentive to original fiction by local authors. This, however, did not occur, and no imaginative literature seems to have been produced in any of the non-Amharic vernaculars of Ethiopia.

It was also during the last decade of the century that the missionaries introduced the printing press.[9] The earliest printed books in Amharic were produced at the St. Chrischona mission press in Switzerland in the 1870s. It was there that Martin Flad edited Gäbrä Giyorgis Terfé's Amharic version of *The Pilgrim's Progress* in 1892. The first local press was founded at the Swedish Evangelical Mission in Menkullu in 1885; it was transferred in 1895 to Asmara which the Italians had made the seat of the colonial government: it issued many works in Tigrigna, and also a few works in Tigré by Karl Gustav Roden. In contrast, it was not until World War I that Catholic book production made a start, in both Asmara and Dire Dawa.

Important though the missionary contribution to the emergence of modern writing and printing in Amharic may have been, the main steps in its development were an outgrowth of the deliberate modernizing policy of Menelik II and his successor Haile Sellassie I. In order to bolster the inner unity of this large, heterogeneous country, and in order to maintain its independence in the face of Western colonial aggression, they had to fight against both the unruliness of the feudal lords and the resistance of the Coptic clergy. They had to foster a sense of nationhood and to introduce technological innovation. The key was education, of a type utterly different from that offered by the traditional monastic schools, whose curriculum was limited to the Ge'ez language, *qenè* composition, theological discussion, and liturgical music. With this end in view, Menelik, in 1887, sent a few gifted young men to Europe to acquire a modern education. One of these, Afäwärk Gäbrä Iyasus (1868–1947) was to become Ethiopia's first novelist: as an assistant in Semitic languages at the Instituto Orientale in Naples, he wrote a book entitled *Fictitious Story* (1908), which combines the narrative techniques characteristic of oral art, the overtly moralizing intention of all Ethiopian writing, and a remarkable mastery of the resources of the Amharic language.[10]

Afäwärk's book was printed in Rome. But when Ras Tafari (the future Emperor Haile Sellassie) was proclaimed regent in 1917, one of his first acts was to acquire a printing press, the first in Ethiopia proper. This was directed by a bright young man of humble origin, Heruy

Wäldä Sellassie (1898–1938), who was to be appointed Ethiopia's first Foreign Minister in 1930. Side by side with his many political and administrative duties, Heruy managed to become the real founder of modern Amharic literature. Not only did he write a large number of edifying and didactic moral and historical treatises, as well as collections of *qenè*, but he also authored the next two Ethiopian novels. *The Marriage of Brehane and Tseyon Mogasa* (1931–1932) was a critique of the widespread custom of child-marriage. *The New World* (1932–33), his second novel, may very well be the first African novel dealing with the fate of a protagonist educated in Europe; it is a biting satire of the superstitious beliefs and immoral customs that he perceived among the lower clergy and the illiterate masses; it contains a strong plea for Western technology; at the same time, it advocates a return to the pristine purity of Christian ethics, unencumbered by the heavy coating of misoneism spread upon it during centuries of conservative clerical omnipotence.

5. The Flowering of Amharic Literature

The Italian conquest in 1936 brought the efforts of Heruy and of a handful of other, lesser writers to a temporary stand-still. Part of the Ethiopian élite was massacred by General Graziani. Access to higher education was efficiently prevented. As has been usual with Latin colonial powers, vernacular writing was discouraged. Ethiopia's subjection fortunately did not last for more than five years. Yet it was responsible for wide-ranging changes in creative literature. This became apparent soon after the liberation (1941) in the novels and plays of Mäkonnen Endalkačäw (1892–1963). A prominent representative of the wealthy feudal class, Mäkonnen played an important role in the political life of the country. But although he executed the emperor's modernizing policies with unflinching loyalty, his writings were exceedingly conservative in outlook. Between 1947 and 1963, he published some fifteen novels and plays which testify to the revulsion of the traditionally-minded element in the Ethiopian intelligentsia against the Western cultural traits which had been so strenuously advocated by Heruy. Only a few of Mäkonnen's works can be dubbed anti-colonialist, in so far as they deal with patriotic resistance against the Italians; but even these are ultimately designed to glorify martyrdom in the service of church and nation. Mäkonnen was addicted to tireless propagation of the ideals of the Coptic church, stressing the vanity of earthly things and absolute subservience to God's will as against the Western values of individualism and economic progress.

The only noteworthy writer who pursued Heruy's modernizing ideas was Germačäw Täklä Hawaryat (b. 1915), a member of the younger

generation that also emerged upon the Ethiopian literary scene in the
1940s. Like Heruy's *The New World*, his only novel, *Ar'aya* (1948–49)
centres on a young man who is educated abroad and attempts to put
his new skills at the service of his people; significantly, Germačäw's hero
is thwarted by court intrigues in government circles rather than by the
general misoneism of clergy and peasants as was the case for Heruy's
protagonist. It is also worth observing that Germačäw's only play, *Tewodros* (1949–50), presents the nineteenth-century emperor not as an
ambitious upstart but as the precursor of modern Ethiopia, and stresses
his determination to subdue both the clergy and the feudal landlords—
a view which is utterly different from that later to be proposed by Mäkonnen Endalkačäw in one of his novels, *Taitu Bitull* (1957–58).

Not unexpectedly, Germačäw was the only writer of his generation
who was truly appreciated by the budding intellectual élite bred in the
modern secondary schools created after World War II, at the University
College of Addis Ababa (founded 1950), and in English and American
institutions of higher learning. During the 1940s and the 1950s, intense
literary activity, usually under official sponsorship, resulted in a large
number of novels, poems, and plays. Most of these were of a regressive
nature. Praise poems in honour of the emperor's birthdays and of other
state occasions were a recurrent feature of Amharic literary life; so were
novels and plays warning against the dangers of devilish foreign habits
ranging from alcoholism and prostitution to individualism in love and
lust for money and comfort. Patriotism was mandatory. Vice was to be
condemned and punished, virtue to be extolled and rewarded with relentless explicitness. Apart from Germačäw, the only writer who departed from this tradition of conformity was Käbbädä Mikael (b. 1915),
who deserves recognition for creating modern stage drama in Addis
Ababa. Even though the many historical and allegorical plays which he
has published since 1942 illustrate the same orthodox alignment in
theme and outlook, his wide-ranging knowledge of Western literature
and languages enabled him to attain new levels of theatrical skill in plot
construction and dialogue.

Yet even Käbbädä's work was not of a kind to stir much enthusiasm
among the younger members of the Ethiopian intelligentsia, men who
were very conscious of the agonizing social and moral problems of the
day, which elder writers chose serenely to ignore. As one of them,
Menghistu Lemma, was to observe in a newspaper of the capital in 1965,

*The vice that bedevils contemporary Amharic literature is not its preoccupation
with topical subject matter and theme, but the flood of crude didacticism that
overwhelms it. In such a state of affairs replete with all sorts of bogus pro-
fundities, every peddler of moral platitudes assumes the robe of the prophet and
moral philosopher.* [11]

In the political field, the coup engineered by a group of junior army officers against Haile Sellassie in December 1960 made it palpably obvious that the educated young were no longer satisfied with the slow tempo of cautious modernization that the emperor had managed to impose upon his country in the face of opposition to such a policy on the part of powerful segments of the aristocracy, the clergy, and the peasant masses. Whereas the Ethiopian élite had remained for centuries confined in confident self-satisfaction and—with the exception of a few forward-looking men, usually of humble origin, whom Haile Sellassie had selected to execute his designs—confident in the unparalleled excellence of their beliefs, traditions and culture, the slow but steady growth of education opened the eyes of the young to the outside world. They became aware that full self-government was no longer Ethiopia's monopoly in subsaharan Africa; they realized that new independent nations were arising with more progressive institutions, and stronger orientations towards social democracy and economic growth. Their desire for change reverberated in literature as well. Already in 1956–57, two younger writers of Galla origin, Taddäsä Libän and Beka Nämo, had produced prose fiction whose realistic style and outlook marked a revolutionary departure from the usual rigidity and conventional sanctimoniousness of Ethiopian writing.

This new trend was brought to the stage in 1962, when Menghistu Lemma (b. 1925) produced *Snatch and Run, or Marriage by Abduction*,[12] a witty satire aimed at the misguided attempts of youthful Ethiopian intellectuals at establishing some artificial form of syncretism between old traditions and Western manners. This comedy was extremely successful among the intelligentsia of the capital and established Menghistu as the literary leader of the new generation. It showed decisive evidence that modern Amharic creative writing was at last freeing itself from the mental authoritarianism that had dominated countless generations of Ethiopian authors. So, the critical outlook that had been daringly but prematurely introduced by Heruy decades earlier, was now expressed in a spirit of mild-hearted satire rather than ponderous moralizing: it is obvious in Menghistu's *The Marriage of Unequals*,[13] a light comedy that deals with the antagonism between family authoritarianism and the individualistic idealism of the educated young in the sphere of work and marriage.

6. Ethiopian Creative Writing in English

A revealing manifestation of the Ethiopian intelligentsia's determination to overcome its age-long isolation and to establish contacts with the outside world was the emergence of creative writing in English during the mid-1960s.[14] This urge had even earlier led to Ethiopian *literati* translating some of their Amharic works into European languages. An English version of three plays by Mäkonnen was published by his son in 1955,[15] and Käbbädä turned into French several of his own plays, only one of whose translations, however, reached print.[16]

Original composition in English first took the form of a couple of clumsy chapbooks. One of them, *The Savage Girl*, was an uninspiring "play" by Abbe Gubegna (b. 1934), who was Ethiopia's only full-time writer and a best-seller of a sort in Amharic. Later, he participated in the International Writing Program instituted by the University of Iowa, and produced a fine novel about the Italian occupation, *Defiance* (1975).

Tsegaye Gabre-Medhin (b. 1935), produced several plays, his best, *Oda Oak Oracle* (1965), being the first Ethiopian work to be published in London. A haunting poetic tragedy of a kind that had never been attempted in Ethiopia before, Tsegaye's drama turned away from the usual preoccupation of earlier writers with Coptic otherworldliness. The plot takes place in an unidentified pagan society, swayed by the erratic, inhuman demands of the ancestors as conveyed by the oracle-man; as such, it perhaps provides a more faithful reflection of the actual creed and ethos of large segments of the Ethiopian population than any earlier writing. While Tsegaye unostentatiously brings out the cruelty and frustrations resulting from crude superstitions, he also shows himself aware of the deep logic that underlies traditional communal life; and while the only Christian character is exposed as a weakling and a coward, the playwright makes it clear that virtue and a man's worth do not lie in formal adherence to any fixed set of beliefs, but in personal courage and inner integrity.

Meanwhile, the existence of a very active Department of English at the University of Addis Ababa was leading, firstly, to improved standards of English among Ethiopian students, and secondly, through a literary journal unassumingly entitled *Something,* to an increased output of imaginative writing in English, chiefly in the form of poems and short stories.

The complexity of the modern Ethiopian writer's linguistic predicament is well illustrated by the case of Sahle Sellassie Berhane Mariam (b. 1936). His first book was originally written in one of Ethiopia's minor languages, Chaha, chiefly as an ethnographic and linguistic document; it was translated into English as *Shinega's Village* (1964). This was followed by another, predominantly documentary novel, *The Afersata* (1968), which dealt with traditional judicial procedure. Sahle Sellassie then wrote several articles and short stories, in English and in Amharic, for Ethiopian and East African journals. He was also said to have published a novel in Amharic by the time he issued his third English book, *Warrior King* (1974), a historical novel about Tewodros, a monarch who seems to hold a peculiar fascination for recent Ethiopian writers.[17]

The latest comer to have joined the ranks of English-writing Ethiopians is Daniachew Worku (b. 1936). His remarkable novel, *The Thirteenth Sun* (1973), which was practically banned in Ethiopia until the revolution of 1974, brings out in a sombre mood some of the tensions that have been building up and undermining the fabric of traditional Ethiopian society ever since the country came more closely in touch with European culture and power in the middle of the nineteenth century. It seems inevitable that these and similar works reflecting European and American influences will force Amharic literature into a more dynamic direction.

At the time of writing (1978), it is too early to evaluate the possible consequences of the revolutionary coup that ended the Haile Sellassie regime in 1974. Much will depend on the linguistic policy that is adopted. Heightened nationalism and resistance to any suggestion of western neo-colonialism are certainly not likely to foster the further growth of English language writing at home. On the other hand, the revulsion against traditional Amharic supremacy that characterizes the policies of the present government might well encourage the study of other Ethiopian languages and the development of creative writing in them. Whether the deep religious faith that has permeated Ethiopian literature for many centuries will remain paramount is obviously very doubtful. But, in the long run, it is equally doubtful whether Ethiopian writers will embrace the westernizing attitude that had characterized such pioneers and innovators as Heruy and Germačäw. All that can be noted of recent developments are the sycophantic poems about the new authorities which have appeared in local journals, poems very similar in tone and style to the panegyrics that used to be issued every year on the emperor's birthday.

PART II

THE LEGACY OF ISLAM

CHAPTER TWO
WEST AFRICA : ARABIC WRITING

For several centuries, written composition in subsaharan Africa remained confined to Ethiopia and the Ge'ez language. With the advent and dissemination of Islam in the seventh century, a second Semitic wave brought the skill of writing and Arab culture to further areas. As far as literary history was affected, two main streams of Muslim-Arabic influence can be discerned: one that thrust southward along the shores of the Indian Ocean, and one that came to the black populations of West Africa along the caravan routes across the Sahara and the Sudan.[1]

Already by the ninth century, the Arabs in the Maghrib had established contact with the wealthy empire of Ghana, which controlled large tracts in present-day Senegal and Mali. Islamization, however, was achieved not by the Arabs but by the Tuareg Berbers, who were responsible for trans-saharan traffic. It was among these that Muslim expansion gathered new momentum in the eleventh century with the Almoravid movement. Its meaning has been explained by R.A. Nicholson:

> Murabit *is literally "one who lives in a* ribat," *i.e. a guardhouse or military post on the frontier. Such buildings were often occupied, in addition to the garrison proper, by individuals who, from pious motives, wished to take part in the holy war* (jihad) *against the unbelievers. The word* murabit, *therefore, gradually got an exclusively religious signification, "devotee" or "saint," which appears in its modern form,* marabout. *As applied to the original Almoravides, it still retains a distinctly military flavour.*[2]

The Berber Almoravids, who ruled from 1056 to 1147, aimed simultaneously at military conquest and religious reform and propagation. While one branch of the movement, starting from their desert stronghold in present-day Mauritania, overran Morocco in 1069 and, by 1103, had brought the whole of Spain under their control, another branch, led by Abu Bakr b. Umar, turned southward and undertook to conquer and convert the land of the Blacks *(bilâd as-Sûdân)*. The comparatively small kingdom of Tekror, near the mouth of the Senegal River, was apparently the first black community to be converted to Islam, towards the middle of the eleventh century.

About 1062, Abu Bakr began attacking the great empire of Ghana, noted for the wealth of its gold mines, which would also assure the opulence of the succeeding empires of Mali and Songhai. The capital fell after fierce resistance in 1076; but Abu Bakr himself was killed in 1087: the Ghana empire and Almoravid predominance in black West Africa were thus brought to an end almost simultaneously.

This, however, did not stop the growth of Islam. For the Soninke merchant community, who formed the nucleus of the Ghana population, perceiving the commercial benefits of orderliness under Muslim law, went over to Islam. Their example in turn led to the conversion of the Mande traders, who played a decisive role in the Mali empire. On the other hand, the local rulers, freed by the disintegration of Ghana, were equally quick to perceive the political, administrative and economic advantages to be gained by assimilating some, at least, of the elements of the more sophisticated Arab culture. One of the earliest surviving documents, written locally, is a *mahram* or letter of privilege granted by the first Muslim ruler of the Bornu-Kanem empire, Umme Jilmi, who reigned during the last two decades of the eleventh century.[3] Yet Arabic literature did not really flower in the Sudan until the days of the Mali empire, founded by the Mande ruler and convert to Islam, Sundiata (1230–1255).

The building up of an indigenous Muslim culture in West Africa was the work of Sundiata's illustrious successor, Musa, who reigned from 1312 to 1335. Not only did he enlarge the Mali empire, which now stretched from the Atlantic coast to the Niger delta, but on the occasion of his pilgrimage to Mecca, his enormous wealth—which reportedly caused a 12 per cent drop in the value of gold on the Cairo market—enabled him to recruit Arabic scholars and to establish close cultural links between Mali and Egypt. While in Mecca, he even persuaded an Arab poet from Granada, Abu Ishaq as-Sahili al-Garmati at-Tuwayhin, to follow him to Timbuctoo, where he died in 1346.[4] Musa thus laid the foundations of Timbuctoo as a centre of Islamic learning.

1. Timbuctoo (15th to 17th Centuries)

Originally a camp of Tuareg nomads at the junction of the Niger river and the Sahara, Timbuctoo had already become an important trading post in the African kingdom of Songhai. It was annexed to the Mali empire by Kango Musa, who had the first mosque built there by an Egyptian architect, and who encouraged local scholars to study in Morocco. After many vicissitudes resulting from the decline of Mali and the rise of the Songhai empire, Timbuctoo was reincorporated into the latter by Sonni Ali (1464–1492) in 1468. The city reached its peak of prosperity during the fifteenth and sixteenth centuries under the Askiya dynasty, a learned family that had originally migrated from the Futa Toro.

Under *Askiya* Muhammad Toure (1493–1529) and *Askiya* Daud (1548–1582) Timbuctoo went through a phase of unprecedented prosperity. While the administrative capital of the Songhai empire was Gao, Timbuctoo was its commercial and cultural centre. Caravans from Morocco, Tunis and Cairo, brought in the products of Arab civilization, while gold, slaves and local fabrics came from Ashanti and the Guinea Coast. This opulence had its intellectual implications: "Here in Timbuctoo," Leo Africanus wrote at the beginning of the sixteenth century, "there are great store of doctors, judges, priests and other learned men, bountifully maintained at the king's cost and charges. And hither are brought diverse scripts or written books out of Barbary, which are sold for more money than any other merchandise." The city was renowned for its schools and scholars, who were in constant touch with the intellectual centres of Arabia, Egypt and the Maghrib. They in turn attracted from all over Sudanic Africa students who wanted to learn the fundamental disciplines of Muslim humanities: theology, law, history, grammar, logic, rhetoric, ethics and astrology.[5]

While many of the Timbuctoo doctors were Berbers whose families had settled there in the course of the previous two centuries, the main feature of the city's culture was undoubtedly its broad humanistic outlook, its tolerance and understanding, its respect for learning as such, and its rejection of racial definitions. Indeed, one of the most widely respected and influential teachers was a Mande, Mohammed Bakhayoko, and most of the works which have been preserved, or at any rate rediscovered, were by demonstrably black African authors. But whatever the authors' origins, their culture tongue and the language they wrote was Arabic. Although many manuscripts have already been traced, few of them have as yet been edited, translated, and made available to a wider audience.

Four Timbuctoo writers are of special interest for the information they provide about the civilization of the city and the history of the Songhai empire. Mahmud al-Kati, who was born in 1468 and allegedly lived to the ripe old age of 125, was a Soninke scholar. He was a personal adviser of *Askiya* Muhammad, and began writing the *Tarikh al-Fattash* ("Chronicle of the Researcher") in 1519. The work was carried on by his descendants, and completed by his grandson Ibn al-Mukhtar about 1665.[6] J. Spencer Trimingham describes it as "a chronological history of the Askiya dnyasty of Songhay which incorporates legends and notes about earlier dynasties and ends in the year 1599, shortly after the Moroccan conquest."[7]

Toward the end of the sixteenth century, the Songhai empire became vulnerable to the expansionist enterprise of Moroccan sultans who, having been driven out of Spain, now turned to the goldmines in the south. In 1591, a Moroccan army defeated Songhai and captured Timbuctoo. Among the prisoners they took to Marrakesh was Ahmad Baba (1556–1627), a Berber and the best known among Timbuctoo writers. About a dozen of his works have been recovered, most of them treatises on Islamic law. His library was renowned and his teaching and writings brought him international fame in the Muslim world. In Marrakesh, under pressure from the local intelligentsia, he was soon allowed to teach. He was the author of some fifty treatises on grammar, Malikite law, and other subjects. His best-known work, *Nail al-ibtihâj bi-tatrîz ad-dibâj* ("The gaining of bliss through the embroidering of brocade")[8], was meant to be a continuation of *ad-Dibâj al-mudhahhab* ("The golden brocade"), a collection of biographical notices of Malikite jurists compiled by Ibn Farhum, a Medina writer of the fourteenth century. Ahmad Baba's book is our earliest source of information on Islamic writing in West Africa. It was printed in Fez (1908), and was even reprinted, together with Ibn Farhun's own treatise in Cairo (1932).

The Moroccan pashas soon gave up all pretence of loyalty to the sultan, and the former Songhai empire fell into a state of complete anarchy. Yet, while generalized pilfering and various attempts at liquidating the learned class precipitated the decay of the once brilliant civilization of Timbuctoo, scholarly activity was not brought to an end altogether.

Abd al-Rahman al-Sa'di (1596–*c.* 1656) was born in Timbuctoo, probably of Fulani parentage, and served as an official and diplomat. He wrote the *Tarikh al-Sudan* ("History of the Blacks"), which Heinrich Barth discovered in Northern Nigeria in 1853. His purpose, he said, was to "record all that I myself could gather on the subject of the Songhay princes of the Sudan, their adventures, their history, their achievements and their wars", adding to this "the history of Timbuctoo from the foundation of that city, of the princes who ruled there and the scholars and saints that lived there." For this, Abd al-Rahman relied heavily on Ahmad Baba's biographies.[9]

"Books of this type", says Trimingham, referring to the works of Mahmud al-Kati and Abd al-Rahman, "were arranged according to subject matter and to some extent chronologically as a series of disconnected facts, a succession of rulers, wars, dynastic intrigues, and rebellions; and, being modelled upon the few Islamic chronicles which filtered into the Sudan, show all the defects of their models: indiscriminate incorporation of legends and traditions, eulogies of the reigning dynasties and denigration of their enemies, and taste for biographies and obituaries of the *Ulama* class to which the compilers belonged."[10] Of a different type is the anonymous *Tadhkirat an-Nasyan (History of Sudanese princes)* composed in the eighteenth century by an unnamed author who was born in Timbuctoo in 1700, and seems to have been of Fulani origin; Trimingham describes it as "an alphabetical inventory of the various pashas, *almamis*, and *gadis* of Timbuktu-Jenne from 1590 to 1750, a collection of the notes of three or four generations of Songhay clerks."[11]

Although, as a number of African and other scholars of the present day now consider, Timbuctoo civilization testified in many respects to a successful integration of African culture into that of Islam, it is noteworthy that West African chroniclers of the sixteenth, seventeenth and eighteenth centuries found it advisable to record—or more likely, to invent—fictitious genealogies ascribing Arabic, usually Yemenite, ancestry to the rulers they were celebrating, in the same way as the Ethiopian dynasty claimed descent from Solomon.

2. Stagnation and Reform (18th Century)

While the fall of Timbuctoo did not bring composition in Arabic to an end, the Moroccan victory over the Songhai empire ushered in a period of religious and cultural stagnation for the Sudanic subcontinent: "After it the Sudan returned to its characteristic pattern of small independent states. In religion it was marked by the eclipse of Islamic universalism and the ascendency of local religions. Islam was neutralized by being emptied of all elements of challenge to African ways of life and Muslims were accomodated into Negro society", so that as a result of what is sometimes called "mixed Islam," it can be said that "the period between the collapse of Songhay and the formation of Islamic theocracies forms an interregnum of eclipse in the fortunes of Islam."[12] This theocratic trend emerged in the course of the eighteenth century among some Fulani communities in Futa Toro and Futa Jalon, and reached both its political and literary apex in the constitution of the Sokoto empire, in present-day northern Nigeria, in the early years of the nineteenth century. Mervyn Hiskett has succinctly brought out the resulting pattern:

> ... the development of a tradition of reform which, having remote origins in the Almoravid movement of the eleventh century, achieved literary expression in the Muslim empire of Songhay, at the beginning of the sixteenth century, and which was continued in the Habe kingdoms almost three centuries later.[13]

The rise of Arabic learning in Hausaland seems to have begun in a peripheral way while the Timbuctoo literature was in the making. One prominent intermediary was Muhammad b. Abd al-Karim al-Maghili (d. 1504), "a Muslim theologian, preacher and politician from Tlemcen in Algeria."[14] He was the most influential exponent of the Malikite doctrine, which was based on strict adherence to the Koran and to the codification of Medina customary law effected by Malik b. Anas (731–795). He visited Songhai in 1502, and his correspondence with *Askiya* Muhammad is of utmost interest for our understanding of the problems connected with the penetration of Islam into a basically animistic society. But al-Maghili travelled widely throughout the Sudan, and taught in such places as Kano and Katsina in present-day northern Nigeria. His treatise, *The Obligations of the Princes,* is said to have been written for the ruler of Kano.[15] Ahmad Baba himself taught in Kano on his return from Mecca in the mid-1580s. There thus arose, in Hausaland and in the adjacent areas, a school of Arabic writing independent of Timbuctoo. The first attested writer was at-Tazadhti (*c.* 1469–*c.* 1529), a pupil of al-Maghili, who had studied in Cairo and Mecca before he settled at Katsina as *kadi*.[16]

From the early years of the seventeenth century, most of the small Hausa states were strongly influenced by the Bornu empire, the only definitely Muslim state in the central Sudan. Bornu has a tradition of Arabic writing of its own, to which all too little attention has hitherto been paid: for example, towards the end of the sixteenth century, Ahmad b. Fartua, the chief imam of Bornu, wrote a chronicle of the reign of Sultan Idris III (1570–1602), who consolidated the Bornu-Kanem empire at a time when Songhai power was crumbling.[17] Hausa writers did not fail to contribute to the corpus of Arabic writing in Bornu. At the beginning of the seventeenth century, Abdullahi Sikka from Kano wrote *al-'Atiya li'l-mu'ti* ("The Gift of the Giver"), which, Hiskett says, "is the earliest example of locally composed *nazm* or versification based on material drawn in the first place from one or more existing prose sources";[18] in its contents, which is strongly reminiscent of Sufi mysticism, the work illustrates the advance in Islamic knowledge achieved in Hausaland.

Some time later, a Hausa poet and commentator, Dan Marina, whose Arabic name was Ibn al-Sabbagh, composed a poem to celebrate the victory of the Bornu king Ali b. Umar over the pagan Kwararafa tribes of the Benue valley in northern Cameroon about the year 1670. His treatise *Mazjarat al-fityan* ("Admonition to Young Men") is of historical interest because it shows that at the time "nearly all the important branches of Islamic learning were familiar to a small scholarly elite centred in the Hausa city of Katsina."[19] Dan Marina was also the teacher of the most influential jurist in Hausaland at the time, Dan Masanih (*c.* 1595–1667), also from Katsina.

The increasing prominence of Hausa scholars in the eighteenth century is connected not only with political, but also with economic developments:

> *Bornu remained a strong kingdom throughout most of the seventeenth century. But by its close, and in the eighteenth century, its kings and ministers—like some other oriental potentates in history—had become more and more involved in the intricacies of their rich life at court, and were becoming less and less effective in governing the state and in defending it against invaders, particularly the Kwararafa from the south and the Tuareg from the north. Thus when after the Moroccan conquest of Songhay, the commercial system of the Sudan began to decay, it was the small Hausa states between Bornu and the Niger, rather than the larger, but increasingly effete, Sefawa kingdom of Bornu-Kanem, which were able to gain the most advantage from the eastward shift in the trans-Saharan trade routes.[20]*

This helps account for the fact that the tradition of Arabic writing after the decline of Timbuctoo was perpetuated in the comparatively weak Hausa states, even though scholars were active in other parts of the Bornu kingdom and not all writers working in Hausaland were necessarily of Hausa origin. But whether the authors were Hausa or Fulani, or perhaps indeed Berbers, whether they were active in Katsina, Kano or Bornu, whether they wrote in prose or in verse, Arabic literature in the Sudanic area became more and more didactic as the eighteenth century wore on, returning to the fundamentalism of Malikite Islam once preached by al-Maghili.

One of the best-known verse compositions of the early eighteenth century is the *Shurb al-Zulal,* sometimes ascribed to Imam Muhammad b. Abd al-Rahman from Bornu. It was so widely known that a commentary of it was written in Cairo early in the nineteenth century. The author was a highly learned man, and it is significant that many of the authorities he quotes are Egyptian; the eastward displacement of the Sudanese centres of learning favoured Egypt's influence at the expense of the Maghrib. According to Bivar and Hiskett, who provided an English version of the *Shurb al-Zulal,* the purpose of Muhammad, and the reason for the great popularity of his poem with West African readers of Arabic, can be described as follows:

> *No doubt the author was concerned to introduce the beginner in Islamic law to certain generally accepted doctrines. Equally, it seems, he was impressed by apparent contradictions between the theoretical code . . . as taught by the Maliki jurists, and the everyday actions of his local contemporaries. Muhammad b. Abd al-Rahman was thus a forerunner, and of course not the only one, of the more thorough-going reformist movements of the early nineteenth century, those of Shehu Usuman dan Fodio in Hausaland on the one hand, and of Muhammad al-Amin in Bornu on the other.*

It was only in the late eighteenth century that the topical relevance of the *Shurb al-Zulal* became obvious. Meanwhile, a number of other writers had done their best to preserve and disseminate Muslim law and science.[21] A Fulani from Katsina, Muhammad b. Muhammad (d. 1760), wrote treatises, some of them in verse, on logic, grammar and astrology.[22] A writer sometimes identified as Muhammad al-Tahir b. Ibrahim al-Fallati (d. 1776) produced, besides some satirical poems, a medical treatise in verse on the diagnosis and treatment of haemorrhoids. But the religious inspiration of the *Shurb al-Zulal* reappeared with far greater explicitness and polemical virulence during the second half of the eighteenth century in the writings of Sheikh Jibril b. Umar (d. *c.* 1795) of Agades in present-day Niger. Jibril, who is said to have been of Hausa origin,[23] was very influential in Hausa towns, especially in Gobir, because of his preaching. This aroused the enmity of the Hausa rulers. His condemnation of their effete and immoral way of life went to such extremes that he equated their departure from the strict letter of Muslim moral law with the cardinal sin of unbelief. Even though he was later reproved for this by his former pupil Usman dan Fodio, Jibril contributed considerably to making articulate and effective the discontent which was to lead to the Fulani *jihad*.

3. The 19th-Century Revival: Hausaland

Jibril's teaching was only part of a large-scale revolution which originated in the spreading of the *qadiriyya* throughout Muslim West Africa. The *qadiriyyas* were fundamentalist fraternities initiated in Bagdad by Abd-Kadir al-Jili (1077–1166) as an aftermath of the mystical movement known as Sufism. From the sixteenth century onwards, says Fage, "the Qadiriyya established themselves smoothly and peacefully in the towns and along the trade routes of the Western Sudan. The results were the spread of Koranic schools, the development of an organised proselytising movement, and, in the westernmost Sudan, the conversion of whole peoples to the Muslim way of life. By the eighteenth century, one of these peoples, the Tukolor, had developed a significant clerical class, the *torodbe*."[24] The Tukolor, who have close ethnic connections with the Fulani, were the descendants of the Tekror kingdom in the Futa Toro area of present-day Senegal. Centuries earlier, it will be recalled, Tekror had been the first black African people to adhere to Islam.

The extremely complex history of Muslim West Africa and of its literature from the eighteenth century onwards was dominated by two decisive factors. One was the reformist movement within the Islamic élites; as the Muslim faith had degenerated among the local rulers throughout the area after the fall of the Songhai empire, educated clerics were determined to restore doctrinal purity to the extent of establishing genuine theocratic states. Further, the main instrument of this important religious and political development, at least in its early phases, were the Fulani: these were highly mobile pastoral people who had spread throughout West Africa, acting as shepherds in the service of animistic agrarian populations; their conversion to Islam, which had begun on a small scale in the sixteenth century, soon gathered momentum; it gave them a sense of intellectual and moral superiority over their "pagan" employers and, in some places, over "pagan" Fulani rulers. The political consequence of this process was the establishment of a number of Fulani theocratic states in the Sudan during the eighteenth and early nineteenth centuries.[25] Their example was to be imitated by non-Fulani reformers in the course of the nineteenth century, but these later attempts were mostly foiled, at least on the political plane, by the onset of European colonization.

The process followed the war-and-propaganda pattern which had been set by the Almoravids in earlier days. The Muslim reformers found it necessary not only to conquer pagan peoples, but also to convert them to Islam. For this latter purpose, they proceeded as Christian, and especially Protestant, missionaries were to do in the nineteenth century: they fought against illiteracy, but realizing the difficulty of teaching the subjected people the Arabic language, they used the Arabic script to transcribe the vernacular languages. They thus gave rise to an *ajami* type of literature.

Though this was undoubtedly the most striking novelty to have occurred in West African writing since its inception, the appearance of *ajami* literatures did not mean the vanishing of a literate tradition in the Arabic language. Throughout the nineteenth century, and even later, learned West Africans, and especially the great reformist leaders, continued using Arabic for their writing, often leaving it to their followers to convey their message in the indigenous tongues. Indeed, the early decades of the nineteenth century, which witnessed the spreading of *ajami* writing, were also a flourishing period for Arabic scholarship and literature, due primarily to the triumph of the Fulani *jihad* in the Hausa states of present-day northern Nigeria.

Usman dan Fodio (1754–1817),[26] who launched the holy war in 1804, was a Fulani born in Gobir, but his ancestors had immigrated from the Futa Toro. A pious Muslim and a keen learner with a gift for languages, he completed his studies at Agades. On his return to Gobir, he soon acquired great fame as a preacher, urging the Hausa people to give up their corrupt customs and to return to Islamic orthodoxy. His prestige aroused the jealously of the emir, who threatened to attack him. In defence, Usman rallied his many followers and proclaimed a *jihad* which, between 1804 and 1810, spread to all the Hausa states and some of the neighbouring areas. Local rulers were replaced by Fulani emirs; these vowed allegiance to Usman, who set up his capital in Sokoto in 1809. In 1808, he had divided the administration of his empire between his son, Muhammadu Bello, and his brother Abdullahi.

For all his military successes and the magnitude of his political achievement, Usman was primarily a scholar and a theologian, whose many Arabic works constantly emphasize his reforming purpose. According to Hiskett, his writings "can be divided into two main categories: general works of a rather theoretical nature, products of the more academic period of his life before the *jihad;* and then, after the *jihad,* a collection of shorter, often polemic, works, dealing with specific problems that arose in the newly established Islamic state."[27]

The very title of one of Usman's first treatises, *Ihya al-sunna wa-ikhmad al-bid'a* ("Revivification of Orthodoxy and Extinguishing of Innovation"), which was probably completed before 1793, "precisely states the Shehu's primary purpose": "to revive the *Sunna* or orthodox way of the Prophet and banish 'innovation'—a term which, in the context of Islamic theology, really means the syncretic practices whereby animist and pre-Islamic custom continued to thrive in the environment of mixed Islam."[28] Likewise directed against syncretism is his *Nûr al-albâb* ("The Light of the Minds"), which later reached print in Cairo.[29] *Masa'il muhimma* ("Important Matters", 1802) "is less theoretical than 'Revification', for it begins to show his increasing preoccupation with the practical problems of the day"; "it marks the transition from the rather scholarly attitudes of a teacher to those of the active reformer and revivalist."[30]

Usman's mystical experiences of the early 1790s culminated in a vision of the founder of the *Qadiriyya,* who appeared to him as an envoy from the Prophet, and girded him, as Usman himself was later to record, "with the Sword of Truth, to unsheath it against the enemies of God."[31] This seminal experience provided the occasion for a poem in Arabic, *al-Qasida al-sudaniyva* ("The Sudanic Ode", 1794). As to the moral justification of the *jihad,* it is fully set out in the *Kitab al-farq* ("Book of the Difference between the Government of the People of Islam and the Government of the Unbelievers").[32]

Hiskett claims that the focal work of the post-*jihad* period is *Bavan wujub al-Hijra 'ala al-'ibad* ("Explanation of the Necessity of Hijra to the Worshippers"):

Whereas 'Revivification' is concerned with the salvation of the individual soul, 'Explanation' is a practical work, concerned with how the Islamic community should conduct its affairs in the temporal world. Its relevance to the circumstances of the day in Hausaland is obvious. What also emerges from it is the intense concern of its idealistic and juridically minded author for the

moral and legal justification, through the correct interpretation of divine rev-
elation, for every step along the way that he and his community had followed.[33]

More specific points were dealt with in *Sirj al-ikhwan,* ("The Lamp of
the Brethren"), which shows Usman's concern with the unity of his
followers, challenged at the time by various attempts on the part of
some of the empire's high officials to establish themselves as independent rulers.[34]

Both of Usman's immediate successors, his brother Abdullah b. Muhammad (1766–1829) and his son Muhammad Bello (1781–1837), were
competent scholars and wrote many works in Arabic. The former,[35] who
was equally fluent in Hausa and translated some of Usman's vernacular
poems into Arabic, is especially noted for *Ida' al-nusukh* ("Depository of
Texts"),[36] which is of considerable interest for the history of Arabic
culture in the Sudan, for it deals chiefly with the education of the author
and his elder brother, and with the books from which they drew their
knowledge of Muslim doctrine in matters of faith and law. His *Tazyin
al-waraqat* ("Adornment of the Manuscripts") is one of the many biographies that were to be composed about the Shehu, and offers a
chronicle of the holy war.[37] But Abdullah was also interested in the
theory of right government, and, towards the end of the *jihad,* he composed *Diya al-hukkam* ("Light of the Jurists", *c.* 1808), to help the
people of Kano in setting up an Islamic government.

The revival of Arabic learning in Hausaland reached its apogee during the reign of Muhammad Bello (1817–1837),[38] when Muslim divines
came from far afield to the court at Sokoto. In his *History of Sokoto,* Hajj
Sa'id later claimed that Muhammad himself

> *was much occupied with composition, and whenever he composed anything he
> used to issue it to the people, and read it to them, then become occupied with
> another composition. . . . If he was asked about a question he composed a
> composition on it, and if it reached him that so-and-so and so-and-so were
> disagreeing on a matter he composed a composition on it.*[39]

Like his father and his uncle, Muhammad was preocuupied with the
theory of government, as can be seen from *Usul al-siyasa* ("Roots of
Politics"). But his most important treatise is *Infaq al-maisur* ("Expend-
iture of What is Available"),[40] which is of peculiar interest because it
contains the correspondence exchanged between Muhammad and the
champion of the rival state of Bornu, Muhammad al-Amin ibn Muhammad al-Kanami (d. 1837), who was the effective ruler of Bornu from
1810 to his death. The latter was described by Hodgkin as essentially
a Muslim scholar like Usman dan Fodio, but with closer connections
with the Arab world. The correspondence, Hodgkin adds, "ranges over

the main questions in dispute between . . . Sokoto and Bornu. Was the
Fulani *jihad* justifiable on accepted Muslim principles? That is to say,
was it conducted against states which were in the strict sense 'pagan'?
. . . Was Bornu in fact such a state? Were there appropriate precedents
for such a *jihad*? Was its real purpose the spreading of the frontiers of
Islam, not of Fulani imperial power?", etc.[41] Further, al-Kanami was
a poet of no small ability. Dixon Denham, who travelled throughout
West Africa in the 1820s preserved the translation of a song he had
composed on meeting his favourite wife after a military expedition in
1821.[42]

The example of al-Kanami shows that the areas under Fulani control
were not the sole centres of Arabic writing in early nineteenth-century
West Africa. Indeed his letters and poetry take their place in a continuous tradition proper to the state of Bornu-Kanem, and which still
awaits adequate investigation.

Much of the literature produced in Hausaland during the first decades of the Sokoto empire was focused on the life and ideas of its first
leader and on the military and political circumstances of its foundation.
This was also true of *Raud al-jinan* ("Meadow or Paradise") by *Malam*
Gidado dan Laima. Gidado was a son-in-law of the Shehu, having married his daughter Asma, herself a well-known poet in Hausa. On Muhammad Bello's accession to power in 1817, he was appointed vizier
of Sokoto. His book is an important source for the biography of Usman
dan Fodio.

The death of Muhammad Bello did not put an end to what has been
called "the extraordinary outpouring of Arabic writing during the period *c.* 1800-1850."[43] Much of it is of historical interest, as the viziers
of Sokoto were in the habit of writing annals of the ruling dynasty. Of
Muhammad's successor, his brother Abu Bakr Atiku, who ruled from
1837 to 1842, it was said that "the dissipated and the sultans hated him,
but the learned and the upright loved him." This judgment is to be
found in the *History of Sokoto,* by al-Hajj Sa'id, who was Koranic reader
to Atiku's successor, Muhammad Bello's son, Aliyu Babba, who
reigned from 1842 to 1859; of the latter, Sa'id said that "He did not
dispute theology with anyone without vanquishing him", and that "he
did not leave off learning by night or day."[44] So far, however, this later
Arabic writing from Hausaland has not received the learned attention
it deserves. For although Sokoto rulers in the second half of the century
departed from the missionary zeal and the austere ideals of Islam, and
despite the effects of both British conquest and the assimilation of Fulani
into the Hausa population, the Arabic language has been used for literary purposes to this day, and a number of the learned men who are
known at present for their works in Hausa are also practitioners of
poetry in the Arabic language.

4. The 19th-Century Revival: Northern Ghana

There are three areas in which further research is likely to reveal much about Arabic writing in the Sudan: one is the literature that was produced in Hausaland itself after the middle of the nineteenth century, when the structures of centralized power began to dissolve in the Sokoto empire; another is the literary production in other Islamized parts of the Sudan; and thirdly, much is still to be learnt about the literary consequences of the Hausa trade, which extended throughout West Africa.

In this latter respect, one area at least has been seriously investigated in recent years. It is known that Hausa merchants had been trading in kola nuts in areas which are now parts of northern Ghana as long ago as the middle of the fifteenth century.[45] Nevertheless, Arabic learning seems to have come to northern Ghana and the adjacent territories along a north-western trade route chiefly frequented by Dyula merchants.[46] Already in the eighteenth century writing in Arabic was common among Gonja Muslims for correspondence, private and commercial, and for recording genealogies.[47] A significant section of this production was composed of magical treatises, one of which at least is known to have been written by a Fulani scholar from Katsina, Muhammad b. Muhammad al-Fulani al-Kashinawi, and became popular in East Africa after being printed in Cairo.[48] Of greater intrinsic interest is a chronicle which was completed, as early as 1752, by Al-Hajj Muhammad b. Mustapha; it recounted the legend of the kingdom's origins and provided a yearly chronicle of events from 1710; "an addendum was written for the years 1763 to 1766 by Imam Umar Kunandi b. Umar. Both of these were learned men and their horizons took in part at least of the Mediterranean World."[49]

Ashanti dominance over northern Ghana during the greater part of the nineteenth century was a setback for the Muslim religion and culture. But the Ashanti were defeated by the British in 1874, and, in the last quarter of the century, the Hausa kola trade was resumed and expanded.

The arrival in Gonja of a Hausa merchant's son, Umar ibn Abu Bakr ibn Uthman al-Kabbawi al-Kanawi (1858–1934) led to a renaissance of writing. Umar was a prolific author. He is claimed to have composed as many as 1200 poems, most of them in Arabic, but some in Hausa. According to Thomas Hodgkin, his contribution "might be described as making poetry the vehicle of social commentary, social criticism and reflections on the history of his time":[50] Most of his writing was done between 1877 and 1917. It includes "theological works, historical verses, poems of anti-Christian protest, a letter-writer's handbook and writings of a more ephemeral character."[51] Several of these works were later to reach print in Cairo, as for example, his epistolary manual, *Kitaâb as-*

sarhat ("Book of the Blooming Flower"), *Tarbî az-zuhd* ("Tarbi Poem
on Asceticism", 1947-48), and *Ta'rikh iqlim Ashanti* ("History of the
Country of the Ashanti", 1950), which deals mainly with the progress
of Islam in the Ashanti part of present-day Ghana.[52] Specialists have
come to the conclusion that Umar should rank "as one of the major
literary figures in West Africa."[53] Together with his contemporary al-
Hasan (d.*c*. 1433) who, however, wrote only in Hausa (see p. 61), Umar
was responsible for the growth of Gonja into a centre of literary activity,
which was later illustrated by the religious poems composed in Arabic
in the early 1920s by Ali b. Muhammad Baraw al-Salghawi.[54]

5. The 19th-Century Revival: Senegal

The vast Islamic reform movement of which the Sokoto empire was
the most visible early political achievement had its origins among the
torodbe class of the Futa Toro. The liveliness of Muslim thinking in the
area, and its vicinity to centres of learning in the Maghrib suggest the
reasons why present-day Senegal should have produced a significant
contribution to the corpus of Arabic writing in West Africa. But although a wealth of information has recently become available about the
Arabic literature of Senegal, thanks mainly to the labours of the Senegalese scholar Amar Samb,[55] even his thorough investigations have
failed to reveal the existence of any such writing earlier than the mid-
nineteenth century. This dearth of documents may largely be due to
French indifference, if not downright hostility, to the indigenous cultural life of the native populations: about the only local Arabic work to
have been translated and published during the colonial period was a
late-nineteenth-century prose chronicle of the Futa Toro, composed by
Sire Abbas Soh,[56] which illustrates once more that, side by side with
their concern for spreading Islamic theology and law, Arabic-speaking
scholars in West Africa were very much interested in recording the
history, lore and customs of their own people. It is also possible that all
the writings of the early reformists in Senegal have been lost, or that
their teaching was essentially by word of mouth.

The fact remains, however, that the West African reform movement
originated among the Tokolor clerical class, in the early decades of the
eighteenth century. But "though their centre was in Senegalese Futa
they had clerical representatives scattered throughout the whole Sudan
belt in both Muslim and pagan villages where they were tolerated by the
chiefs who made use of them as practitioners of magic and granted
them a plot to cultivate."[57] Their rebellion against traditional rulers in
favour of theocratic states was launched in 1725 in the Futa Jalon, in
present-day Guinea. A similar revolution did not occur in the Futa Toro

until later in the century, and, although no literary documents have been recovered from this early period, the movement must have been accompanied by intense intellectual effervescence, for it was strengthened, at the turn of the century, by the spiritual influence of a Moroccan reformer, Ahmad al-Tijani (1737–1815). He was the founder of a *tariqa* (brotherhood), the *Tijaniyya*, which soon became second only in importance to the *Qadiriyya*, and easily swept over the whole of West Africa because of "its relatively uncomplicated prayers, litanies and exercises, the facility of which facilitated the understanding of its teachings and practices by uneducated followers."[58] It still occupies an important position in Senegalese Islam, where it dominated until the late nineteenth century.

As far as is known at present, the renascence—or perhaps the birth—of Arabic writing in Senegal and, more generally, in the western Sudan, was the outcome of a movement of spiritual reform and military conquest that was led by al-Hajj Umar ibn Sa'id Tall (1794–1864). "As the son of a cleric, he received a religious education, and in 1826 he set off to perform the pilgrimage to Mecca where he was initiated into the Tijaniyya *tariqa* and, so he claims, appointed *Khalifa* for the Sudan. He acquired a considerable reputation during his return journey, which lasted many years, by way of Bornu under al-Kanemi and Sokoto under Muhammad Bello where he remained three years taking part in the wars and acquiring a considerable booty of slaves."[59] In the early 1850s, he sought to gain control of Futa Toro, his native land, but he was soon halted by the French advance, which prevented him from establishing his authority over Senegal. In about 1857 he began to turn eastward, and succeeded in conquering a vast empire in Masina, in present-day Mali.[60]

Although Trimingham describes Umar as "a new type of Islamic adventurer whose vast conquests threw western Sudan into a state of complete anarchy,"[61] he was a scholar, as learned as the members of the Fodio dynasty, and he made a serious contribution to Arabic writing in West Africa.[62] His best-known work is *Rimah hizb al-rahim 'ala nuhur hizb al-rajim* ("The Lances of God's party against the Throats of the Satanic Faction").[63] The author tells us that what he calls "this blessed book," was completed in 1845, seven years before he embarked on his *jihad*. It provides a survey of the ideas and customs characteristic of the *Tijaniyya* brotherhood, and contains a wealth of biographical information, concerning his pilgrimage to Mecca, his stay in Sokoto, his dealings with Muhamad Bello, and his controversy with al-Kanemi. According to Abun-Nasr, "since Hajj Umar's death, his book al-Rimah has become one of the most important books of the order, and when *Jawahir al-ma'ani*—the autobiographical work that Ahmad al-Tijani, the founder, had dictated to one of his Moroccan disciples, Ali Harazim b. al-Arabi

Barada—was printed in Cairo in 1927, the *Rimah* was printed in its margin." Umar's epic career and tragic destiny inspired a number of biographical works, such as *Iqd al-jumân* ("A Pearl Necklace"), where Ahmad al-'Adnani recounts some of the miracles wrought by the Sheikh.[64]

Until the death of Umar in 1864, Futa Toro had remained the main stronghold of Islam in Senegal itself. But the French occupation, which was completed in the ensuing years, was one of the factors responsible for the conversion of the Wolof, who make up the bulk of the country's population, for they "realized intuitively that their old [animistic] religion was incapable of carrying them through the next phase of history heralded by the early impact of the West. By adopting Islam *en masse* they were able to preserve their social life and all essential institutions intact."[65] A case in point is that of Lat-Dior, *damel* (king) of Cayor, the heartland of the Wolof country. After a heavy defeat inflicted by the French, Lat-Dior converted to Islam in 1864 in order to gain the alliance of neighbouring Muslim regions and thus to keep his throne; and even after paying allegiance to the French he actively promoted the spread of Islam in Cayor, so that "the conversion of the whole of the Wolof was accomplished within fifty years."[66]

Inevitably, the development of Islam was accompanied by the diffusion of the Arabic language and script and, consequently, the growth of poetry in Arabic. This rapid conversion was first operated under the aegis of the *Tijaniyya*, but the last decades of the century witnessed the constitution of new local brotherhoods, such as the *Muriddiya*, as learned men founded religious centres of learning and devotion (*zawiya*) throughout Senegal. There was much interlocking of Tukolor and Wolof Islam, as young Muslim scholars toured the various *zawiyas* and often studied in Mauritania to complete their education.

One of the earliest Arabic poets in Wolof country was Madiakhate Kala (1835–1902), an uncle and adviser of Lat-Dior.[67] An accomplished writer, his originality resides in his inspiration, which is not only didactic and devotional, but also epic and satirical, as when he sings the wars of Lat-Dior, or casts doubt on the sincerity of the king's conversion to Islam. This exceptional feature may be due in part to Kala's own temperament, and in part to his proximity to the oral tradition of the *griots*.

Far more conventional was a younger kinsman of his, al-Hajj Malik Sy (*c.* 1855–1922), who was "extremely well educated in Islamic literature and juridical studies and was the author of numerous scholarly treatises on law, theology and sufism."[68] According to Abun-Nasr, "he came from a Fulani family which lived in Wolof territory and intermarried with the Wolof, so that it lost command of the Fulani language and came to use the Wolof instead." In 1902, he founded his *zawiya* in Tivaouane, in Cayor, and it was under his leadership and that of his successors that the Senegalese Tijani order began to grow so that it was to become the most important branch of the *Tijaniyya* in West Africa. In the course of time, Malik's *zawiya* became not only the chief centre of the *Tijaniyya* in Senegal but also a centre of Islamic and Arabic studies. Through his writing and preaching, he fought superstition, fanaticism and rebellion, advocating union and concord among the Senegalese, and acceptance of French rule. As Abun-Nasi points out, "this continued loyalty did not go unrewarded; for the French authorities arranged for twenty-two of his theological and linguistic tracts to be published by Bel-Hassem Frères in Tunis at the expense of the Tunisian government in 1914–15."[69]

Malik Sy's progeny included several gifted poets, such as his sons Ababakar Sy (d. 1957), al Hajj Mansour Sy (1892–1957) and al Hajj Abdoul Aziz Sy (b. 1904), as well as Ababakar's own son, Cheik Tijâne Sy, all of whom have been respected scholars, noted writers, and leaders of the Tijani brotherhood.

The most influential figure among the Wolof Muslims was a contemporary of Malik Sy, Amadou Bamba M'Backé (1850–1927),[70] a kinsman of Madiakhate Kala, who taught him the techniques of Arabic versification. His family was of Tukolor origin. He set up his own *zawiya* in Touba around 1886, and was the founder of the *Muridiyya* brotherhood. For a long time the French authorities suspected him of intending to launch a holy war, and he spent several years of his life in exile in Gabon and Mauritania. Actually, Amadou Bamba had no confidence in armed rebellion, and he was instrumental in bringing about the submission of Lat-Dior and other Senegalese leaders to the superior power of the French. His teaching was responsible for a thorough reorientation of the traditional Islamic outlook, for he instilled into the Murid movement a sort of work ethic which turned a large part of the Wolof population into agriculturists, and encouraged them to settle and exploit arid lands well beyond the traditional borders of their own country, while others turned to trade, and later to banking and industry, founding prosperous communities in the towns of Senegal.[71]

Amadou Bamba was a prolific writer, whose works have remained immensely popular in Senegal to this day. Fernand Dumont lists forty-one pamphlets, mostly in verse; they are usually extant in manuscript copies, but some of them have been printed at the expense of Bamba's disciples, in Dakar, or even in Casablanca, and in some cases in Tunis. It is surmised that the total output of Bamba's works comprises some 20,000 copies per year.[72]

Murid means disciple, and as the core of Amadou Bamba's doctrine is saint-worship, it is not surprising that an important segment of Senegal's Arabic writing should consist of hagiographical treatises and poetic panegyrics on the founder of the brotherhood. Samb lists six Arabic

works on Amadou Bamba and his teachings.[73] One of the most important in spite of its hagiographic tone is *Irwa en-Nadim min 'adb hubb el-
Hadim* ("The Guest Quenches His Thirst at the Sweet Love of the Servant"), by Mamadou Lamine Diop Dangana (d. 1967).[74] Though this
has remained in manuscript, a compendium entitled *Hayatu es-Sheikh
Ahmed Bamba* ("Life of Sheikh Ahmed Bamba") composed by a younger
Senegalese writer, Moustapha Ane, was later printed in Dakar and Casablanca.[75] Two of those biographical accounts were written by Mauri-
tanian scholars. At least one prominent follower, Ibra Diop Massar
(1888–1932) seems to have devoted most of his work to praise-poetry
in honour of the master.[76] Apparently, however, the most valuable of
Bamba's biographies is the one produced by the fourth of his twelve
sons, al-Hajj Muhammad el-Bachirou M'Backé (1895–1966), under the
title *Minan el-Baki el-Qadim fi ma'atir es-Sheikh el-Hadim* ("The Good
Deeds of the Eternal, or the Memorable Deeds of Sheikh the Servant"),
printed in Morocco in 1969, because the writer exhibits a genuine sense
of history, which is often missing in purely hagiographical writings.[77]

As in the case of the Sy dynasty, the art of poetry has been carefully
cultivated among the descendants of Ahmadou Bamba. His two eldest
sons, Mustapha M' Backé (1895–1966), who succeeded him at the head
of the *Muridiyya,* and al-Hajj Falilou M'Backé (1889–1968), who succeeded his brother, also wrote some poetry, as did the latter's son,
Cheikh M'Backé, who is better known, however, as the representative
of the brotherhood's industrial and banking interests.[78]

Since the death of al-Hajj Umar, nearly every generation has seen the
foundation of one or more *zawyas* in Senegal. The tremendous success
of the *Muridiyya* did not put the *Tijaniyya* out of business, and several
new branches of the Tijani brotherhood were founded at the turn of
the century. They are important centres of Arabic writing because their
renown can thus extend far beyond the borders of Senegal, whereas a
large proportion of Murid writing is done in Wolof. Cheikh Moussa
Kamara (*c.* 1864–1963),[79] who was born in the district of Matam, Futa
Toro, founded his *zawiya* in Ganguel in 1883. The greater part of his
work deals with religion and law, but he also wrote commentaries on
Arabic grammar and poetry and on the pre-islamic poets, and several
historical treatises, one of which, the *Life of al-Hajj Umar,* was translated
into French by Amar Samb.[80]

Another prestigious *zawiya* is the one at Kaolack, which, since early in
this century, has been under the leadership of the Niasse family. Mou-
hammadou Niasse (1881–1957) and his brother Ibrahima (b. 1902),
who succeeded him, both of them venerated and influential though
slightly quarrelsome figures in the Tijani brotherhood, had a *Diwan*
(collection of poetry), of dual authorship, printed in Kano, a fact which
goes to show that their renown extended as far as northern Nigeria.[81]

It is noteworthy that Samb also extols the poetry of Roqaya, Ibrahima's daughter, the only woman-writer to be mentioned in his survey.[82]

The interaction of the various *zawiyas* is illustrated in the case of Cheikh Hadi Touré (b. 1894),[83] whose father was a pupil of Madiakhaté Kala, while he himself benefited by the teaching of al-Hajj Malik Sy, one of whose daughters he married. He is one of the Tijani poets, and his *Diwan* does not comprise more than about fifty poems, some of them fairly lengthy; but he is chiefly renowned for his learning in the Muslim sciences of arithmetic and astronomy.

Lack of reliable data makes it difficult to appraise the impact of westernization on this Arabic-language literature. At first sight it would seem that the younger educated generations were little attracted to this traditional form of literacy; among recent writers Samb mentions only two, both of them born in 1924: Sheikh Tijane Sy,[84] a descendant of Malik Sy, who was appointed Senegal's ambassador to Egypt after independence, and Moustapha Ane,[85] a widely travelled man, who studied at Al-Azhar university in Cairo, and is well-known, as a journalist and pamphlet-writer, for his determination to bring about a modernization of Islam.

Senegal's age-long familiarity with Islam and its proximity to the centres of learning in the Maghrib may well be responsible for the remarkable contribution of that country to the corpus of Arabic writing in West Africa. But on the other hand, it is equally possible that the difference between Senegal and other countries in the area is simply due to the fact that no scholar has yet gone to the trouble of investigating the history and scope of Arabic writing in those other countries. René Baesjou, in an article already mentioned,[86] tantalizingly drops a few names which suggest that Senegal may be rather less exceptional than has hitherto been thought. Among the pupils of al-Hajj Umar of Northern Ghana, he lists Ahâni Abdulahi in Togo. The concepts of the *Tijaniyya* have been propagated in Mali by Uthman ibn Abî Bakr, one of whose works was printed in Tunis; the same brotherhood is also active in Kumasi (Ghana) with authors like al-Hajj Ahmad Bâbah and Ahmad Nûruddin, author of *Nibrâs al-mudidîn* ("The Lamp for the Disciples"), which was printed in Cairo (1971). It is also noteworthy that much Arabic poetry has been composed by those West African writers who are better-known for their vernacular works, transliterated in the Arabic script, to whom the next chapter is devoted.

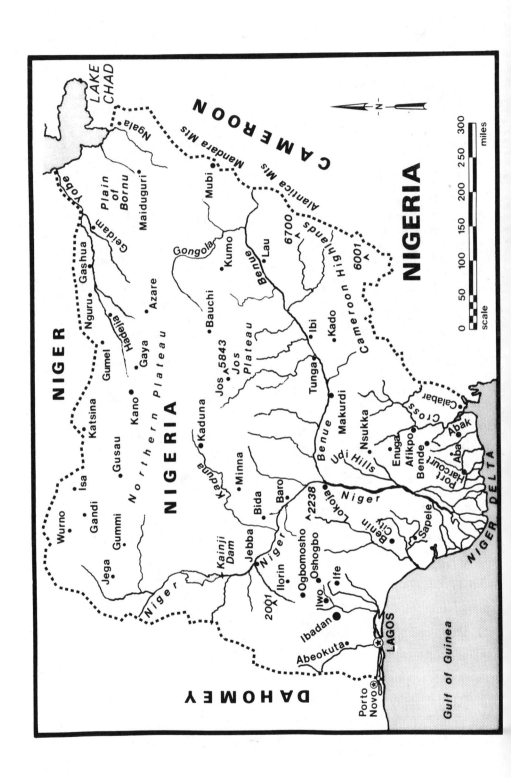

CHAPTER THREE
WEST AFRICA : THE *AJAMI* TRADITION

1. Fulani

At an early stage in their drive for an Islamic revival, the Fulani clerics felt the need to depart from the time-honoured custom which restricted the use of writing to the holy language used by Allah in dictating the Koran to Muhammad. If the movement was to obtain popular support and to lead to genuine mass conversion, it was necessary to address the illiterate people in their own language and, therefore, to produce texts that might usefully be read out to them. While the first literary consequence of the Muslim revival was the renascence of Arabic writing, its second result was the emergence of the written art in some of the West African languages.

Mervyn Hiskett has clearly brought out the part which must have been played by the traditional Islamic educational system in this phenomenon. Discussing the intellectual evolution of Usman dan Fodio, Hiskett points out that "his education, like that of his companions, took place in schools which, as the sources show, were the early equivalents of what are known in Hausa as *makarantun ilmi*, schools of higher Islamic learning." These, he claims, may have grown up "in imitation of the Sufi seminaries which were so important in the cultural life of North Africa, particularly Morocco, during the seventeenth century." Hiskett describes the method of instruction in these schools as follows:

The teacher reads a phrase or brief passage from the Arabic text, then follows with a commentary in Hausa or Fulfulde[1] *(for certain schools are still the special resort of Fulfulde speakers), while the students listen, make notes, and occasionally ask questions. It soon becomes apparent that these vernacular commentaries are known by heart. . . . They are handed down through* isnad, *or chains of authority, in exactly the same way as other Islamic religious material, and the word-for-word integrity of the commentary is jealously preserved. It is,*

therefore, clear that, in addition to their main effect of disseminating higher
Islamic learning, a side effect of these schools has been to produce literary, or
"malamaic," forms of Hausa and Fulfulde into which the ideas, imagery and
style as well as the vocabulary of classical Arabic literature have been absorbed.
. . . This has been important in influencing the vernacular literate verse-tra-
dition, which . . . the reformers exploited for the purpose of religious propa-
ganda.[2]

Though this hypothesis is both plausible and attractive, there is no
firm evidence, as Hiskett himself acknowledges, that the Fulani language, or any other West African vernacular, was written down before
the lifetime of Usman dan Fodio, who thus may claim to be not only
the main agent of the Arabic renascence, but also one of the founders
of the *ajami* tradition. It is known that already in his early 'twenties he
had composed poems in praise of the Prophet, both in Arabic and Fulani. At a later stage, while he was preparing for the *jihad*, his brother
Abdullah records that Usman composed much vernacular verse during
his mission journeys. Some of these were in Hausa, but the majority
were in Fulani. Much of this production, says Hiskett, "is better described as versification than as poetry because it was intended for mne-
monic and instructional purposes—verse accounts of the intricacies of
Islamic inheritance or how to perform correctly the involved rituals of
ablution and prayer."[3] But one of his longer Fulani poems, composed
in 1791 and preserved in a Hausa translation by Usman's son Isa dan
Shehu, is written in praise of Muhammad and "demonstrates most
clearly the source of his inspiration and the intensity of his feeling of
dedication."[4]

Likewise, during the period of his visions in the mid-1890s, Usman
composed a vernacular ode in honor of the *Qadiriyya* and its founder,
which has been preserved in an Arabic version by his brother Abdullah.

The course of historical events after the *jihad* did not prove favourable
to the expansion of Fulani writing in Northern Nigeria. The Fulani
were a ruling minority in the Sokoto empire. Even during the first few
decades of the nineteenth century, the literary activity of the Fulani
clerics was mainly in Arabic, as we have seen, and in Hausa, as we shall
see. A process of linguistic assimilation set in, and the Fulani minority
was absorbed into the Hausa community, so that the main effect of the
Islamic reform on the literature of the Hausa states was the promotion
of Hausa writing.

● ● ●

The easternmost point reached by the Fulani in the course of their
long dispersion was northern Cameroon where, by the eighteenth cen-

tury, they had settled in large numbers, moving and living among the local pagan tribes. The example of Usman dan Fodio inspired one of their leaders, a cleric *(modibo)* named Adama, "who had received a religious education in Bornu˙and had been on pilgrimage":

> *Hearing of Uthman's* jihad *he went to Sokoto in 1806 to offer allegiance, was invested with a flag, and returned to inaugurate the* jihad. *He succeeded in the difficult task of getting his authority accepted by the Fulbe and unified them temporarily through appealing to their racial and plundering instincts. He began his* jihad *in 1809 and subdued the pagans of the north "for the religion," as the chronicles affirm, and not in order to capture slaves and increase his* harim *as was the case with his successors." . . . He founded Yola on the Benue in 1841 as his capital and died there in 1847–8.*[5]

There are indications that written poetry began to flourish at Yola in the middle of the nineteenth century, for the town became a genuine centre of learning, even if it did not reach the fame of Sokoto. Tradition has preserved the as yet unpublished works of a poet of the time who wrote under the pseudonym of Tan Ililel. In the late 1930s, G. Pfeffer obtained some information about Adamawa literature from the court poet of the Emir of Yola, a man named Amadu, who communicated to her a small collection of poetry and prose in the Fulani language: some of this was claimed to date from the foundation of Yola and "had been copied and recopied for several generations", while the rest consisted of records of purely oral traditions.[6] The classification established by Mrs. Pfeffer is of considerable interest because it reveals criteria of literary value not unlike those that prevailed in early medieval Europe, when only the authors of works endowed with religious significance saw their names preserved, while most written material dealing with non-Christian subject-matter remained anonymous, however higher its literary quality may now appear. The Fulani literature of Adamawa comprises a large number of stories, riddles, songs and tongue-twisters which properly belong to oral lore, although much of this was recorded in Arabic script together with stories that seem to be of Arabic origin. The criterion of selection for recording seems to have resided in the moral significance of the narratives. Finally, there is a body of material that undoubtedly belongs to literature *stricto sensu* rather than to folklore, because it consists of works that were composed in written form by identifiable authors. This includes songs in praise of eminent persons, songs with a moral idea, and religious songs; but the same category also contains a considerable amount of narrative prose, chiefly moral stories, and semi-historical legends dealing with the origins of Fulani customs and social structure.

No further information concerning Fulani writing in Adamawa was

available until 1965, when French scholar Pierre Lacroix collected a
corpus of poems composed between 1930 and 1960 by six poets, four
of whom—Haman Bello, Sambo Dibi, Hamaseo Gire and Isa Dembo
(d. 1959)—were born *c.* 1900, while the other two—Moodi Yaawa and
Buuba Jariida—belong to a younger generation, born *c.* 1925.[7] From one
generation to another, little evolution is to be perceived. The comparative autonomy which Adamawa enjoyed under the Germans and later
under the French and the British, apparently made for the perpetuation
of an exceedingly conservative society. Further, none of the colonial
regimes really tried to overthrow the political, social and economic structures of the Adamawa emirates. Even attempts to eradicate slavery were
very cautious and largely ineffective. The poetry, therefore, contains
little criticism, whether direct or ironic, of European colonialism, even
though some of the poets suggest that the western impact is responsible
for the introduction of alcoholism, adultery and female disobedience.
A very elaborate piece by Hamaseo Gire is filled with hyperbolic praise
of western technology as exemplified in a variety of contraptions that
range from the bicycle and the telegraph to the airplane and the gramophone. Yet the Muslim background is everywhere obvious: in the *contemptus mundi* theme—"the world," writes Moodi Yaawa, "is but a vain
delusion, the dirty abode of lie"—and especially in the many poems
written in warning against women's frailty and wiles.

By far the largest segment in the corpus gathered by Lacroix is
made up of praise poems which reflect the strongly hierarchical, aristocratic character of Adamawa society. Many were composed in honour
of chiefs and other noble persons, in the hope of gaining patronage.
Others were presumably paid assignments written in praise of members
of the emerging African middle class such as butchers, shop-keepers or
truck-drivers: "The smoke of your truck," writes Buuba Jariida, "is as
fragrant as sandalwood; its tires leave their imprint on the road like a
seal."

The transition to independence, which led to considerable unrest in
the neighbouring Bamileke country, occurred all the more smoothly in
Adamawa as the dominant party, the *Union Camerounaise*, had its main
strength in the Muslim north: it was led by Ahmadou Ahidjo, who became the country's first prime minister in February 1958, and its first
president when it gained independence on 1 October 1961. Haman
Bello wrote several praise poems in honor of Ahidjo. These are of special interest because of the light they throw on the way traditional theocratic attitudes persist even after the outward apparel of parliamentary
democracy had been introduced. Bello makes no mention of parties or
elections, or of the fact that the *Union Camerounaise* won only by a bare
majority; he is aware that a new type of power structure has appeared,
since, as he states, "sovereignties have always been hereditary since the

beginning of our religion"; but, he goes on, "Ahidjo obtained his power from the Almighty," and "when he gives an order, all are obliged to abide by the will of the Almighty." Implicit is the concept that western-type electoral procedures are just another way for Allah to manifest his will: "The gift of God is enough for him who received it to obtain everything. He whom He has rejected obtains neither throne nor glory." In another poem, presumably written after 1962, when the large scale revolt organized among the coastal populations by Dr. Félix Moumié's *Union des Populations Camerounaises* had been put down with the help of French troops, Haman Bello hailed Ahidjo for bringing all the benefits of peace and freedom to the country: tribal fighting is over, trade, agriculture and cattle-breeding are prosperous, colonial controls and interdictions have been abolished, airplanes are taking pilgrims to Mecca. And the poet stresses that the counterpart of power is respon- sibility—on a nation-wide scale: "Since God delivered this country unto your hands, Ahidjo, you are responsible for anything a Cameroonian may suffer." This was a very rare example of modern-type national consciousness as distinct from traditional ethnic loyalty.´

The Fulani's proud sense of superiority, which they derive from their religious affiliation and their Arabic culture, is very prominent in a praise poem by Buuba Jariida, where Ahidjo is described, somewhat unexpectedly, as "the handsome European from Garwa," "the white Arab," "the white man from Paris"! Moodi Yaawa never disguises his contempt for thick-necked slaves and black pagans, and the comparative prosperity which trade brought to the South is to him a source of puz- zlement: "Allah has blessed those people," he exclaims incredulously in his verse account of a trip to Yaounde: "look at that black pagan, whose house is covered with corrugated iron."

Such a surprising reaction, expressing a deeply conservative outlook, is the price that Adamawa society has to pay for living in sheltered isolation. None of the Adamawa poets has received much of a western- type education. On the other hand, the many francophone writers who appeared in Cameroon in the 1950s came from the South and were unaware of Fulani poetry. Even such a knowledgeable scholar as Rupert East could claim in 1935, that "Fulani is dying out in some places and deteriorating in others, because there is no literature by means of which it can be preserved in classical purity after it has ceased to be spoken."[8] Whether Fulani will cease to be spoken in the foreseeable future is very doubtful. In the 1960s, an attempt was made by the important Came- roonian publishing house, the *Centre de Littérature Evangélique*, to bridge the literary gap between the Muslim North and the more westernized South by publishing Eldridge Mohammadou's *Contes et Poèmes Fulbe de la Benoué*, so that there is some prospect that Fulani writing from Adamawa may one day become integrated into modern Cameroonian literature.

•   •   •

There are Fulani communities in many parts of West Africa and the area which was to become, as far as we can make out in the present state of our knowledge, the main centre of Fulani writing was the mountainous Futa Jalon in present-day Guinea. Important Fulani groups coming from Masina had migrated there in the last quarter of the seventeenth century. By 1725, a theocratic federation of Fulani states had come into being in the Futa Jalon, where the first learned writer who relinquished Arabic in favour of the vernacular seems to have been a contemporary of Usman dan Fodio, Mohammadou Samba of Mombeya (c. 1765–1852).[9] In *Oogirde Malal* ("The Goldmine of Eternal Happiness"), he described his purpose as follows:

I shall explain the dogmas in the Fulani language
To make them understandable to thee: hearing them, accept them.
Only one's own language enables one
To understand what the original says.
Many among the Fulani doubt what they read
In Arabic, and so remain in uncertainty.[10]

Thus Samba did in the Futa Jalon what the Dan Fodio family were doing in Hausaland. Written by learned men deeply committed to the spiritual betterment of their people, this early Fulani poetry was characterized by its other-wordly outlook, its emphasis on religious learning, its fatalism, its ethical preoccupations, its uniformly lofty, but highly refined, style and versification.

It was also during the first half of the nineteenth century that Samba's disciple, Saidou Dalen (d. c. 1850) composed a treatise on Fulani grammar and versification which codified the indebtedness of *ajami* writers to the verse forms and metres of classical Arabic poetry. His own poetry exhibited the same orthodox didactic trend as his master's. One of his books was entitled *The Prophet's Praises*, and one of his poems, "Brothers, Listen and Learn," was a verse restatement of the essentials of Islamic religion, a genre as widely spread throughout Muslim Africa as homilies and verse sermons used to be in medieval Europe, both east and west. Islamic learning was cultivated in such centres as the town of Billeh, which E.W. Blyden, the famous scholar from Liberia, visited in 1873. He called it "a University town—the Oxford of the region." It was the seat of a "Muslim University" of some 500 students. Its President, Fode Tarawally, was, Blyden says, "the great literary celebrity of this region." When Blyden, together with the Governor of Sierra Leone, Pope-Hennessy, and the other members of the expedition went to see him, he showed them what Blyden's report describes as "a wonderful collection of Arabic manuscripts on various subjects—some copies of books brought from Arabia, and some original African compositions."[11]

Together with asceticism, the need for Koranic learning remained a central theme in the growing body of poetry produced by the learned scholars called *tierno*, a large amount of which has been collected and preserved through the labours of Gilbert Vieillard and, more recently, of Alfa Ibrahima Sow. The trend was pursued well into the twentieth century by such writers as Alillou Bouba-Ndiang (1845–1927),[12] and his son Chaïkou Manda (b. *c.* 1900). But the dissemination of literacy through the Islamic schools also favoured the emergence in writing of a more popular type of literature in rhymed prose. This was already represented in the 1850s by Bademba Issaga, one of whose love poems contains interesting allusions to trade with the European posts on the Guinea coast. According to Alfa Ibrahima Sow, the two main themes of this secular literature were the praise of women and the praise of cattle, the latter a not unexpected interest in a pastoral society, similar in this respect to those of Lesotho and Rwanda.

The French conquest of Futa Jalon in 1896 was to bring new topics within the compass of Fulani poetry. In theory, the kingdom was a protectorate, but the French soon proceeded to destroy the ancestral structure of Fulani society, deposing and replacing all traditional authorities that did not conform to the instructions of the governor in Conakry. Here as in many other parts of French Africa, the colonial administration undermined a well-established and highly respected hierarchy. Kings and noble lords were stripped of their power. The only traditional rulers left with some authority were the village headmen, who became little more than low-class auxiliaries of the French administration: their main function was to collect taxes and to recruit manpower.

A number of hitherto anonymous poems, which were gathered by Vieillard around 1910, but not published until 1937, illustrate the ambiguous impact of those events on the Fulani writers. Some of them have a decidedly militant note:

> *Destroy the arrogance of the rebels, the French and their Negro slaves, Almighty!*
> *Return vigour to religion in Futa Jalon*
> *Destroy the Europeans in all Futa.*
> *Permit us to recover our slaves, our troops, and our women, All-powerful One!*

Return abundance to Futa Jalon
Permit us to control Futa Jalon, replace us in possession of Futa, in justice.

One suspects that further research might unearth a number of similar protest poems, which Vieillard may have neglected for obvious reasons. On the whole, however, the most intriguing feature of this poetry is that there seemed to be little active resistance to colonization. In the main, such poems from the beginnings of the colonial period as have reached print, while outspokenly rancorous, reflect the writers' Muslim fatalism and otherworldliness, especially in connection with the taxes levied by the French through the village headmen:

God is putting us to the test, that is why he has made us know
The tax collectors, who are deprived of bliss in the other world.
Let us pay the tax, that they may eat it. We will observe our religion,
And God will feed us in the other world.

In his slow, circuitous way, the poet gradually becomes more violent in tone: worldly wealth is carrion, taxes are a dog's vomit, which only dogs will swallow back; soon further complaints against the colonial system are introduced:

The tax eaters, let them also swallow carrion, liquor
And pork, since they choose the present above the future.
Let them practise usury and adultery: they have chosen.
They are with the Whites, who will be deprived of bliss in the other world.

And the poet ends with the hope that the expected Mahdi will soon come and drive the tax collectors to the Gehenna. The work may therefore conjecturally be ascribed to the early years of the twentieth century, for in 1907 one of the most honoured *tiernos* of the Futa Jalon began to preach openly against colonial injustice and predicted the imminent coming of a Mahdi to end French oppression.

This strange combination of ascetic acceptance and outspoken protest found expression in slyly ironic form in a poem which Mohammadou Louda Dalaba allegedly composed for Gilbert Vieillard in the early 1930s. Entitled "Let Us Accept the French," it begins with a praise of Allah, "who makes us live in these days of French rule;" the poet then explains that it is everyone's duty to do the will of God, and that after all the French are no worse than the Pharaohs and other oppressors, whose power was conspicuously transient. After granting that France enrolls African soldiers not of her own will but because of her enemies, Mohammadou Louda goes on to praise the chiefs and soldiers who help the French, for the very pragmatic reason that "It is thanks to them, indeed, that the Faithful can practice their religion under French rule."

While many Fulani poems of the colonial days deal with colonial rule in a spirit of resigned acceptance or militant protest, an important group of poems in Sow's anthology, *La Femme, la Vache, la Foi,* lament the moral decay which, it is claimed, resulted from the impact of the western way of life upon the ethical structure of Fulani society. This included the intrigues deriving from the disintegration of ancestral power patterns, the abolition of slavery, and also, perhaps most prominently, the growing aspiration of women for a more independent status than was afforded them by the Islamic tradition.

Different attitudes came to the fore with the generation of poets who were born after the French conquest. Even though most of them remained loyal to the Muslim creed and to the traditional technique of starting and ending their poetic compositions with praises of Allah, many had also received some degree of western-type education. They were aware of the secular values of the modern world, to which mastery of the French language was the key. Mahdillou Daka (b.c. 1905) wrote in French and Arabic as well as in his own language, and he provided Fulani translations of Christian scriptural texts for the Labé station of the American Bible Society. Where most earlier poets emphasized the need for Koranic learning, he advocated that all work, including manual work, should be for the benefit of the whole country. This secularizing trend was even more conspicuous in the poetry of Abdurrahmane Ba (b.c. 1917), which decidedly favored modernization. One of his major poems, "Hymn to Peace and to Futa Jalon," written in celebration of the termination of World War II, begins with the traditional invocation to God; the poet then reminds his listeners and readers of their sufferings during the war, when the Vichy regime obliged them to increase the production of rubber as a contribution to the war effort, when forced labour was the rule, and when migrant workers were sent to Senegal to help with the groundnut crops. All this is now over, he says gladly, and a man can now loiter in his compound from sunrise to sunset without fear of being disturbed by the local headman in search of taxes or manpower; and the learned man can meditate on the Koran at leisure. But while Abdurrahmane advises his readers to have their children brought up in the Muslim faith, he also adds: "Teach them French, so that they can manage the affairs of the world," and he stresses Guinea's urgent need for lawyers and engineers, doctors and teachers.

This is no recantation of Islam, but rather an updating of its outlook. Another of Abdurrahmane's poems, entitled "The Wonders of Our Time," mentions air travel, road building, improvements in housing, but also notes that broadcasting enables the faithful to listen to the Koran being recited in Cairo, and that new techniques make it possible to build larger, fireproof mosques that will outlast the centuries. This poem was written in the late 1950s, for it alludes to the author's leaving the *Bloc Africain de Guinée*, a conservative political party led by the chiefs, in order to join Ahmed Sekou Touré's *Parti Démocratique de Guinée;* indeed, the central purpose of the poem was to extol the latter and to denounce the traditional chiefs' exploitation of the common people.

There are still, however, a number of poets reared in traditional Koranic learning, whose work seems to be hardly touched by any modernizing ideas. To this group belongs Diawo Pellel (b.*c*. 1900), a Koranic school-teacher. One of his longer poems, "Advice to the True Subjects of the Eternally Living One," is an account of the many holy men, scholars and poets, who built up the pure Islamic tradition of Futa Jalon. A more impressive example of the permanence of devotional inspiration is a poem edited with critical commentaries and a French translation by Christiane Seydou in 1966. Entitled "Who Does Not Know God Is Lost," it was written by a woman, whose name is supposed to be Rahmatullahi. It is a verse homily in the Malikite tradition, but of exceptional quality because of its clear structure, vivid imagery and artistry in versification. After exhorting the reader to knowledge of and obedience to, the Prophet's law, it provides an almost Dantesque description of the fate that awaits the wrong-doer in the Gehenna.

Yet, despite the persistent liveliness of this tradition, it is clear that on the eve of independence the once almost absolute prestige of religious and didactic inspiration had been sufficiently muted to make room for a critique of traditional political structures, for the acceptance of western technology, and for a type of nationalism that disregarded the formerly aristocratic character of Fulani society, and thus enabled Muslim scholars to sympathize with the socialist outlook of many among the new political parties in Africa. But while the French literature of Guinea, scant as it may be, is at least able to reach a wider audience, very little is known about recent developments in vernacular writing. The evolution of Fulani poetry during the last few decades of the colonial regime suggests that it was capable of fitting effortlessly into the cultural patterns characteristic of the new African states. A renowned chronicler, Farba Ibrahima, reciting the genealogy of the Diallo of Labé, takes one of the princely branches down to the Minister of Co-operation of the early 1960s; although the version supplied by Sow in *Chroniques et récits du Fouta Djalon* was tape-recorded, the work must have been composed in writing, as it ends with the words, "Here the pen stops." And *La Femme, la Vache, la Foi* contains a highly interesting poem by Mohammadou Woûri Sagali (d. 1962): entitled "They Say We Know Equality," it shows that the poet was aware, most articulately and at a very early stage, of the corruption and social injustice with which Guinea, like most African states, was plagued in the years following independence.

• • •

There is a report that when El Hajj Umar, the great Senegalese reformer, visited Futa Jalon a few years before launching his *jihad*, he congratulated Mohammadou Samba for writing his *Oorgirde Malal*, but at the same time he cautioned him against future translations from the Arabic into the vernacular, for, he said "You will cause the Arab language to disappear." It is likely that the exceptionally close links of the Futa Toro with the Arab-speaking centres of learning in the Maghrib prevented the emergence of an *ajami* tradition as early as in other areas equally affected by the Fulani reformation. But in spite of the Sheikh's unswerving personal loyalty to the sacred tongue of Islam, the requirements of propaganda among the illiterate population made themselves felt in the Futa Toro and the neighbouring areas as they had done in Hausaland and in the Futa Jalon. While the example of Umar himself led to the promotion of Arabic writing in Senegal, a number of his disciples found it expedient to resort, in their written works, to the Futa Toro dialect of the Fulani language.

Most of the poems that have been thus produced belong to the Arabic genre named *qasida*, a rhymed ode of pre-Islamic origin. Their purpose is to reach the vast audience who could not be expected to read or understand Arabic. They are designed to be learned by heart and recited or chanted by beggars and students. They are usually focused on the personality, doctrine and career of Umar. They have seldom more than two or three hundred verses, and they are all fundamentally religious in outlook. Several *qasidas* dating from the Sheikh's lifetime are still well known in the Futa Toro. They include work by such contemporaries of Umar as El Hadj Mahmadou Lamine (d. 1887), and especially Lamine Tafsir Ahmadou Dyamabou, whose *qasida* centres on the military exploits of Umar.

The most ambitious *ajami* poem from the Futa Toro is a long epic *qasida* of Umar's life history, by Mohammadou Aliou Tyam (*c.* 1830-1911).[13] Mohammadou was still a very young man in 1845, when he was one of the first to join the Sheikh, who had just returned from Mecca to the Futa Toro. He followed Umar almost until the latter's death, and took part in most of his campaigns against the pagan Bambara and the Fulani of Masina. After Umar's death in 1864, Mohammadou lived with the prophet's son and successor, Amadou Sekou, in Segou, in present-day Mali, where he worked at his *qasida* for more than twenty years. It is a long chronicle of more than 1180 verses, all ending on the same rhyme, on the Arabic model. It tells the life story of el-Hajj Umar from his pilgrimage to Mecca to his death; it recounts many details of his formative years, and of his religious and military career, which would not be otherwise available.

Such poetry of religious or historical inspiration is the more respected segment of *ajami* writing among the Futa Toro Fulani. After Umar's death, the tradition was continued by such poets as Ahmadou Tidyani (d.*c.* 1930). But there is also in existence another, lighter and more popular vein of poetry, which may be erotic or satirical. Partly derived from Arabic love poetry as transmitted through Mauritania, and partly imitative of the art of the *griots*, oral bards held in low esteem by literate Fulani, this poetry has been recently exemplified in some pieces by Oumar Ba (b. 1914).[14] These vernacular poems, provided with his own French translation, often reflect the usual homiletic type of Muslim piety, but others, of a more mundane character, express with terse, almost aphoristic irony, the writer's sly wisdom on women, on politics and politicians and on the character of other ethnic groups. Besides being a notable linguist and Islamic scholar, Oumar Ba has also published in French his reminiscences of the days when he was an interpreter in Mauritania.[15]

2. Hausa

The emergence of an *ajami* tradition in Hausa was the third major literary consequence—besides the Arabic revival and the birth of Fulani writing—of the Muslim renascence under Usman dan Fodio. Being more fluent in Arabic and in Fulani, the Shehu produced only few poems in Hausa: "it therefore seems likely that, whereas the Shehu addressed himself mainly to those who understood Fulfulde or Arabic, it was [his brother] Abdullah and others of the Shehu's companions, for instance the Zamfara poet Muhammadu Tukur, who composed the message for the Hausa-speaking congregations."[16] One of Usman's Hausa poems, *Wallahi, wallahi* ("I Swear by God"), composed between 1809 and 1815, is of pecular interest because of its intensely personal note, so uncommon in Muslim poetry: here, the leader of the *jihad*, while severely indicting administrative corruption and greed, angrily defends himself against those who claimed that he was moved by personal political ambition.[17]

It was chiefly under the reign of Muhammad Bello (1817–1837) that the foundations of Hausa writing were laid by Usman's brother, Abdullah b. Muhammad (1766-1829), his daughter Asma'u (also known as Nana) bint Shehu (1794-1863), and such of his early disciples as Asim Degel and Muhammadu Tukur. They handled in Hausa the favourite genres and the main themes of Islamic writing: they produced panegyrics of the prophet Muhammad and of other saintly men, chiefly the founders of the brotherhoods. This could hardly be distinguished from the so-called biographies (*sira*) such as Abdullah's *Wakar sira* ("Song of Biography") and Asim Degel's *Wakar Muhammadu* ("Song of Muhammad"), both of which deal with the Prophet. Asma is mainly remembered for her *Wakar gewaye* ("Song of the Wandering"), which was perhaps originally composed in Fulani, and which recounts the life of her father from the days of his exile until his death.[18] Abdullah and Muhammadu Tukur wrote the earliest Hausa poems of admonition, warning the reader against the fickleness of earthly life and its poisonous allurements.[19] Those early poets also transferred to Hausa poetry the interest in numbers, astronomy and astrology in which Arabic poets and learned men had traditionally been much absorbed.[20] And they inserted the budding Hausa literature into the honoured tradition of didactic verse, providing rhymed treatises on law and theology.[21]

After the death of Muhammad Bello, a period of decay began for the Sokoto empire as Fulani leaders departed from the missionary zeal and austere ideals of Islam, indulged in internecine fighting and treated the territories of their neighbours as a source of supply for the profitable slave trade. Then it was that the Shehu's posthumous son, Isa (1817–1880) provided Hausa versions of several of his father's Fulani poems and adapted into Hausa, as *Wakar karamomin Shehu* ("Song of the Shehu's Miracles"), Gidado dan Laima's Arabic account of the miracles attributed to Usman.[22] While the production of edifying verse went on unabated, new themes and new moods crept into Hausa poetry. The concept of political morality had not been absent from early Hausa writing. But whereas it had been handled in such a way as to indict the "mixed Islam" of the Habe emirs, learned poets now turned increasingly to moral criticism of the corruption and divisiveness that had emerged among the Fulani rulers themselves.[23] An early representative of this new trend was Muhammadu Na Birnin Gwari, who flourished *c.* 1850, and who was incensed at the way a break-away dynasty of the Sokoto house, the Nagwamatse, had set up a new emirate at Kontagora and terrorized their Muslim neighbours by their slave-raiding. This lasted until British intervention brought the empire to an end: at the close of the nineteenth century the *imam* of Daura inserted political attacks against the local Fulani rulers into an otherwise fairly conventional didactic poem. And the point was reached when a grandson of Usman, Hayatu dan Sa'idu, could write a long satire in macaronic verse skilfully mixing Hausa and Arabic, against the whole of the Sokoto establishment.

Those were tumultuous days for Hausaland. On top of this inner decay, strife was stirred by the claims of the Mahdi of the Eastern Sudan, and European penetration was beginning to show the extent of its threat. These upheavals strengthened the *contemptus mundi* attitude which had always been a commonplace of Muslim homiletic poetry, and encouraged thoughtful men to seek solace and hope in the mercy of God and in the intercession of the saintly men who acted as intermediaries between Allah and mankind. This sense of apocalypse inspired such writers as Buhari dan Gidado, the grandson of Muhammad Bello's vizier, who was himself vizier of Sokoto when the British captured the city in 1903. It lasted well into the twentieth century, and one of its most eloquent exponents was Aliyu dan Sidi, who ruled over Zaria from 1903 to 1920.[24]

• • •

The British conquest of Hausaland at the turn of the century was bound to produce deep changes in Hausa writing. Yet, these were not very conspicuous at first: the resilience of Islamic societies against threats to their cultural autonomy must be taken into account. The didactic tradition was to enjoy its monopoly for several decades. It remained dominated by the usual religious outlook and themes. Even European occupation failed to make much of an impact. As Hiskett put it,

Protest was fragmentary, directed at certain specific inconveniences, and at the general upset that the occupation and the campaigns that preceded it, caused to the traditional Hausa way of life. There is some evidence of a sense of moral outrage against the aggressive intrusion of the foreigner; but this is not the dominant sentiment. Hausa society viewed the events of c. 1900 at several different levels. First, they were simply steps on the way to the final apocalypse. . . . Second, when this final catastrophe failed to materialize immediately they were seen as part of all the other tensions and clashes of interest that already made up the pattern of Hausa relations. And, finally, the poets seem as much preoccupied with the inadequacies of their own society as with foreign intrusion.[25]

Not altogether surprisingly, one of the fiercest opponents of European rule, with the quill as with the gun, was the slave raider Ibrahim Nagwamatse (1857–1922), who composed songs to extol Muslim resistance to the troops of Lord Lugard. But although he may have been partly prompted by fears for the future of his own trade, one of his poems revealingly "ends with his fears for the liquidation of the Islamic religion in the North [of Nigeria]. He saw European education as essentially Christian, and its influence therefore negative."[26]

The rapid establishment of the *pax britannica* was not viewed unfavourably by Hausa traders, whose Muslim devotion did not prevent them from keeping in mind the interests of business. A remarkable example of this ambiguity is provided by al-Hajj Umar ibn Abu Bakr (1858–1934)[27] the Hausa kolanut merchant who, as already mentioned, prompted the appearance of a school of Arabic writing in Northern

Ghana (see pp. 39-40). In 1903, five years after he had composed an Arabic poem lamenting the arrival of the Europeans, Umar wrote a Hausa poem, variously known as *Labarin Nasara* or *Wakar Nasara* ("Song of the Christians"), where his comments were rather ambivalent, showing "awed respect for Christian prowess" and "*Schadenfreude* at the defeat of local rulers", thus indicating that "reaction to the British occupation of Hausaland was not one of simple disapproval or outrage."[28]

Nor was Umaru the only writer of Hausa in Gonja. Another active figure was Malam al-Hasan (d. *c.* 1933), a scholar of half-Fulani origin, who used Hausa for his historical accounts of various Sudanic kingdoms. "He should be regarded as a colleague, rather than a disciple of al-Hajj Umar", but although "the School of Salaga may be seen as drawing its strength in the late nineteenth and early twentieth centuries principally from these two scholars, al-Hajj Umar appears to have attracted far more students."[29] While the majority of these chose to write in Arabic, one at least, Yusuf Abin-Nema, is remembered for a Hausa poem which he composed after World War I and which deals with the period of European penetration in northern Ghana.

It is perhaps no sheer coincidence that these troubled times seem also to have witnessed the writing down of verse chronicles in Hausa, as if Hausa poets, sensing the threat from modernity, were eager to stabilize the image of their people's identity as embodied in the oral tradition. The best-known of these is the *Song of Bagauda*, a verse chronicle of Kano.[30] It is remarkable for providing an account of the early, legendary, history of Kano, and for devoting considerable attention to the pre-*jihad* history of Hausaland. It was first written in the late nineteenth century, but successive anonymous authors brought it down to the 1950s. By contrast, the *Chronicle of Sokoto*, completed in the 1920s by Abubakar dan Atiku, makes no reference to the early history of the country. These verse chronicles, and other ones dealing with lesser towns, were not simply regarded as historical documents perpetuating the memory of the past, but are heavily marked by characteristic Islamic moral didacticism: they are at many points dominated by the *ubi sunt* and *memento mori* attitudes which underlie the greater part of Muslim homiletic writing.

•   •   •

The most significant consequence of European penetration, in Hausaland as in other parts of Africa, was the introduction of the roman script, leading to the emergence of digraphia and the birth of imaginative prose in Hausa.

Christian missionaries had been active in the area long before the

colonial conquest. The Gospel of St. Matthew had been translated into
Hausa in the 1860s, and in 1877 part of a translation of St. John had
even been printed in Arabic script: this was the work of Jacob Friedrich
Schön (1803–1889).[31] Under British rule, repeated attempts were
made to introduce the Roman alphabet. But in actual fact, use of the
new script was practically limited to European scholars—Germans such
as G.A. Krause, R. Prietze, A. Mischlich, and K. Krieger, and later,
British students of the language and its literature—mainly for the recording of oral lore. This trend culminated in 1913, with the almost
simultaneous publication of Frank Edgar's *Litafi na Tatsuniyoyi na Hausa*
("Hausa Tales and Traditions"),[32] A.J.N. Tremearne's *Hausa Superstitions and Customs* and R.S. Rattray's *Hausa Folk Lore*. Because it was
printed in the indigenous language, Edgar's collection was later to provide an example and useful encouragement to modern Hausa writers.

Apart from Christian texts and traditional lore, the new script was
also used for a number of educational pamphlets. But, as Czech scholar
Petr Zima has pointed out,

> *The first reactions of Hausa readers were not altogether favourable. The Ar-
> abic script and literacy in it had the advantage of being already in use; re-
> stricted though Ajami literacy may have been at that time, it was established.
> The Roman script, on the other hand, was automatically associated with for-
> eign, "pagan" or unbelievers' ideas. The common name given to this Roman-
> script-based literacy—*boko—might well have been associated both with the
> English word "book" and with the Hausa original sense, which means "de-
> ceit" or "fraud."*[33]

As a result, for several decades, educated Hausas simply ignored the
new script; they also ignored the possibilities for a prose fiction in the
indigenous language which had been opened up by Edgar, and they
confined themselves to the tradition of *ajami* poetry.

But in the early 1930s a Translation Bureau was set up in Northern
Nigeria under the management of an education officer named Rupert
East. Its main purpose was to provide Hausa translations of school textbooks, but original authorship was not neglected: already in 1931, the
Bureau published two books dealing with the history and customs of
the Hausa and their neighbors. This ampler scope became formalized
when the institution was turned into a Literature Bureau, which was
situated in Zaria, and which deliberately tried to foster Hausa creative
writing in the Roman script.

East has provided a revealing account of the obstacles he had to overcome in prompting educated Hausas to write prose fiction on the western model:

The first difficulty was to persuade these Malamai that the thing was worth doing. The influence of Islam, superimposed on the Hamitic strain in the blood of the Northern Nigerian, produces an extremely serious-minded type of person. The art of writing, moreover, being intimately connected in his mind with his religion, is not to be treated lightly. Since the religious revival at the beginning of the last century, nearly all the original work produced by Northern Nigerian authors has been either purely religious or written with a strong religious motive. Most of it is written in Arabic, which, like Latin in Medieval Europe, was considered a more worthy medium for any work of importance than the mother tongue. . . The art of story-telling is, of course, well known to all people of West Africa, but in Northern Nigeria, as elsewhere, it is looked upon as a pastime for the amusement of women and children, somewhat below the dignity of a man who has attained to the status of a malam. For generations the same stories have been passed from mouth to mouth, and never written down except at the instigation of the European. . . . To these people, therefore, the idea of writing a book which was frankly intended neither for the edification of the mind, nor the good of the soul, a "story" book which, however, followed none of the prescribed forms of story-telling, seemed very strange. The historical novel, which presented itself as a possible link between history, which they understood, and fiction writing, which they did not—in other words, the practice of deliberately mixing truth with falsehood under the same cover—appeared to some to be definitely immoral. In short, it was necessary to explain to a very conservative audience a conception which was entirely new, and of doubtful value if not morality. [34]

East's efforts were successful to the extent that he persuaded several young Koranic scholars, who had also received some western-type training as school-teachers, to write five short novels, which were printed by the Zaria Literature Bureau in the mid-1930s. One of these, *Jiki Magayi* ("The body is the one that tells") was in fact written jointly by himself and Malam J. Tafida (b. 1909). The theme is the revenge taken by a young man, who has lost his bride's affection to a wealthy older man versed in the use of magic. The manner of his vengeance launches a chain of events dominated by something very much akin to the immanent logic of crime and punishment in Greek tragedy. An English version of the story was later produced, without acknowledgment, by the Igbo Writer Cyprian Ekwensi in *An African Night's Entertainment* (1962). [35]

Love, hatred and revenge, which play a conspicuous role in *Jiki Magayi*, are significantly absent from the works of purely local authorship that were composed during those years. The best of these was *Shaihu Umar*; [36] its author, who signed himself Abubakar Bauchi, was none other than Abubakar Tafawa Balewa (1912–1966), who was to become the first Prime Minister of independent Nigeria. It tells the story of a fictional

Hausa *malam* of the late nineteenth century. It illustrates the usual characteristics of early African endeavours in the alien art of prose fiction:
concentration on the anecdotal narrative of incidents, indifference to
the subtler shades of character depiction and psychological analysis, and
heavy-handed moralizing. There is, however, a revealing contrast between the resilience of the title character and of his mother and the
picture of the harsh world in which they move. As in many early vernacular works in other parts of Africa, much emphasis is laid on the
general insecurity of life and society: Umar's step-father is evicted from
his native place by court intrigues; Umar and his mother are separately
captured by Arab slave-traders; Balewa provides a grimly realistic picture of the trans-Saharan slave trade. The sense of general impotence
before the hostility of nature and the inhumanity of man to man goes
a long way to account for Muslim fatalism and stoicism: *Shaihu Umar*
helps the non-Muslim reader to grasp this important point. Yet Balewa's somewhat sombre picture of man's life is not without its redeem-
ing features. For all the horror that is built into the slave-trade, the
traders themselves are not portrayed as beasts of prey in human attire;
indeed, it is one of them who, in Egypt, sees that Umar receives the
Koranic learning for which he will become famous first in Egypt and,
later, in his own country.

Balewa's realistic description of the hazards of life in pre-colonial
Hausaland helps us to understand a different trend which emerged in
the work of another pioneer of Hausa prose fiction, Muhammadu
Bello's *Gandoki*. A scholar of the classical Islamic type, Muhammadu
Bello (b.1890) is the author of a number of pamphlets and poems in
Arabic which never reached print but were disseminated in manuscript
form. His only novel, which he wrote for the Zaria Literature Bureau,
relates the high deeds of an imaginary Hausa warrior in the days of the
British conquest. After his defeat by British troops, Gandoki leaves his
country to fight against the *jinns*. After years of fanciful adventures, he
comes back to his native place in the hope that he will now succeed in
driving out the infidels. Much to his surprise, he finds that the country
is peaceful and well-governed, and that the people are satisfied with
British rule. He admires the white man's achievements in agriculture,
and he sends his son to the missionary school. It is tempting to assume
that the book was written in order to please the colonial authorities. But
Shaihu Umar had described the sense of fear and insecurity which permeated a decadent pre-colonial society, and this is the historical background to *Gandoki*. It must be remembered, too, that the British system
of indirect rule first implemented by Lord Lugard in northern Nigeria,
allowed a considerable measure of autonomy to African societies and
enabled them to preserve much of their cultural identity, while introducing the *pax britannica* and checking the more blatant abuses of the

emirs. There is therefore no reason to doubt that *Gandoki* faithfully reflected the viewpoint of a large section of the educated class in the middle of the colonial period.

The peculiar mixture of realism and fantasy, together with its luxuriant style and the praise-poems with which the narrative is interspersed, earned *Gandoki* the first prize in a competition organized by the Zaria Literature Bureau, while *Shaihu Umar* which was more austerely didactic and written in simple, straightforward language, received the third prize. The second prize went to a story by Muhammadu Bello's younger brother, Abubakar Imam (b. 1911), whose *Ruwan Bagaja* ("The Water to cure all ills") has a sort of picaresque plot, with a hero setting out on a quest, undergoing various trials among the *jinns* and encountering loosely connected adventures in each place he visits. As in *Gandoki*, much of the action takes place in a world of magic and fantasy, but Imam added a note of humour and satire, which is part of the folklore legacy rather than of the written tradition. The protagonists are two corrupt *mallams* who anticipate the satirical portrayal of venal *marabouts* later to be found in the French stories of Birago Diop.

These three writers, together with Muhammadu Gwarzo (b. 1911), whose novella *Idon Matambayi* ("The Eye of the Questioner") appeared in 1934, may truly claim to have laid the foundations of modern prose fiction in Hausa, with its peculiar blend of Muslim piety, earthy folk humour, and oral tradition. *Jiki Magayi*, however, is different from the others, perhaps because of its dual Hausa-English authorship. Here, indeed, as Neil Skinner has observed, "the darker sides of human nature—jealousy, hatred and revenge—are painted, and the atmosphere is that of Verdi's darker operas. Suffering and death are not matters for quiet resignation, for submission, as in *Shaihu Umar,* but are causes of resentment to the characters and of sympathy in the reader. It is of interest too that the start of all the trouble in *Jiki Magayi* is the passion of a man for a woman, a theme rare in Hausa written literature, except for drama."[37] But as formal drama in Hausa did not arise until two decades later, Rupert East may well have been responsible for this kind of emotional activism, as well as for the recognition that what Skinner calls "the primitive emotions of passion, cruelty, vindictiveness and hatred," hitherto confined to oral art, were valid material for the written art as well.

Abubakar Tafawa Balewa and Muhammadu Gwarzo later turned to politics. Muhammadu Bello entered the administration, ultimately to become *wali* of Katsina. But Abubakar Imam never desisted from his interest in the promotion of a modern literature among the Hausa. In 1935, he was assigned to the Zaria Literature Bureau and composed a three-volume collection of stories, *Magana Jari Ce* ("The Art of Storytelling is a Valuable Gift") which appeared in 1940: the tales, which

are supposed to be narrated by a parrot so clever that he has been made
a *vizier*, are drawn from a wide variety of sources, African, European,
Arabic, and Oriental. In 1939, Abubakar Imam was instrumental in
bringing about the foundation of the first Hausa newspaper entitled
Gaskiya Ta Fi Kwabo ("Truth is Worth More than a Penny"). In 1945,
he contributed to the setting up of a government-sponsored Hausa publishing house, the Gaskiya Corporation, which supplanted the Zaria Literature Bureau. The Gaskiya Corporation remained the main publisher
of vernacular material in Northern Nigeria until the foundation of the
North Regional Literature Agency (NORLA) in 1954. Side by side with
these new activities, Imam went on composing stories designed as reading matter for schools; he also produced a number of educational works
dealing with natural science, Islamic history and the Muslim faith. His
Six Hausa Plays, published in the late 1930s, are the earliest examples of
modern-type drama in Hausa.

Gaskiya, the Gaskiya Corporation, and, from the late 1950s, NORLA,[38]
provided invaluable encouragement for vernacular writers in Hausaland, which, incidentally, did not produce any creative writing in English
until the early 1970s. In 1951 and 1952, the Gaskiya Corporation issued
such short novels as *Iliya Dan Maikarfi* ("Iliya, Son of a Strong Man")
by Ahmadu Ingawa, *Sihirtaccen gari* ("The Enchanted Town") by Amada
Katsina, and *Da'u Fataken Dare* ("Dau, the Night Raider") by Tanko
Zango. These are slight, 40-page booklets: extended prose fiction does
not seem to hold great attraction for Hausa authors. *Nagari Na-Kowa*
(1958) by Jabiru Abdullah Mashi with its 112 pages, is often considered
the first "full-length" novel in Hausa; it is a picaresque story without
much interest in plot organization or character development.[39] More recently, Umaru A. Dembo (b. 1945) reverted to the shorter form with
Tauraruwa Mai Wutsiya ("Shooting Star," 1969), which combined the
influence of the *Arabian Nights* already at work in *Gandoki*, with that of
western space fiction.

While these showed no marked improvement upon the prose fiction
of the 1930s, formal drama, initiated by Abubakar Imam, was consolidated in the late 1950s by a younger writer, Shu'aibu Makarfi (b. *c.*
1918), with *Zamanin Nan Namu* ("These Times of Ours," 1959) and
Jatau Na Kyallu ("Kyallu's Jatau," 1960); these are typical of Hausa
drama, on which Neil Skinner commented as follows:

> . . . plays—*in contrast with poetry, which views a wider field*—*have on the
> whole been concerned with domestic situations and, in particular, marriage
> and divorce in a polygamous household and the tensions that arise there. Such
> situations are treated with considerable realism and are used to point out a
> moral which is often driven home through the medium of an Announcer,
> playing the part of the Greek chorus as well as helping the author fill the*

audience in on any action that has occurred offstage. The evils of drink, profligacy, the rejection of traditional ways or—in contrast—the refusal to grasp the opportunities offered by modern education are all pointed out at some length.[40]

The problems connected with marriage in societies undergoing cultural change often provide topical subject matter for modern African dramatists. But the Hausa form an obdurately conservative society which does not seem to have been deeply affected by the impact of European beliefs and mores. Consequently, Hausa playwrights prefer to treat traditional Muslim marriage either as a target of moral criticism, or as a source of slapstick comedy. *Uwar Gulma* ("Mother of Mischievous Tale-telling," 1968) by A. Mohammed Sada (b. 1942) has been described as one of the first serious literary works in Hausa. It focuses on a messenger and his young wife, whose marriage is destroyed by parents and so-called friends. With savage irony and harsh realism, it provides a very damaging picture of a decaying society. But *Tabarmar Kunya* ("Mat of Shame," 1969), by Dan Gogo and Dauda Kano, is the farcical comedy of a young man who tries to win back his offended wife from the home of her parents

That the playwrights' intention is usually didactic and/or comic confirms Neil Skinner's generalization that "Hausa literature does not encourage its audience to feel—to enjoy tears and emotionalise over suffering. In this of course, it merely expresses the culture, in which people endure suffering silently, if it is their own; but if it is the suffering of one with whom they are not concerned, are apt to laugh at it."

● ● ●

Although drama, especially in broadcast form, seems to have become increasingly popular in Hausaland, experiments with the alien genres of the novel and formal stage drama have remained rather exceptional. Poetry is still the most highly valued of the literary forms, and poets seem to enjoy greater esteem than prose writers or playwrights.

The most widely renowned Hausa author of the first half of the twentieth century is Aliyu Na Mangi (b. *c.* 1895), known as the blind poet of Zaria, who composes orally, although his works have reached print both in *boko* and in *ajami*. A piously traditional writer, he is the author of *Wakar Imfiraji* ("Song of Comfort"), an ambitious poem in eight long cantos, in which he "succeeds in expressing the urgency and passion of his desire to worship and conveys his spiritual experience of a close, personal relationship with the Prophet."[41] But his attachment to the Islamic ethos does not prevent him from writing occasional satirical poems, which, however, likewise reflect his basic traditionalism. One of these, dwells on the dangers of marrying a slovenly woman, while *Wakar Keke* ("Song of the Bicycle") is a verse dialogue between a bicycle and the rider it has thrown down, a comic warning against the new-fangled contraptions coming from Europe.[42]

Aliyu's poems were actually the first to be printed in the *ajami* script, but there are many among the older writers who choose to keep to this traditional medium. Mohammadu Dan Amu (b. 1903) composed his *Wakokin Madahu* ("Songs of Praise to the Prophet") in compliance with the highly formalized requirements of the Arabic panegyric called *madh*. Sometimes he even gives Arabic titles to his Hausa poems.[43] He claims that his poetry is chiefly designed to help Koranic students understand Islamic law and theology.[44] But such otherworldly concerns did not prevent him from bringing the verse chronicle of Sokoto up to modern times.

Yet, the pressure of social change made itself felt even among the writers of this older generation. Hiskett notes that Akilu Aliyu (b. 1912), dealing with the evils of present-day society, "has moved on from traditional satire of the prostitute herself, based on Islamic moral precepts, to attack the social causes of prostitution."[45] The turmoils of the Nigerian civil war inspired his *Wakar Soja* ("Song of the Soldier").[46]

This new trend became increasingly apparent as younger poets were coming to the fore. Most prose writers of the 1930s and many of their successors were school teachers reared in Northern Training Colleges—especially the one at Katsina, which was opened in 1928—where they received little more than a modicum of modern schooling. There is some evidence that Hausa writers tended to revert to the verse tradition, the higher and the more westernized the type of education they received. More elaborate education was provided by the Higher College opened in 1934 at Yaba, near Lagos, which aimed at training African secondary school teachers to replace expensive European staff. Northerners were often reluctant to spend years in the South for their professional training.

The first Hausa writer to do so was Sa'adu Zungur (1915–1958).[47] He was also the first to exhibit a full intellectual awareness of the problems facing his country. His *Wakar maraba da soja* ("Song of Welcome to the Soldier") is a praise poem in honour of the Hausa soldiers returning from World War II. As such, it is couched in the traditional mould, celebrating warlike prowess and satirizing the enemy. But the poem ends on a note that is far from traditional, as Sa'adu describes the mood and expectations of the returning soldiers, who want freedom and justice, prosperity and gratitude. The preparation for independence in Nigeria prompted the writing of *Arewa, Jumhuriya ko Mulukiya?* ("The North—Republic or Monarchy"), where Sa'adu warns his readers against the danger of a Nigeria dominated by the non-Muslim, republican South. While eulogizing the system of government inherited from the Sokoto empire, the poet also issues a sort of ultimatum to the traditional emirs, exhorting them, if their power is to survive, to accept the reforms, especially in matters of justice and education, that will enable their region to catch up with the South. This poem contains a curious passage, which shows how national feeling of a modern type was beginning to supplant the old religious definitions, for the writer implores Allah to protect the North, wholly, completely:

> *Muslims and Christians, all of them,*
> *Yes, and pagans too, the beer goblins,*

a prayer which, for all the ambiguity in its wording, signals the emergence of "a sense of common identity and a shared culture, on which certain Islamic values became widely accepted beyond the limits of confessional adherence to Islam."[48]

Basically similar premises underlie the poetry of Mu'azu Hadejia (1920–1958), whose *Tutocin Shaihu da Waninsu* ("Flags of the Shehu and Others") celebrates the traditional leaders of Hausaland. His main interests, however, are less overtly political and more decidedly moral than those of Sa'adu Zungur. His poems on the value of education, or on the social evils of harlotry and beer-drinking are little more than the stock response of one who feels his values threatened and merely resorts to "the secular sanction of the popular praise-singer—that is, public satire—and the Islamic sanctions of the Muslim moralist—that is, social ostracism and the threat of divine punishment—to deter the deviant and enforce conformity."[49]

Such poems exhibit complete indifference to the conditions that create ignorance, alcoholism or prostitution, and utter disregard for the advisability of social, moral, and intellectual reform. Some of the youngest poets, however, depart in various ways from this established pattern. The influence of western poetry is probably at work in the occasional appearance of lyrical themes which are outside the mainstream of both African inspiration with its highly communalized outlook and Muslim poetry with its strongly didactic character. *Wakar Damina* ("Song of the Rains") by Na'ibi Wali (b. 1929) contains fine descriptive passages within the framework of a praise-poem in honour of the rainy season.[50] The polemical inspiration, which is part of the tradition, has at times been placed in the service of causes which have no apparent connection with Muslim orthodoxy. During the 1950s, Mudi Sipikin (b. 1930), showed his radical anticolonial inclination in a "Song in Praise of Russia," which was casually printed in the *Daily Comet* under the British administration. But Zima reports that Sipikin later "abandoned his radical opinions and joined . . . the ruling conservative party," becoming "particularly interested in religious poetry" and "writing both in the Arabic script and in *boko*."[51] Finally, recent literate poets are apt to use the written art in a direction which used to be the preserve of oral bards: personal satire and abuse, which is basically different from the vein of moral satire exemplified by their elders. An uncommonly subtle example is *Wakar Bushiya* ("Song of the Hedgehog"), whose author is Isa Hashim (b. 1933), a Hausa poet of Fulani descent, who writes in both Arabic and Hausa. The theme of the poem is his "frustration and resentment against unfair treatment by a man placed in authority over the poet. . .". One of its chief features is "the contrast between the violent abuse of the words, conventionally fitted into a religious frame, and the sad, pensive, almost feline quality of the tune" to which it is to be chanted.[52]

Three articles published in 1965–1966 in *Kano Studies*[53] give some idea of the extraordinary complexity of the literary situation in Hausaland with regard to poetry. To begin with, oral composition is still very much alive and each emir seems to maintain his court musician, while the services of praise-singers are also resorted to by wealthy businessmen, "who see their praise-songs as an indirect advertisement; other songs that deserve attention are those from musicians attached to prominent farmers, butchers and hunters." With regard to the written art, some of it is still produced in Arabic, but "only the prominent Mallams at the head of the two major religious sects—Qadiriyya and Tijjanya— and a few of their lieutenants are capable of writing Arabic poetry of a satisfactory standard"; even these, however, prefer to write in the vernacular because "the moment the poets decide to write in Arabic, they limit their audience to the top layer of Mallams."

By far the larger proportion of the poetry written by the few dozen poets whose names are mentioned in the *Kano Studies* articles is in the vernacular. It constitutes an impressive body of remarkable diversity, with regard both to language and to the way the writers reach their audience. While the dialect of Sokoto is generally taken to be standard literary Hausa, each of the main towns in Northern Nigeria—Kano, Katsina, Kaduna, Zaria, and others—produced poetry in its own dialect. This is disseminated throughout Hausaland in a number of ways: poems circulate in manuscript form; they are broadcast from the Nigerian Broadcasting Corporation stations in Kano, Kaduna and other places; they are printed in *boko* (Roman script) or in *ajami* (Arabic script) in *Gaskiya* or by NORLA; and in Kano, *ajami* poets can rely on several private printing presses.

Nevertheless, for all the changes that have occurred in Hausa writing since the end of World War II—the growth of prose fiction and drama, thematic innovations in the traditional poetic forms, the use of printing and the modern media—its evolution has remained grounded in a rigid linguistic misoneism: Hausa literature has stubbornly resisted the encroachment of the colonizer's language which has been so successfully adopted by the other two main ethnic groups of Nigeria, the Ibo and the Yoruba. This is largely due to the vicissitudes of history: "Supported by Lugard's policy of Indirect Rule, the Northern Emirs have been able to consolidate their power, maintain traditional institutions, and limit social change in the past fifty years. As a consequence, the North was, at independence in 1960, by far the least developed Region, the literacy rate in Roman script being only 2 per cent against 16 per cent in the East and 18 per cent in the West."[54]

It is only in the early 1970s that the need to use a foreign language in order to communicate with the outside world began to make itself felt among Hausa writers: in 1968, curiously enough, *Kano Studies* printed a poem in French, by Muhammad Awal Ibrahim, an assistant lecturer at the Abdullahi Bayero College in Kano. Of wider significance, no doubt, and of less curiosity, was the appearance, in Kaduna in 1970, of the first issue of a new magazine, *Images*, which contained writing in Hausa and in English, showing signs, in Neil Skinner's words, "of an effort to describe things as they are, rather than to escape into the other worlds of stars and jinns or humorous fantasy."[55] The year 1970 also saw the foundation of *Harsunan Nijeriya*, a scholarly periodical which was first entirely printed in Hausa, but which has now come to include substantive essays in English on topics connected with the Hausa language and literature. This may be taken as an indication that Hausa *literati*, without renouncing their pride in possessing a widely-spread language with a long, venerable literary tradition, are beginning to adopt an attitude more responsive to the interest of outsiders.

3. Wolof

As the main vernacular language of Senegal, Wolof has come to be used as a *lingua franca* by most other Senegalese tribes. It is usually assumed that Islam began to supplant the original animistic religion of the Wolof as early as the eleventh century, at about the time of the conversion of the neighboring kingdom of Tekrur. From evidence gathered by European travellers in the fifteenth century, it seems that while the bulk of the Wolof population remained pagan, the leader class were in the habit of surrounding themselves with *marabouts* from the Maghrib. As in Futa Toro, the closeness of Arabic centres of learning may have prevented would-be Wolof writers from putting their own language to written purposes. At any rate, "the adoption of Islam by the Wolof was a slow process until in the second half of the nineteenth century a people's movement developed."[56]

A written literature might have arisen at an early stage as a result of French influence. "During the eighteenth century, the Senegalese towns of Saint-Louis and Gorée saw the growth of small but influential communities which were Afro-European in culture, and to some extent genetically also. . . . This community was quite small. Estimates of the 1770s suggest that between twelve and fifteen hundred free Negroes and mulattoes lived in Saint-Louis, and perhaps 250 at Gorée."[57] This appeared sufficient, however, for some attention to be paid, at a remarkably early date, to the local tongue: the Wolof language was reduced to writing, dictionaries and grammars were printed in the second quarter of the nineteenth century.[58] Further, "in the colonial towns the government gradually undertook to provide schools for the children of the *habitants* and such African children as could benefit from them."[59] It is interesting to note that the medium of elementary instruction was Wolof, so that a vernacular literature in roman script could conceivably have emerged as it was soon to do in South Africa, and later, in other British territories, if Wolof had not been replaced by French as early as 1829. As Hargreaves observes,

> This important decision did not entirely succeed in its purpose of replacing African cultural influences by French (since, to the despair of the Fathers, even mulatto children were still addressed by their mothers in their native Wolof, and thereby taught "superstitious ideas, obscene songs and stories"); but it inhibited the progress of all but the most adaptable African children.[60]

Accordingly, literary production under western influence was delayed for about a hundred years. As to non-literary writing, it is significant that of the two major documents for the precolonial history of the Wolof kingdom of Wâlo—both, of course, recordings of oral traditions—one, the note-books of Yoro Dyao (1847–1919)[61] was written in French, while the other was dictated in Wolof by Amadou Wade (1896–1961) on the basis of notes written in Arabic[62]: the latter thus appears as an outgrowth of the Arabic literacy that had been introduced among the Wolof as a consequence of the spreading of the Tijaniyya through Al Hajj Malik Sy and his contemporaries (see pp. 42–3).

As far as we know, creative writing in Wolof emerged in the late nineteenth century as a belated effect of the wave of Muslim expansion that had swept over the whole of West Africa. On the territory of present-day Senegal, this culminated in the foundation of the Murid brotherhood by Ahmadou Bamba M'backé. Although Ahmadou Bamba's own writing was in Arabic, he was deeply convinced of the need for reciprocal integration of Islam and the indigenous cultures. His disciples soon realized that genuine conversion of Kayor and of the neighbouring Wolof kingdoms could only be achieved through vernacular writing which could be sung or read out to illiterate village audiences. This attitude was in line with the activities of the Fulani reformers in the Futa

Jalon and in Hausaland, but in direct opposition to the Arabism of Al Hajj Umar and of his followers, who were afraid that *ajami* writing might lead to the neglect and disappearance of the sacred language in West Africa.

There thus arose a body of Wolof poetry,[63] whose main representative seems to have been an early disciple of Ahmadou Bamba, Moussa Ka (1890–1965)[64]; some of his poems have recently been made available in French. One of these, entitled "I will Try to Rise Once More...",[65] is a *memento mori* homily in eighty couplets, where the poet first reminds his readers of the many illustrious men whose power, opulence and even holiness did not allow them to escape death; after which he evokes—in terms reminiscent of François Villon and other dance-of-death poets of fifteenth-century Europe—the body's decay, and also the moral torture which awaits every man after death unless his piety and charity enable him to escape eternal damnation; he then conjures up with almost Dantean rhetoric the eternal punishments that Resurrection will bring to evil men, and he closes with the hope that Ahmadou Bamba's guidance will allow him to eschew the *gehenna* and to be welcomed in Paradise by Allah's *huris*.

Besides providing a Wolof translation of the Koran and Wolof versions of Ahmadu Bamba's Arabic poems, Moussa Ka was also addicted to another favourite Muslim genre, praise-poetry. Like all Islamic writers, he wrote praises of Allah and of the Prophet, and eulogies of his master, on whose death in 1927 he composed a funereal ode. *Jaaraama* is a panegyric of Ahmadou Bamba's mother.[66] According to Pathé Diagne, Moussa Ka's most ambitious work is an epic entitled *Barjân*. Written in the form of an imaginary dialogue between God and the Prophet, it is said to owe much to oral tale technique and to the dream vision characteristic of Arabic fiction.

Moussa Ka's assertion that

> *Wolof, Arabic, and all other languages are equally valuable:*
> *All poetry is fine, that aims at praising the Prophet,*

fostered the emergence of many poets writing in Wolof, whose output is of considerable diversity. Anta Diop mentions the satirical poetry of Aliou Thioune, the polemical epistles of Mor Talla Fall, the anguished descriptions of hell of Mor Kayré. And Amar Samb claims that the most gifted disciples of Moussa Ka were Messa Dâf and Sheikh Fall Trâhir.

Although Diop states that Murid poetry, in its musicality and rhythm, reflects the Africanization of Islam which was effected by Ahmadou Bamba, written composition in Wolof did not remain a monopoly of the Murids. In the wake of al-Hajj Umar, Tijani *marabouts* had been very active throughout Senegal. Although the Tijani movement soon spread to Wolof country, especially under the impulse of Al-Hajj Malik Sy, Tijani contributions to the literature of Senegal seem to have been mainly in Arabic, a signal exception being Mohammadou Aliou Tyam's famous ode in the Fulani language. According to Pathé Diagne, the only Wolof author of Tijani obedience who can bear comparison with Moussa Ka is Sheikh Hadi Touré (b.1894), a distinguished writer in Arabic, who composed poems in Wolof in praise of the founder of the brotherhood and of its Senegalese khalifs, Abukabar Sy and Abdul Aziz Sy. The latter is a well-known poet, who composed praise poetry in Arabic interspersed with Wolof verse in honour of his predecessors and, of other Tijani holy men such as Hadi Touré.[67] But as the *tijaniyya* is more widely represented throughout West Africa than the *muridiyya*, it is not surprising that Tijani poets and scholars should have a preference for Arabic, which enables them to be known internationally.

During the colonial period, this vernacular poetry received no official encouragement and hardly any attention, except in so far as the teachings of the *marabouts* contributed to the development of nationalist sentiment. Although the prestige of French culture remained especially strong in Senegal, this situation changed after independence. A number of *ajami* poems in Wolof were printed locally in pamphlet form. But in Senegal as in many others parts of Africa, broadcasting is the most efficient medium for the diffusion of vernacular poetry, which is generally sung. Amar Samb has pointed out that a number of Wolof works nowadays are recited at Radio Senegal, including the committed songs of a popular female singer, Maasa Thiam, and the topical poems on political subjects of El Hajj Mortala Diop. A decree of 1972 aiming to introduce the national languages into Senegalese education should, if it is implemented, prove beneficial to modern Wolof literature.[68]

CHAPTER FOUR
MADAGASCAR

1. *Ajami* Writing

The Western reader is familiar with the history of the Muslim conquests in Europe, which developed in two main waves: in the eighth century, Arabo-Berber invasions were launched from the North African coast; after the fall of Constantinople (1453), Turkish armies overcame the Balkan peninsula and nearly captured Vienna in 1529. We have briefly described the far-reaching results of the thrust towards black West Africa that was an outgrowth of the former of these movements. But for a proper understanding of literary history in other parts of Africa, it is necessary to keep in mind that Muslim expansion, whether carried on by Arabs or Turks, also moved eastward and southward, along the shores of the Indian Ocean. What concerns us here is that these other movements led to two further types of *ajami* writing: one, which was short-lived and not very productive, arose in Madagascar; the other, which proved, by contrast, extremely fruitful and persistent, centred on Zanzibar and the nearby towns along the eastern coast of present-day Kenya and Tanzania. Muslim expansion also resulted in some literary writing, especially in Arabic, among the Somali.

Little is known as yet about the way man first reached Madagascar.[1] But at the beginning of the Christian era, the introduction of Hinduism in Indonesia led to the creation of powerful sea empires that availed themselves of oceanic currents to carry out large-scale trading activities throughout the Indian Ocean. According to the twelfth-century Arabic geographer El Idrisi, brisk trade had been going on for a long time between the Sumatra-Java kingdom of Strivijaya and Eastern Africa, including Madagascar, which the Arabs called Qomr, a word preserved in the name of the Comoro islands. Indeed, linguistic and other evidence shows that the bulk of the Malagasy population is of Indonesian origin, and suggests that Indonesian colonization began in the first few centuries of our era.

Islamic influence in Madagascar occurred at a later stage as a result of complex developments that extended over a long period of time. It seems that trading-posts were established on the northern coasts by Arab merchants as early as the tenth century; these early colonizers were mainly interested in commerce and while introducing Islam they do not seem to have made any serious attempt at spreading the Arab culture, language and writing. The situation was entirely different on the south-eastern coast, mainly peopled by a tribe known as Antaimoro. The French governor of Fort-Dauphin, writing in the middle of the seventeenth century, claimed that the Koran, writing and schools were brought to this area by the Arabs two centuries earlier.[2] However, Pierre Boiteau is of the opinion that these Muslim societies possessed features less characteristic of Arab than of Indonesian Islam, which had been influenced by the Hindu substratum.[3] Whether the new culture was brought by the Arabs or the Indonesians, the fact remains that the Antaimoro, or at any rate certain clans or social classes among them, were responsible for the emergence of the written art on the island.

The earliest European mention of Malagasy writing[4] comes from a Portuguese sea-captain, Paulo Rodriguez da Costa, who landed at Nosy-Fanjahira on the eastern coast on 4 November 1613; he reports that he concluded a treaty with the local ruler for sending the latter's son to Portugal: this document was written in the Malagasy language and in Arabic script. Yet writing was not put solely to such utilitarian uses: some time later, two English agents of the East India Company actually bought a manuscript—for six oxen. And in the middle of the seventeenth century, Flacourt managed to obtain a few specimens of these *ajami*-type books and sent them to Paris. The earliest of these are sometimes claimed to date back from the thirteenth to the sixteenth centuries.

Those manuscripts, known as *sorabe* ("Great Writings"), are jealously guarded by a caste of diviners, the *ombiasy*, most of them of Antaimoro origin: the oldest of these books have never been seen by Europeans,[5] even though a number of other manuscripts have been studied and edited, especially by French scholars, since the middle of the nineteenth century.[6] From what is known about the Malagasy manuscripts, it appears that the Antaimoro clerics put the written art to two main usages. A large proportion of the material is of an esoteric nature, dealing chiefly with divination and astrology: it was their magical knowledge in such recondite matters that conferred special prestige and power on the *ombiasy*.[7] While it has been shown that Malagasy astrology was definitely of Arabic origin, it is a peculiar feature of this Muslim culture that Arabic influence did not entail any significant use of the Arabic language nor, for that matter, any truly religious importance being attached to the Koran.

But the Malagasy manuscripts also include several works that are of genuine historical interest, and which, therefore, have received most attention from French scholars. One of them recounts the arrival on

Madagascar of one Ramakararube, coming from Mecca in search of a suitable settlement and thus introducing Islam, allegedly in 1164 (A.H. 542): as is usual in non-Arab Muslim countries, the leading clans are in the habit of claiming Meccan descent.

Another interesting example is a manuscript which was sent to the Ecole des Lettres in Algiers by General Gallieni in the early years of this century.[8] The first twenty pages are genealogies, an exceedingly important genre in traditionalistic societies, where a man's identity and status are defined by his lineage rather than by his personal qualities or achievements. The bulk of the manuscript consists of a narrative of tribal wars in south-eastern Madagascar. But some twenty pages are of especial interest because they are the earliest local document to deal with European contact: they recount the resistance of the native rulers and people to the ventures of a Frenchman called La Case in the years 1659–1663. The first part of this account seems to have been written down soon after, if not during, the events described: it is a very dry chronicle, mentioning only facts, but with remarkable precision as to chronology and in the listing of dead warriors and burnt villages. But the second part was composed in the late nineteenth century by one Ramahasitrakarivo, a descendant of one of La Case's main opponents; it testifies to a deliberate attempt at a more stylish and structured form of narrative, which suggests that Ramahasitrakarivo copied the first part verbatim from some older manuscript, but composed the second personally on the basis of other documents, presumably drawn from family archives.

This example shows that *ajami* writing was still in use in Madagascar long after the island authorities had officially adopted the Roman alphabet. Indeed, it may be claimed that the Arabic script was on the verge of a process of rejuvenation and expansion at the end of the eighteenth century. There are indications that when the Merina of the central highlands began to evolve from their archaic tribal organization into a feudal kingdom in the sixteenth century, some of the more powerful and enterprising chieftains called upon the services of Antaimoro witch-doctors. In the late eighteenth century, Andrianampoinimerina (1787–1810), the ruler who achieved the unification of the various Merina tribes, paid a considerable sum to bring literate Muslims from the south, together with their sacred books; though he himself was illiterate, he realized that these people had other than simply magic powers. Several of these "scholars" were appointed as teachers to the monarch's son and heir, Ramada, who reigned from 1810 to 1828 and was familiar with the Arabic script.[9]

The failure of *ajami* writing to achieve in Madagascar the exalted status it received in Hausaland and on the Swahili coast is probably due to the convergence of two factors. One was the remoteness, physical and intellectual, of the spiritual and historical sources of the island's Muslim culture: limited to esoteric and historical purposes, the script never reached a level of creative vitality at all comparable to what occurred with Hausa, Fulani or Swahili. This led to inner degeneracy: apart from a few genuine "scholars", writing became more and more confined to the composition of talismans. The second factor was that just at the time when the Malagasy script was about to receive royal support in a unified island kingdom, the influence of the West and of Christianity began to make itself felt, together with the economic impact of British and French expansionism. The fact that a vast number of manuscripts were burnt, throughout the nineteenth century, by European missionaries and local converts, as vestigial remnants of heathenism, will prevent modern scholarship from establishing how far *ajami* writing had spread in Madagascar. But the destructive efficiency of religious zeal was not the only force at work. During the second decade of the century, Ramada I was instructed in the roman alphabet by an Englishman named Hastie and a Frenchman named Robin,[10] and he came to the conclusion that this new script was better suited for the transliteration of the language.

2. Christianity and the Roman Script

After obtaining a modicum of information about the European languages, Ramada, in 1823, thus opted in favour of the roman alphabet and decided that the Malagasy language would be transliterated by means of French vowels and English consonants, insisting that each sign should correspond to one sound only. Meanwhile, in 1818, a representative of the London Missionary Society had been allowed to set up a station and a school on the island. While this early experiment failed, Ramada himself organized a palace school where members of the royal family and high officials were to be educated. In 1820, a missionary school was founded in Antananarivo. A printing press arrived in 1827. By the time the last missionaries were driven out by Ramada's successor, Queen Ranavalona (1828–1861), in 1836, a sizeable amount of printed material had been issued, consisting mostly of spelling booklets and translations of the Scriptures, but including the first part of a Malagasy version of *The Pilgrim's Progress*. The latter immediately became "a favourite with the earliest Malagasy Christians, and prized as next in value to the Scriptures themselves."[11] Indeed, when Christian missionaries were allowed to return to the island in 1862, the first batch of books they sent from Mauritius comprised 2,370 copies of Bunyan's work.

In 1828, the press had turned out 800 copies of a small volume of vernacular hymns for public worship; in 1836, a second edition of 4,500 copies was printed. Those hymns had been composed not only by Eu-

ropean missionaries, but also by the more literate among their converts.[12] Further, as part of their programme to supply edifying reading-
matter, the missionaries translated thirteen fables of Aesop, which were
printed on the L.M.S. press between 1827 and 1834 under the traditional title *Angano* ("Fables"); this collection became highly popular: it
was reprinted in 1867 and 1875.

The literacy program sponsored by Ramada I met with considerable
success. It has been estimated that by the time of his death in 1828
there were more than 4,000 Malagasy literates who could read in their
own language, and 28 schools had been established in Imerina alone,
as well as 14 other schools catering to the needs of other parts of the
island.[13] But the new script was not used solely for purposes of religious
conversion. An impressive number of so-called "Merina manuscripts"
are still extant; they were never printed, but they provide a more reliable
index of the Malagasy élite's interests than the printed works. One of
the earliest surviving documents of local authorship is a transcription of
the last recommendations addressed by Andrianampoinimerina to his
son and his advisers; there are at least two versions of this document,
both of them originally written in 1825. Other manuscripts, probably
written during the early years of the reign of Queen Ranavalona I,
contain the speeches (*kabary*) of Ramada.[14]

The Queen correctly perceived the European presence as a menace
to her power. Further, she was under the impression that the Bible
contained the history of the Europeans' ancestors. The missionaries
were gradually expelled between 1832 and 1836. Once this was done,
the Queen undertook to have the history of her own ancestors fixed in
writing. This resulted in intense historiographical activity beginning in
1844, when one old adviser named Rabetrano dictated, or perhaps
himself wrote down, lists of the Queen's ancestors, together with their
high deeds, for use in political oratory. Another fascinating offshoot of
this type of preoccupation is a manuscript in English, of some 8,000
pages, which was composed during the years 1853–1855 by Raombana
(1809–1855), one of the Queen's advisers, whom Ramada had sent to
England for his education from 1821 to 1828.[15] Yet another historical
manuscript, written during the late 1860s, is ascribed to an anonymous
ombiasy of Ranavalona I.

These and other manuscripts were later used, together with oral traditions, as sources by a French Jesuit named Callet for his pioneering
Tantara ny Andriana eto Imerina ("History of the Kings of Imerina"),
whose three volumes appeared between 1873 to 1881. They were also
exploited by a Malagasy high official, Rainandriamampandry, whose
Tantara sy Fombadrazana ("History and Customs of the Ancestors") was
printed in 1896, at the very end of Queen Ranavalona III's reign, and

shortly before the author himself, by then a minister in the royal government, was condemned to death by Galliéni.[16]

Nor was historical research, which cannot be dissociated from nationalist and royalist propaganda, the only concern of early Malagasy writers. Already under Queen Ranavalona I, and presumably with her encouragement, two palace secretaries, Raharo and Raharolahy, who had been among the first students of the L.M.S. Royal Missionary College set up under Ramada I, wrote down a collection of the typical Malagasy poems known as *hain-teny*.[17] There is no doubt that more such manuscripts will come to light, even though much of this early indigenous production was destroyed after the return to Christianity under Ramada II (1861–1863) and even more after the French conquest (1895).

With the death of Queen Ranavalona I in 1861, Madagascar became open once more to outside influences. In a way, intellectual change was stimulated by the rivalry between French and British, Protestants and Catholics, for economic, cultural and religious control. Until the establishment of a French protectorate in 1895, the island experienced a period of impressive intellectual development. Many missionary schools were founded. Printing presses were imported. Several periodicals were launched, such as the L.M.S. *Teny Soa* ("Good Words") in 1866, and the Catholic *Resaka* ("Talks") in 1874. The *Antananarivo Annual* began publication in 1875. Promising students were sent to Britain or France.

One of the first Malagasy authors to have reached print did so as a result of the return of the missionaries: he was a convert of the first generation named Razaka (*c.* 1814–1885), who weathered the queen's persecutions, was sold into slavery, was taken to Réunion island, where he successfully resisted the Jesuits' efforts to convert him to the Roman Church, and returned to Madagascar on Ranavalona's death. The missionaries asked him to write an account of his life, which was first published by instalments in the L.M.S. journal in 1883, and, according to the Rev. T. Matthews, was later reprinted "as a small booklet, hundreds of which have been given away as school prizes."[18]

As the Protestant, mainly British, missionaries had a clear lead over the Catholics, and as Madagascar was still an independent nation, it is not surprising that all literary activity during this period was in the Malagasy language. Further, the coalescence of local reverence for public oratory with the Protestant emphasis on the importance of sermons led to the emergence of a number of highly esteemed preachers. The most prominent of these was Josefa Andrianaivoravelona (1835–1897), who was born of noble and presumably Christian parents. One of the first students of the L.M.S. Theological Institute which had been opened in Antananarivo in 1869, he was also one of the first Malagasy ordained ministers. According to Sibree's report, "he often preached four or five times on a Sunday without any apparent fatigue," he gave valuable assistance in the revision of the Malagasy Bible, and he was a prolific hymn-writer, over thirty of his compositions being included in the L.M.S. hymn-book. In 1872, when the five Protestant missions in Antananarivo decided to undertake the revision of the Malagasy Bible, Andrianaivoravelona was prominent among the nine Malagasy members of the committee, whose activities lasted for 14 years, until the new Bible was published in 1888. Meanwhile, Andrianaivoravelona had also been of considerable help to the Rev. Richardson for his Malagasy-English dictionary (1885). As one of the chaplains of Queen Ranavalona III's Palace Church, he also enjoyed some influence at court, and when the French abolished the monarchy in 1897, Andrianaivoravelona was imprisoned and exiled to Réunion in spite of courageous protest by the French Protestant missionaries of the Paris Evangelical Missionary Society.[19]

It was under Queen Ranavalona III and her Prime Minister Rainilaiarivony that Britain and France began contending in earnest for control of Madagascar as part of the scramble for Africa. French influence on the spot was chiefly fostered by the Jesuits. They were based on the northern island of Nosy Bé, which had come under their control in 1840. The first Catholic writer was a contemporary of Andrianaivoravelona, Basilide Rahidy (1839–1883), who came from a Sakalava chiefly family of Nosy-Bé. He studied in Jesuit schools, first in Réunion and later in France, and was the first Malagasy Jesuit priest. After his return to the island, he was soon attached to the Catholic press. Apart from his many devotional and linguistic works in the Malagasy language, he earned a special place in the history of vernacular writing with his *Fanoharana* ("Fables," 1889), which first appeared in *Resaka*. These were free adaptations of the fables of La Fontaine, skilfully arranged to illustrate Malagasy proverbs. Rahidy's work was very popular with local readers and reached its fifth edition in 1955. During the same period, however, the increasing influence of European powers prompted a nationalistic reaction of more immediately topical interest: the first dramatic performance, of which an account has been kept, almost by accident.

The Malagasy have a highly developed dramatic sense, and possessed a vast repertory of plays in which music and dance were as important as action and dialogue. The reason why it has been claimed that "the drama is not an indigenous genre"[20] in Madagascar, is that the traditional performances used neither theatres nor scenery, and their function was not "aesthetic" in the Kantian sense of the term: they were dramatic representations still closely rooted in their religious and social origins. Performances often took place on the occasion of such ceremonies as circumcision or burials. They usually took the form of competitions between companies of actors known as *mpilalao*.[21] It would seem that European influence fostered the emergence of a transitional type of play, for in 1890 the *Antananarivo Annual* carried an anonymous account of a play which must have been performed in the late 1880s and which is alleged to have been printed "at the Queen's press", founded in 1881.[22] The author's name is not mentioned. He is described as "a clever-looking specimen of young Imerina, the Gilbert and Sullivan of the entire entertainment, who supported the chorus" by playing on a harmonium.

As in the indigenous *mpilalao* tradition, songs and dance figured prominently in the performance, but this play, entitled *Fitiavan-Tanin-Drazana* ("Patriotism"), was different in three significant respects: it was composed in writing; it was acted on a formal, if somewhat improvised stage, which was "nothing more than the bare tiled floor of the schoolroom"; and it carried a political message, which the reporter, in his condescending flippancy, seems to have missed completely. Judging from his not very coherent summary in the *Antananarivo Annual*, the play is mainly concerned with the travels of a Portuguese sailor, João Gomez d'Abreu, the first Westerner to have visited Madagascar in the early sixteenth century. Significantly, continental Africans are described as cannibals and west coast Sakalavas as robbers; the latter, however, after despoiling the voyagers, "gave them a great deal of information about the island, and also demonstrated its fatness, produced monster roots of manioc, and sweet potatoes from the soil, called lemurs from the forest and employed them to fetch honey, hooked eels and fish from a neighbouring pond (a big bath-tub surrounded with brushwood)." After thus displaying the wealth and attractions of the island, the Sakalavas escort the travellers to the Merina governor, who welcomes them most hospitably: "they were fed until they slumbered of repletion and visibly expanded in the evening clothes which they had produced somehow under stress of distinguished society." The reporter does not seem to have been aware of the satirical parody taking place on the stage as "a graceful native dance by the young girls" gave way to a show by the Europeans who, "in the western war-paint of swallow-tails and fashion-book robes, enlivened the scene with a neatly-executed schottische and a mazurka", and the actors "indulged in a laughable imitation of the vigorous white-man's prancing, which the Malagasy do not all affect, their taste both in music and dancing being as quiet as that which they manifest in colours and patriotism is loud."

The play was performed before an audience that included "the Sovereign of the island and Her Consort the Prime Minister, the French Resident-General accompanied by several members of his staff, and the Vice-Consul of Great Britain, accompanied by his wife." The European visitors may have enjoyed the show, but there is no doubt that the play held a definite message for the Malagasy spectators: a message on which the *Antananarivo Annual*'s reporter almost unwittingly gives several tell-tale hints. As the curtain opened, the whole company sang a chorus calling upon all and sundry to "behold a kingdom maintaining its independence, gliding swiftly into glory, a couch immense but not big enough for two." This, surely, was an allusion to the unholy designs of the European powers, which France was soon to bring to fruition. The play is nationalistic in more senses than one. First, it glorifies the courtly manners of Merina society as compared with the dubious hospitality of the Sakalava robbers. Second, it celebrates the wealth and gracious living in Madagascar as compared with the alleged savagery of the African continent. Finally, it is mildly, but caustically satirical about the Portuguese travellers. The generous hospitality of the Merina governor implicitly brings out the greed of the Europeans whose main concern is to exploit the wealth of the island for their own benefit. The actors' "prancing" in imitation of Western dance styles must have been intended as a sarcastic comment on the agitation and lack of dignity in European social behavior. The play opens with an introductory scene culminating in the funeral of Marco Polo, which the reporter describes as follows: "when the officiating priest came on, wearing a solemn mask with a rubicond nose, a swaying chasuble and a mitre, and graced the procession with a peculiar ecclesiastical stunt, the whole audience, including the Queen on her dais, broke into peals of laughter." No doubt, they had recognized a satirical imitation of Christian, and more precisely Catholic, funeral rites.

3. The French Regime

This seems to be the only recorded manifestation of Malagasy nationalism as expressed on the stage while the island was enjoying its last few years of political independence. On 30 September 1895, Queen Ranavalona III and her Prime Minister had to agree to the establishment of a French protectorate. On 6 August 1896, the French Parliament voted the annexation of Madagascar as a colony with General Galliéni as its first governor-general. From the very beginning he set out to destroy the educational system that had been established in the course of the nineteenth century by the missionaries with the approval of the Malagasy authorities: French was to become the sole medium of education in all schools, at all levels; and intellectual pursuits were to be discouraged in favour of a curriculum designed to provide industrial and agricultural manpower for the French settlers.[23]

This was the type of "cultural" policy that applied throughout France's African empire. But in Madagascar, it largely failed to yield the intended results. The main reason is that unlike the colonies of the continent, the island already had a powerful tradition of literacy and

writing in the native tongue. The young intellectuals of the late nineteenth century, the class that was to provide the first writers under the
French regime, had been trained in their own language in excellent
schools, where textbooks and teaching were in the vernacular. Besides,
there was a vernacular press of considerable vitality, which the French
never managed to curb, and which was to provide a ready outlet for
much creative writing throughout the colonial period. The nineteenth
century had also seen established a tradition of literary writing in the
local language, practised by both Malagasy and European missionaries:
while part of its inspiration was devotional and designed to promote the
spreading of Christianity, much had also been done towards the preservation in writing of various aspects of the oral traditions. The priority
of English and Protestant influence on the island largely accounts for
the exceptional position of Madagascar in the literary life of the French
Empire: like a number of British colonies, it produced a significant
amount of creative writing in the vernacular.

The Malagasy writers' attachment to their own language as a literary
medium was also a by-product of a national pride which manifested
itself chiefly in the many political movements that grew up on the island
throughout the period of French occupation. An early example was the
V.V.S. conspiracy during the first World War:[24] in 1913, a Protestant
minister, the Reverend Ravelojaona (1879–1956) published in the
L.M.S. journal *Mpanolotsaina* ("The Adviser") a series of articles extolling the way in which Japan had managed to preserve its independence
and traditions while becoming a truly modern nation. This led to the
constitution of a secret society known as V.V.S., for "Vy Vato Sakelika"
(Iron, Stone, Network), grouping a number of younger students together with some Protestant ministers and Catholic priests. They were
vaguely determined to drive out the French and restore Madagascar to
its earlier independence. In 1915, the V.V.S. was accused of conspiring
to poison the European population. More than three hundred suspects
were arrested. In January 1916, a handful of them were condemned to
heavy sentences. They included a number of young writers. Although
an amnesty was granted in the early twenties, one consequence of the
repression was to radicalize anticolonial opinion in Madagascar. Supported by the French communist party, it now put forward two entirely
different claims: one for full French citizenship, and the other for complete political independence. Whereas such a French-language poet as
Jacques Rabemananjara (b. 1913) played a significant part in the anticolonial struggle, it seems that vernacular authors found it advisable
henceforth to show their nationalist feelings in more indirect ways, by
treating historical topics, exalting traditional values, or, conversely, advocating a spirit of modernization.

It was, however, the peculiar paradox of Malagasy literature that the

early years of the French regime saw the consolidation of modern-type
creative writing in the vernacular. This was largely the product of the
educational system that existed prior to the annexation to the French
empire. The Palace school and the missionary schools had trained a
number of gifted, many-faceted personalities who devoted part of their
activity to the secularization and modernization of creative writing.[25]
The process is exemplified in the career of three authors who were in
their twenties at the time of the annexation.

The Reverend Andriamatoa Rabary (1864–1947), who had been educated at the local L.M.S. teacher-training college and in France, became
a teacher in L.M.S. secondary schools from 1890 and took up a parish
of the Mission Protestante Française in 1914. Keenly interested in politics, he became a prominent member of the V.V.S. society and was
arrested in 1915. On his release, he devoted himself entirely to his pastoral duties and the editorship of Protestant journals, where he published in serial form such sentimental and moralizing novels as *Nivoahan-
dRefanoela* ("Rafanoela's Exit", 1933), and a few others which were
issued in book form after his death. A very prolific writer, Rabary is
rightly prized, however, less for his fiction that for his historical accounts
of the growth of Protestantism on Madagascar.

Justin Rainizanabololona (1861–1938) had acted as secretary to
Prime Minister Rainilaiarivony during the last few years of the reign of
Ranavalona III. In 1910, he founded a weekly, *Ny Lakolosy volamena*,
which he edited under various titles until his death. He was well known
as a poet, and wrote the first modern Malagasy treatise on versification,
where he recommended experimenting with rhyme and metrical schemes
based on Latin and French prosody.

Tselatra Rajoanah (*c.* 1863–1931) had also held high office during the
monarchy. He had already become famous for his eloquence. He does
not seem to have been politically active under the French, but was chiefly
renowned for his literary and journalistic production. This included a
large number of novels, published by instalments in local journals, and
many poems in the traditional genre known as *hain-teny*.

But the main contribution of Rainizanabololona and Rajoanah—as
also of Alexis Rakotobe, about whom no biographical information is as
yet available—was the creation of modern Malagasy theatre, a most unexpected consequence of French influence. Mention has already been
made of the indigenous *mpilalao* tradition, which was one of the favourite forms of entertainment among the Malagasy people, and we
have seen that the elements of modern stage drama had begun to
emerge towards the end of the monarchy. The missionaries had fought
relentlessly against the *mpilalao* performances which they considered
highly pernicious to public morality. They liked to think that "Christianity has brought much greater brightness and variety" into the daily

lives of the Malagasy.[26] The latter may have enjoyed community singing and pulpit oratory but it is highly doubtful whether they found any pleasurable excitement in the pious and rather lame Sunday school entertainments which the missionaries offered them in lieu of the allegedly orgiastic performances of the *mpilalao*. French ideas about what constituted an adequate cultural policy for Madagascar were not quite in tune with the austere outlook of the British missionaries, who were understandably dismayed when the French authorities soon introduced their own Gallic notion of what a proper week-end should be: "Races and other amusements," Sibree wrote, "were commenced by government patronage on the Sundays, and fêtes and public festivals were generally arranged for on that day."[27] Matthews lamented that "the quiet Sabbath day is a thing of the past, as bands now play, games and races go on, theatres are open, and there have even been bullfights on the Sabbath." And he noted that there arose controversies "with regard to Christians—especially pastors, preachers, and Sabbath-school teachers—countenancing theatres, operas and balls. The poison of so-called civilization, frivolity and indecorum had been introduced and was affecting certain sections of the community."[28]

Highly influential—though, perhaps, indecorous—as regards the literary evolution of the island were the visits by French performing companies brought in from 1894 to provide entertainment for the military, the small settler community and, at the same time, for the theatre-loving Malagasy population.[29] Both the French and the Malagasy had a soft spot for the operetta. It was not, perhaps, the most sophisticated sample of French culture and art that one could think of, but in the eyes of the islanders it had a familiar ring, combining as it did a love story with plenty of songs and dancing. The favour of the operetta among the colonizers was, to the colonized, decisive proof that their own *mpilalao* tradition was by no means an uncouth and primitive genre, good enough for illiterate pagan savages, as they had been led to believe. The operetta brought the approval of civilized taste to native drama, and led to the mushroom growth of the dramatic genre—a trend without precedent or parallel on the African continent. As Malagasy poet M.R. Robinary was later to reminisce, the indigenous middle class, imbibed with Victorian values, attended such shows as *Phi-Phi* or *Miss Elyett* with pious disapproval and hypocritically concealed delight.[30] But there arose a generation of writers with decidedly secular gifts, who created the modern Malagasy musical comedy, fusing together the native *mpilalao* tradition with the influence of the French operetta, often adding, for good measure, the sermonizing touch required by missionary Christianity.

Rainizanabololona, Rajoanah and Rakotobe are generally hailed as the founding fathers of modern Malagasy drama. They lavished teaching and encouragement on a remarkable constellation of younger authors, who were born at the beginning of the French period and who, although they had their schooling in French, remained faithful to their mother tongue. Thumbing through Rajemisa-Raolison's *Dictionnaire historique et géographique de Madagascar*, one is amazed at the large number—and the literary versatility—of playwrights who deserved to be listed there for their contribution to Malagasy drama. They include Charles-Aubert Razafimahefa (1880–1936, pseud. Dondavitra), also well-known for his poems and short stories; Wast Ravelomoria (1886–1951), often deemed the best Malagasy playwright for his comedies of manners, although his novels of love and adventure enjoyed considerable popular success; Romain Andrianjafy (1888–1917), who, like many others, himself composed the music for his plays and who launched one of the first theatrical companies, "Tananarive-Théâtre"; Jasmina Ratsimiseta (1890–1946), who was also a poet and short-story writer; Justin Rajoro (1893–1949), who shares with Andrianjafy the honour of founding one of the first theatrical companies; and his friend Naka Rabemanantsoa (1892–1943), who launched several other companies after making his literary beginnings as a hymn writer.

Little of the theatrical output of this generation ever reached book publication; many manuscripts lie in the archives of the Malagasy Republic, but they still await scholarly study and recognition. From what little information is available, it is possible to infer that the playwrights of the colonial period, besides their specifically literary, musical and theatrical talents, did not rest satisfied with exploiting the love theme which they had inherited from the *mpilalao* drama and the French operetta: they also dealt with social and political problems, often in a cleverly ironic manner. M.F. Robinary has provided a summary of a play entitled *Ny najara tsi-fantatra* ("Fate is unknown") by Ramanantoanina (1891–1940; pseud. Ny Avana [The Rainbow]), who was much more famous as a poet than as a dramatist; the play shows a mother and her two daughters living in destitution in order to pay for the studies of the only son in Paris; its purpose is to stir indignation towards the young man, who, after taking advantage of his family's selflessness, returns home with a French wife. Robinary describes this as a "nationalist drama" and there is some reason to believe that anticolonialism and a revulsion against assimilation into French culture were central themes in a number of early Malagasy plays.

The youngest among the writers who were arrested in 1915 as members of the V.V.S. was Arthur Razakarivony (1897–1967; pseud. Rodlish), who was to become, with Ravelomoria, the most successful of the Malagasy dramatists between the two world wars. A bright and precocious young man, he had been influenced, prior to his arrest, by the lyrical dramas of Gabriele d'Annunzio. The love theme remained central to his two masterpieces, *Ranomody* ("The whirlpool", 1926) and

Sangy mahery ("Violent games", 1931). Both plays deal with the problems raised by the traditional Malagasy caste system, as their heroes fall
in love with girls of a higher social status. In *Ranomody*, the girl remains
loyal to her lover although her father wants to marry her to a Sakalava
prince; but the prince poisons the young man with a substance that
drives him to madness; the girl follows her lover to the lunatic asylum,
but when he recovers, he imagines she has betrayed him. Ultimately, he
manages to force the prince to confess his criminal deed. The father
then allows his daughter to marry the man she loves, while the prince
becomes mad in his turn. According to one critic, the play is designed
to assert the necessity of love in marriage, to denounce the obstacles
which the rigid caste system erects in the way of love, and to show that
evil deeds are a whirlpool into which their author becomes irresistibly
engulfed through the workings of immanent justice.[31] *Sangy mahery* handles the same theme but in an atmosphere of spiritual inwardness rather
than social criticism: the lover hero sublimates his love to the extent that
he sacrifices his life in order to save his rival and the happiness of his
beloved; on his tomb, the young woman proclaims that in the next world
she will love him with an everlasting spiritual passion.

While the flowering of stage drama was undoubtedly the most striking
and original feature of Malagasy writing during the colonial period,
poetry was successfully practised too. The modernization of prosody
which had been advocated by Rainizanabololona was actually effected
by Edouard Andrianjafitrimo (1881–1972; pseud. Stella). He studied
at the Palace school and the L.M.S. teacher-training college, but after
a short spell at teaching, he made his professional career as a business
accountant. As early as 1906, he was one of the founders of *Basivava*
("The Tatler"), the first non-official, non-denominational vernacular
weekly in the country. This was suppressed by the administration in
1910, and in 1915 Andrianjafitrimo launched another weekly, *Ny Lo-
harano*, which disappeared when its editor was arrested during the
repression of the V.V.S. movement. A few years after his return from
exile in 1921, he launched yet another weekly, *Sakafontsaina* ("Food for
the mind", 1928–1936). In this and other local journals, he published
a large number of poems, essays and short stories. His poetry evinces
the sense of disillusionment and the nostalgia which are constant features of contemporary Malagasy poetic inspiration.

The best representative of this trend, however, is often claimed to be
Ramanantoanina, whose melancholy poetry provides an outstanding illustration of the sombre mood that affected Malagasy intellectuals after
two decades of French colonization. Admiration for western civilization
had decreased steadily with the experience of colonialism at work; many
came to doubt the inherent superiority claimed for French culture; their
subordinate status in colonial society—Ramanantoanina died a humble

clerk at a bookseller's—led to a sense of alienation and impotence and to a kind of hopeless *Sehnsucht* which is also conspicuous in the French verse of Rabearivelo. The experience of exile, which Ramanantoanina shared in 1915 with so many other budding writers seemed to crystallize a fundamental aspect of Malagasy life: estrangement from the familiar beauty of his native island appeared to repeat the original pattern of exile which had taken the Malagasy people far away from their Indonesian homeland.

Among the many versatile and prolific writers who were born before the establishment of the French regime, special mention must be made of the Rev. Maurice Rasamuel (1886–1954), a Church of England priest and L.M.S. teacher, who, according to Rajemisa-Raolison, did more than anyone else to preserve the legacy of native oral lore and the memory of the island's historical past. A frequent contributor to the vernacular journals issued by the L.M.S., he wrote a large number of books and pamphlets, most of them devotional, historical or linguistic. His *Ny fitenin-drazana* ("The language of the ancestors", 1948 sqq.) is a large collection of Malagasy proverbs systematically arranged, where he also tried to bring back to life the difficult genre of *hain-teny* poetry. He also published collections of discourses (*kabary*) for various occasions. His most important contribution to creative writing is a historical novel, *Tao Manjakadoria* ("Formerly in Manjakadoria", 1942), which deals with the wars of the past.

Historian Pierre Boiteau has rightly emphasized the part played by men such as these in bolstering Malagasy resistance to what he calls French "cultural oppression."[32] This took a variety of forms. During the first decades of the colonial regime, the number of pupils in schools dropped sharply: it was not until 1925 that it reached the same level it had known in 1882. Ineffectual steps were repeatedly taken to hamper publication of journals in the Malagasy language. French was imposed as the sole medium of instruction. The inefficiency of such measures was largely due to the resilience of the transitional generation whose work has just been described.

Inevitably, however, the best-known feature of the next literary generation is the emergence of the first French-language poets: M.-F. Robinary (1892–1971) and J.J. Rabearivelo (1901–1937), who do not fall within the scope of this study. While choosing the European language as their artistic medium, they gave close attention to the vernacular tradition: Rabearivelo wrote articles about vernacular poets, and Robinary commented profusely about *mpilalao* drama and the early written Malagasy theatre. Nevertheless, the bulk of the literary output remained in the local language, thanks mainly to the efforts of Andrianjafitrimo and Ramanantoanina, both of whom influenced and encouraged a number of younger writers such as Rajaonarivony (b. 1898; pseud. Jean

Narivony), Charles Rajoelisolo (1896–1968), Fredy Rajaofera (1909–1968),[33] and others, whose poems appeared in the journals and little magazines of Tananarive, where many of them still lie buried. As to prose fiction, it was continued in the 1930s with such novels as *Bina* (1933) by Auguste Rajaonarivelo (1890–1957; pseud. Rajon), *Veromanitra* ("Citronella", 1932) by Rafanoharana (b. 1902; pseud. Bolespara), and with the short stories of Elie Raharolahy (1901–1949).

In the period between World War II and accession to independence, literary developments in Madagascar were influenced by the same trends which were at work throughout French Africa. One was the coming to fruition of the colonial linguistic policy, which led to the emergence of a significant corpus of lyrical poetry in French. Jacques Rabemananjara (b. 1913) was the only member of this new generation to be at all closely associated with the *négritude* movement. Malagasy writing in French, when compared with the French production of the continent, has two peculiar features: first, the majority of these writings reached book-form publication on the spot; they include such verse collections as *Tananarive* (1946) by Elie-Charles Abraham (b.1919), *Illusoire ambiance* (1947) by E. Randriamarozaka (b. 1919) and *Une gerbe oubliée* (1948) by Paul Razafimahazo (b. 1907). A further point of interest is exemplified in the work of the best-known of the local French-language poets, Flavien Ranaivo (b. 1914): his three volumes of verse — *L'ombre et le vent* (1947), *Mes chansons de toujours* (1955) and *Le retour au bercail* (1962)— are not affected by the rather lame academicism of much francophone Malagasy poetry; indeed, Ranaivo reversed the trend initiated by Rainizanabololona earlier in the century, and instead of adapting the local language to classical French prosody, he transposed into French the style and techniques peculiar to Malagasy oral poetry, especially the *hain-teny*.

More generally, the period also witnessed the swift growth of the nationalist movement. Colonial policy became increasingly repressive, culminating in the massacre that followed a rebellion in 1947. As part of the repression, stricter measures were taken to curb the use of the Malagasy language and to suppress the more outspoken of the vernacular journals.[34] This is probably the reason why only one significiant new vernacular writer emerged between 1940 and 1960: Jean Verdi Salomon Razakandrainy (b. 1913; pseud. Dox), who gained some renown as a lyrical, elegiac poet; he also wrote a few historical and biblical plays, and provided translations of some of Corneille's and Racine's tragedies.

The peculiar combination of absorption into the French cultural sphere and indomitable pride in the national traditions, linguistic and literary, is apparent in a third trend which is without parallel in French Africa: the emergence of authors whose creative abilities extend to the two languages: Fidélis-Justin Rabetsimandranto (b. 1907) was already well-known as a vernacular poet, novelist and playwright when he tried his hand in French and published *La Nymphe dorée* (1958), a rendering in classical French verse of an old Malagasy legend of love and deception. Among younger writers, Régis Rajemisa-Raolison (b. 1913), who had been associated with Jacques Rabemananjara in launching the *Revue des Jeunes de Madagascar* in 1935, inaugurated his literary career with *Les Fleurs de l'Ile rouge* (1948) before he wrote his short stories and plays in Malagasy.

Little scholarly attention has so far been paid to literary developments since Madagascar became fully independent in 1960. As was the case in other parts of the former French empire, there was a noticeable decline in creative activity in French, as such writers as Jacques Rabemananjara and Flavien Ranaivo were appointed to high political or administrative office. Both of them left the island after President Tsiranana was replaced by General Ramanantsoa in 1972. On the whole, it would seem that the most fruitful among such new trends as may have occurred is the growth of the novel with Alphonse Ravoajanahary's *Tao anatin'ny sarotra* ("In big trouble", 1967), Jean-Louis Rasamizafy's *Mandrakizay ho doria* ("For ever", 1967) and *Valin-keloka* ("The punishment of sin", 1968) by Michel Paul Abraham-Razafimaharo (b. 1926). According to M.R. Robinary's preface, this latter novel, which deals with adultery and its retribution, should rank as a turning-point in Malagasy prose fiction because the writer is not interested solely in the linear narrative of events regardless of context or verisimilitude, but is also concerned with psychological motivation and ethical analysis.

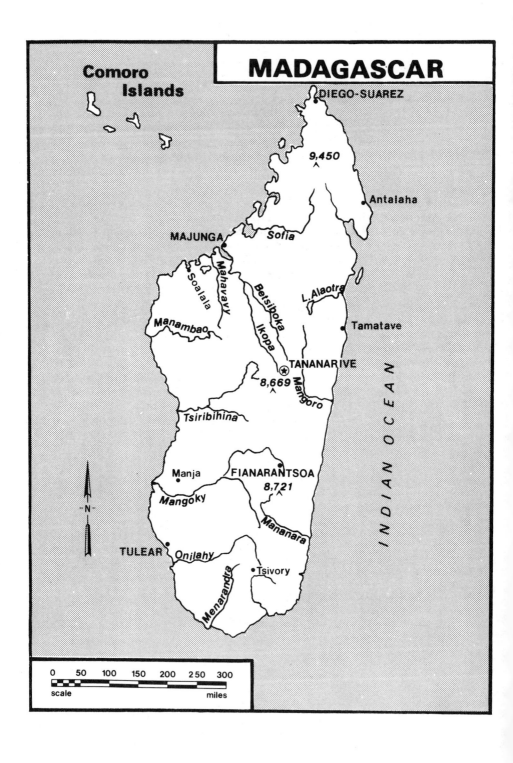

MADAGASCAR

Comoro
Islands

DIEGO-SUAREZ

9,450

Antalaha

MAJUNGA
Sofia

Soalala
Mahavavy

L. Alaotra

Manambao
Betsiboka

Ikopa
Tamatave

TANANARIVE
8,669
Mangoro

Tsiribihina

INDIAN OCEAN

Manja
FIANARANTSOA
8,721

Mangoky
Mananara

TULEAR
Onilahy
Tsivory

Menarandra

-N-

0   50   100   150   200   250   300

scale   miles

CHAPTER FIVE
EAST AFRICA : SWAHILI

1. Early Works

Direct commercial contacts between the Middle East and the eastern coast of Africa had existed since the first century A.D., possibly earlier.[1] The rise of Islam added religious zeal to the Arab and Persian trade in ivory and slaves, whereas internecine quarrels often caused migrants from Southern Arabia to seek safety and freedom in the area known as Zenji-bar, *i.e.* the Coast of the Blacks. As those people of Middle Eastern stock intermarried freely with local inhabitants, the Swahili civilization that emerged was a distinctly composite culture. In its first flowering, at the beginning of the present millennium, it shaped itself into the so-called Zenj Empire, which was actually a loose conglomeration of more than thirty towns, extending from Mogadishu to Kilwa and, at times, as far south as Mozambique and Sofala. Although their relations were characterized by frequent rivalry for commercial supremacy, they were united in a common faith: when the Moroccan traveller Ibn Battuta visited the Coast in 1331, he clearly felt that he was in Muslim country.[2]

The Zenj empire enjoyed increasing prosperity from the tenth to the late fifteenth centuries, when Vasco da Gama sailed to Mombasa (1498). The first period of European domination was one of steep cultural and economic decline for the native population of the East Coast. Portuguese rule came to an end in 1699, when the ruler of Oman took advantage of the rivalry between Dutch, English and Portuguese trading companies to evict the latter from what few coastal towns they were still holding. This, however, merely started a new era of disturbances, as the Omani rulers strove to establish full control in the face of local resistance. Nevertheless, the restoration of Muslim culture promoted the appearance of creative works composed in Swahili and written in the Arabic script.

There is some reason to believe that writing was not unknown on the Swahili coast prior to the Portuguese conquest, but no documentary evidence has been unearthed so far. Nor is there any objective support for the local traditions about a warrior-poet named Liyongo Fumo who is alleged to have been active on the island of Lamu (*c.* 1150–1204). Although the Arabic and Swahili chronicles make no mention of Liyongo, many tales about him are in circulation, as well as a number of very archaic poems attributed to him. His legend and several poems connected with it were first recorded from oral sources by Bishop Edward Steere in *Swahili Tales as Told by the Natives of Zanzibar* (1870). Steere relates that "the poem of Liyongo used often to be sung at feasts and then all would get very much excited and cry like children when his death was related, and particularly at the point where her mother finds him dead."[3] Some of the shorter poems attributed to Liyongo have lingered, often in very corrupt form, in the memory of the Swahili. The legend inspired later poets, most notably Muhammad Kijumwa, who composed the *Utendi wa Liyongo Fumo* ("Songs of Liyongo Fumo") in 1913.[4]

According to the legend, Liyongo's father, Fumo, was the ruler of Lamu island. When he died, his subjects chose his younger son Mringwari as ruler because they were fond of him, and because Liyongo's mother was a mere concubine. Liyongo wanted to assassinate his brother, but the latter was informed of this and organized a great feast in the course of which Liyongo was arrested after drinking. In his prison, he composed a song for his mother, asking her to bake a loaf of bread and hide a file in it; this poem, known as the *Song of Saada*, is one of the more archaic elements in the story. Liyongo then asked his brother, as a last favour, to organize a *gungu* ceremony, *i.e.* a dance with songs to the accompaniment of a dish-shaped gong named *gungu*. This was granted, and while the people were loudly singing the chorus of a tune which Liyongo himself had composed—another poem of archaic character—the prisoner cut away at his chains and managed to escape. But Liyongo had a son who allowed himself, on reaching manhood, to be bought by Mringwari. As he was the only person whom Liyongo trusted, he knew that his father could only be killed with a copper knife. After Liyongo's death at the hand of his son, it is sometimes said that his town, Shagga, was destroyed by Sultan Omar of Pate. This might be Omar ibn Muhammad 'Fumo Mari,' who died in 1392.

Liyongo is a typical heroic character. Being invulnerable, except to one definite weapon, he is an African Achilles or Siegfried. The magnifying imagination of the people endowed him with superhuman size and strength: like Roland at Roncevaux his breath splits the war-horn that he blows. Yet, there is hardly any supernatural element in his make-up. He is a sheer human being, thrown on his own natural resources of strength, skill and cunning. At the banquet, when his brother, planning to shoot him treacherously, proposes that each guest in turn should climb a palm-tree and throw down the fruit for the others, Liyongo cleverly uses his bow and arrow to bring down the fruit. An archaic poem known as *The Warrior Song*[5] typically illustrates the pride of the warrior, who disdains and despises the comforts of city life and places his self-esteem in his lust for warlike fame and in his disregard of danger:

> I dwell not in the city to become a worthless object.
> I go into the forest to be eaten up by the alien.
> If the alien siezes me and devours my flesh,
>   Well, that is the fortune of war to be killed by the enemy.
> A nobleman is like an elephant: he does not die in bed,
>   But by the keen-edged sword which kills in battle.
> A nobleman is a spitting cobra: he dies hard.
>   If he comes and goes this is no gentleman.

Prestige and power are the rewards Liyongo seeks, and it is his being deprived of his legacy that launches the epic action. Yet his fate is tragic: for all his struggle and determination, he falls into the hands of his enemy; it is not his bravery but his cunning which enables him to outwit his brother, and at the end he is treacherously killed in his sleep by his cowardly son.

The ethos of the Liyongo story reflects attitudes which are undoubtedly characteristic of a heroic, pre-Islamic society. Nevertheless, by the thirteenth century, Muslim influences from Arabia, Persia and western India had merged with the local culture to create the syncretic civilization of the Swahili. Fishing villages had grown into towns and city states; stone mosques had been built, dialects of Swahili, a Bantu language with a strong admixture of Arabic elements, were spoken over a vast area along the coast and on the off-shore islands; and it is possible that a written literature of the *ajami* type had begun to arise. According to Wilfred Whiteley, "the early poets seem to have lived and worked on the northern coast of Kenya, perhaps in and around Pate, writing religious and didactic verse in the Arabic script and using one of the northern dialects of Swahili. Their inspiration was Islam, and Islamic culture and thought impregnate all the early verse."[6] One of the earliest writers whose name has been preserved was Sayyid Muhamad al-Mudaffa, a poet who also taught Koranic law in Pate during the last few decades of the thirteenth century. But it must be noted that when Ibn Battuta visited Kilwa considerably further south in 1332, he reported meeting with native poets, who composed lyric and epic works in Swahili.

In the sixteenth century, the many poems of Malenga al-Kilifiy (1515–1592) dealt mostly with the tribal wars that went on around Mombasa at the same time as the Portuguese were consolidating their power over the city. Whether they were originally written works, or oral compositions later committed to writing, is of course difficult to ascertain. In the former case, they might be taken as evidence that the writing skill was used at a fairly early stage to deal with secular matters and especially to preserve the memory of contemporary events, which is one of the most important functions of traditional oral art.

2. The Emergence of Swahili Writing

"The seventeenth century," says Basil Davidson, "was a time of violent competition by sea and land between Europeans struggling for control of the Indian Ocean and its seabord, and of renewed attempts by the peoples of the Coast and Islands to win back their former independence."[7] In this, the Swahili were greatly helped by the Arab state of Oman, which had managed to throw off Portuguese domination in the middle of the preceding century. The Portuguese were not evicted from Mombasa until 1729, but Omani influence, which was to culminate in full control in the 1810s, began to make itself powerfully felt in the late seventeenth century. As far as we can make out, it was this historical development that led to the flowering of Swahili writing. Further, as Basil Davidson observes, the revival of Swahili civilization in the eighteenth century "occurred along those parts of the coast where resistance to the Portuguese was more successful, and where the Portuguese remained weaker than in the far south. Here it was, at Pate, Lamu, Mombasa and elsewhere, that the language of the Swahili now underwent a new expansion."

According to Jan Knappert, "the oldest poem in the Swahili language is the *Hamziya*," and "its language is so archaic that it cannot be dated later than the seventeenth century, although the earliest extant manuscript is dated 1749."[8] Its author, Saiyid Aidarusi b. Athumani from Pate was a scion of an Arab family from Hadramaut, which had reached Berbera in the mid-sixteenth century, and had then spread as far away as Zanzibar, northern Madagascar and the Comoro islands.[9] This, his only surviving work, is an interlinear Swahili version of an Arabic poem of 465 stanzas upon the life of the Prophet, by a thirteenth-century Egyptian poet, Muhammad ibn Said al-Busiri. Originally entitled *Umm al-Qura* ("Mother of Cities"), it was popularly known as *al-Hamziya* because it was composed in the rhyme scheme called *hamziya*. The title was transferred to the Swahili version, although the latter did not preserve the rhyme scheme of the original.[10]

The earliest surviving manuscript in Swahili was written for the Sultan of Pate in 1728. Composed by an author who identified himself as Mwengo bin Athumani, the poem is known as *Chu cha Tambuka* ("The Book of the Battle of Tabuk") or as *Utenzi wa Herekali* ("The Epic of Herakleios")[11]. The word *utendi* (or, in the dialect of Zanzibar, *utenzi*) originally refers to an extended narrative poem.[12] It is conveniently, if not altogether satisfactorily, rendered by "epic". Such poems obey very strict prosodic rules, as each stanza is composed of four eight-syllable lines, of which the first three rhyme together, while the fourth carries a rhyme that is repeated as the terminal rhyme throughout the poem; this stanza form later spread to poems which are by no means narrative. The *Tambuka* epic is typical of the early Swahili *utendi* tradition, which was started in the form of vernacular versions of Arabic poems of the so-called *maghazi* type, *i.e.* recounting historical or semi-legendary events during the wars of the Prophet after Hegira.

The historical framework of Mwengo's poem is constituted by the attacks of Mohammed's troops against the Byzantine empire during the reign of Herakleios, in the early decades of the seventh century. After being attacked by the Persians in the 620s, the emperor had restored his authority over large stretches of his Asian possessions by 629. Historical sources say that Mohammed, meanwhile, had sent an army toward Syria in order to avenge the murder of an envoy: the Arabs were defeated at Mn'ta, south of the Dead Sea, in 628 or 629, and in the summer of 630, the Prophet sent a powerful army to Tabuk, on the border of the Byzantine empire. There is no historical evidence that any large-scale fighting took place there, although it is with the battle at Tabuk that the *Utendi wa Tambuka* is mainly concerned.

The poem recalls in many ways the Christian feudal epics of the Western middle ages. While its general theme is the struggle between the Cross and the Crescent, lust for fame and thirst for revenge play a significant part in the motivation of the characters. The action starts when Mohammed is informed of the death of his nephew Jaafar, and the angel Gabriel orders him to undertake a campaign against his Byzantine murderers. Like the old French *chansons de geste,* the *utendi* offers a crude black and white contrast between the upholders of the true faith and their "idolatrous" opponents. Miracles and supernatural interventions are plentiful. Yet, in this case too, the religious element is not internalized, and the poem reflects a primitive, warlike society. The author explicitly states that the Prophet's companions loved war; the bulk of the work consists in descriptions of battles and single combats; while the Muslims, for the sake of variety and plausibility, are allowed to suffer occasional defeats, the poet is generally careful to give them the most overwhelming victories; at one point, he even specifies that 5,000 Christians were duly sent to hell, whereas only 30 Muslims reached the gates of Paradise. The poem's inspiration is ostensibly religious, and the author expatiates at length on the vanity of worldly goods; yet, in the course of the narrative, much is made of the amount of booty plundered by the faithful, many of the miracles are connected with the provision of food, and Mohammed invites the Muslim warriors to meet their death cheerfully, since "tender nymphs" are waiting for them at the gates of Paradise. In compliance with epic tradition, many of the heroes utter boasts and praise-poems about themselves, both before and after battle. But there is a great deal of truth in the author's humble assertion that he is not instructed in the art of poetry; this is especially conspicuous in the structure of the work, which is rambling and repetitive, with little attempt at aesthetic organization of the material.

Many later *utendi* were to evolve from the *maghazi* tradition. Another early example is the *Utenzi wa Katirifu*,[13] which was probably composed in the third quarter of the eighteenth century by the son of Mwengo, Abu Bakari. While several passages are obviously imitative of the *Tambuka*, the later work does not have the same primitive vigour, and the eventful plot is launched in a more roundabout, romantic way. The title character is a wealthy man who wants to marry Hasina, the daughter of a tyrannical pagan king; she is a widow, whose first husband was killed while fighting against the Prophet and his companions. She therefore demands Mohammed and his son Ali as bride-price. This conspiracy is reported to the Prophet in Medina by a converted Jew: thus begins a string of battles with many ups and downs, at the end of which the Muslims, strongly helped by the angel Gabriel, emerge victorious.

As is usually the case in Swahili poetry, the author identified himself at the end of his poem saying that he originated from Lamu although he lived in Pate. He further added that his purpose had been to tell an Arabic tradition in the vernacular (*Ki'ajami*). Spanish literature in Arabic script was commonly referred to as *aljamiada*, and similar Hausa writing is generally known as *al'ajemi*. But according to Jan Knappert, who edited the epic, this is the only occurrence of the word *ajami* in the sense of "Swahili".

3. The Golden Age of Classical Swahili Literature

The most gifted of Swahili writers in the late eighteenth century was a kinsman of Aidarus, Saiyid Abdallah b. Nasir (*c.* 1720–*c.* 1820). Two of his best poems, the *Takhmis wa Liyongo* and the *Utendi wa Inkishafi* (also known as *al-Inkishafi*) are of outstanding quality, and may serve to illustrate the dual system of values reflected in the literature of the Islamized Swahili society.

The *Takhmis wa Liyongo* receives its title from the Arabic five-line stanza scheme which the poet was the first to use in the vernacular.[14] In the first stanza, Abdallah announces that he will sing of Liyongo. The poem itself is placed on the lips of the hero as he is held captive by his brother.

The intrinsic interest of the *Takhmis* lies in Abdallah's skill in defining a code of behaviour which is based on the antithetic values of gentleness and warlike fame. This takes the form of a series of balanced statements which provide an accurate description of ideal conduct: "I make myself a slave to my friends . . . but I do not submit to abuse nor to occasion for humiliation. I am gentle and yield gently when people hold me, but I am a warrior-slayer when I hear ill-word's infamy;" "I love any man as long as he loves me, but if my own kinsman should bring evil to me, then I am . . . like a killer of birds seizing them out of the flock." This is a far cry from the *Warrior Song* already quoted, which, though recorded in writing at a considerably later date, represents a more archaic inspiration, based on single-minded self-assertion. On the whole, however, it is noticeable that even in Abdallah's *takhmis*, considerable emphasis is placed on warlike fame; as Liyongo (and the writer) warm to the subject, the neat equipoise between meekness and prowess is ruptured:

By God I swear that these words of mine are not just proud boastings.
When I strive for honour, though I be black, I become white.
And when I turn my face to my foe, he must give way.
I am like a vulture in strife with an antelope, or with a beast on the grass-
    plains, or on the high mountain peaks.

Although the poem contains numerous invocations to God, these merely bring religious sanction to attitudes which are characteristics of a secular shame culture. Liyongo's highest reward is public praise, which is obtained through heroic deeds: "He who strives for honour is honoured as he strives." Lip-service is paid to the righteousness of the cause: "The man of gentle birth is bound to cast away evil." But it is the prowess that matters above all: "For I am a brave young man well-pleased with the cries of the [enemy] dying." The only thing that Liyongo really fears is not Allah's judgment, which is not alluded to in the poem, but the judgment of society: the shame which public opinion heaps upon the man who allows himself to be slighted by slander and upon the cowards who choose life and safety rather than danger and death; this last idea is expressed twice in climactic end couplets:

How can a man behold the rising of shame and yet be unwilling to die before
    remorse comes?
I am as a lion proud to die fearing only disgrace and that my enemy should
    find me in the back-ranks.

The code of heroic-aristocratic behaviour extolled in the *takhmis* is, for all the religious wording that is woven into it, in complete contrast with the philosophy expressed in Abdallah's other remaining poem, the *Utendi wa Inkishafi*, which he composed at the end of his life.[15] In essence, this is a homiletic poem on the vanity of earthly goods, as frequent a theme in Islamic poetry as it was in the Christian literature of medieval Europe. But whereas many poems of this kind merely expound the doctrine and lack the concreteness that makes for good poetry, the historical situation, combined with his own talent, enabled Abdallah to treat the theme with unparalleled grandeur and urgency. It will be remembered that this otherworldly inspiration—connected with such themes as *vanitas*, the *contemptus mundi*, the *ubi sunt*, and the *memento mori*, which are all present in the Swahili poem—reached its apogee in fifteenth-century Europe, as part of the aftermath of the havoc wrought by the Hundred Years' War and the resulting disintegration of medieval culture and society. A local equivalent to this shattering experience was provided at the end of the seventeenth century by the economic decline of the Pate sultanate. Abdallah wrote the decay of the once opulent and elegant city-state into his poem as the central metaphor conveying with poignant immediacy his sense of the transitoriness and worthlessness of earthly power and prosperity. Although the musical values and many of the emotional connotations of the poem are lost in translation, its careful structure and its wide-ranging imagery remain sufficiently perceptible.

The title of the poem has been variously rendered as "The Soul's Awakening," "Self-Examination," or "It is revealed." The work itself is an address of the poet to his heart, "which is overcome by the lusts of the world." The first five stanzas are devoted to the customary listing of the names of God, and to the prayer to Allah, after which the poet describes both his purpose and his technique. His object in giving counsel to his soul is to obliterate the "darkness of ignorance" so that "whosoever reflects [on what I write], let it be pardon to him who repents." The poem's projected structure is then described in a revealing—although, in Swahili poetry, somewhat commonplace—metaphor:

> *My inner intention is to make a necklace entwining it,*
> *Shining with large pearls and to put little pearls at the end.*

The symmetry of introduction and conclusion is a usual feature of Swahili homiletic poetry: the invocations to God at the beginning are balanced at the end by prayers and humble requests to the reader to pardon any error or lack of skill. In Abdallah's *utendi*, the central segments of the poem, moreover, are unified by the single thread of his purpose: to convince his own heart of the vanity of earthly delights. At key passages in the graded demonstration, the writer chides his heart for keeping to its terrestrial attachments and admonishes it to heed his further arguments.

The discussion begins with a general statement of the *contemptus mundi* theme, first in metaphorical form: "The world is a raging sea . . . responsible for every loss;" "it is like a well without bottom," where no one can quench his thirst; it is a "mirage" where the false appearance of water only hides "the sun's fire." The theme is then formulated in abstract terms—"the world is corrupt," "it pursues only what is evil,"—after which the poet passes on to his main topic, which is not so much the evil of the world as its transiency and therefore the futility of earthly allurements. The introductory verses of this section deal with death and are neatly symmetrical with those that dealt with the world, as explicit statement is followed by metaphoric expression: "life is a lantern put out by the wind," "a roaring fire extinguished by the rain."

Apparently, the poet's soul is not convinced by such generalities, so that he turns to the more concrete approach which is the distinguishing feature of the poem:

> *This world that thou desirest, what is its good that you so love it? It has no eternal quality, it does not last. If thou hadst dominion over it, what wouldst thou do with it?*

After briefly mentioning Solomon, who had to depart from his earthly kingdom although he was "ruler of men and jinns," Abdallah, in his leisurely, roundabout way, calls upon his soul's own experience:

> *How many rich men have you seen, who shone like the sun, who had control of the weapons of war, and stored up silver and gold?*

Only later will it become clear that he is thinking of Pate in the heyday of its prosperity. But although the picture temporarily remains anonymous, it is an admirable description of power and prestige, of opulence and gaiety, of elegance and sensuous enjoyment, which, apart from its intrinsic poetic quality, provides valuable insights into the Swahili way of life in the eighteenth century. Incidentally, v. 38 contains the only literary reference to the Chinese porcelain used by the wealthy, an interesting illustration of the poem's unique place in a literature whose spirituality generally precludes any sense of the concrete and the particular. Because of the fullness of this picture of a prosperous past, the contrast is all the more striking as the poet abruptly turns to the description of the present: rotten corpses and derelict houses. The wealthy, elegant people are now buried, "maggots pass down through noses and mouths": in its lurid details, the picture is as effectively nauseating as anything in Villon or in the funeral sculpture of fifteenth-century Europe, and the description of the ruined town itself is the very image of the destructive power of time.

The controlling principle in the poem's structure is one of increasing concreteness and immediacy. After the initial generalizations on *vanitas* and the strongly particularized picture of transiency and destruction, this movement culminates in a section which is devoted to the *ubi sunt* motif in completely personalized terms. The poet rhetorically asks where are his father, and other ancestors and kinsmen: "Where now is Abi b. Nasir, and his brother-in-law Abu Bakr, and Sharifs Aidarus and Muhadhar?" And the pattern of dealing not only with man, but with man's proudest works is maintained as he goes on to ask what has become of the aristocratic quarters of Pate: "Where is Kiungu and those who filled the halls? And the good Sheikhs of Sarambi?" After which the poet unobtrusively brings the *ubi sunt* motif to a more impersonal, and generalized conclusion: "There were lords and viziers," "there were judges, dispensers of justice, students of books who proved things, leaders of people in the right paths;" "where are the dove-like women, balm for the eyes, soothers of passion?" The questions lead naturally, after a renewed appeal to the heart, to a consideration of the Last Judgment.

This last section begins with a brief mention of the rewards in store for those who have been oppressed in life, but the poem is brought to a close, as is suitable when its purpose is recalled, with a more extended description of the retribution meted out to the damned in hell. The awe-inspiring picture of death, decay and damnation is designed to turn men away from the transient pleasures of earthly life. But while the poem is a general admonition to heed the will of God, it contains an interesting undercurrent of social criticism: the proud men who deal "in merchandise and arrogance" are of course the powerful and the wealthy, and as the poem moves toward the description of the Last Judgment, a clear distinction is established between those, and "the oppressed" who will accuse them and to whom God will give the eternal rewards of virtue.

•   •   •

The *Inkishafi* bears witness to the decline of Pate and of the neighbouring island of Lamu, which had been the centre of literary production in the eighteenth century. At the same time, Abdallah ushered in the extraordinary flowering that characterized the growth of Swahili literature during the following decades.

Meanwhile, however, as Whiteley has pointed out, "by the beginning of the nineteenth century the poetic tradition was moving south to Mombasa."[16] This was partly the result of historical circumstances and of new political tensions that disrupted the Swahili coast at a time when Omani overlordship was gaining ground, sometimes in the face of serious opposition. The sultan of Muscat, Sayyid Said ibn Sultan, who held nominal suzerainty over Zanzibar and the East Coast had become ruler of Oman in 1806 by murdering his brother. In order to consolidate his power, he sought the alliance of the British. Through the Moresby Treaty of 1822, in exchange for restrictions to the slave trade, he obtained formal recognition of his overlordship in East Africa. He soon proceeded to establish effective power by undertaking to curb the unruly proclivities of the Mazrui, an Omani family who had been governing Mombasa since 1727. By 1837, the town had come under his firm control, and in 1840 Sayyid Said had practically moved his capital from Muscat to Zanzibar.

The poetic witness of those troubled, innovative days, was Muyaka bin Hajji al-Ghassaniy (c. 1776–c. 1840),[17] whose main contribution was threefold: he departed from the Muslim tradition, and "brought poetry out of the mosque into the market place;"[18] "he is accredited with having brought to perfection the other main form of Swahili verse, the quatrain (shairi);"[19] and he is remembered as the first political poet in the language.

Muyaka was born into a family of allegedly Syrian origin. An occasional political adviser to the Mazrui rulers of Mombasa, he wrote poetry on a great variety of subjects. Many of his quatrains comply with the pious fatalism of Islam:

> He that fled from Fate, a journey of sixty years, he went and there it was waiting for him, sitting in the gutter; And it said, "come, let us sit down, friend, my friend!" And he asked it: "Who are you?" and it said: "Am I not your Fate?"

But Muyaka also celebrated more secular, warlike impulses as in the following song about sea-fighting:

> I roam the sea, a hunter bold, in waters deep I slay!
> And in my fearsome grip I hold, relentlessly, my prey.
> My foes would rend my flesh! Behold! Tis them I hold at bay!
> For I am fierce and valiant, aye! The lion of the seas
> When high the surging rollers leap and squalls toss white the spray,
> When back and forth the wild winds sweep, I hunt my hunter's way!
> I sink in the depths of the waters deep, whose surge no ship may stay!
> For I am fierce and valiant, aye! The lion of the seas.

It is also to Muyaka that we owe some of the earliest Swahili love poetry to be duly authenticated:

> When the messenger came and told me the news, I was sitting waiting for you,

and you did not appear. What happened to you, gorgeous one? What kept you away? Today you do this to me—what will you do me tomorrow?

But Muyaka's chief claim to fame is the poetry of political inspiration which sometimes causes him to be considered "the first nationalist poet"[20] of the Coast. Actually, there is little reason to classify him as a champion of any sort of African independence: the struggle between the Mazrui governors of Mombasa and the Sultan of Muscat was a dispute between Omani Arabs. Muyaka wrote as a devoted upholder of Mazrui rule, in order to stiffen resistance to the new wave of invaders from Oman:

> *The previous threat, which, you recall became war, hustled up the men, the women, and those at home; you people of Pate, Lamu, and Mombasa fortress, I tell you it is not like that today.*
>
> *Tighten your loincloths, take up sword and shield: these are your vessels. They may have come from their parts; let us intercept them, and challenge them if they come; let us join with them when they come out on to the field of battle. . . .*
>
> *They have come bringing trouble on themselves . . . To want what you cannot have is idiocy. Each day we will kill them and cut them down with our swords; when this year ends, they will not come next.*

They did come back, however. Indeed, Muyaka may well have been writing this poem out of sheer loyalty and against his better judgment. When Abdallah b. Hemed became governor of Mombasa in 1814, the poet vainly advised against his refusal to pay the usual tribute to the Sultan of Muscat. This, and Abdallah's invasion of Pate in 1819, provided Sayyid Said with a pretext for taking armed action against the Mazrui. The war lasted for nearly twenty years. When Abdallah died in 1823, Muyaka wrote an obituary poem. He subsequently placed his talents in the service of the new governor, Salim b. Hemed, who ruled over Mombasa from 1826 to 1835. He even remained loyal to Salim's unpopular successor, Khamis b. Hemed. But in 1837, Sayyid Said took advantage of dynastic quarrels within the Mazrui family to subdue Mombasa, thus becoming the undisputed master of the East coast and the off-shore islands. These included Lamu, where the wars were seen from the other side, and where local resistance to the aggressiveness of the Mazrui was celebrated by such contemporaries of Muyaka as Zahidi bin Mgumi (*c.* 1760–*c.* 1830) and Muhammad bin Abubakar al-Lamuy (*c.* 1760–*c.* 1827).

•   •   •

Under Sayyid. Said, Zanzibar and the coastal towns reached unprecedented prosperity. The Sultan enjoyed British protection, and the sphere of his influence extended from the Persian gulf to the Great Lakes. The introduction of clove-growing considerably increased the resources which Said's treasury had drawn from the trade in slaves and ivory. While British interests remained paramount, Indian traders were attracted in large numbers, and commercial treaties were signed with the United States (1833) and France (1844). Although Islamic influence retained its supremacy over Swahili writing, economic growth apparently strengthened poetic interest in this-worldly matters, so that even the *utendi* form came to be used for secular topics. This important change was effected by a group of writers who were born at the turn of the century. Side by side with the didactic trend characteristic of Muslim writing, they exhibited increasing concern with historical themes of contemporary relevance, such as Sayyid Said's struggle to establish his control over Mombasa, or, after the sultan's death in 1856, the rivalry between his eldest son, who inherited Oman, and Sayyid Majid, to whom he had bequeathed Zanzibar.

Sheikh Muhyi 'l-Din b. Sheikh Kathan al-Waiti (1789–1869) was born on Lamu, which was the cradle of Swahili creative writing. He was of purely or predominantly Arab stock. In his poem *Dua ya kuombea mvua* ("Prayer for Rain"), he claimed descent from a lineage "in Arabia, free men of good stock." When he was appointed judge (*kadhi*) in Zanzibar—where, as Lyndon Harries observes, "the tradition of verse-making had a very slender hold" — "he adopted the literary conventions belonging to the poets of the north."[21] "His *Prayer for Rain*[22] is composed in the usual devotional manner.

The poet tries to placate Allah with proclamations of remorse and appeals for pity: "Though we have rebelled . . . take not vengeance on us." He praises God's omnipotence and ends with widening the scope of his requests:

We ask for peace from your wrath, O Powerful One,
Here on earth and at the Resurrection, the day of dread.
Place us in Paradise, let us rest within that roof,
Give us your favours, choice women and good, together with boy servants
*   to adorn us before and behind.*

In compliance with poetic usage and good manners, Muhyi 'l-Din winds up with the customary, almost ostentatious, display of humility:

And though I do compose, I know not the art; it is only a desire.
I do not know how to arrange the good pearls with the coral.
I only choose beads that are smooth and worthless.

And for all ye minstrels, when you see there is a mistake,
Correct the foolish error, for when you do this you are rewarded.

Another poem of his that has survived is a dialogue between a *kadhi*
and a witch-doctor's customer.[23] The *kadhi* voices the viewpoint of the
orthodox Muslim scholar, claiming that witch-doctors have no medical
knowledge, that they exact "wages for doing nothing," that there is
nothing in the Koran about "jinns and dancers" as the cause and cure
of illness, and he charges sorcerers with fornicating with their women
clients. After a brief and feeble defense by the witch-doctor's patient,
who retorts that such accusations are lies, but nevertheless asserts his
great desire to keep the esteem of the judge, the latter restates his views
and expounds the true Muslim doctrine of trusting the benevolence of
Allah:

The one who gives alms and who prays at worship.
If he is ill he recovers, and the blessing is increased.

Muhyi 'l-Din is also to be credited with one of the earliest Swahili
versions of the Arabic story known as *mi'raj*.[24] The word means "lad-
der" and originally refers to Mohammed's own account of a dream
in which he was transported from the Ka'ba to the Temple at Jerusalem, and thence up to the seventh heaven, where he received his mission
from Allah. In Arab literature, the tale was soon embellished with fantastic accretions, some of them of pre-Islamic origin. In this form, it
became exceedingly popular among Swahili writers. According to
J.W.T. Allen, the university library at Dar es Salaam contains twelve
Swahili versions in *utendi*, *qasida* and *takhmis* form.[25] One of their main
sources was the *Mishkatu 'l-Masabih* ("The book of light"), compiled at
the beginning of the twelfth century by Husain al-Baghawi.
    There seem to be two main reasons for the extreme popularity of the
miraj story. One is "its abundance of miraculous episodes".[26] The other
is that it combines into one story three motifs which are of paramount
importance for the Muslim audience: the glorification of the Prophet
is brought to a climax in his vision of God; the ascent is an occasion for
a description of the whole universe; and the tale culminates in the institution of the ritual prayers around which the daily life of the faithful
revolves.[27]
    Perhaps the most remarkable feature of Muhyi 'l Din's *Miiraj* is that
it is not composed in the *utendi* meter which is usual for narrative purposes, but in 15-syllable lines known as *ukawafi* . This is the oldest known
form of Swahili prosody, as it is the metre of the *Hamziya*; but whereas
the *Hamziya* verses are arranged in distichs, Muhyi 'l Din's poem is the

first occurrence of the use of this metre for quatrains, which are sometimes graced with inner rhyme.[28]

Another writer of the same generation, Umar b. Amin b. Umar b.
Amin b. Nasir al-Ahdal (1798–1870), was a judge at Siu, on Pate Island, at the time when Sayyid Majid captured the town in 1861. He was
highly regarded as a poet, and some of his compositions are still recited
in East African mosques on the Prophet's birthday. Two of these, which
were printed in the early 1850s, are uncompromisingly loyal to the
pious Swahili tradition: the poet hammers home the Islamic philosophy
of non-attachment and unquestioning subservience to the will of Allah.
When the pre-ordained function of serious literature is to repeat the
same truths over and over again, carefully avoiding any deviation from
accepted ideals, the specifity of poetry as an art is almost necessarily
confined to its formal values, and the quality of a poet tends to be
appraised in terms of his skill in inventing new and ever more difficult
prosodic forms. Umar was particularly esteemed in this respect, and he
is considered a master of Swahili acrostic poetry, in which the Arabic
alphabet provides the framework.

A good example of this is his *Dura mandhuma*.[29] The title, says Lyndon
Harries, is "a Swahili rendering of the Arabic words 'al-Durr al-Man-
zum', or 'Strung Pearls'. Such a title is frequent in Arabian literature,
for the Arabs liken the verses of a poem to strung pearls, and prose
they liken to unstrung pearls." Each of the poem's 29 four-line stanzas
corresponds to one Arabic letter, with which each of its first three lines
begins; further, the letter is accompanied by three different vowels, but
always in the same order: the first three lines in stanza 2 thus begin with
the syllabes *Ba* -, *Bi* -, *Bu* -, in stanza 3 with *Ta* -, *Ti* -, *Tu* -, etc. This
elaborate system is combined with a rigid *aaab* rhyme scheme, *b* remaining constant throughout the poem.

Another of Umar's poems, known as *Waji Waji* ("Didactic poem")
is again an acrostic piece, but in *takhmis* form, with 29 five-line stanzas.
A didactic admonition on man's life, duties and sins, from conception
to resurrection, it is widely popular among Swahili audiences. J.W.T.
Allen lists eight manuscripts, three of them in roman script, and four
tape recordings.[30]

It was probably also Umar bin Amin who wrote the *Utendi wa Ayubu*
("The Epic of Job") which was completed in June 1835.[31] According
to some reports, the work was based on a much earlier poem, dating at
least from the early eighteenth century. Whoever the original Swahili
writer may have been, he states at the beginning that it was translated
from the Arabic; here again, however, no exact Arabic equivalent has
been traced, although it is clear that the ultimate source is to be found
in Koranic commentaries and that the original author was unacquainted
with the Biblical Job story.

As it is, the *utendi* is the work of a highly talented writer. It is remarkable for the simplicity and clarity of its composition and for its psychological perceptiveness. After a conventional opening, the poet describes both the wealth and piety of Job. Iblis (the Muslim name for Satan) goes to God and claims that if Job were destitute he would forget the Lord; the devil thus obtains permission to try Job "in all ways [by which] thou dost wish to enter his mind." As Iblis conveys the welcome news to his sons, their crude minds are evidenced in their manner of rejoicing.

That we may put war in their hearts
So that people may love to quarrel
Or to commit adultery and steal.

Satan, however, has subtler schemes in view, and he waves their gross intention aside: "Leave all those things alone." His purpose is to turn Job against his Creator. This he proceeds to do with carefully graded strategy. First, he destroys Job's property, beginning with his goats and herdsmen; as this does not seem to weaken Job's faith, he goes on with killing his horses, camels and cattle. He then goes back to God claiming that if Job remains steadfast, it is because he feels assured that his property will be restored to him. God gives him permission to try Job on his progeny. Accordingly, Satan causes the schoolbuilding to crash on the ten children, who are all killed; disguised as a teacher, he then reports to Job and invites him to rise up against the Lord who has made him "utterly miserable, like a man who has never had any children at all." Job is almost persuaded: "His liver turned round in him, his tears started flowing, they rotted his chest." But he recognizes Satan under his disguise and bids him leave. The devil then repairs to God with a request, which is granted, for permission to try Job in his body.

This last trial is vastly expanded, but always according to the triadic pattern which controls the whole structure of the epic. Job is attacked in three ways: in his wealth, in his children, and in his person. This last temptation grows through three stages: first, Job is struck with a hideous illness; next, the devil urges the people to banish him from the town; finally, remembering perhaps his previous success in dealing with Adam through Eve, the devil turns all his attention to Job's wife, Rebecca.

Rebecca too is submitted to three temptations. In order to get some food, she first has to work for the neighbours, but when the story of Job's illness begins to spread, she finds all doors closed; Satan tries to stir her resentment at the loss of her wealth, beauty and status, and advises her to leave her husband; but she refuses, and Job tells her who that stranger is. The second temptation occurs when the devil, disguised as a handsome knight, offers her wealth and power if she agrees to marry him. Some time later, she meets Archangel Gabriel in all his glory, and listens to him; not until he advises her to give up her obstinacy and to abandon Job to God's wrath does she realize that this is Satan in disguise once more.

Because of Rebecca's unyielding loyalty, Job's ordeal comes to an end, and the Lord sends him a miraculous spring which cures him, while Gabriel comes down with new garments. The poem ends with pious reflections and recommendations.

•   •   •

Both Muhyi 'l-Din and Umar b. Amin, continuing the inspiration of *al-Inkishafi* , were outstanding representatives of the mainstream of Swahili art poetry, as defined by Jan Knappert:

> *The main theme of traditional Swahili poetry is invariably religious. It deals with moral precepts and instructions regarding ritual, praises of God and His Prophet, the horrors of Hell and the pleasures of Paradise. Where the moral rules are not given directly, they are given, by implication, in the form of* Historia Sancta, *the legendary history of the Prophet, his family and his followers. As such these legendary stories are of the greatest importance to members of the traditional Swahili society: they provide the individual with a sure guide to life in this world. The perfect example of the Prophet and his followers is the model of life that must be imitated by everyone who desires to attain Paradise. These legends are not entertainment, they are* elimu , *knowledge required for all who want to lead a righteous life.*[32]

Although the author of *al-Inkishafi* had managed to incorporate into his poem realistic allusions to historical events of the day, these were completely subordinate to the otherworldly moral to be inculcated. It was, therefore, a significant departure when a writer of the next generation used the epic form to chronicle events of purely secular interest, of which he had been an eye-witness. This was Abdallah b. Masud b. Salim al-Mazrui (1797–1894), with his *Utendi wa al-Akida*.[33] Abdallah was already the author of the *Utenzi wa Mwana Hasina na Rashida Walii*, the story of which, in Jan Knappert's summary, runs as follows: "A Princess falls in love with a saint, who resists her attempts to seduce him. On her request her father the sultan has a hermitage built for her where she can have lessons from the saint without disturbance. The prudent teacher castrates himself and gives the sultan his 'charms' for safe keeping. When the princess is found pregnant, the chaste teacher is able to prove his innocence." As is so often the case in Islamic writing, woman is depicted as a vessel of iniquity, a pattern from which Umar b. Amin had departed in the *Utendi wa Ayubu*. But the point is that Abdallah b.

Masud used the *utendi* form for a tale which, however edifying and didactic, has no connection with the holy history and legends that had provided inspiration for most earlier Swahili epics.

Even more definitely secular was his *Utendi wa al-Akida*, a historical verse chronicle apparently composed shortly after the events related, which took place in the mid-1870s.

When Sayyid Said vanquished the rebellious Mazrui governors of Mombasa in the late 1830s, he appointed one Abdallah bin Mbarak as *akida* (commandant) of the city. Abdallah died while his son Muhammad was still an infant, but when the latter was old enough, he was appointed to his father's office. The new *akida* soon surrounded himself with soldiers from Hadramaut, whose allegiance went to him rather than to the Sultan, and a competition for power began to develop between the commandant and the governor of the town. Open hostility was launched by the leader of the *akida's* opponents, the poet Suud b. Said al-Maamiry, who went to Zanzibar and intrigued against the commandant at the Sultan's court. After several months of indecisive motions, actual fighting broke out in January 1875, when Muhammad bombarded the governor's house from the fort where he had regrouped the garrison. There was some looting, but Muhammad surrendered to the Sultan's forces after the British representative in Zanzibar, whose name was Prideaux, had guaranteed his safety and that of his followers. In view of the many discussions concerning the historical value of African vernacular chronicles, it is noteworthy that the poet's narrative of events fully concords with more recent historical accounts which are based on Prideaux's dispatches.[34]

But Abdallah bin Masud also provides an interpretation of those historical facts which is definitely moral, although unobtrusively so. Muhammad's rebellion is presented as a genuine tragedy, for the *akida* was "a man beloved by the people, a man in whom the Sultan had great confidence." The reason why he ended up betraying his legitimate ruler is traced to the treacherous behavior of Suud, who is the villain of the story: "There is no ruler who is loved by all, but there is sure to come an evil person who seeks to do him ill." Suud, however, is not alone: he is supported by the "elders of the town," although they are unable to substantiate their complaints against al-Akida to the Sultan's vizier. Nevertheless, the poet does not fully empathize with Muhammad; although he has the latter convey his righteous indignation at being summoned before the Sultan "like a corrupt slave who had done wrong," the writer is aware that al-Akida's reaction is marked by "rage" and "arrogance," and he sympathizes with the Baluchis, the soldiers from Baluchistan, who are victimized because of their loyalty to the Sultan:

He drove them from the Fort, the poor Baluchis, in humiliation and sorrow.
They were scattered about the villages.

This note of objectivity, which has its stylistic counterpart in the sober matter-of-factness of the writing, is preserved to the end, as the British "Admiral" promises to stand surety for Muhammad, and as the Sultan implements his guarantee. Muhammad, a noble but embittered man, must be exiled, the Sultan feels, not only for the sake of the common good, but also for his own safety:

Do not keep him in Zanzibar. I foresee danger there for him,
For he is a mischievous person, and will harm my subjects.

In his aloofness, Abdallah b. Masud maintains an exceptional measure of objectivity throughout the narrative. Yet his own viewpoint is expressed in the very first line of the poem, where one can sense a definite nostalgia for the days when the seat of Arab power was in Arabia: "First in the Name of God, if you want the truth, the Swahili country is no place for us to live in." His tragic interpretation of al-Akida's story appears when, after describing the fury of Muhammad and the first shooting, the poet exclaims:

Alas, this destruction! We are a famous people,
But because we are divided, that is why we are destroyed.

The divisiveness, of course, is due to the envy of Suud and of the elders of Mombasa. But in its own way, Abdallah's *utendi* dramatizes the tragedy of power which, the more it grows, the more it heads to destruction through the workings of jealousy and discord.

•   •   •

It was also apparently during the second half of the century that the verse dialogue and epistolary verse became a favourite, although minor, genre in Swahili poetry. As Lyndon Harries points out, "it is not always possible to know if the dialogue verse is actually of dual authorship, but dual authorship can generally be attributed to poems in which a theme is developed in a fairly long sequence of verses and similarly answered."[35] Such documentary evidence as is available suggests that the genre goes back at least to the late eighteenth century. Harries mentions a dialogue between the author of the *Utenzi wa Katirifu*, Abu Bakari b. Mwango and Ali b. Sheikh Abdullah, "concerning the custody of a young girl (referred to as *dura* or *love-bird*)," and he adds that in the scripts belonging to Sir Mbarak Ali Hinawy there is another dialogue

poem of thirty-five verses in which Sheikh Ali b. Saad of Lamu writes
to the same Abu Bakari "seeking legal advice for a mother of children
who had been neglected by her husband." Of single authorship was
Muhyi 'l Din's dialogue poem between a judge and a witch-doctor's
client already mentioned.

Although one of Muyaka's poems is a love dialogue, dialogue verse
had mainly been used to argue points of law and ethics. That this continued to be one of its usual functions in the second half of the nineteenth century appears from a poem in which Suud b. Said al Maaamiry
(1810–1878) and Muhammad b. Ahmad al-Mambassiy (1820–1895)
engage in a learned discussion concerning the legal status of a family of
Bantu origin who were living in Mombasa. Of greater historical interest
is another verse dialogue by the same two writers, which is known as
the *Forge Song*, because nearly all the quatrains end with the same line:
"The cooling of the tongs does not mean the end of the forging." The
occasion of the poem was Suud's coming to Zanzibar in order to undo
the *akida* of Mombasa. Muhammad's letter of seven verses advises his
friend to see people of high rank and to tell the sultan of the *akida's*
conduct; he also strongly urges him to be cautious and secretive, and
not to despair, even though his sympathizers may seem reluctant to
support him openly. Suud's reply begins with directions to the boatman
carrying his letter to Muhamad, and ends with intimations of his intentions and hopes.

This example, together with Abdallah bin Masud's epic on al-Akida,
suggests that the setting up of Zanzibar as the capital of the Omani
empire in East Africa had been favourable to the growth of secular
types of poetry with more than latent political implications. This is confirmed by some of the writings of Ali b. Athmani, usually known as Ali
Koti (*c.* 1820–1895). One of his poems is a conversation piece between
himself and another learned man, Mwalimu Musa al-Faman: it concerns
such minor points in Muslim religious observance as what becomes of
the duty of daily prayer when the believer has no water for the prescribed ceremonial ablutions that are supposed to accompany it![37]

But Ali Koti is better known as the author of the so-called *Mzigo* song
("The Load"), a topical poem referring indirectly to the disturbances
in the Sultan of Zanzibar's dominions. Ali Koti was a friend of Ahmad
b. Fumoluti, who belonged to the house that had ruled over Pate until
1848. In 1861, Ahmad and some other local leaders rebelled against
Majid Said. They were vanquished by the Sultan's troops and retreated
to the mainland in 1862; Ahmad, known by now as Simba (the lion),
built a fortified post at Witu, and it was there that Ali composed the
Mzigo song. The subject is an insulting gift addressed by Simba to Fumo
Bakari, the new ruler of Pate, who was an ally of the Sultan. In Lyndon
Harries's summary, "the poet instructs a man to take a load of millet

to his enemies at Pate and to divide out to each what in the contemporary context would be regarded as very small quantities indeed. The sting is in the meagre offering to be made to each . . . To send a special messenger across the water from the African mainland to the island of Pate and to dole out 18 lbs of maize to be divided between the Sultan and his First Minister, was to say the least an uncourtly gesture."[38]

Besides these poems, narrative or otherwise, dealing with secular topics of contemporary political relevance, the middle years of the nineteenth century saw the appearance of the first Swahili woman writer on record, Mwana Kupona binti Msham (c. 1810–c. 1860 from Pate. She was the widow of Sheikh Mataka ibn Mbaraka (1779–1856), who had successfully resisted Sayyid Said's attempts to control Siu; she married him in 1836, and the *Utendi wa Mwana Kupona*[39] was composed in 1858 as a sort of educational treatise for her daughter, who was then 17 years old. Mwana Kupona makes no high literary claims for the work:

The reason for composing is not poesy nor minstrelsy.
I have a young innocent child, and I wish to instruct her.

But it is indicative of the sophistication in well-to-do Swahili circles that she should have been able to write it in highly polished verse. For the modern reader, it offers an engaging glimpse into family life and the condition of women in the middle of the nineteenth century.

Mwana Kupona may not have been quite as exceptional as current prejudices about the inferior status of women in Swahili society may suggest. Alice Werner claims that girls on Pate and Lamu received a considerable amount of instruction, and that many Swahili women were not only fond of reading poetry, but also adept at composing verse. It is likely that many works of unidentified authorship that have been preserved were composed by female writers. In more recent times, Lyndon Harries, one of the few western scholars to have paid some attention to non-classical forms of Swahili literature, has emphasized the contribution of women poets and singers in Zanzibar.

● ● ●

For all these innovations, the strict Muslim tradition of devotional verse was maintained throughout the second half of the nineteenth century. In 1895, a long homiletic poem upon the due observance of Islam was composed by Sheikhan b. Ahmad b. Abu Bakr al-Husein, a descendant of the same Hadramaut Sayyid family that had already produced Aidarus in the late seventeenth century and the author of the *Inkishafi* poem. He claimed that this poem was revealed to him in a dream by his sixteenth-century ancestor, Sheikh Abu Bakr b. Salim.[40]

More important, however, was his kinsman Sharif Sayyid Abu Bakr
b. Abd al-Rahman 'l Husseini (*c*. 1828–1922) from Lamu.[41] As both his
parents claimed to be descendants of the Prophet, he was usually known
as Sayyid Mansab. After studying theology and law at Mecca and under
the learned men of Hadramaut, he was appointed *kadhi* in Zanzibar by
the Sultan Sayyid Majid, who reigned from 1856 to 1870. At the death
of the Sultan he returned to Lamu, where he was later appointed *kadhi*
by his successor, Sayyid Bargash, who reigned from 1870 to 1888.

Sayyid Mansab authored many homiletic poems of which ten at least
have been preserved. One of his early works is *Ukawafi wa Kisshanaiya*
("Poem of the Blanket"),[42] composed in 1854. Based on sura 73 of the
Koran it is a praise-poem in honour of the Prophet and of his family,
whose God-ordained pre-eminence it is designed to extol. It tells how
Mohammed, suffering from a fever, goes to his daughter Fatima and
lies under a blanket. In succession, several members of the family and
archangel Gabriel are attracted by the "sweet odour" and the "wonderful light" that emanate from Mohammed, and come to lie with him
under the blanket. Hasan then sings a poem in praise of himself and of
Mohammed's family: they all participate in the glory of the Prophet,
for whose sake, he claims, God created man and the universe, and to
whom the Lord has given sway over the whole world. At several points,
the writer emphasizes the importance of the story: "This poem is a great
and high symbol. Read it, my brothers, that you may understand its
meaning," he says at the beginning. And at the end, he has the
Prophet's son-in-law, Ali, ask the Lord to pardon "him", "and also
him who cannot read it, but who will hold it" in his hands, and to
shower his "favours upon those who will lend it."

Like Mwana Kupona, Sayyid Mansab turned epic verse to educational
uses in his *Utendi wa Akida Tu' l Awani* ("Poem of the Doctrine for the
Common People"). Under the title *Tabaraka* ("Evening prayer") he
translated an Arabic poem denouncing the transiency of worldly things
and advising the reader to put all his trust in God.[43] But his best-known
work is the *Maulid Barzanji*, extracts from which are still read in mosques
and in private houses on Muslim feast-days. In Arabic literature, *maulid*
poems are narratives of the birth of Mohammed. Sayyid Mansab's
poem, composed in 1891, is a Swahili adaptation of a nineteenth-century
abridged Arabic version by Zain al-'Abidin al-Barzanji, who claimed to
be the grandson of the early eighteenth-century author of the original
poem.[44]

According to some reports, Sayyid Mansab once asked the governor
of Lamu, Abdallah b. Hamedi, to arrange for the publication of a collection of his poems. An Indian sea-merchant agreed to take the manuscripts to Bombay for this purpose, but later claimed that they had

been lost at sea. But for this, Sayyid Mansab might well have become the first Swahili writer to have his books printed in the original Arabic script.

Many of these epic writers were connected with the northern part of the Swahili area and continued the *utendi* tradition as it had arisen in Pate and Lamu. During the latter part of the century, however, verse writing had spread from Mombasa to Pemba, where, according to Wilfred Whiteley, "all the poets seem to have lived in or around the main centres and the clove-plantations and to have enjoyed the patronage of wealthy Arab landowners." They established a tradition of social verse in the quatrain vein popularized by Muyaka: "they acted as commentators of daily life, vying with one another in their efforts to record their feelings on such diverse topics as hunger, love, hardship, the spirits, politics, and notable people." [45] Many of the elegant quatrains that are still in existence must have originated in Pemba in that period, and it is to be hoped that future research will solve the many problems of dating and authorship which they raise.

4. The European Conquest and Its Consequences

While these developments were going on within a society whose sole link with outside civilization had been through Islam, European interest in Eastern Africa had begun to make itself felt.

A German missionary, explorer and scholar, Ludwig Krapf, landed in Mombasa in 1844. He was in the service of the London Church Missionary Society, and besides his other achievements, he has a claim to having been the first European to encounter Swahili creative writing. In 1854, he brought back the first Swahili epic manuscripts to Germany; they were not published until 1887, when colonial enterprise had greatly stimulated interest of all kinds in Africa. Meanwhile, British scholars had also been active in the field, most notably Bishop Edward Steere, of the Universities Mission to Central Africa, whose collection of Swahili tales had appeared in Zanzibar in 1866.

The Berlin Conference (1884–1885) gave the scramble for Africa tremendous impetus. The Germans had already begun to undermine the suzerainty of Zanzibar by signing more or less spurious treaties with local chieftains and rebel leaders on the mainland. In 1890, the treaty of Heligoland placed Zanzibar under British protection and apportioned Tanganyika to German, and Kenya to British influence.

During the latter part of the nineteenth century, then, German and British scholars, colonial administrators and missionaries revealed the existence of Swahili literature to the outside world; while the latter admittedly paid little attention, workers in the field were fully aware of

the importance of their discoveries. With laudable diligence, they en-
gaged in the work of tracing manuscripts, recording oral tales and
poems, editing, printing and translating them into European languages,
especially German and English. The succession of Krapf and Steere was
first taken up by Carl Buttner and Carl Meinhof. In the early years of
the twentieth century, a host of other scholars joined their ranks: Carl
Velten, and later Ernst Dammann, on the German side, Alice Werner
(a German by birth), W.E. Taylor, William Hichens, Roland Allen, and
later Lyndon Harries and J.W.T. Allen, on the British side; the extensive
research done by a Dutch scholar, Jan Knappert, has also added considerably to the body of classical Swahili literature that is now available.

In this, Europeans were helped by native Swahili speakers, writers,
reciters, copyists and manuscript collectors, such as Hemedi b. Abdallah
b. Said b. Abdallah b. Masudi al-Buhriy, Sheikh Muhammad Jambein
al-Bakari, Muhammad Abubakr bin Umar Kijumwa Masihii, and Sir
Mbarak Ali Hinawiy. As a result of this cooperation—which received
valuable support from the East African Swahili Committee when
Wilfred Whiteley became its secretary in the early 1950s—a large
amount of manuscript material has been collected which, in spite of
considerable repetitiveness, provides an impressive picture of the abundance and formal sophistication achieved by Swahili writing. As literary
topics in Swahili are mostly dictated by the Islamic tradition of narrative
and devotional composition, it is hardly surprising that poets should
concentrate on form. Perhaps inevitably, albeit unfortunately, this is also
true of students and critics. Much research has been devoted to defining
the rules of Swahili prosody and to analyzing the nature of the literary
genres. Problems of authorship and dating, however, have been comparatively neglected, with the result that the available material is not yet
fit for historical treatment. As more data comes to light, further research, historical, thematic and stylistic, will probably help solve the
many intricate problems which must be solved if a reasonably complete
and reliable historical account of Swahili literature is ever to be provided.

●   ●   ●

It is characteristic of the cultural resistance that Islamized societies in
Africa were able to put up against European influence that the classical
and oral traditions of the Swahili remained alive and productive well
into the twentieth century, a feature which the East Coast has in common with Hausaland and with Fulani areas. Indeed, the interest demonstrated at an early stage in the colonial process by German and British
scholars may well have proved an incentive for Swahili literati to copy,
re-write, or compose a number of works in the traditional style.

An outstanding example is the work of Hemedi b. Abdallah b. Said al-Buhriy from Tanga, who was already active in the 1890s. Several of his more ambitious compositions are in the *maghazi* tradition, but they exhibit uncommon skill in style and structure and greater depth in outlook than had been usual in Swahili epics. The *Utenzi wa Seyyidna Huseni bin Ali*,[46] narrates the rebellion of the grand-son of the Prophet, Hussein, against Yazid, the Umayyad Caliph of Damascus in the late seventh century. In compliance with Muslim tradition, Yazid is described as an irreligious, effeminate tyrant: "he ate and scented himself extravagantly," "he dressed with pomp and display," "he wore a crown as bright as a lamp," and "sat on a throne of pearls, rubies and emeralds;" he "sat alone, drinking wine at riotous parties, and he frequently ate pork." Hussein on the contrary, is described as an otherworldly person, who refuses for a long time to yield to the entreaties of those who spur him to rebellion:

I do not wish for this world. I want to worship God. That is my desire. I will not be king. I will be poor. I do not wish to fight that country. I will remain in Mecca and worship the Lord and never go away until my death.

It is only after angel Gabriel's intervention that Hussein finally agrees to take up arms with his family and a small retinue. Like Roland at Roncevaux, he refuses such help as is offered him; not, however, in order to increase the glory that he may expect from the battle, but for the very different reason that Allah's will is going to be done anyway.

After the death of Hussein the story focuses on his brother Muhammad ibn Khanif, whose wrath is aroused by the news. His anger is described in terms which cannot but call to mind the hyperboles of the Irish epic tales:

When Mohammad heard this, he was very angry indeed and his expression was furious. His nostrils quivered, his eyes were red, his muscles stretched all over his quivering body. He became tense and he roared like a dragon or a lion, and he ran with sweat. The people were amazed by his wrath. His blood boiled and his body was tense and he frothed. When he stopped wailing but was still angry, he stood up and ordered his horse. When he came he put on him his war panoply, the armor that could drive into the host. After his horse he girded himself, and if you want his array described, I will tell you. He wore three iron head pieces bound with cloth of mail. Each head piece was so heavy that ten men could not lift it. On top a mailed turban strong as a mountain or a storm. He covered his face with the fringe of the turban. He was mightier than the leopard, the dragon and the lion. The cloth covered his neck and chin and the whole of his face except his eyes. On his body he wore twenty one plates of steel, a belt of copper and shining steel, and he put on his ninefold leggings that you could not look on near or far. His steel leggings he put on and over all an eightfold cloak and he wore fourfold boots. He girded his dagger for the war and his sword, "Master of India," and his mace, like a black snake. He took the shield of his grandfather Hamza.

Though Muhammad ibn Khanif was out to seek revenge, he never reached Yazid's country, for in the midst of the desert, he suddenly found himself hemmed in by rocks, and he heard the voice of the Grace of God proclaiming:

"Here you will never die . . . Remain here among the rocks until the last days when I will take you out. You shall go and wreak vengeance of the son of Haider, on the backs of the unbelievers, the Christians and the Jews . . . but first be patient and let the unbelievers have the power until the time for the fulfilment of your promise." Then the rocks closed in on right and on left and the Lord placed him inside in a secret place and his name was Mahdi.

Although the ending of the epic repeats in a different key the pattern of failure already illustrated by Hussein's brief fighting career, it also serves to convey "newer hope" by announcing the coming of the Mahdi, a saviour descended from the Prophet, who will ensure the triumph of Islam and establish the reign of God. Hemedi's poem shows greater subtlety than earlier *tendi*, where the power of God manifests itself mostly through instant military victory for the faithful. The introduction of the Mahdi legend places the whole tale in the wider perspective of large-scale history and Muslim eschatology.

The intricate problems of authorship built into the literature of a conservative society whose authors keep drawing on a limited fund of topics can be illustrated through a consideration of Hemedi's *Utenzi wa Abdirrahmani na Sufiyani*,[47] which tells of the conversion of Abdurrahman, a brother of the Prophet's wife, and of the ensuing war between the Muslims and Abdurrahman's father-in-law. At the end of the *utenzi*, which has one thousand four-line stanzas, Hemedi writes as follows:

Know that I learnt this poem of Abdurrahman long ago and it was my grandfather (Said) who told it to me. I saw it when I was a boy, for a few days, and then the poem was lost, without anyone knowing who knew it by heart, or being able to tell it; but I knew it all. Moreover my grandfather's composition was lost and had disappeared, and I was recently seized with a desire to save it, and I said I will do my best. I cannot tell the poem of my grandfather Said word for word so that every detail is correct. This utenzi is a wonderful one which was composed by my grandfather . . . I put down the poem of my grandfather in my own arrangement.

In 1940, Ernst Dammann had edited a shorter poem of the same title which was supposed to have been copied by a female slave on Pate island.[48] The two versions are utterly different, even though they tell the same story. They probably represent final stages of two distinct traditions going back to Arabic originals. It seems certain, however, that Hemedi's poem should be regarded as an original composition, based on his recollections of a poem composed by his grandfather, who himself had been inspired by a pre-existing manuscript.

A detailed comparison of the two published poems would bring out Hemedi's immeasurably greater narrative skill. It is noteworthy that the Dammann text, although shorter, should devote twenty-three stanzas to the usual pious invocations, whereas Hemedi manages with just eight verses. The Dammann version has a more strongly marked religious character throughout. Hemedi, it would seem, was chiefly concerned with spinning a good yarn: devotional matter is kept to a minimum, the incidents follow each other at a fast pace, and the space devoted to breath-taking battle descriptions is twice as large as in the other version. Further, although Hemedi concluded his poem with the mandatory prayers and invocations, he also had some rather revealing things to say about his personal purpose as a writer:

> To tell this tale is a way to make myself known here and in some sort to exalt myself. Some men are famous for wealth, others by their journeys, others for showing courage and strength. Some are renowned for their authority and power, and some by their birth in great houses. I, Hemed Buhry, am well-known by my verses; the world sings my songs, and thereby I have reputation.

Seldom has lust for fame been so openly acknowledged as a major purpose of poetic activity in Swahili writing.

• • •

While Muslim subject-matter remained paramount in Swahili literature, colonial enterprise fostered the growth of a trend which had begun with Abdallah bin Masud: the use of epic forms for handling secular topics and contemporary events. German rule had not been welcomed by the inland population, who in many cases already had behind them a long tradition of rebelliousness against the Sultan of Zanzibar. One of the resistance leaders in the late 1880s was an Arab, Abushiri, whose family had opposed Zanzibari rule for more than a century. In 1889, Bismarck sent an army to fight Abushiri; in his despair, the latter sent to Tanga for Hemedi bin Abdallah al-Buhriy, who, besides his literary fame, also enjoyed quite a reputation as an astrologer. Hemedi's prophecies were most ominous and, as it turned out, also most accurate, for

Abushiri was captured and hanged later that year.

These events were to prove important for the development of Swahili literature, for Hemedi soon provided his own, largely autobiographical, version of a story in which he had played some part.[49] The author was surprisingly well-informed of the European background, for after the customary invocations, the first part of the epic describes how the "Sultan" of Germany made enquiries about the Swahili coast and decided to place the whole undertaking in the hands of the merchants of the German East African Company, who describe their intentions in the following terms:

> *We have seen a great war come over Europe. We have looked for a place to go and prosper, and we have discovered the country of the Coast. We wish to settle there, to set up whom we like, to put down whom we will, to have servants to serve us. We will build houses and adorn them magnificently, and if anyone opposes us, we will show him no mercy.*

At one point, one "Mushti Kirofu" (presumably Mr. Krapf) describes Zanzibar and its ruler for the benefit of the German emperor: the physical and moral portrait of Sultan Khalifa is an excellent example of praise-poetry:

> *The Sultan is unmistakable; he is beautifully built; I have not seen his equal. His face is round, as round as the moon, you cannot gaze at it for its beauty. His face is round and his nose like a scimitar. His complexion is wonderfully bright. When the Sultan comes to the audience, he is fierce as a lion terrible to behold. He has a sword in his hand and a fine scimitar. Even a brave man would be afraid and fear would come on him. When he puts on his turban and sits like a lion, the stoutest shrink under his accusation. His character is quiet and untroubled. This Sultan has no doubt or hesitation. His judgment is noble; if you go to him you will be heard; even if you are poor, you will receive justice. An eye for an eye, and an ear for an ear, a tooth for a tooth and a life for a life.*

In connection with the treaty which was signed with the Sultan on 28 April 1888 the poet insists that the concession of the coastal strip and its harbours entailed no territorial ownership: the Sultan gave his agreement, "provided that you give me the money and do violence to no man. Do not oppress the people with soldiers and unlawful acts. You have rented the country, you have not bought it"; and to the population the Sultan explains: "I have given him no more than control over the shipping. If he does anything else, do not consent. If he wants land, this is not in the agreement; kill them, let them not return, as God is my witness I give you this order."

The Germans, it appears, soon made themselves undesirable for a variety of reasons: "At Kilwa and Dar es Salaam there was a plague of Europeans. There was no free speech, they held the country." Their demands for housing were bitterly resented: "We were assured that Europeans were living in the houses of the town of Pangani"; "To Tanga they came daily asking for houses, and some who had obtained them were already established." They showed open contempt for Muslim custom: "We were assured that, with Europeans about, the festal prayers had not been said in the mosque. They had entered in, with their great dogs too, and the Governor had fled and could not bear to remain." They also openly flouted the Sultan's sovereignty: "They cut down the flag and still it lay. They confiscated all the gunpowder in the shops. They struck the flag of Islam and now proposed to raise their own." There was some sporadic fighting, and the Germans complained to the Sultan about the attitude of the Governor. The cunning, noncommittal answer of Khalifa deserves quoting:

> The Seyyid replied: "Perhaps you have been causing damage. Those things would not have happened without a cause. We discussed his [the governor's] work; I did not tell him to fight, nor did I give him ammunition or weapons for battle; but the people of the mainland are not my slaves, they have freely agreed to join me and to accept my sovereignty. Now, if they wish otherwise, I am not their king. Do not come to me with your charges if you go and are killed. You have my agreement for you to change customs, but the towns are their own. I cannot interfere with them."

Dissatisfied, the Europeans, says Hemedi, "left shame-faced and they made an order to use force."

Here begins the narrative of Abushiri's rebellion. From other records, it appears that the resistance groups met with some success in several places, but were defeated at Dar es Salaam, as a result of which Hemedi was called to Abushiri's camp. The scope of the story, which at first had embraced Europe as well as Africa, now narrows down and focuses on the poet's own part in the tale. What the poem loses in range, it gains in human immediacy, as Hemedi's complex personality comes to the fore.

The defeated rebels realize that their setbacks are due to deficient organization: "War is a skilled art and requires a magician, an adept to come and make spells for us. We should look for an astrologer." Upon which, two of Abushiri's companions inform him they know the right man:

His name is Hemedi, an outstanding expert of astrology and poetry. . . . He can enter a house when the owner is asleep and utterly deceive you so that you suspect nothing. You may put on locks and chains, but he will defeat them and undo them all . . . What he does is miraculous.

After this flattering self-portrait, Hemedi tells how he set out for Abu-shiri's headquarters and made his terms clear:

I said, "Sir, if you wish for my skill I will put all that I know into the hand of God. I will pray to the Lord and the house will be open when I put my hand to it, if the Lord guide me. When it is open, with them inside, all that you desire I will do for you." And I told him my terms, "If the Subtle favours me, give me not less than a thousand rupees, and two boy-slaves, good ones of pleasing appearance, and two girl-slaves with necks slim as bamboos. Then will I do the work that you give me. And what I and my people take is to be our own. Do not later ask me for a contribution in time of war. What I shall have taken, seize it not back again from me. If you are satisfied with this, I will use my art for you."

Hemedi does not conceal the fact that his attempts at spying were a dismal failure. This did not seem to detract from the confidence put in him: "I was in great favour with the Sheikhs and councilors. I conjured a day for the attack." Unfortunately, the warriors simply failed to arrive, and Hemedi, in dismay, studied his books once more, with the help of a few colleagues: "We found war and the death of many men and much looting of persons . . . We, the experts, consulted together and we saw disaster." Abushiri, however, refused to believe these ill omens, and when the Germans actually attacked, Hemedi tells us, he "leapt up to praise the Merciful, the Glorious, the Almighty," — though whether out of joy at being proved right or in the hope of special protection, is not made clear.

When it became evident that the rebels were routed, Hemedi recounts, "our leader was the first to flee. I was watching him there inside the stockade and I saw a good place to jump. I jumped out second." While Abushiri was going to his death, Hemedi made his way back to his native town of Tanga, which surrendered without fighting, and the poem ends—"to go further would be to spoil it," "everything has its proper size to grow and be complete"—with renewed praises of Allah.

In 1905, a few years after Abushiri's resistance had been put down, a far bloodier rebellion broke out in the area north of the Mozambican border. The story was related by Abdul Karim bin Jamaliddini in his *Utenzi wa vita vya Maji-Maji* ("Epic of the Maji Maji rebellion"), the text of which was collected as early as 1912 by A. Lorenz in Lindi.[50]

The poem begins with a description of the amazement with which the news of the rebellion was first received:

We were relaxing, resting and eating well, when suddenly we heard news that the pagans had rebelled and were advancing on the fort, weapons in their hands, pillaging the hamlets. We, for our part, treated the matter with some contempt: how could these folk act in such outrageous way? . . . These pagans are fools, working themselves up pointlessly.

In order to understand the viewpoint intimated in this passage, it is necessary to remember that the German colonizers had perpetuated the system of local administration which had been used by the Zanzibari sultans: they appointed chiefs generally chosen among the Muslim élite; these were rarely natives of their district, and were often contemptuous of what they saw as heathen customs. Abdul Karim was a Koranic teacher *(mwalimu)*, and belonged, therefore, to the class from which the Germans originally recruited many of their administrators *(akida)*, governors *(liwali)*, and magistrates *(kadhi)* .

By the early years of the century, however, the status of the *mwalimu* in colonial society had become considerably more ambiguous. While remaining spiritual "leaders of Swahili society", they were beginning to be deprived of such power as the Germans had conferred upon them at first: "Their Koranic education excluded them from employment in European service and brought them into conflict with the better-equipped institutions of western education." Some of them became adherents and even leaders of a newly-formed radical branch of the Qadiriyya known to the Germans as *zikri*, which grew after the *maji-maji* rebellion and combined "eschatological teaching uneasily with aspirations towards improvement". It is indicative of the tensions within Swahili society that in 1910 Abdul Karim was convicted by his own brother, the *kadhi* of Lindi, of "leading a movement to permit women to enter the mosques and officiating at a funeral at which dancing and singing women were present." He was also described by the German district officer as "a radical teacher . . . and as an adherent of zikri".[51]

Although Abdul Karim, in his verse chronicle, went so far as to call the non-Swahili inland people *Washenzi* ("savages") and openly ridiculed their ill-advised attempt to overthrow European rule, he did not identify himself with the German cause. His peculiar status in East African society enabled him to achieve a measure of objectivity in depicting the attitudes of the non-Muslim inland peoples, as well as in clarifying their resentment. While die-hard colonialists interpreted the Maji Maji rebellion as a regressive, savage response to progress introduced by European colonization, "those who were less committed to the German regime," Iliffe notes, "found their explanation of the rebellion in administrative abuses. They pointed to taxation and the brutal methods

by which it was often collected, to forced labour required for road construction or by European settlers, to the misgovernment of the Arab
Ikidas, and to other specific forms of misrule," such as the enforce-
ment of cotton cultivation. This is the type of motivation which is explained in the poem by some captive rebels.

*We are tired of being under orders. We would rather die and have done with
it. This is our choice. We have to cultivate our fields, pick cotton in the
evenings, then build our houses, and look for our tax-money. A heavy burden
as we saw it. All night we talked things over, we plotted revolt, and have
chosen to die. Us you have caught, but there are others.*

Yet the indigenous population was not of one mind in this affair.
While the rebellion was launched and carried out by local chieftains,
witch-doctors and free warriors, the pagans' slaves were reluctant to
fight and often betrayed them to the Germans. They were kept in tow
by the terrible oaths which they were made to swear, and also by fear
of indiscriminate German reprisals; this they willingly acknowledge once
they are captured and have little left to lose:

*Bwana, the pagans have betrayed you. Their leader is Hongo-Hongo. Every-
one acknowledges him. What he says is done, no one dares to refute him, so
great a fear does he inspire. Yet he is a poor man. He has deceived the people
and has gathered a host. We have warned them but our advice was ignored.*

And they go on to describe their dilemna:

*If we were to go to the [German] Fort, we should be handcuffed and die in
goal. This is our danger! Let us turn our backs on the Fort and follow Hongo-
Hongo, even if he is a liar. We shall get a chance to move about freely.*

In local parlance, *hongo* was the term used for the emissaries who
spread the rebellion from its original outbreak in the Rufiji Valley in
1905 to the whole of German-occupied territory. In Iliffe's view the
hongo was the central figure "who arrived at a village, summoned the
surrounding people, persuaded them to fight, and administered maji,"
a magic concoction of water mixed with millet and maize, from which
the rebellion drew its name, and which was supposed to make the fight-
ers proof against German bullets. In the hands of the *hongo* , Iliffe goes
on, "the movement acquired millennial characteristics, claiming power
to rid African societies of the two incalculable evils, European control
and sorcery [i.e. evil magic]. Here, it would seem, where the rebellion
had merged with an established pattern of popular religion, the recur-

rent millenarian movements to eradicate sorcery which have been widespread in East and Central Africa."[52] These wider purposes can be seen in the poem in the character of Hongo-Hongo. In spite of all the disparaging remarks permitted to be placed in the mouths of slaves and prisoners, Abdul Karim is not oblivious to the streak of purity without which no true revolutionary leader could gain a following. For Hongo-Hongo, the specific grievances of the African population simply reflect the paramount fact that they have been deprived of their freedom, the token of their manhood: "You were thirsty for manhood," he exclaims. His aim is the eviction of the white man, and he concentrates on this with single-minded, ruthless obstinacy: "First," he orders the warriors, "do not carry out any looting, concentrate on killing; that is when my medicine will prove itself." When the rebels complain that the magic water does not protect them against the German-led *askaris*, Hongo-Hongo blames the failure on their refusal to comply with his instructions:

> *The source of our damage is the greed of your young folk. Their hearts are full of greed. Hence this trouble. Try my medicine. I have tried it myself, but you have abused it; that was how we suffered loss. You enjoyed yourselves too much, and did not heed my words. For example you plundered. I told you not be commit rape, nor to pillage houses, nor to commit murder on the way; you paid no heed to my words . . . Today, you can see the trouble this has caused. It is patent. Now, return all their property to young and old . . . If you don't return it, then understand you'll be finished.*

Like many medieval chroniclers in Europe, Abdul Karim is prone to ascribe historical processes to the workings of individuals. While this is an oversimplification of historical truth, it also makes for human interest, as can be seen from his narrative of how the rebellion came to an end. After the death of Hongo-Hongo, one of the major leaders, Hassani bin Ismaili, decides to drink the magic water and to submit to the sexual taboos that strengthen it. His wife, however, resents this enforced abstinence although she outwardly agrees to it:

> *The woman saw that this was a serious matter, although she was livid with resentment; she was not an old woman, but still a mere child: she thought hard. They agreed to abstain from pleasure and swallowed their ill-feeling; this they did from choice. They swore to each other a solemn oath, the wife to abstain from fornication, and the husband, likewise, to abstain from taking a second wife.*

A similar oath was taken by all members of Hassani's household, who were made to drink the magic water. Unfortunately,

*On the sixth day, the woman began to regret her action. She called her boy-
slave—she had changed her mind—and said to him, "My dear, don't run
off, come back to me every day, but not in the daytime."*

Filled with supernatural terror at the prospect of breaking the taboo,
the young slave runs away and, presumably to seek protection against
his mistress, goes to the German officers, to whom he spills the whole
story. Thus warned, the Germans are able to organize an expedition in
which "all the war leaders were captured." And the poet concludes:

*The pagans have no intelligence: the pauper has no guts. Everyone simply
agreed with everything he said. The Makonde and the Yao, their hearts failed
them; they and their children were daily killed by shooting. Not a single one
of any importance managed to escape. They were all hanged. Now all is peace
and happiness.*

The events narrated by Hemedi and by Abdul Karim provided inspiration for a number of other writers. As Whiteley says: "Similar
poems sought to document, often from the German point of view, the
punitive expeditions against the Hehe, under Mkwawa, the campaigns
around Kondoa, and against Hasan bin Omari, between 1893 and 1897,
but again there is no evidence at all as to the audience for whom they
were composed. They were collected by the German scholar C. Velten,
published with a German translation, and have remained in libraries
ever since."[53] Included in Carl Velten's *Suaheli-Gedichte* (1918), and
maybe commissioned by him, are to be found an anonymous *Utenzi wa
Hasin bin Umar*, whose hero led an Arab revolt in the Kilwa hinterland
in 1894, and the *Utenzi wa Mkwawa*, where Mwengo Shomari b. Mwengo
Kambi told the story of the Hehe warrior chief Mkwawa, an ally of
Abushiri, who was killed in 1898.[54] It may be supposed that these verse
chronicles were written for the semi-privileged audience of literate people of Arab stock in German employment. But while they deal with
African responses to European impact, in style and technique they exhibit no trace whatever of European influence: they are within the tradition that had been started by Abdullah bin Masud in the *Akida* poem.

•   •   •

By 1900, the Swahili-speaking areas had been carved out into three
zones with different regimes. While Zanzibar had become an English
protected territory in 1890, the Germans had established themselves on
the southern mainland coast, whereas the British administered the
coastal strip north of Tanga, in present-day Kenya. In Zanzibar, Mombasa, Lamu, and other places under British influence, creative writers

of the early decades of this century remained loyal to the *ajami* tradition, as did their colleagues in Tanganyika. The manner of British administration, however, did not provide them with the same kind of material as had inspired Hemedi bin Abdallah and Abdul Karim bin Jamaliddini in the German colony, and Islam remained their main source of inspiration.

One of those writers was Muhamcd Jambein al-Bakari, of whom we know only that he was already active in Mombasa and Lamu at the beginning of this century; by the 1930s, he had become one of the most esteemed informants of such European scholars as Ernst Dammann. His *Kiongozi cha Banati* ("A Guide for Daughters") is an educational treatise in verse in the line initiated by Mwana Kupona. He also authored a poem on the nativity of the Prophet, *Maulidi ya Jambeni*,[55] which, according to Knappert, "is remarkable for its poetic form as well as for some of the motifs that are not found in other Swahili Maulids but which do feature in the Maulid narratives in other languages of the Islamic world." The Prophet's ascension to heaven is the subject of his *Utenzi wa Miiraji*.[56]

Muhammad b. Abubakar b. Umar al-Bakari (c. 1860–c. 1940) already enjoyed some reputation as a writer in the 1890s. Better known as Muhammad Kijumwa, he added to his name the word "Masihii" (follower of the Messiah) in 1932, when he became the first Swahili scholar of Arab origin to be converted to Christianity.[57] A many-faceted personality, he was at one time a dancer at the court of the Sultan in Zanzibar. But he spent most his life on Lamu, where he was active as a painter, a sculptor and a musician. He rendered invaluable service to Swahili literature through his co-operation with several generations of European scholars, from W.E. Taylor and Alice Werner to Ernst Dammann. An indefatigable copyist, he was responsible for the preservation of large segments of the Swahili tradition; but since concern with originality and authorship was not widespread among Swahili writers, it is often difficult to assess his own contributions to the works that he is alleged to have merely copied.[58] For example, his *Utendi wa Liyongo*, which was written is 1913, is based on traditional oral material and incorporates several songs of a very archaic character.[59] Such works as are definitely his own—for example his didactic poem *Utenzi wa Kijumwa kumuusia mwanawe Helewa Siraji* ("Poem of Kijumwa's last will addressed to his child Helewa Siraji")—are epigonic in form and may well be indicative of some decay in classical Swahili poetry.

At the same time, he acted as an innovator, turning the favourite *utendi* verse form to new uses. Three of his poems which were edited by Dammann in the early 1940s are highly revealing in this respect. *Nasara wa Arab* ("Christian and Arabs", 1936) should probably rank as the first Swahili poem of Christian inspiration. Resenting, perhaps, the unfriendliness of other Muslims after his conversion, Muhammad Kijumwa offers a rather rosy picture of European life as he could observe it in Lamu: Christians use handkerchiefs, they evince cleanliness and discretion in their table manners, they are monogamous, they show charity and tolerance to poor people and to members of other religions, they deal impartial justice to poor and rich alike, they have no slaves, they are diligent and inventive, so that "God has blessed them: on his order did they gain supremacy over us." Perhaps for fear of offending the Muslim reader, Muslim habits are not directly opposed to those of the Christians, but the poet lays considerable emphasis on the divisiveness that characterizes Islamic brotherhoods. The general purpose of the poem is a plea for tolerance and understanding: "Each ship has her captain, on whom all rely, but the harbour is the same." Unfortunately, on each ship "all travellers say of themselves, 'We are those bound for paradise, the others are destined to Hell'."

Kijumwa's antiquarian interest in the past of Lamu, exhibited in his activity as a copyist, was also apparent in another poem which gives a detailed description of a marriage ceremony on old Lamu. This poetic account of old customs, Dammann claims, is an innovation in Swahili poetry. And so is the third of the poems *Dammann* edited, *We safari utendi* ("Story of a journey," 1937), a verse report of a journey undertaken in the Lamu archipelago by the poet, the German scholar and the latter's wife.

The career of Muhammad Kijumwa covered almost the whole of the colonial period. Indeed, this kind of creative and scholarly activity went on throughout and well beyond the days of colonial rule. Among the many Swahili scholars who co-operated with European scholars in the preservation and retrieval of classical Swahili writing, special mention must be made of Haji Chum, whose *Utenzi wa vita vya Uhud*[60] provides a remarkable example of the way traditional subject matter could be submitted to a rather extraordinary refining process. It is as yet impossible to make out which was Haji Chum's personal part in the remoulding of the version that he used; this version originates in an oral tradition which ultimately goes back, as usual, to an Arabic narrative. The author of the earliest Swahili version must have been an Arab too, for it is said in one of the introductory verses: "This work I wish to compose in their language which is known as Kiswahili."

The poem deals with the battle of Uhud (625), an episode in the long struggle between the Prophet and the other Qoraish, the Meccan tribe to which his own clan, the house of Hashem, belonged. The factual contents of the poem is of the slightest: thanks to Muhammad's excellent strategy, the fighting first turns to the advantage of the Muslims; but part of the Prophet's army then leave their assigned position to pursue the enemy and share in the spoils. This enables the Qoraish to turn about and regain the lost ground; they even reach Muhammad himself, who inflicts a deadly wound on one of the opponents but is injured by a stone. Not until the Qoraish have withdrawn with their dead do the Prophet and his closest friends dare to emerge from their hiding-place. He first decides to take revenge, but the Lord speaks to him; Mohammed then vows to abstain from vengeance and returns to Medina with his faithful. Historical evidence does not seem to support this interpretation: according to Nicholson, it was the Qoraish who "made no attempt to follow up their advantage, while Muhammad, never resting on his laurels, never losing sight of the goal, proceeded with remorseless calculation to crush his adversaries one after the other."[61] Historical facts, it would seem, had all the elements for an epic of the traditional type, ending in a resounding victory for the faithful. We are bound to wonder why the poet rounded off the narrative with an admission of military defeat, thus choosing a pattern basically similar to that of Hemed's *Huseni* epic. For lack of outside information on this point, the answer must be sought in the poem itself which, in fact, is less an epic than an anti-epic using epic techniques to downgrade the epic values of warlike courage and glory and to proclaim a gospel of forgiveness and inwardness.

It is a convention of the Swahili *utendi* that the writer must make a great show of humility, at the beginning or at the end, apologizing for his defective talent and inviting readers and other poets to improve on his mediocre work. This is usually done in a more or less casual way. In the *Uhud* poem, however, the tendency towards self-disparagement is pushed to extreme ends. After the initial invocations to Allah, the author devotes twenty-five stanzas to an orgy of self-depreciation: he is a destitute "wanderer," unfit to undertake writing the poem because he is "neither skilled in writing nor well-informed in composing"; he is liable to make spelling mistakes because he is "short of teeth and cannot distinguish between the letters 'z' and 'dh'"; his speech is "harsh and halting"; and in the confusion of his mind he is apt to omit words. The poem is metaphorically described as a painful mule journey through the desert, and this conceit recurs in such continuous and elaborate manner that it creates at times an unusual impression of Chaucerian humour.

Yet the desert image operates at several distinguishable levels: it signifies the painful progress of the Prophet and his followers as they march towards and retreat from Uhud; even more explicitly, it denotes the dreary progress of both poet and reader (or listener) through the work itself and through the monotonous succession of fights that it describes. The Prophet's and the Poet's odysseys are overtly linked at the end, as Mohammed comes back to Medina:

> *The Prophet has now arrived safely in Medina, and now I have reached an*
> *end and unload my mule.*
> *We have reached the city we intended as I told you at the start.*

Not only is the finishing of the poem the writer's own Medina, but the
equation receives new, ethical overtones as the writer begs his readers
for pardon:

> *I crave forgiveness for taking you through the wilderness*
> *And for everywhere I went, and the wars I got into, and every hill I climbed,*
> *I beg your patience.*

In the author's mind, the hills of the desert and its "sandy wastes,"
the "stones and holes, mountains and great rocks" through which he
has been wandering are a correlative, not only of the difficulties he
experienced in writing the story, but also of the battles he has narrated.
And the forgiveness he asks of his readers has its equivalent in the
pardon granted by Mohammed.

Here indeed we have reached the heart of the matter and the key to
the purpose of the poem. In a conventional Swahili epic, the victory of
Mohammed's enemies could not have been final: the infidels would
have to be beaten in a further war, and the treacherous, disobedient
soldiers would have to get their deserved reward. But what the *Uhud*
story leads up to is precisely the vanity of this endless chain of crime
and punishment, and the efficiency of moral behavior commanded by
inner values. True, the first idea that occurs to the beaten Mohammed
is to take bloody revenge on the Meccans:

> *The Beloved said, "May I defeat the Kureish!*
> *I must slaughter a full seventy of them for his."*

But the point is that this vengeful impulse, backed by the primitive
ethics of shame and prestige, of military power and defeat, is checked
by orders from above:

> *When the Prophet had spoken, straightway the two verses came down to him*
> *and entered his mind.*

This is a reference to verses of *sura* 16 in the *Koran,* which recommends
generosity, patience and resignation: how contrary they are to Mohammed's innate proclivities is evidenced not only by his earlier intentions, but also, more dramatically, in a long episode where the Prophet
kills a man who had insulted him in Mecca. The message from above
initiates a startling change in Mohammed:

It was then that, without delay, he broke his oath and rescinded his pronounced intention . . . If he defeated the Kureish, he would not take revenge by slaughtering them; he repudiated vengeance and annulled it entirely.

Furthermore, it must be remembered that the defeat was not due solely to the superior power of the enemy, who carried the day only because of the treasonable disobedience of the Prophet's own soldiers. Yet these too are to be pardoned:

Also on that day came down the texts concerning forgiveness of the men who had run away.

It is now possible to define in what sense the *Uhud* poem can be considered an anti-epic. The essence of the epic outlook lies in Vergil's phrase, *Arma virumque cano*. But what the Swahili poet sings is neither the arms nor the man who knows how to wield them. The wars he has been reporting can be equated with the hills and rocks and sands of the wilderness because they too are in the nature of obstacles: warring does not achieve what it aims at; warring itself is the stumbling block on the way to the victory that is its assigned target. Fighting is not only irrelevant—which is why the author begs his readers' forgiveness—but altogether inefficient. And the ultimate meaning of the poem is that acceptance of physical defeat is the right way to spiritual victory. In his repetitious way, the poet had intimated as much at the beginning, when, after listing the more prominent among the Qoraish opponents of Mohammed, he said:

Further, it was these people, these gentlemen we have named, who, in the end, were all on the side of the Prophet.

Moreover, they were converted, and became Believers, and acquired the leadership in the war command.

They became the army commanders and were responsible for its orders; they made a speedy appearance whenever there was action.

They were famous people, and when they had dropped their ignorant beliefs, they became the friends of the noble Prophet.

Whether this was a device of Haji Chum's own invention, or was already present in the original source, it has been the purpose of the poem all along, in the author's devious and often ironic manner, to describe how spiritual conversion can only be operated through the virtues of inwardness.

5. Western Influence and Swahili Literature

Whiteley noted the irony in the fact that, while Kenya—with Mombasa and the islands of Lamu and Pate—had produced the major part of classical Swahili writing, it was in German-occupied Tanganyika that the first decisive steps were taken towards the modernization of Swahili literature.[62] This resulted from the introduction of roman script, printing presses and western-type schools by the German administration. Swahili poets remained for a long time as impervious to those novelties as their Hausa contemporaries. But side by side with the *ajami* verse chronicles of the German period, a few historical prose works were written in roman script. The pioneer in this new genre was Abdallah b. Hemedi b. Ali el Ajjemy (b. *c.* 1835), born in Zanzibar of an Arab father and a Hehe mother from central Tanganyika. After serving the Shambala chief Kimweri za Nyumbai, he entered German service, occupying several posts as *akida*, and was appointed *liwali* (governor) of Lindi from 1905 to 1912. His *Habari za Wakilindi* ("Chronicles of the Wakilindi"), was printed in three volumes (1895, 1904, 1907) by the Universities Mission to Central Africa on their press at Magila, near Tanga.[63] It was a recording of oral traditions concerning the history of the Shambala, a non-Swahili tribe.

The writing of chronicles has been a very important genre in Swahili culture. In the early years of the sixteenth century, Portuguese navigators brought to Lisbon a copy of the Arabic chronicle of Kilwa, a translation of which was printed by J. de Barros in his *Decades da Asia* (1552).[64] In 1856, the French historian M. Guillain made use of a copy of the Mombasa chronicle dated 1823.[65] The manuscript of the chronicle of Pate, which recounted the history of the town from the thirteenth century to 1885, was destroyed during the rebellion of 1890, but its contents survived in many memories so that several independent versions were published in the early decades of the twentieth century.[66] In 1928, William Hichens published a copy of the Lamu chronicle which had been made in the late 1890s by one Shaibu Faraji.[67] Their manuscripts were the outcome of a long *ajami* tradition of historical writing, which remained productive until the European conquest: around 1880, Sheikh Ali b. Hamed wrote his *Habari za Mrima* ("History of the Tanganyika coast"), which was printed in the journal *Mambo Leo* in 1935.

This type of research, and the writing of it in roman script, was undoubtedly encouraged by the Germans. By the end of World War I, the files in the office of the *Bezirksamtmann* in Tanga contained typescripts of a *History of Mombasa and Tanga* written in the early years of the century by Sheikh Omari bin Stamboul, (d. *c.* 1918), who was then *Kadhi* of Tanga, and of a *History of Africa,* which had been completed in 1914 by Sheikh Hemedi bin Abdullah. E.C. Baker, who later published an English translation of the latter, wondered "whether such records are worth publishing, for much of the contents is legendary, the facts are often garbled and the genealogies are incomplete, but we have so few records of past events in East Africa that every item of information is worth preserving."[68] The sycophantic ending of Hemedi's *History of Africa* may make it easier to understand the peculiar outlook illustrated in the *utendi* verse chronicles of the period:

> *During the rule of the Germans we have gained happiness and prosperity and many beautiful things. May their rule be great, for they love the people greatly. It is now twenty-six years since the Europeans began to rule: they have done away with twenty-six bad things and have brought twenty-six good things to the country.*

This esoteric playing with numbers is substantiated in the form of such diverse items as plentiful imported food, stone houses with corrugated iron roofs, modern transportation (trains, steamers, roads and bicycles), European script and schools, hospital medicine, agricultural growth and general security.

The British, for their part seem to have been more concerned with the provision of reading-matter for schools. For many decades, this took the form of Swahili translations prepared by European educationists. As early as 1867, Bishop Steere made some of Charles Lamb's *Tales from Shakespeare* available to juvenile leaders in mission schools; they were printed in Zanzibar under the title *Hadithi na Kiingereza*. This was followed by a few translations—some of Kingsley's tales (1889), selections from *Aesop's Fables* (1890)—printed locally or in London. No further translations appeared until the 1920s, when the need to provide more vernacular reading matter began to make itself felt throughout British Africa. A Swahili version of Bunyan's *Pilgrim's Progress* appeared in 1925, followed, during the next dozen years, by bulkier translations from such writers as R.L. Stevenson, H. Rider Haggard, Rudyard Kipling and Jonathan Swift. These were printed in London, as were several volumes of selections from *The Arabian Nights*. A new phase began when a native Swahili speaker, David E. Diva, gave a revised translation of *Aesop's Fables* (1937), although it was not until 1950 that this type of activity passed almost entirely to African hands. Nor did London remain the sole centre of production for such works: from 1957, brief Swahili versions of Russian creative writing began to appear in Moscow, with Omar Juma as their most prolific translator. And in 1964, a Swahili translation of Chinese short stories was printed in Peking.[69] All these works were intended as class-room material and for popular reading, but they did bring prose fiction as a legitimate literary genre to the attention of prospective Swahili writers, in whose traditional culture verse was the only recognized literary art form. Translation was raised to a considerably higher level of literary achievement with Shaaban Robert's rendering of Edward Fitzgerald's own version of the *Rubaiyat* of Omar Khayyam (1952), and when the president of the Republic of Tanzania, Julius Nyerere, published his Swahili translation of Shakespeare's *Julius Caesar* (1963).

By 1920, Tanganyika had become a mandate territory under British administration as part of British East Africa, together with Kenya and Uganda. Although the new authorities did not maintain the incipient German policy of making Swahili the language of the administration, English officials, missionaries, scholars and educationists did encourage the promotion of Swahili as a sort of *lingua franca*, not only along the coast where it was the native language, but also in inland areas where it had first been introduced by Arab traders. Under German aegis, the U.M.C.A. had issued the earliest Swahili newspapers, *Msimulizi* ("Teller of Tales," 1888) and *Habari za Mwesi* ("Monthly News," 1895). In 1923, the British launched *Mambo Leo* in Dar es Salaam, and this became the most important medium for modern-type literature by Swahili writers long before publication of indigenous writing in book form was achieved. At the same time, literate knowledge of Swahili spread further and further inland with the result, as Whiteley points out, that "if Swahili was the language of the country in Tanganyika, in Kenya it was the language of the towns, especially Nairobi, where people from all parts of the country found it a convenient bulwark against the loneliness of city life as well as a ready tool to exploit the attractions which the city offered."[70]

According to A.B. Hellier, "the beginning of the 'modern period' may confidently be dated from 1925," when an Education Conference was convened by the Governor of Tanganyika on the assumption that it would be "an incalculable advantage that a common vernacular language should be as widely used as possible" in schools throughout British East Africa. After several years of negotiations and progress, the Inter-Territorial Language Committee came into being in 1930. As Whiteley recounts, the I.L.C., which later became known as the East African Swahili Committee, was first "based in Dar es Salaam, but moved to Nairobi in 1942; in 1952 it moved to Makerere, but it moved back to the coast ten years later, to Mombasa, before finally returning to Dar es Salaam in 1963. There, in 1964, it was finally incorporated into the Institute of Swahili Research, one of the Research Institutes of the University College, Dar es Salaam."[71]

The fundamental purpose of the Committee was "to promote the standardization and development of the Swahili language" in the Zanzibar dialect, which had been selected at an early stage. Some of the ways to do this were described in its constitution as "giving advice to all prospective authors concerning books which they proposed to write," and "giving encouragement and assistance to authors whose native tongue is Swahili." Actually, the Committee proved to be mainly concerned with problems of linguistic study and standardization, and with research into classical Swahili literature. By 1940, A B Hellier could legitimately remark that "the encouragement of Native authorship has not produced anything very striking so far." In 1948, the literary function originally assigned to the Committee was taken over by the East African Literature Bureau, but a number of modern works—poems, stories, short novels—had been and went on being, published by London presses as part of their overseas educational programs.

In the years immediately following independence, although considerable support was given to Swahili as a prospective national language in Tanzania, it was in Kenya that the majority of modern Swahili works were published, not only by the local branches of such British publishers as Longman, Heinemann and Oxford University Press, but also, significantly, by a local press which was founded in Nairobi in 1965, the East African Publishing House. For a long time, however, the main outlet for modern work was the government-sponsored paper *Mambo Leo,* out of whose backfiles a three-volume anthology of poems *Mashairi ya "Mambo Leo "* (1966) was later compliled. This was published in London by the Sheldon Press, as had been other early works of genuine Swahili authorship, such as Akiri K. Kyabongo's prose stories, *Hadithi za Wasiboro* ("Tales of the Wasiboro", 1939), and James Juma Mbotela's *Uhuru wa Watumwa* (1934), a semi-historical narrative which was later translated into English as *The Freeing of the Slaves in East Africa* (1956). This was of peculiar interest as it suggested that the new Swahili literature was being born outside the traditional literate circles. Mbotela told the story of his grandfather, who had been taken into slavery by Arab traders in the vicinity of Lake Nyanza, was freed at sea by a British ship as he was being carried to Arabia, and settled at Freretown near Mombasa; Mbotela continued the story with reminiscences of his own father, who witnessed the events of 1880, when Mombasa Arabs and Swahili raided the freed-slave settlement at Freretown but were defeated by the missionaries and by British troops sent in from Zanzibar.[72]

Uhuru wa watumwa was presumably commissioned by the missionaries for school use. It undoubtedly falls into the category which Janheinz Jahn has called "apprentice literature", meaning "the literature which in its style follows European models, and in its content adopts the ideology and social forms of colonialism or approves them without argument or reflection."[73] It is understandable, however, that the ex-slaves and their descendants should have stayed loyal to the British, to the missionaries, and even to the East Africa Company, which, Mbotela says, "sent white men to teach them so that they could take a step up in civilisation. The citizens of Freretown were very pleased when they saw that they were also being taught English . . . The Company brought many tools and ploughs for them to use, and trained them . . . Truly our grandfathers were awakened from their sleep of ignorance." That this loyalty was genuinely felt appears from the fact, mentioned by the English translator, C.G. Richards, that one of Mbotela's sons "was assassinated in 1953 for his bold stand against those who were attempting to bring a new kind of terror to this land"—a reference to the state of emergency that was declared in Kenya as a result of the Mau Mau insurrection. But Mbotela's little tale is important for the history of Swahili literature because it exemplifies how a new trend was arising in modern-educated circles that were alien and even hostile to the predominantly Muslim and/or Arabic elements in traditional Swahili culture.

These attempts at renewal, however, did not come to fruition until after World War II. As has been usual in the formative stages of vernacular creative writing throughout black Africa most of the works issued during this early phase were designed for juvenile readers. Two writers proved exceptionally prolific in this sphere. In 1948, David Edward Diwa, who had previously appeared in print with Swahili versions of some of Aesop's fables (1937), published *Mtoto mwivu na hadithi nyingine* ("The lazy child and other stories") and in 1949, Omar C.A. Shariff inaugurated his career with *Isa bin Tajiri na hadithi nyingine* ("Isa the trader's son and other stories"). These and many subsequent collections of short prose fiction for school use were published in London.

As to formal drama in Swahili, it did not make a start until the late 1950s, under the sponsorship of the East African Literature Bureau, with Henry Kuria's *Nakupenda, lakini* ("I love you, but . . .", 1957), a murderous tragedy dealing with the conflict between traditional and modern ways of life in rural Kenya. This was followed by another Kenyan play, *Nimelogwa nisewe na mpenzi* ("I have been bewitched, I have no lover," 1961), by Gerishon Ngugi; it centres on "topics such as payment of dowry, marriage, conflicting values between generations, petty jealousy and fruitless rivalry between indiviuals," and it has been rather contemptuously dismissed by one East African critic as "no more than an unsuccessful maiden effort, with a number of half-baked ideas . . . characterized by rather poorly mastered dramatic techniques."[74]

While modern Swahili prose fiction was making such humble beginnings in the decade following World War II, poetry too underwent the effects of the winds of change that were sweeping over black Africa. One interesting, though not widely spread, development, was that Swahili scholars and poets of the traditional Islamic school began to avail themselves of the advantages of print. In this respect, the most remarkable figure was perhaps Abdullah Saleh el-Farsy. At that time he was *kadhi* of Zanzibar, but he became the Chief *kadhi* of Kenya after the Zanzibar revolution of 1964. Although Knappert describes him "as the most notable Swahili poet of the Islamic World,"[75] he is better known as a Islamic scholar and a translator of the Koran.[76] He embarked on his career as a writer with a biography of *Seyyid Said bin Sultan* (1942); this was printed in Zanzibar, as were most of his later works, which concern points of Muslim law and custom. But some of his translations of various Koranic *suras* were printed in the early 1950s as far away as Bangalore: they include the Arabic texts, and Swahili commentaries in verse.

The decisive figure in the modernizing process that affected Swahili literature was Shaaban Robert (1909–1962) from the Tanga area in Northern Tanganyika. Though he started writing poetry in the 1930s, his first volume, *Pambo la lugha* ("Beauty of the language"), did not appear until 1948, when it was issued in the "Bantu Treasury" series published in Johannesburg. This was the first of many works in prose and verse which made him, in the words of Wilfred Whiteley, "the most notable literary figure to have appeared on the Swahili scene in this century."[77] Because of his exceptional position as a professional man of letters, because of the abundance and diversity of his literary output, and because of his deep knowledge and subtle handling of the Swahili language, he enjoys an exalted reputation among Tanzanian literates and Swahili scholars. He has even been called "the Shakespeare of Africa."[78]

Shaaban's parents both belonged to the Yao tribe of present-day Malawi, but he himself was born on the northern coast of Tanganyika, and was obviously an intellectual product of Swahili culture. Because of this dual situation, he was very conscious of the desirability of striving for the cultural unification of the whole of East Africa through the spreading of the Swahili language, instead of limiting his concern, as classical Swahili writers had done, to the Swahili community in a narrow sense. The ending of his *Utendi wa Adili* ("Poem of Good Conduct")[79] is clearly indicative of the poet's unusual pride in his African identity:

I have not betrayed my tribe.
I am an honest African.
Do not think of me otherwise.
I am not of mixed lineage
Neither on my mother's nor my father's side.
However fine [other lineages] may be
I am not sprung from it
I am no Arab nor a European.
I am not of Indian descent.

I tell this to the world,
So that the curious may know.

And he clearly defined his purpose—and his choice of Swahili rather
than English—in an essay where he wrote:

> *Perhaps better literature than that from my own wretched pen already exists*
> *in East Africa, but the disadvantages of the foreign language in which it is*
> *written are not negligible. Africans are forced to get knowledge from it with*
> *much difficulty, like children fed from the bottle instead of from their mother's*
> *breast. My writing will be in the one important language of East Africa. By*
> *this many people will be able to receive knowledge from the breasts to which*
> *they are accustomed. In this way I will help in some small measure the progress*
> *of my country. I have had no higher education, but I do have a sufficient store*
> *of language to use and depend upon always in my writing.*[80]

Actually, when these words were printed, East African creative writing
in English was practically non-existent. It was therefore Shaaban's exceptional merit to show that the vernacular tongue and its resources
were not limited to the classical Muslim tradition, however impressive
this might be, but could also be successfully used as a medium for introducing western literary genres into Swahili literature.

Nevertheless, immersed as he was in the classical Swahili tradition, it
was inevitable that he should conceive of literature as primarily didactic
in purpose. As Harries observes,

> *Traditionally, the Swahili writer loved to moralise. His values were the con-*
> *ventional ones. Shaaban Robert was in his element— and in the tradition of*
> *his people—when he was postulating moral, conventional principles of no*
> *individual application. This results in an astonishing lack of humour, and*
> *surely the ability to laugh is an African characteristic.*[81]

Not only, then, was Shaaban a practitioner of traditional genres and a
master of classical versification, but most of his poems are straightfor-
wardly didactic and homiletic, as exemplified in the *Utendi wa hati*
("Poem of the written homily"), or in the later *Marudi mema* ("Good
Advice"), a 400-stanza homily designed "to guide the poet's own heart
through this world to future joy."[82]

Shaaban's determination to make Swahili poetry accessible to a wider
audience than the coastal Muslims appears in his frequent habit of ap-
pending a glossary at the end of his works, as well as in a curious innovation, conspicuous in *Kielezo cha Fasili* ("Explanation of the *fasili*,"
1968), the provision of a prose paraphrase of some of his poems. On
the other hand, his desire to widen the literary horizon of his country-

men is manifest in his translation of Fitzgerald's version of Omar Khayyam's *Rubayat,* which he had received from an English friend.[83] While the translation was perhaps partly prompted by his eagerness to introduce the Swahili reader to non-Arab literature other than the English juvenile stories and novels of adventures that had been adapted by British missionaries and educators, he must have found the task peculiarly congenial because of the fact that the original poet was a Persian and a Muslim, although, as Harries points out, it must have been difficult for him "to recognize the pessimistic and cynical rationalism of the poem which even he would not have dared to teach in his orthodox Muslim environment."

It was probably the example of the nineteenth-century authors of chronicles in *utenzi* form that prompted Shaaban to the writing of *Utenzi wa Vita vya Uhuru* ("Epic of the war for freedom"), a 12,000-line poem where he tried to narrate and explain, for the benefit of his countrymen, what he himself described in his autobiography as "the history of an event which had momentous consequences for the world in the century in which I lived," namely, the second World War.[84]

But Shaaban was also interested in the promotion of a more popular type of Swahili poetry. In *Wasifu wa Siti binti Saad* ("An account of Siti binti Saad," 1958), he published a number of poems by a famous female singer-poet of the first half of the century, Siti binti Saad (*c.* 1880–1950), who was exceptional among African Swahili women in that she received instruction in the language of the Koran as part of her apprenticeship under the popular African Swahili poet Maalim Shaaban (b. *c.* 1893). According to Harries,[85] she was one of several singer-poets, such as the the blind Mbaruk Talsam (1892–1959), who compose and sing with no other purpose than to entertain others and to please themselves and who found their audience "in the many musical clubs which have featured so prominently in Swahili coastal life." While "it was, and still is, customary for the songs to be written down before performance," and while one of the best-known Zanzibar clubs had a number of them recorded in Bombay, little attention was paid to them by literary scholars until Shaaban's anthology; it is perhaps as a result of this that a selection of the song-poems of Maalim Shaaban, Mbaruk Talsam and Siti binti Saad was later publishd in Dar es Salaam under the title *Waimbaji wa juzi* ("Singers of Yesteryear," 1966).

The most important contribution of Shaaban to the modernization of Swahili literature is no doubt his addiction to prose writing. His first composition in this respect was probably the first part of his autobiography, *Maisha Yangu* ("My life"), which won first prize in the 1936 East African Literary Competion, but did not reach print until 1949. The second part, entitled *Baada ya Miaka Hamsini,* ("After Fifty Years") was completed in 1960 and published in 1966.[86] Autobiography was not an

altogether new genre in Swahili writing. There are autobiographical
elements in al-Buhriy's epic poem on the German conquest, and the
famous Arab trader of the nineteenth century, Muhmad Hamid bin
Muhammad, generally known as Tippu Tip, had left a fairly detailed
account of his life and travels[87] but this was an exceptional work. The
theocentricity and otherworldliness of the Swahili literary tradition precluded excessive concentration on personal experience and, of course,
prose was not considered an artistic medium at all. Shaaban's autobiography, therefore, was an arresting novelty, and it may well be held
responsible for later occurrences of the genre, such as *Maisha ni kitu aali*
by Paul O. Ogula, or *Safari ya ndoa saba* by G. Mhina.[88]

The transitional quality of Shaaban's work is perhaps best exemplified in his prose narratives, which seem to have much in common with
Hausa novellas. While the medium itself is of western descent, these
tales exhibit a taste for the marvellous which is partly of African origin,
but was also no doubt influenced by the *Arabian Nights* tradition. The
main novelty is that the heavy moralizing inherent in much Swahili
writing is now concerned with a specific secular problem which might
be described as the problem of correct leadership in a changing society.
One of Shaaban's earliest prose stories *Kufikirika* (completed by 1946,
printed 1967), is probably the first Swahili work that attempts to face
the question raised by the intrusion of foreign innovation in a highly
conservative state. The title is the name of an imaginary kingdom, whose
rulers have to decide whether to follow their ancestral customs or to call
upon the help of modern science, in this case medicine. The action is
dominated by a mysterious character who appears in the guise of a
soothsayer, a progressive teacher, and a wise peasant. Shaaban's attitude is that the law exists only for man's welfare: it should not be
observed to the point of endangering his very survival.

Kusadikika, chi iliyo angani (1951) narrates the trial of a young man who
is indicted for advocating the introduction of legal studies in the imaginary country of Kusadikika. In order to defend his views against the
impressive public prosecutor, a die-hard reactionary bent on preserving
the vested interests of the ruling hierarchy, he tells a parable about
ministers of state sent to various foreign countries, whose reports, on
their return, were completely ignored by the rulers. The very title shows
that this is a companion piece to the earlier story. Shaaban has now
enlarged his perspective: where modern medicine was the only para-
digm of modernity, he now takes in wider problems of intellectual, social, and economic advance. As the accused is described as a commoner,
and as the public prosecutor makes the point that the greatness of the
kingdom has been due to people of nobler origins, there is an element
of social criticism which may well refer, albeit ambiguously, to the aristocratic strucure of Swahili society or to the inequality in colonial society.

In the absence of any extraneous evidence, it may be supposed that *Adili na Nduguze* ("Adili and his brothers," 1952), was written earliest, for the element of fantasy is much closer to the folklore and Arabic traditions, and the moralizing is of a more personal nature, than in the other two tales. The story centres on the sea travels and marvellous adventures of a protagonist of inordinate goodness, Adili, who suffers exploitation at the hands of his brothers; unlikely incidents pile up as he saves a centipede from a snake and sees it turned into a beautiful damsel, meets the princess of a ruined city, and sees his brothers turned into apes as a deserved reward for their jealously and cruelty. Although harmony and justice are restored at the end through the agency of a bountiful king, the purpose of the tale seems to be simply to advocate selflessness and to indict undue attachment to worldly goods.

In later years, with the coming of independence, Shaban turned his sermonizing proclivities to more topical political purposes, at the same time strengthening the realistic trend that had been introduced recently into Swahili prose fiction by a few journalistic writers in Tanga. In *Utubora mkulima* ("Utubora the farmer," 1968), the name of the title character has the Bunyanesque meaning of "Mr. Best Human Nature." In compliance with the Tanzanian government's efforts to check the rush from countryside to congested cities, Utubora sacrifices a well-paid job in Zanzibar in order to work on the mainland as a hired gardener. Shaaban's edifying and societal intentions bring him close to many vernacular writers throughout black Africa, whose main task as they see it is to contribute to the moral and material progress of their own people. *Utubora* clearly reflects an idea that is central to the political thought of Julius Nyerere: the notion that one of the main keys to African development is the common citizen's adherence to the work ethic, with the concomitant reappraisal of rural activities and values. This shift to the very concrete problems with which a country like Tanzania is faced accounts largely for the increasing realism in Shaaban's narrative art.

The twofold nature of Shaaban's progress—the widening scope of his message, and the increasing sophistication in his novelistic technique—were much in evidence in his last piece of prose fiction, *Siku ya watenzi wote* ("The day of all creators," 1968). Like *Utubora*, it deals with concrete characters precisely located in time, and there is no appeal to the fantastic and the marvellous. Shaaban's contains the first occurrences of town slang in Swahili literary writing. Indeed, it is more recognizably a novel than the earlier tales, both in length and in complexity of the plot, which involves a comparatively large number of clearly delineated characters. It also deals with a greater variety of themes such as the condition of women in the new African society and, significantly, the need to overcome the divisiveness that results from religious sectarianism.

• • •

Shaaban's emphatic assertion of his African origins—although in spite of his Yao ancestry he was a genuine Swahili—his insistence that he was neither an Arab nor an Indian, are significant indications of the great change that affected Swahili literature as a result of the fact that linguistic policy in independent Tanzania prolonged and intensified trends that had been initiated by the German rulers. Until the advent of Western imperialism, Swahili writing had been mainly produced by two categories of authors: the majority were of Arab, or of mixed Arab-African ancestry; they usually claimed patrilineal descent from some Arab ancestor; they thought of themselves primarily as Arabs rather than as Africans. Others were Africans fully assimilated to Islam, but who had kept close links with their tribal culture on the coast; they called themselves *shirazi* in order to distinguish themselves from the so-called Arab Swahili and in reference to traditions concerning the arrival of migrants from Shiraz in Persia before the thirteenth century. In addition, there was of course a fairly large population of illiterate, hardly Islamized Swahili speakers, whose literary activity had perforce to be oral. It was the latter class that rose to literacy—in roman script—in the missionary schools, and its representatives were strongly instrumental in modernizing the Swahili language and literature. In the linguistic sphere, they tended to define themselves in opposition to the hitherto unchallenged influence of Arabic over Swahili. As Lyndon Harries pointed out, Shaaban Robert, who was still under the sway of Arabic cultural "assimilation," realized "that he was writing for Africans less familiar than himself with Arabic words. In several of his books he provided a glossary of Arabic terms with a simpler equivalent, together with an explanation of some terms of his own coining which look as though they were of Arabic derivation, but in fact are not." But for wider than literary purposes, other members of his generation were happy that they could now turn to English rather than Arabic for the new words necessary for modern-type assimilation.

One of these was Sheikh Amri Abedi (*c.* 1906-1965), who, as minister of Community Development and National Culture in independent Tanzania, was very much concerned with the development of Swahili as a suitable medium for expressing the emergent African national culture of the country. Himself a poet of some distinction, Abedi was the author of the first modern Swahili treatise on the art of poetry.[89] But although he was aware that any modern Swahili poetry had to be designed for reading, his practical advice with regard to poetic form is conservative in the extreme: "he leaves no doubt that the writer must learn to imitate what others have written . . . His instructions are concerned mostly with the techniques of dealing with the fixed syllabic measure, the caesuras, and the rhymes. . . . For the average writer, these were the techniques to be mastered, not because they were the most convenient means of expression or the most likely of appealing to the readers, but because this was the way Swahili poetry had always been written."[90]

More notable as a creative writer was Mathias E. Mnyampala (c. 1919–1969), who was born in Dodoma, in the remote interior of Tanzania. His first two creative works, published by the East African Literature Bureau, were a short novella, *Kisa cha mrina asali na wenzake wawili* ("The adventures of a Honey-gatherer and his two Friends," 1961), and a collection of poems, *Diwani ya Mnyampala* (1963). But his most ambitious venture was the *Utenzi wa Enjili Takatifu* ("The Epic of the Holy Gospel," 1963), the originality of which can be compared to that of Alexis Kagame's long Christian epic in Kinyarwanda. What makes this first Swahili epic of Christian inspiration remarkable, says Jan Knappert, "is that it is written entirely in the old Utenzi-tradition; it uses the real literary Swahili. But the poet, being a man of our times, has been able to bring in a more personal touch which is rarely found in the old Utenzis, so that to the epic movement of this poetry is added a lyrical beauty entirely its own."[91] Shortly before his death, Mnyampala attempted to put poetry into national service by initiating the public performance of Swahili song-poems, many of them composed by himself, with the express intention of teaching the audience "good conduct, indigenous culture, and national politics, especially African Socialism and Self-Help."[92]

It was also in 1963 that the East African Literature Bureau issued the *Diwani* of another poet of the same generation, K.H.A. Akilimali Snow-White. Meanwhile an attempt at renewal had been made in prose writing with *Mzimu wa watu wa kale* ("The Home of the Spirits of the Ancestors", 1960), a thriller which had earned its author, Muhammed Said Abdulla, the first prize in a short-story competition organized in 1957–58. At about the same time, the Bureau printed *Kurwa na Doto* ("Kurwa and Doto") by Muhammed Saleh Farsy; Lyndon Harries describes it as one of the few prose narratives of truly Swahili origin "in which the writer succeeded in dealing with an indigenous love-story without being influenced by European sources, and free from the moralizing that deadened so much African fiction in the vernacular." Careful consideration of these and a few other works, such as Kharusi's *Usinisahau* ("Don't forget me") or Faraji Katalalambulla's short mystery novel *Simu ya Kifo* ("Phone call to death," 1963), has led Carol Eastman to conclude that they all deal "primarily as entertainment with mystery or romance. In the fictional short novels produced before the 1970s, there is apparently no motive to document or interpret Africa to the outside world or to preserve the African past . . . Accounts of wars or protests are generally treated in the medium of traditional poetry . . . The ma-

jority of fiction uses violence as a means to move a plot geared to entertainment rather than to make a political point or raise social consciousness."[93]

The most innovative and popular development in the Swahili prose
fiction of Tanzania occurred in the Tanga area in the mid-1960s, when
young journalists published short stories in such local vernacular journals as *Mwafrika*. In their appeal to the ordinary reader, they deliberately rejected the conventions, moral and stylistic, of all previous Swahili
literature, whether classical or "modern." Here, says Harries with obvious relief, "is sin in plenty": "Writers like Bawazir, Vuo, Semwaiko are
known to many in Tanzania. The Swahili they write has been called,
unflatteringly, the language of 'the bums'. Indeed the stories are all about
bums and tarts. Mr. Bawazir has expressly written: 'I penetrate
the secrets of the harlots and pimps of the Tanga coastal regions'. In
reading these tales from Tanga, one feels that the sordid events described are things that really do happen: they are about real people.
The amazing richness of vocabulary reflecting current speech by at least
a small section of the community, especially in reference to 'the cup that
cheers', is surely the expression of a reality. The traditional Swahili love
of moralizing, at least in literature, is kept to a minimum, and sometimes, thank goodness, is omitted altogether because the story may speak
for itself. The writing is realistic, and for Africans to write realistically,
is, with the deepest respect, something of an innovation in East Africa.
These stories have much in common with the modern vernacular literature that is sold from stalls in the Nigerian market-places. It represents the beginnings of a modern indigenous literature, and is far more
genuine as an art form than most books written by Africans in a foreign
language."[94]

This almost revolutionary trend, whatever its ethical and aesthetic
value, also appeared in Kenya. It may indeed have originated there, for,
as Wilfred Whiteley notes, "the weekly *Tazama* had a circulation of
nearly 17,000 in 1954, and one of the incentives for reading it seems to
have been its fiction content, which included the serialization of a Peter
Cheyney type novel and a translation of [Sotho writer Mopeli-Paulus's
English novel] *Blanket Boy's Moon*."[95]

In retrospect, it seems obvious that the inchoate modernization illustrated by the various phenomena that have been dealt with so far was
a kind of preparation for the renewal that was to occur in the early
1970s. But side by side with the introduction of western genres, the
spreading of authorship inland from the coast, and the introduction of
non-Islamic subject matter, whether of Christian or African origin, traditional modes of oral production not only survived, but even received
unprecedented scholarly attention. This trend had been initiated in
1966, when Wilfred Whiteley sponsored the collecting and editing of

Waimbaji wa juzi. In the same year, Lyndon Harries edited a collection of gnomic verses by Ahmad Nasir bin Juma Bhalo (b. 1937) of Mombasa.[96] In his introduction, Harries observed that "the general purpose of most of the poems was to make generalizations and platitudes. For the poet no doubt this purpose was not consciously held, but he is strongly aware of his function as guardian of the spiritual interests of those for whom the poems were originally intended." Ahmad Nassir's message offers little originality and can easily be summed up in a few statements: "The world is not to be trusted, nor is it to be played with. It is a place of deeps, it has no goodness; nowhere can it be fully controlled. The world is above all changeable—a place of confusion, a merry-go-round or whirligig. But there is hope for mankind. Man must take the measure of the world. Human nature is noble; we share a common humanity. Frailty is our common lot. The real people are those who love one another." Such poetry may be termed syncretic inasmuch as "Islamic teachings are not inconsistent with African ideals, nor are the echoes of African morality necessarily at variance with Muslim tradition"; indeed, the poems may as well contain echoes from such western Christian values as are also part of some vague universal ideal.

Such poems, which are comparable with gnomic art, whether oral or written, in all early world literatures, are highly popular in Mombasa, for they fullfil one of the main functions of literature in conservative societies: to express, and so perpetuate, the accepted values of the community. Nevertheless, as Harries points out, "it would be a mistake to think that these poems were meant for some backward village people with no awareness of political and economic change"; on the contrary, "the many Mombasans who know and value [them] are modern Africans, fully aware of the changes taking place around them, and in which they play an active part, in industry, administration or business"; furthermore, many of Ahmad Nassir's poems "were written especially for performance at the Mombasa radio station and so reached a much wider audience than the traditional poet ever thought possible." Indeed, they are an interesting example of the way conservative cultural traits obstinately survive in the midst of the turmoils of social change, and of how audiences cling with nostalgia to their traditional wisdom and literary forms even though most of these may have become irrelevant to their new experience and purposes.

Nor is this the only way in which the vernacular tradition has successfully survived Western encroachments. In 1968, Lienhardt edited an epic poem of more than 1500 lines which narrates a mysterious incident in the Kilwa area.[97] It tells how a woman was murdered by three sorcerers, who were subsequently unmasked by a famous medicine-man named Nguvumali. The poem is a mine of information about the inland cultures where adherence to Islam had not destroyed magic

beliefs and practices which Muslim orthodoxy expressly condemns. It
is also interesting in its departure from the actual facts at the end of the
case: in his eagerness to extol the beneficent power of the medicine-
man, the author, Hasani bin Ismail, refrains from mentioning that for
lack of conclusive evidence of their participation in the murder, the
alleged culprits were sentenced to short terms of imprisonment for
being in possession of instruments of witchcraft. But the main point is
that *Swifa ya Nguvumali*, which was recorded in the late 1950s, is an oral
composition.

In the preface, Lienhart emphasizes that "Hasani bin Ismail is able to
write Swahili in Arabic script, and indeed made a few notes during the
evenings to remind himself of the order of the verses, but he had never
written the whole poem down. ... In public performance, the poet
changed his ballad to a tune, and when asked about some lines that
seemed—on paper—to scan irregularly, he referred them to the tune,
not to a count of syllables. Once or twice when I suggested emendations
which would have brought up the written line to a 'regular' eight syllables instead of an apparent seven, Bw. Hasani rejected them as being
too long for his tune." In a "Note of the form and language of the
poem," Professor M.H. Abdulaziz further observes that "a striking
feature of this poem, when analysed on paper, is that the author seems
to depart from the conventional rhyming rules in a number of places.
Apparently he does this in order to suit the tune when the poem is
recited, but it is also possible that he does not want to sacrifice the
meaning by an over-rigid adherence to the rhyme-pattern." Abdulaziz
adds the interesting remark that "among poets from Tanzania such
deviations are accepted as normal, and this fact is an important step
towards freeing Swahili from an over-rigid insistence on the rhyme-
patterns which some critics have felt to be a weakness of Swahili poetry
generally." In his comments on the literary quality of the work, Abdulaziz also points out that "the author uses a simple straightforward
style, almost like that of the English ballad, eschewing elusive language
and artificial word-order—a device often employed to meet the exigencies of rhyme—and concerning himself little with far-fetched metaphor.
... By the subtle use of direct speech and sudden changes of person
the poet succeeds in portraying vividly the attitudes of his characters
and creating an effective sense of drama. ... The poem is written mainly
in the dialect of Kilwa, and there is little attempt to introduce the traditional northern lexical and grammatical features beloved of poets of
an older generation. ... Far from adhering slavishly to tradition, we
find the poet using loan-words from English, not all of which are by any
means fully assimilated nor in general use."

These observations are of considerable value. The oral tradition seems
to have remained very much alive on the Swahili coast, simultaneously

with the written classical tradition, and its verbal aspect is kept subservient to the musical aspect. At the same time, although Abdulaziz claims that Hasani's straightforward manner is "in keeping with the narrative style of Swahili poetic diction," it is obvious that the poet has relinquished the element of preciosity and the artfully repetitive manner typical of the Muslim *utenzi*, in favour of speech directly accessible to the audience, such as was generally used by the authors of classical epics with topical contents.

6. The Post-independence Period

The years immediately following the gaining of independence witnessed a swift process of differentiation concerning the status of Swahili in the three nations that had once constituted British East Africa. In Uganda, it was decided that the language of government should be English, and Swahili is only one of the many local languages that are used at primary-school level and on the radio. While classical Swahili poetry of the past had originated on what is now the Kenya coastline, official preference was given to English, and although Swahili was recognized as "*the* important language of communication and perhaps also of 'pop' culture" at least for the area of Nairobi,[98] no African language was granted preferential treatment over the others in basic school education. Tanzania, then, is the only country where Swahili has become the official language. It is the language used by the administration; it occupies a pre-eminent status in the transmissions of the Tanzania Broadcasting Corporation; there are more than forty Swahili newspapers; and deliberate efforts are being made, with official encouragement (such as the foundation of the National Swahili Council in 1967), to enrich, modernize and standardize the language. Once limited to the island and coastal areas, Swahili had begun to spread inland under the impact of the Arab slave-traders and later of the colonial administration. Its further dissemination and extraordinary progress during the 1970s was largely fostered by official policy.

This was crystallized on 6 June 1968, when President Nyerere, in the wake of the Arusha Declaration of 1967, "took positive action to bring Swahili poetry into the service of the state. He invited a group of Tanzanian poets to use their talents in order to promote a better understanding by the people of the land (*Wananchi*), of national policies, and particularly the responsibilities of the citizen resulting from the implementation of the Arusha Declaration."[99] The first organizational consequence was the foundation of the Society for Swahili Composition and Poetry (*Chana cha Usanifu wa Kiswahili na Ushairi Tanzania*), known as UKUTA, whose first chairman was Mathias E. Mnyampala. The ultimate aim of this new policy in linguistic and literary matters was to promote the production of *ngonjera,* a word which, as defined by Prime Minister Rashidi Kawawa, was intended "to apply to any art-form, such as a play, a poem or an action-song, that helped to fulfill a threefold purpose. First, to give the people a new fluency in Swahili so that they would be able to explain in public and with ease the politics of the nation. Second, by learning the words by heart, the people would be familiarizing themselves with national aims as envisaged in the Arusha Declaration, the *Ujamaa* village projects, the concept of self-reliance, etc., and they would come to know just who their national leaders in the various segments of the political organization were. Third, the people would achieve a consciousness of their national culture and would learn to reject any foreign culture."[100]

To the outsider, directives of this sort do not sound very likely to lead to high literary achievement. And it is not surprising that Harries should be of the opinion that *ngonjera* verse, "like so much Swahili poetry, has become something of a literary curiosity in which the sociological content takes precedence over literary merit." Such strictures may well apply to Mnyampala's two-volume collection of verse, *Ngonjera na UKUTA* (1970–1971), or to the enormous amount of well-meant verse that has been flooding Tanzanian newspapers and journals, or to the adaptation of traditional poetic forms for the expression of modern nationalistic ideas as already exemplified in R.W. Maruka's *Utenzi wa Jamhuri ya Tanzania* (1968), an 800-stanza epic on the history of Tanzania from the days of the Arab slave trade to the present.

But, as will perhaps be most clearly perceptible from the third part of this book, literature has a manner of exploiting "official" encouragements in ways that had not been foreseen by their promoters. President Nyerere's recommendations of 1968 obviously released literary energies that, in earlier days, had been largely smothered by the overwhelming prestige of the conservative tradition of Muslim conformity. All of a sudden, writers found themselves invited to explore and innovate, and this they did, not only along the prescribed lines, but also in several new directions.

Perhaps the most unexpected aspect of the renewal was the rapid growth of the modern novel, which had been tentatively initiated by Shaaban Robert. Until the late 1960s, the greater part of Swahili prose fiction consisted of small collections of folk tales and animal stories designed for school use, especially for the elementary and intermediate teaching of Swahili. But 1969 saw the publication of the first Swahili novel about the Mau Mau emergency, *Kaburi bila Msalaba* ("The Grave without a Cross") by P.M. Kareithi. In the same year, the East African Publishing House issued *Kuishi kwingi ni kuona mengi* ("To Live Long is to See Much") by John Ndeti Somba (b. 1930). This was of particular interest because Somba was the first Swahili writer to embark upon a path already well-trodden by vernacular authors in Southern Africa: the critique of the new urban society. His protagonist, Katua, is a young man who has given up all traditional attitudes and beliefs, and who leaves the village for the city; as usual in novels of this type, he is soon disillusioned and condemned to unemployment and misery. Returning to his village, he marries a Christian girl, but, in his boundless pride, refuses to practise her religion. This leads to connubial unhappiness, from which he finds a refuge in the religion of his ancestors. The realistic depiction of modern experience characteristic of the Tanga tales is here combined with the traditional didactic purpose of Swahili writing. But the main originality of Somba in the context of Swahili literature seems to be his advocacy of a return to traditional tribal mores.[101]

In the early 1970s, there appeared a number of new Swahili novelists, most of them young university graduates, who tried to combine the popular appeal of the detective novel introduced ten years earlier by Muhammad Said Abdullah, with the equally popular themes of witchcraft and violence, and with the didactic determination to diffuse *ujamaa*, the mixture of consensus and participation which characterizes Nyerere's brand of socialism. They often do so with an outspoken realism that is entirely foreign to the traditional reserve of Swahili writing, suggesting that they have appropriated the lessons of the Tanga journalists of the previous decade. The most promising of those younger novelists was Euphrase Kezilahabi[102] whose *Rosa mistika* (1971) concentrates on a problem which seems to occur frequently in modern Tanzania: the abuse of school girls by their teachers; it is significant that the book was banned for school use, not only because the writer was severely critical of the Ministry of Education, but also because several scenes in the novel were felt to be too outspoken for school reading.

Such works undoubtedly represent a decisive new step in the maturation of the Swahili novel, a process that has been taking place for two decades. In contrast, formal stage drama in Swahili was practically nonexistent by the late 1960s, when two very young writers, Ebrahim Hussein (b. 1943) and Crispin Hauli (b. 1945) started producing short plays with serious intent, such as the former's social comedy *Alikiona* ("He saw it") and the latter's political drama, *Dunia Iliyofarakana* ("The departed world"), while G. Uhinga's *Rejala* boldly dealt with "racial conflict in a love affair between an African boy and an Asian girl."[103] The printed stage was reached with Hussein's *Kinjeketile* (1969). This semi-historical lyrical drama deals with the Maji Maji uprising, but the playwright has re-shaped the facts so as to convey his own subtle interpretation of history.[104] The title character is the leader of the rebellion; possessed by Hongo, he has brought the magic water to his people. But the play centres on his inner puzzlement, which has a twofold origin:

first, he is disturbed because Hongo, although a powerful spirit, has no power over matters of life and death, so that he is not entitled to launch a war where thousands of men are bound to die; second, Hongo's prophecy is highly ambiguous: he has announced that if the rebels succeed in defeating the Germans, they will become the children of the Arab Sultan in Zanzibar. As the rebellion begins and develops, Kinjeketile becomes disturbingly aware that belief in the magic water is nothing more than a crude superstition, which could only become meaningful if the tribes were truly united, which they were not: he realizes that "A word born of man grows strong, and ends by enslaving him." Yet, after being caught and tortured by the Germans, Kinjeketile steadfastly refuses to proclaim the falsity of his message in the certainty that it will one day become true: "A word has been born. Our children will tell their children about this word. Our great grand-children will hear of it. One day the word will cease to be a dream, it will be a reality!"

After writing *Mashetani* ("Devils," publ. 1971), which Micere Mugo considers to be his best play so far, with "an intricate plot that is so very neatly put together that one has to peel off several layers of psychological meaning to reach its full depth," Hussein returned to his central preoccupation with the tortuous workings of history and time in *Wakiti Ukuta* ("Time Is a Wall," 1971). Focussing on the conflict of generations, an obsessive topic in a society caught in the acculturation process, "the playwright seeks to expose the mistakes of both parties for assuming that they can either arrest time or speed its movement."

Peninah Muhando was not the first woman playwright in East Africa: she had been preceded by Rebecca Njau, whose English play, *The Scar* had been published in 1965. But she was certainly the first female dramatist in the Swahili language. The heroine of *Hatia* ("Guilt," 1972) is a young country girl, who confronts the harshness of city life in her attempt to make a living; she is made pregnant by a lover who denies his responsibility, and she becomes enmeshed in a complicated (and murderous) plot, until she learns (in the words of Micere Githae Mugo) "to accept herself and her responsibility instead of taking flight into a negative escapism." In her next play, *Tambueni Haki Zetu* ("Recognize our Rights," 1973), Peninah Muhando turned to a more ambitious theme, which bears some similarity to Hussein's preoccupation with the dialectics of history. The story deals with the fate of an imaginary tribe, the Watone, who have been cunningly tricked into accepting the suzerainty of their neighbours: this may well be a parable for colonial oppression. Ultimately, they became ready for their chief, Mundewa, to lead them into a liberation war. On Mundewa's death, however, the ancestral spirits deny him entry into the world of spirits, alleging that he has violated the promises that had been made by his forefathers. As L.A. Mbughuni points out, the theme of oppression and justice is han-

dled at two different levels: the play denounces the injustice of the alien
intruders whose oppression inevitably provokes a violent reaction; but
the spirit world, too, is indirectly criticized for adhering to the letter of
the Watone's promises, instead of taking into account their inalienable
right to independence.

Alongside the great leap forward effected by the Swahili novel and
the emergence of written drama in Swahili, the renewal of the early
1970s also affected poetry. This statement does not refer only to the
tremendous outpouring of *ngonjera* verse that was the most obvious
result of official promptings, for these, after all, were still in the didactic
and societal tradition characteristic of much Swahili, and indeed Islamic,
poetry. But deeper changes were also at work, in at least two directions.

In 1971, Abdilatif Abdalla el-Kindy (b. 1946) from Mombasa published his *Utenzi wa Maisha ya Ada na Hawaa*,[105] which purports to recount, in 637 stanzas of impeccably traditional verse, the Koranic-Bibl-
ical story of the Fall. But side by side with some minor technical
innovations, such as the introduction of dialogue and author's commentary, Abdilatif found in his topic "a pretext to express his own philosophical and poetical conception of human nature."[106] In traditional
accounts, whether Muslim or Christian, Satan-Iblis is the impersonation
of evil, Eve is his instrument, and Adam succumbs a victim to the wiles
of his wife. According to Jan Knappert, however, we find in the Swahili
poem (as in *Paradise Lost*, which Abdilatif never read), "a certain sympathy for Iblis (Lucifer) when he rebels against God's decrees, and
more clearly, an inclination of the poet to side with Eve who wants to
live to the full, against Adamu, the haughty husband whose narrow-
mindedness robs him of some of his human features."[107] Such a re-
interpretation of the Fall story implies a definite departure from the
other-worldly outlook that was traditional in classical Swahili writing. It
also chimes in with the interest in terrestrial love which is beginning to
make itself felt in Swahili prose fiction.[108]

Even before he was thirty, Abdilatif has been described as "the modern Muyaka" and "the youngest major modern poet-politician in East
Africa."[109] It is probably significant that this faithful adherent of traditional poetic forms, a close kinsman of Ahmad Nasir, should have
originated in Kenya: modern Tanzanian writers, many of whom are,
ethnically speaking, not Swahili at all, have less respect for the tradition.
It is even more significant that the poet spent three years in prison,
from 1969 to 1972, because of his activities as a militant member of
Oginga Odinga's socialist-oriented KPU Party, which was soon to be
banned. He gathered the poetic fruit of this term in jail in *Sauti ya Dhiki*
("Voice of Agony," 1973) which was paradoxically published by the
Kenya branch of the Oxford University Press after its author had found
refuge in Tanzania.[110] Those poems are entirely consonant with the

mood of disillusionment and rebellion which, since the late 1960s, had found expression in the English works of several Kenyan novelists. As M.M. Mulokozi aptly observes, "this is not the classical bourgeois disillusionment with life, but rather disillusionment with those who have been entrusted with the duty of guiding and safe-guarding the lives and rights of millions of African working people; disillusionment with the system that has failed to meet the people's cherished hopes, that has flattened their will and damped their energy." Some of the poems in the collection have been blamed for "an unmistakable tinge of pseudo-Islamic didacticism in the Shaaban Robert tradition," and for "condemning practices such as abortion, prostitution, etc. without delving deep into their social-economic causes and necessities." On the whole, however, Abdilatif's second volume has been praised not only for its "intellectual compactness" (Ohly), but also because it marked "the beginning of a new era of committed proletarian verse" (Mulokozi).

This changed outlook, however, was bound to generate new forms, for it was not to be expected that the zest for renewal and experimentation fostered by Tanzania's policy-makers would remain confined within the narrow, societal, limits they had first been assigned. The foundation of a modern state and the young intellectuals' access to world culture could not fail to stimulate the new generation of writers, most of them highly educated university students and graduates, in deeper and more far-reaching directions. By the mid-seventies, bold experimenters such as Euphrase Kezilahabi, already known as a modern novelist, and Ebrahim Hussein, already known as a modern playwright, had started introducing new forms and new contents into Swahili poetry.[111] They gave up the old obsession with prosodic regularity, experimenting in various ways with blank and free verse, an innovation which launched a fairly high-pitched controversy among Swahili critics. While S. Chiraghdin stated that "if these compositions are accepted as poems, then the status of Swahili poetry will have been reduced miserably to a non-entity," Farouk M. Topan retorted that "the acceptance of this modern form will enhance the status of Swahili poetry, enrich the genre, and widen the scope of its composition."[112]

Nor was experimentation restricted to form: the new poetry also gave shape to new contents. Classical Swahili verse had merely aimed at formulating a pre-existing world view as a fully articulated system of thought, the Islamic values shared by the Swahili community; the new poetry attempted to mould itself as closely as possible to the inner processes of experience and thought, substituting individual meditation for communal dogma, introducing anxiety and doubt where assurance of a somewhat wooden kind and intellectual self-confidence had reigned supreme. It is probably no exaggeration to claim that after the foundation of modern drama and the modern novel, this sudden transformation of poetry, the last bulwark of the literary tradition, marked the creation of a fully modern literature in the Swahili language.

CHAPTER SIX
EAST AFRICA : SOMALIA

1. Traditional Somali Poetry

In the middle of the fourteenth century, Mogadishu ranked as the most important centre of Muslim influence and Arabic trade on the eastern coast of Africa. But Somali society, Hamitic in ethnic affiliation and composed of nomadic pastoralists, did not submit to the same kind of linguistic and literary acculturation as did Swahili society further south. The reason seems to be that, among the Somali, "conversion changed the religious elements of their life and, reinforcing their national consciousness, gave them a different outlook but scarcely influenced their social institutions. Only where we find a settled Muslim polity based on towns and a detribalized society are social institutions changed drastically. Nomadic Somalis, though strong Muslims, were always independent and rejected Islamic law except on matters of cult and personal status."[1] More specifically, despite a century-long exposure to Islam, the Somali failed to produce any substantial amount of writing in Arabic, and even less in their own language. I.M. Lewis accounts for this in the following terms:

This apparent dearth of any strong corpus of locally written literature reflects the fact that only a small proportion of religious men are in fact fully literate in Arabic. In general, knowledge of reading Arabic is more widely diffused than full literacy, competence in which has until recently been the monopoly of a small religious elite . . . . Although a considerable proportion of these sheikhs have functioned as teachers, sometimes with peripatetic students wandering around the Somali bush and largely dependent on charity, they have not brought general literacy to the laity. The exigencies of the nomadic life allow few nomads to attend such schools regularly or over long periods, and teaching is in any case for the most part limited to learning the Qur'an by heart and not directed towards teaching writing as such . . . . Another factor is the high development of oral communication . . . . More directly, Somalis appear to regard oral communication not only as a refined art, but as a basic essential for successful survival. . . . Oral Somali is used, particularly in the

*form of poetry, as an extremely important medium of mass communication.
The power of the tongue and of the spoken word in spreading hostility and
enmity, in countering it, or in broadcasting conciliatory messages, in ruining
reputations or praising men to the skies is very evident in Somali culture.
. . . In fact, the oral tradition is so strongly developed and so highly prized,
that there is also a certain, mainly religious, oral treasury of poetry in Arabic
as well as Somali.[2]*

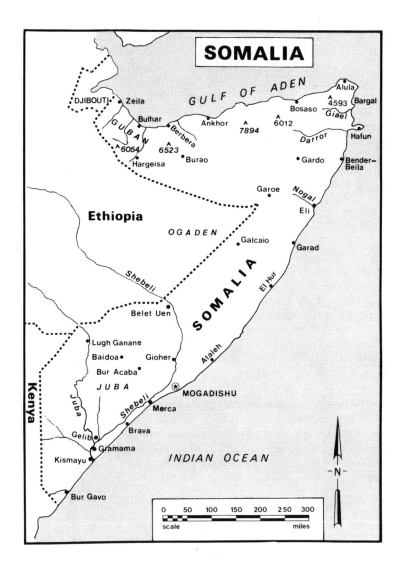

Non-literate peoples have long memories, and the Somali still remember the poems and the names of such bards of olden days as Raage Ugaas of the Ogaden clan, who probably lived in the eighteenth century,[3] Haaji Ali Adirrahmaan of the Majerteyn Sultanate, who died c. 1820,[4] or Sheikh Mahamuud Mahammed Gabyow, who lived and worked in the Benadir region, and died towards the end of the nineteenth century.

As far as we know, it would seem that the need for committing Somali poetry to some sort of writing first arose as a response to colonial enterprise, not only by European powers, but also by Ethiopia, during the last two decades of the nineteenth century. In 1884 the French established a Red Sea coaling-station at Obock on the Danakil coast; during the following year, they expanded eastward into Somali territory, where they set up the port of Jibuti. In 1885–86 Britain took over the northern coast of Somaliland from Egypt and established a protectorate there. After the treaty of Ucciali (1889), the emperor of Ethiopa, Menelik II, annexed large tracts of Somali territory, especially Ogaden. During the 1890s, Italian companies assumed the administration of coastal ports in Southern Somaliland, until the area became a colony under the direct control of the Italian government in 1905. In 1895, Somali areas south of the Juba river had been incorporated into the British East Africa Protectorate.[5]

In spite of their ethnic homogeneity, their common language and their adherence to Islam, the Somali had no sense of national unity. Somali society was divided into a large number of separate and often rival clans. And it was among some of those clans that resistance to foreign domination first arose in the early years of the twentieth century. It was essentially a Muslim rebellion against Christian invaders, and it was led by Mahammad Abdille Hasan (1864–1920), better known in the West as the "Mad Mullah."[6]

Mahammad was born in the eastern part of the British protectorate. He became an adherent of a Muslim brotherhood known as Salihiyya-Rashidiyya when he went on a pilgrimage to Mecca in the mid-1890s. He then settled at Berbera, where he preached reformist doctrines and attracted much opposition from the Qadiriyya, which was the predominant brotherhood among the Somali. At the same time, the activities of a French Roman Catholic Mission near the city and their baptizing of Somali children convinced him that the purpose of the Christian powers was to destroy Islam. He proclaimed a *jihad* against the infidels in 1900, and this holy war lasted for twenty years before the Dervishes, as his disciples were known, were defeated. I.M. Lewis has made the point

that "his brilliant success as a leader was closely connected with his con-
summate powers as a poet, as he made extensive use of poetry as a
political weapon in campaigning for support against his enemies." His
Arabic poems include a praise of Muhammad Salih (1845–1916), the
founder of the Salihiyya brotherhood. While such poems were composed in writing, Mahammad's vernacular poetry, although undoubtedly more influential, was oral. Some samples of it are included in the
anthology of Andrzejewski and Lewis; a few of those poems are addressed to one Hasan, "one of Sheikh Mahammad's constant attend-
ants, whose main function was to memorize and later broadcast his poetry."

Not surprisingly, a large part of Mahammad's poetry is devoted to
extolling traditional Muslim virtues, holding up as an example

> *He who spreads goodness evenly among all the sons of Adam,*
> *He who does not favour those to whom he is close in genealogical descent,*
> *He who does not sow dissension amongst the slaves of God,*
> *He who holds his peace and is silent when evil words are spoken to him,*
> *He who does not tremble with excitement at the prospect of profit and food,*
> *And who does not eat to the last morsel the dish placed before him,*
> *And who does not gorge himself like a glutton gobbling food,*
> *He who does not threaten others with violence, endangering his own house. . .*

Yet, this condemnation of violence does not extend further than Mahammad's disciples. For the poet also speaks out in praise of

> *He who does not follow the Amhara as though they were his fathers,*
> *And who does not fight as an askari for the uncircumcised infidel,*
> *And who does not turn up his nose at the origins and ways of the Somali,*
> *And who does not perform menial services for the wages of the unbelievers,*
> *Or accept without complaint their niggardly wage;*
> *He who devotes himself to the holy war and is garlanded with flowers,*
> *He who turns against the English dogs*
> *And who wins the victory and glory and the shouts and songs of praise. . .*

Side by side with these Islamic and xenophobic elements, Mahammad's poetry is inspired by his genuine nationalistic determination to
unite all Somali clans in resistance to the Christian oppressors, whether
European or Ethiopian. And he gave full vent to his power of invective
when referring to such Somali clans as refused to join his *jihad:*

> *Those who come to me with threats, it is my duty to challenge.*
> *It is my duty to attack the Hagar lineage, with their cankered testicles.*

It is my duty to destroy their dwindling herds,
And those of them who are impoverished and destitute should be driven to the
*   river,*
While those who are left behind should be eaten slowly by birds of prey.
The fate of the Iiddor peoples is to remain forever as stupid as donkeys,
And since the days of Adam, it is their lot to trot in terror behind the infidels;
They are fated to understand nothing and condemned to madness;
Their lot is to hate the faith and despise the Divine Law;
Let them bring upon themselves a curse, these children of the devil:
It is their fate to bring sorrow to those who turn with zeal to the holy war.

This, apparently was not the right way to convince the supercilious Somali, and "the Mullah's attempt to avail himself of Islam to conquer the
old rivalries between the tribes and combine the Somali to drive the
British out of the country, failed both on account of the strength of the
British forces and the fierce resistance, often unconscious, opposed by
the Somali on behalf of their ancient tribal organisation and customary
law."[7]

Although Abdille Hasan is undoubtedly the most important single
figure in the history of Somali poetry, it must be remembered that his
poems, composed orally and disseminated by word of mouth, take their
place in a very long oral tradition. Nor was he alone of his kind. Among
his contemporaries, who were born towards the middle of the nineteenth century, but who in many cases outlived him until the 1930s,
several names emerge, such as Ali Duuh who was "renowned for his
wit, invective and forcefulness,"[8] Farah Nuur, whose poetry is often
concerned with rivalries between the clans although he was aware of the
significance of colonial partition,[9] Qamaan Bulhan, of the Ogaden clan,
who lived in Eastern Ethiopa, and whose reflective poetry has yielded
a number of proverbial expressions,[10] and Salaan Arrabey, who died
after World War II: a well-travelled man, he was familiar with such
foreign languages as Swahili and Hindustani besides Arabic and English,
and introduced a number of loan-words into the language.[11]

As far as we know, most of these poets, besides sharing in the usual
edifying trend of Muslim poetry, were chiefly concerned with clan life.
But while the Mullah's rebellion proved most effective in British Somaliland, in the southern part of the country, his movement met with
considerable opposition from faithful adherents of the Qadiriyya, thus
creating disruptions that superimposed themselves upon the internecine
quarrels between hostile clans and tiny sultanates. One of the best-
known songs in Southern Somalia was for a long time a poem composed
by Hasan Hoday, who had joined the Dervishes before leaving them in
protest against their cruelty. It deals with a battle that took place in

1913, when the Dervishes raided the Sultanate of Obbia, thus compounding with external danger the problems that had arisen from the Sultan's bad management.[12]

It is to another opponent of the Mullah that the notion of using the Arabic script to transliterate poems composed in the Somali language is sometimes ascribed. Sheikh Awes (or Uways) ibn Mahammad, who was born in Brava, south of Mogadishu, towards 1846, and who was killed by the Dervishes in 1909, was a devout member of the Qadiriyya, which, according to I.M. Lewis, "has a high reputation for orthodoxy, is on the whole literary rather than propagandist, and is said to maintain a higher standard of Islamic instruction than its rivals."[13] One of his songs, edited by Cerulli, mourns the pitiful situation of the Somali people, caught between the incursions of the Dervishes and the repressive operations carried out by English and Italian troops. But in general, the works of Awes illustrate the strain of Sufi mysticism which permeates Somali religious poetry. His unpublished manuscript *Tawassul ash-shaikh Awes* is a collection of songs to be sung at initiation ceremonies.

Another unpublished manuscript of the same type is the biography of Sheikh Ali Maye Durogba (d. 1917), who introduced into Somalia the Ahmediyya brotherhood which had been founded in Mecca in the early nineteenth century by Ahmad ibn Idris al-Fasi (1760–1837). According to Cerulli, the work is divided into four parts: the first expatiates on the author's genealogy so as to demonstrate Quraish descent; next comes an account of his youth when he studied grammar, theology and law; the core of the work tells how Ali Maye entered the Ahmadiyya brotherhood and describes his progress in the mystic way; finally, the sheikh narrates the miracles he performed in curing the sick.[14]

In the main, however, Awes Mahammad appears as an isolated pioneer in the institution of an *ajami* type of Somali literature. But whether it remained oral, or made use of some of the various alphabets that will be mentioned presently, Somali composition went on unabated as generation followed generation.

Two younger poets emerged in the early years of the twentieth century. Abdillahi Muuse (b. *c.* 1880) was renowned as the pious author of didactic poems,[15] whereas Ismaa'iil Mire (1884–*c.* 1950), a close friend and trusted adviser of Abdille Hasan, turned to clanic and religious themes after the insurrection.[16] Among the latest generation, Ilmi Bowndheri (*c.* 1908–1941) gave considerable prominence to the theme of love, which was to become fashionable in Somali poetry with the advent of broadcasting,[17] and Sheikh Aqib Abdullah Jama (b. *c.* 1920) of Jigjiga in Eastern Ethiopa, made quite a reputation for himself as "one of the most ardent champions of using Somali for religious purposes," a practice that the more rigid Somali sheikhs had looked down upon as inferior to the use of Arabic.[18]

• • •

While the controversy between the Mahdi and his Somali opponents
had prompted the first attempts at using the Arabic script to transliterate the local language, they also seem to have been responsible for the
first recorded Somali writings in the Arabic language.

Among the Somali as in other parts of Muslim Africa, conversion to
Islam had meant the introduction of Arabic: "As the language of the
Koran, the Tradition and Muslim theological scholarship, Arabic enjoys
enormous prestige and is sometimes referred to . . . as 'the language of
God'. Prayers and invocations in Arabic seem to many Somali people
more appropriate for worship and more efficacious then their mother
tongue. . . . Among the lay public quite a number of people, particularly
in towns, have a good knowledge of Arabic and the new *élite* educated
in government schools in Somalia and universities in Arab countries,
usually reach high levels of proficiency. . . . All men of religion are
expected to know Arabic well and some actually achieve such a high
standard that they compose literary works in it, especially poetry."[19]
Consequently, Somali poetry is characterized by a kind of division of
labour between the vernacular language, which has produced a considerable amount of secular poetry, and Arabic, which is preferred for
religious writing, whether didactic or poetic. Although it seems likely
that literate sheikhs must have used the Arabic language and script as
a literary medium at a fairly early stage as they did in West Africa, there
is no report of Arabic poetry being written until the late nineteenth
century. And while Mahammad Abdille Hasan did compose several
poems in Arabic,[20] the main producers of this kind of literature were,
like Sheikh Awes, affiliates of the Qadiriyya and originated in the southern part of the country. Indeed, they were responsible for the printing
of the first books of Somali authorship.[21]

The oldest poems in Arabic are to be found in the *Majmu'at al-Qasa'id*
("Collection of poems") compiled by a native of Brava, Sheikh Kasim
b. Muhyid'd-Din (d. 1921), himself a noted poet and mystic. According
to Cerulli, this volume (which went through a second edition in Cairo
after World War II) comprises eight poems, two of which were by
Sheikh Awes; four others, in praise of the Prophet and of the founder
of the Qadiriyya were the work of Sheikh Abd al-Rahman al-Zaila'i (d.
1883), who wrote many other mystic poems in Arabic. The last two
were composed by Kasim's teacher, Sheikh Abd al-Rahman ibn Abdallah al-Shashi (d. 1904), a scholar from Mogadishu commonly known as
Sheikh Sufi; a learned man, versed in astrology, he wrote many Arabic
poems such as "The Tree of Certainty," and a curious series of
prophecies on the future of Mogadishu.

In A.H. 1338 (1918–1919), another compilation was printed in Cairo.

Entitled *Al-majmu'at al-mubaraka* ("The Blessed Harvest"), it was the
work of a younger poet, Sheikh Abdallah ibn Yusif, and has been described by Lewis as "perhaps the most important of Somali Sufi literature."[22] According to Cerulli, it consists of a short preface and four
treatises, the first of which characteristically traces the author's ancestry
to the Quraish and his spiritual filiation to al-Jilani, the founder of the
Qadiriyya. The other treatises are attacks against the Mad Mullah's
disciples, who are held to ridicule for their scant learning, and blamed
for exploiting religion with political aims in view. Abdallah's collection
also includes Arabic poems by the two nineteenth-century sheikhs already represented in Kasim's volume, as well as poems of local and
foreign Muslim saints.

2. The Modernization of Somali Literature

Until World War II, none of the colonizing powers had given much
attention to the Somali language and culture. In 1941, however, Italian
troops conquered British Somaliland, which, after a few months, was
recaptured by the British who also occupied Italian Somalia. From that
moment increasing efforts were made by the British: "the old care and
maintenance policy of the past" was "decisively abandoned in favour
of more progressive policies."[23] This was especially conspicuous in the
development of elementary and secondary education, which could not
fail to have an influence on the evolution of literature. The main consequences were: some spreading of writing in the Arabic language, the
emergence of Somali literature in European languages, and the lengthy
process which led to the adoption of an official Somali orthography. It
is, however, a peculiar feature of the recent history of the Somali language and literature, that the process of modernization and standardization first occurred through a modern, but still oral, medium:
broadcasting.

●   ●   ●

The first regular broadcasts of world news in Somali began in 1943,
two years after the English had driven the Italians out of the whole
country. This innovation took place under peculiar conditions that have
been described by Andrzejewski:

*News bulletins were translated from English, and the skill of interpreting at
a high level had to be acquired as a matter of urgency and new demands on
the lexical resources met. A public whose awareness of the aesthetic side of their
language had been nurtured for centuries on fine poetry would not be satisfied*

with slipshod translation; they expected news bulletins and commentaries which were both clear in their sense and felicitous in style and use of words. The early broadcasters rose to the occasion and set a pattern of adaptation which has been followed by their colleagues and successors ever since, both in Somalia and abroad.[24] *Their difficulty lay almost entirely in the field of vocabulary, which was deficient in words connected with modern life. The gaps could have been filled by massive borrowing from English or Arabic, but this would have placed a heavy burden on the listener's memory and would interfere with a full understanding of what was said. Moreover, such a course of action would amount to a humiliating admission of the intellectual inadequacy of their mother tongue, a language of great poets, story-tellers, and preachers. The path which was followed was probably inspired by the tradition of coining new words which pervades all Somali poetry, and may be connected with the heavy demands of alliterative verse, where the same alliteration has to be carried through the whole poem. The Somali broadcasters invented new words and phrases for the purposes of translation . . . Frequently, a broadcaster educated abroad would carefully explain the meaning of a particular English or Italian word or phrase to an old bard and ask him for guidance in coining a Somali equivalent.*[25]

At an early stage in this remarkable experiment, Andrzejewski points out, "programme organizers realized that oral literature and historical traditions could be used both as entertainment and as a form of education. Poets, poetry reciters, storytellers, and experts on traditional sciences and folklore have all found an appreciative, often enthusiastic audience." Modern poets composing in the traditional way, such as Omar Hussein Gorse or Mahammad Nuur Fadal (d. *c.* 1950) became frequent broadcasters. By being thus enabled to address a nationwide audience, they contributed considerably to the spreading of a standardized form of Swahili, based on different but mutually intelligible dialects.

One interesting outgrowth of broadcasting has been the emergence and rapid dissemination of a new poetic genre known as *balwo* or *heello*.[26] A short lyric usually celebrating a hedonistic view of love, it was created in the mid-1940s, and soon became "an important feature of all radio programmes, often being provided with elaborate instrumental and musical accompaniments."[27] Andrzjewski and Lewis give a few examples which illustrate both the sensuality and the epigrammatic terseness of these modern songs:

The oryx does not bring her young into the open,
Why are you doing this with your thigh?

A flash of lighting does not satisfy thirst,
What then is it to me if you just pass by?

When you die you will enter the earth,
Let not the preacher then turn you from your love-song.

It is not surprising that the outlook evinced in such poetry, widely disseminated by the radio, should have prompted irate rejoinders from poets faithful to the austere tradition of Somali Islam, such as this invective in Arabic by Sheikh Muhammad Hasan:

The evil balwo *songs came, bringing corruption and spreading sin,*
And God was displeased with those who wrought such wrongfulness.
They wasted their substance in frivolity and dissipation,
They gathered together in debauchery and hungered after what is prohibited.
Women who became devils lured them astray,
As the holy tradition says: "They are the snares of the devil."
Turn away from them, pay no heed to them, and abandon their places of song.
Achieve instead the success and strength which
God gives, the builder of the Throne.[28]

•   •   •

While creative inspiration was thus being rejuvenated by what was at the time the most modern of the mass media, it is highly characteristic of the dichotomy in Somali society and of the anti-Western bias of Islamic circles, that composition in Arabic by literate sheikhs went on unabated. Much of this production has remained in manuscript and is still hoarded in private collections. Its main trend is hagiographical. Andrzejewski and Lewis quote one poem which, they claim, "is typical of many composed in Arabic in honour of Somali sheikhs." It was written by Abdullahi Haashi in praise of Sheikh Isaac, the saintly founder of one of the most prominent Somali clans, who allegedly migrated from Arabia in the thirteenth century. One reason for this concentration on a single topic—which can be handled in praise poetry or in hagiographical prose derived from oral legends in the vernacular—is that traditional Somali Islam regards saints as the necessary intermediaries between God and ordinary men. It is therefore not surprising that what few books were printed in Arabic by Somali authors, especially the two treatises published in Cairo in 1954 and 1964 by Abd al-Rahman bin Umar, were concerned with the Somali Qadiriyya and its most illustrious representatives such as Sheikh Awes and Sheikh Abd al-Rahman Zayla'i.[29]

But even here, modern ideas and, to some extent, modern scepticism, slowly made their way. In the course of the last dozen years, there has been a reaction among Somali men of religion and educated laymen against the cult of the saints: such critics may have been influenced "both by Islamic fundamentalism which regards the cult as contrary to the belief in the unity of God, and by modernism which regards it as a quaint, even if at times charming, relic of the past which reinforces the conservatism of the masses." In 1961, Sheikh Nuruddin Ali, "the greatest contemporary Somali critic of the cult", published a treatise in Arabic, in which "he launches a closely reasoned attack on the belief in the thaumaturgic powers or super-human qualities of the saints."[30]

• • •

The almost total absence of any Somali written art until very recently was probably due to spontaneous Islamic resistance to acculturation and its innovations. This must have acted as a deterrent to such administrators, linguists and missionaries as might have wished to follow the pattern, usual in British-occupied territories, of reducing the local language to writing in order to spread the tenets of Christianity. Some of the intellectual leaders, though, were aware of the advantages to be gained by resorting to writing.

Sheikh Awes adapted the Arabic alphabet to several local dialects but his example does not seem to have spread to any appreciable extent. About 1920, a non-Arabic script was invented by Isman Yusuf Kenadid; known as Osmaniyya, "this alphabet and script, some of whose characters resemble Amharic, initially enjoyed a limited currency amongst its inventor's close kinsmen and friends. Later, its currency spread through its connection with modern Somali nationalism."[31] Another type of non-Arabic script, devised by Sheikh Abdurahmaan Sheikh Nuur of the Gadabuursi clan in about 1933, met with very little success.[32] Two years later, Muhammad Abdi, in a book in Arabic printed in Bombay, advocated adapting the Arabic script to the requirements of the Somali language.[33] A basically similar, although more refined, procedure was proposed, as late as 1954, by a prominent Somali scholar, who is renowned both as a linguist and a poet, Muuse Haaji Ismaa'iil Galaal.[34]

The failure of all these attempts was probably due to the utter lack of interest evinced by the colonial powers. On the Côte française des Somalis no official attention was paid to the vernacular language; indeed, after the Somali nation obtained its independence in 1960, the French government tried to counter the new republic's designs on Jibuti and the neighbouring area by changing the colony's name to "Territoire des Afars et Issas." From 1950 onwards Italy administered its former colony under United Nations mandate. In Italian Somalia and in British Somaliland entirely different systems of transliteration into roman script had been evolved by the authorities for their own administrative purposes. It is true, as Andrzejewski observes, that "from 1943 onward political changes brought educational progress to

the Somali people, and in the 1950s secondary education at home and
scholarships or secondments abroad began to produce a new educated
élite."[35] But by the time the Somali Republic came into being, and for
a dozen years afterwards, this young nation, which could boast greater
ethnic and linguistic homogeneity than almost any other of the new
African states, still had no unified written language. Andrzejewski and
Lewis point out that "officials with British education usually do not have
a written language in common with those of Italian education. They all
speak Somali, but often have to employ translators in order to read
correspondence between government offices"![36] In 1961, the independent Somali government set up a Linguistic Committee to investigate
the problem: eighteen proposals were submitted to its attention. But by
the late 1960s Somali children were still studying under a system of
four-year elementary education in Arabic, followed by eight years of
intermediate and secondary education in Arabic and English with Italian
as an optional language.

This situation precluded the development of the written art in the
indigenous language. It also made it inevitable that such few would-be
writers as had benefited from a modern education and did not want to
resort to Arabic were obliged to turn to the European languages. Modern Somali literature thus made a start in a way that is absolutely unique
in Africa.

The first Somali writer to have been in a position to reach an international audience was William J.F. Syad (b. 1930), who was born in
Jibuti, but later became a citizen and a civil servant of the Somali Republic. His first volume of poetry, *Khamsine* (1959), was published in
Paris as part of the remarkable expansion of francophone African writing that took place during the 1950s. Two further collections, *Harmo-
niques* and *Cantiques,* appeared in Dakar in 1976.

Meanwhile, a beginning had been made with the Somali novel: *From
a Crooked Rib* (1970) was written in English by Nuruddin Farah (b. 1945).
This writer, who was born and educated in the southern part of the
country, was first schooled in Italian, but later studied at the University
of Chandigarh in India. The title of his novel refers to a Somali proverb
to the effect that "God created Woman from a crooked rib, and any one
who trieth to straighten it, breaketh it." The book deals with woman's
fate in Somalia: the heroine runs away from her home in order to escape
not only the authoritatianism of the family males who want to marry
her off as best suits their own convenience, but also the enslavement of
women in a Muslim society, and, more generally, the monotony and
discomfort of nomadic life. The point of the story, however, is that her
liberation simply creates other sets of problems, to which the writer
carefully refrains from offering any ready-made, theoretical solution.

Finally—at least to the present time of writing—Mohamed Said Samantar (b. 1928) had the distinction of being the only African author who ever published any creative work in Italian. As ambassador of his country in Rome, and later in Paris, he issued a bilingual collection of poems, *La pioggia è caduta/Il a plu* (1973), which was printed in Rome. The title reflects the great preoccupation with drought and rain and the desert wind which was apparent in the title of Syad's first collection, and which has also inspired some poetry in the Somali language.[37] But for Samantar, the coming of the rains is a symbolic event, an objective correlative for the renewed vitality that independence is bound to bring to Somalia and indeed to Africa as a whole.

3. The New Somali Script

After the military take-over of October 1969, the revolutionary government took vigorous steps to put an end to the endless inflammatory controversy that had arisen around the issue of a Somali orthography. The Somali Language Committee was reconstituted and strengthened, and in 1972, an official national orthography in Latin script was finally promulgated. This momentous decision had immediate repercussions upon the development of Somali literature, for the government's directives for the introduction of the new system "were implemented with a speed and thoroughness which surprised not only foreign observers, but also the Somalis themselves."[38] Early in 1973, Somali was adopted as the sole medium of instruction in elementary schools. In April 1973, the task of producing suitable readers became the responsibility of the Curriculum Department of the Ministry of Education and Training. A Ministry of Culture and Higher Education was created, which set up an Academy of Culture, whose task it is to engage in research into all aspects of Somali culture, with special emphasis on the language and literature, written and oral; its staff includes "not only scholars with academic training gained in various foreign countries but also a number of connoisseurs and practioners of oral literature who had have little or no formal education of a modern type but have a deep knowledge of the traditional culture of the country."[39] Above all, Somalia embarked on an ambitious programme of publication.

This programme could proceed with exceptional speed because the new orthography was nearly identical with systems of transcription in roman script which had been used previously by several Somali scholars.[40] In 1956, Muuse Xaaji Ismaaciil Galaal (b. 1914) had published a collection of traditional narratives, *Hikmad Soomaali* ("Somali Wisdom").[41] In the mid-1960s, his *Collection of Somali Literature: Mainly from Sayid Mohamed Abdille Hassan* had been printed in Mogadishu. Another scholar who had been extremely active in the preservation of oral poetry was Shire Jaamac Axmed with *Gabayo, maashmaad iyo sheekoyin paryar* ("Poems, proverbs and short stories," 1965); he was also influential through the literary journal that he edited in the mid-1960s, *Iftiinka Aqoonta* ("Light of Education").

A second important trend of these preparatory years had been the emergence of such alien genres as modern prose fiction and formal stage drama, both of which were initiated by Axmed Cartan Xaange. In 1967, the periodical *Horseed* published his long story "Qawdhan iyo Qoran," which anticipated Farah Nuruddin's English novel in offering a poignant critique of woman's fate and of marriage customs in traditional society; it brought description of scenery to Somali narrative prose. It was also Axmed Cartan Xaange who produced the first modern play in the language. Entitled *Samawada* (1968), it deals with the role of women in the struggle for independence in the period following World War II; it is based on an incident that actually happened in 1948, and celebrates the intelligence, the independent spirit, the patriotism and the ultimate scarifice of its title heroine.

Play-acting was of course not new to the Somali[42] but it is of interest that recent dramatists availed themselves of its popularity to spread newer sceptical attitudes which are foreign to Somali tradition. In Somalia as in other parts of Africa the army has played an important role in the political, social and even intellectual evolution of the nation; in 1969, its Theatrical Ensemble performed a highly successful play, *Waxan jirin bay jaclaysteen* ("They loved what did not exist"), which does not seem ever to have reached print; in opposition to the general unquestioning veneration for religious men, it offers a comic exposure of the way impostors posing as holy men can cheat superstitious people. The same irreverent outlook characterizes *Shabeelnagood* ("Leopard among the women"), which was very successful at the National Theatre in Mogadishu and was serialized on the radio in 1969; in this comedy, which was to be printed in Britain with an English translation in 1974, Hassan Sheikh Mumin exposes the exploits of amiable tricksters who pose as men of religion and arrange bogus marriage ceremonies.[43]

The official introduction of the new orthography led to the rapid creation of a new readership. Not only was the language taught in schools, but public servants had to pass a proficiency test in reading and writing Somali in a matter of months. The rapid fostering of a reading public that was by no means insignificant in size, together with official sponsorship of book publication by the Academy of Culture, could not but give added momentum to the elaboration of the written art in the Somali language.

In the 1970s Somali scholars' zest for retrieving and preserving oral folk art and the works of their major poets led to the printing of several important books such as *Murti iyo sheekooyin* ("Traditional wisdom and stories," 1973) by Cabdulqaadir F. Bootaan and *Sheekooyin Soomaaliyeed* ("Somali stories," 1973) by Muuse Cumar Islaam. *Diiwaanka gabayadii Sayid Maxamed Cabdulle Xasan* (1974) is a new collection of the great Somali leader's poems, edited by Jaamac Cumar Ciise. In 1975, Axmed Faarax Cali "Idaajaa" likewise collected the poems of *Ismaaciil Mire*, as Rashiid Maxamed Shabeele did those of Cilmi Bowndheri in *Ma dhab baa jacayl waa loo dhintaa?* ("Is it true that people die of love?"). The same year saw the publication, by Cumar Aw Nuux, of *Diwaanka gabay-ada Xaaji Aadan Axmed "Afgallooc"*: Aadan Axmed is an oral poet who is said to be over a hundred years old; an ardent supporter of the Somali revolution, he is chiefly concerned with social and political matters.

But the 1970s also witnessed the swift development of more innova-tive trends. To the Somali, verse is the most widely respected medium for the literary art. As John W. Johnson observes, "in their hierarchy of values a talent for poetry can place a person at the very apex of public acclaim, alongside national leaders and heroes; in fact the status of a poet in Somali society would inspire their counterparts on modern Eu-rope and America with envy."[44] Ever since pre-colonial days when their talent was in the service of clannish rivalries, Somali poets have been inspired by political issues. But whereas "in the years before the 1969 Revolution [they] seldom presented any coherent ideology, after the Revolution many poets took upon themselves the task of presenting to the nation its new principles and aims."[45] At first, radio-broadcasting played a major role in the dissemination of this new poetry. But from 1972, "poems in support of the policies of the Revolutionary Govern-ment soon appeared in written form in the daily newspaper *Xiddigta Oktobaar* ("The October Star") and in such periodicals as *Waaga Cusub* ("The New Era"), *Codka Macallinka* ("The Teachers' Voice"), *Hawl iyo hantiwadag* ("Work and Socialism"), *Kacaan* ("Revolution") and *Dhambaalka Akademiyaha Dhaqanka* ("The Bulletin of the Academy of Culture")." Cabdi Muxumud Aamin's *Geeddiga Wadaay* ("Lead the Trek!" 1973) is a volume of verse whose title "derives its imagery from the treks which the nomadic pastoralists undertake in search of new grazing, which the author uses as a symbol of the new Somalia moving on towards progress and prosperity." Axmed Cabdullaahi Qaalib's *Taageerida Kacaanka* ("In support of the Revolution," 1975) is likewise a poetic apology for the Somali brand of revolutionary socialism which the poet seems easily to combine with his deep Muslim piety; the book contains several praise poems in honour of General Siyaad Barre, the President of the Supreme Revolutionary Council.

In 1973, narrative prose fiction received impetus from two short nov-els by Shire Jaamac Axmed: *Halgankii nolosha* ("Life struggle") is mainly set in the years preceding the second World War; the author stigmatizes the inhumanity of traditional education and the cruel futility of tribal fighting; at the end of the story, he hails the coming of modern education with the victory of the British over the Italians during the war. *Rooxaan* ("The Spirits") contains another indictment of what seems to be resented by modern Somali as a particularly repellent feature of traditional society: the abuse of religion by brutal schoolmasters and fraudulent sheikhs. In his novel *Agoondarro waa u nacab jacayl* ("Ignorance is the enemy of love," 1974), Faarax M.J. Cawl goes back to the days of the Dervish rebellion; he uses the story of a love tragedy to illustrate the importance of literacy, while also criticising family authoritarianism in traditional marriage; the story is interspersed with poems, dating from the times of the events, as is his later novel, *Garbaduubkii Gumeysiga* ("The shackles of colonialism", 1978). In the late 1970s, however, much prose fiction was first serialised in the national daily. This was the case, for example, of *Waa inoo berrito* ("We shall see each other tomorrow," 1977), where Axmed Faarax Cali "Idaajaa" inveighs against civil servants who misuse their power and privileges in order to enrich themselves by illegal deals; and in *Wacdahara jacaylka* ("The vicissitudes of love", 1977), Yuusuf Axmed "Hero" used the vernacular tongue to put forward the feminist trend which had already been illustrated in English by Nuruddin Farah.

Whereas playwriting in Somali had mainly taken the form of satirical comedies of manners, one of the latest contributions to the genre was an epic play, *Dabkuu shiday Darwishkii* ("The fire which the Dervish lit," 1975) where Axmed F. Cali "Idaajaa" and Cabdulqaadir Xirsi "Yamyam" present in dramatic form the history of the Dervish struggle for freedom from its inception in 1896 to its unhappy end in 1921.

PART III

THE IMPACT
OF
THE WEST

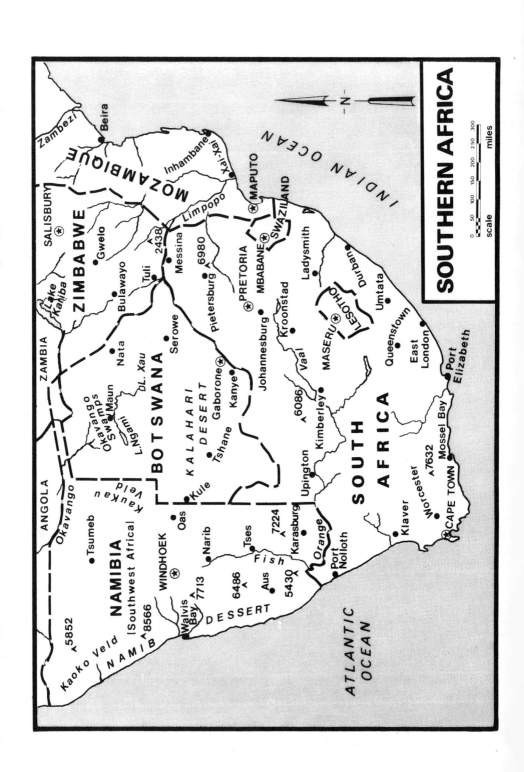

SOUTHERN AFRICA

scale

miles

0 50 100 150 200 250 300

-N-

INDIAN OCEAN

Zambezi

Beira

MOZAMBIQUE

Inhambane

Xai-Xai

MAPUTO

SWAZILAND

SALISBURY

ZIMBABWE

Gwelo

Limpopo

2438

Messina

6980

PRETORIA

MBABANE

Ladysmith

Durban

Tuli

Pietersburg

Johannesburg

Kroonstad

LESOTHO

MASERU

Umtata

Lake Kariba

Bulawayo

ZAMBIA

Nata

Serowe

Vaal

Queenstown

East London

Nata

L. Xau

KALAHARI

Gaborone

6086

Kimberley

Port Elizabeth

Okavango

Okavango Swamps

Maun

L. Ngami

BOTSWANA

DESERT

Kanye

SOUTH

Okavango

Kaukau Veld

Tshane

Kule

Upington

AFRICA

Mossel Bay

ANGOLA

Oas

Narib

Tses

7224

Karasburg

Klaver

Worcester

7632

Kanye

Tsumeb

NAMIBIA

(Southwest Africa)

WINDHOEK

7713

6486

Aus

5430

Fish

Orange

Port Nolloth

CAPE TOWN

5852

Kaoko Veld

Walvis Bay

NAMIB

DESSERT

ATLANTIC OCEAN

8566

CHAPTER SEVEN
COLONIZATION AND LITERATURE

The arrangement of this book has made it necessary at several points to mention the way cultural contact with western Europe affected literatures that had been in existence centuries before the white man made his presence felt in subsaharan Africa. It should be clear, however, that contrary to what the white world has long held to be an unchallengeable assumption, the written art had made deep inroads into the black continent long before it could avail itself of the alleged advantages of western technology. While the majority had of course remained for the most part non-literate, vast areas in Ethiopia, in West Africa and on the Indian Ocean coast had produced a significant élite which had supplemented the oral tradition with a considerable body of writing in Arabic and in African languages. It would be a mistake to underestimate the importance of such novelties as the roman script, the printing press and new thematics for the modernization of Hausa, Swahili and other literatures, but it is equally obvious that a strong element of continuity underlies their evolution into modern times. The fact remains, however, that the impact of the West gradually led to the emergence of literate élites throughout subsaharan Africa with a concomitant diffusion of creative writing throughout the continent.

The present shape of the relationship between independent Africa and the western world represents only the third stage in a historical process that began in the late fifteenth century, when Portuguese sailors and explorers in search of a road to India that would not be subject to Arab control, sailed round Africa and established contact, and in some cases business relations, with some of the coastal kingdoms. This could hardly have anything to do with creative writing. Nevertheless, archives in Portugal have preserved a number of letters from the king of Kongo, Affonso, which show that the Catholic missionaries at Mbanza Congo had made a start with teaching their language and the writing of it to some of the local dignitaries.[1] This was the beginning of a pattern which closely resembled the introduction of the writing skill and the Latin language throughout western Europe in the days of the Roman empire.

If relations between Portuguese and Africans had remained friendly, or at least peaceful, this might have led to such developments as the early spreading of a modern-type system of education, the creation of a literate élite, the diffusion of the European language, and, in time, the emergence of the written art in areas under Portuguese influence.

The experiment aborted, however, and a second stage was reached as the entrepreneurial spirit characteristic of the western mind devised a new rapport with Africa, together with new, egregiously inhuman, uses for its population. Sorely in need of manpower for the plantations that they had established in their overseas territories, not only in Africa (São Tomé) but even more in the western hemisphere, the Portuguese, and later the other European powers, inaugurated a form of the slave trade that was probably the most remunerative (and murderous) business venture ever to have been invented by man. No secure figures are available, but according to some estimates, more than twenty million Africans were thus bought from local chieftains and carried overseas in the course of the following two centuries. Such protracted mass migration was a historical process of unprecedented magnitude. It had manifold consequences, which need not be enlarged upon in the present context. But two points are perhaps worth emphasizing: one is that the underprivileged black diaspora preserved the essentials of its oral lore and produced an art form which, under the name of jazz, was in its turn to conquer the whole of the western world in the first half of the twentieth century. The other is that in the course of the centuries, a number of black slaves or ex-slaves managed to become conversant with the culture of their white masters and, beginning with Phillis Wheatley and Jupiter Hammon, at length created, in the United States and in the West Indies, a substantial body of creative writing that constitutes a significant contribution to literary development.

This latter trend was fostered in the eighteenth century by new attitudes that were no doubt partly due to increasing industrialization and a reduced need for cheap unskilled labour in modern countries. But this economic factor was accompanied by two powerful currents of thought, Pietism and the Enlightenment, both of which, for their diverse reasons, contributed powerfully to the growth of the anti-slavery movement.

The opponents of the slave trade were well-meaning people with very laudable intentions. They wanted to stop the slave trade and to abolish slavery, and in due time they succeeded in doing both. They also wanted to return the black exiles to the continent of their origin, and several serious attempts were made to that effect in the early decades of the nineteenth century. Undoubdtedly, they contemplated an idyllic future for their African protégés. But human nature being what it is, they also wanted to compensate for the disappearance of the profitable slave trade by means of some other, legitimate, form of business. An unholy alliance was thus formed between philanthropists and businessmen, and a third phase began in the relation between Africa and the West: the colonial era. Commercial interests in Europe started an intensive search for material resources in the African continent, and this was the beginning of modern colonialism, which was to crystallize into full-fledged imperialism at the Berlin Conference of 1885.

Europeans had of course been present in Africa before that: there was hardly any western nation that had not established a few forts and trading posts somewhere along the coast, and Dutch and French Protestants fleeing persecution at home had even settled in not inconsiderable numbers at the tip of South Africa. These, however, had all been comparatively small-scale ventures. From the middle of the nineteenth century, the process of exploration and exploitation began in earnest. And to the missionaries' humanitarian desire to combat heathenism and to make the Africans participate in the spiritual benefits of Christianity, was added a new incentive: the self-interest of the European capitalist companies which needed literate indigenous help, capable of working under climatic conditions often murderous to the white man.

Religious proselytism and the requirements of colonialist exploitation were thus the two main elements that were to lead to the growth of literacy, itself the primary prerequisite for the production of the modern written art to which Janheinz Jahn was to give the name of "neo-African literature."

•   •   •

Shortly before his untimely death in 1973, Jahn had published a statistical breakdown of his bibliographical findings,[2] which showed that of the 2130 published works by 1127 writers which constituted the whole of "neo-African literature," as listed in the 1971 version of his great *Bibliography*,[3] 62% had been composed by 56% of the writers in European languages, while 38% had been written by 44% of the authors in 51 of their own, African, languages. Actually, for all the painstaking thoroughness of his research, Jahn had underestimated the number of literary works in vernacular languages. Further investigations are likely to demonstrate that the distribution between European and African languages is nearer fifty-fifty.

This book is not concerned with African writing in European languages. But Jahn's statistics enabled him to observe that "there is no literature in an African language in Portuguese Africa and hardly any in French-speaking areas": nearly the whole of the vernacular writing was produced in the areas that had been controlled by the British. To this important observation, it is possible to add a few points whose significance will soon be made clear. One is that Italian and Spanish colonization in Africa proved singularly barren in the literary field: the period of fascist domination in Ethiopia was chiefly conspicuous for the abolition of publication in Amharic, and no original creative work was ever produced in Italian by any African author, with the exception of Somali poet Mohammed Samantar, whose *La pioggia è caduta* was published in 1973, several years after Somalia had become an independent republic. Likewise, only two novelists wrote in Spanish in the area that has since become Equatorial Guinea. On the other hand, it should also be remembered that German colonization, short-lived as it was, had exerted a strong influence not only on the development of Swahili literature as we have seen, but also on the emergence and early growth of Ewe writing in German Togoland. It is further to be noted that Madagascar is the only part of the French African empire to have produced a sizable amount of creative writing in its own language: this was the aftermath of a trend that had gained momentum during the nineteenth century, at a time when British cultural and commercial influence was paramount. Cameroon, too, has a few creative works in vernacular languages: but then, Cameroon had first been a German colony; it was never a French colony but a mandate territory, like French Togoland.

It is thus obvious that two utterly different patterns determined the literary development of black Africa under European colonial power: where British (and to a much lesser extent German) authority was paramount, the literary use of vernacular languages was encouraged and eventually flourished, so that a bilingual tradition emerged, some of the writers using their own languages, others resorting to English.[4] By contrast, the peoples of the areas ruled by France, Portugal, Spain and Italy produced hardly any writing in their own languages (the exception being the written art of the Muslim communities); in French and Portuguese territories, all the literary energy was released in the languages of the conquerors.

This peculiar configuration is strongly reminiscent of the manner in which the early literatures of western Europe emerged more than fifteen centuries ago. These, too, followed two distinct patterns. In the areas that were incorporated into the Roman empire at an early date—chiefly Italy, Spain and Gaul—the introduction of writing was a by-product of the Roman conquest. For six centuries after the fall of the empire, the writing skill was used solely in the language of the erstwhile conquerors. New literatures in the vernacular Romance languages of the peoples concerned were not created until the eleventh century in Northern and Southern France, the twelfth century in Spain, the thirteenth century in Italy and Portugal. But in the peripheral Celtic and Germanic

areas, where Roman penetration had not been as intense and protracted, such as England, or which the Romans never conquered at all,
such as Ireland, Scandinavia and the greater part of Germany, writing
was introduced not through military and administrative conquest, but
as an instrument for the propagation of Christianity and the development of intellectual life. New literatures thus arose as early as the sixth
century in Ireland, the seventh century in England, the late eighth century in the German part of Charlemagne's empire, and around the
tenth century in Iceland and Scandinavia. These literatures had at least
one feature in common: they were bilingual. Although the Roman empire had disintegrated, Latin remained the language of the Church and
of culture. It was used mainly for religious purposes (hagiographies,
homiletic works, hymnal poetry) and for the writing of history (Bede,
Saxo Grammaticus). But by far the most original and arresting portion
of these new literatures of the early middle ages was couched in the
vernacular Celtic and Germanic languages, chiefly for the recording of
epic traditions dealing with the great warlike events and heroic deeds
of the tribal past: the Irish cycles, *Beowulf*, the *Hildebrandslied*, the Ice-
landic sagas.

It would be unduly rash to claim that the dichotomy in the modern
literary history of black Africa is simply a belated offshoot of ethnic
differences between the colonizing nations, even though the latter fall
clearly into two groups: the Latin/Mediterranean group (France, Portugal, Spain, Italy), and the Nordic/Germanic group (Britain, Germany).
Yet this division of the conquering nations is reflected at a second, more
immediately relevant, level. For in the colonies of the "Latin" nations,
the educational system which was the Africans' sole access to literacy
was mainly in the hands of Catholic missionaries, whereas in the colonies
of the "Germanic" nations it was controlled by Protestant missionaries.
Below the surface were important differences which should not to be
underestimated. The educational policy applied by the "Latin" countries in their African colonies was basically characterized by the ethno-
centricity and cultural and linguistic centralism which had been a characteristic feature of Roman imperialism, and had remained extremely
powerful in the Catholic church until the Vatican council in the mid-
twentieth century. But the very spirit of Protestantism, strengthened in
Britain by its connection with individualism and parliamentary democracy, was oriented in an entirely different direction.

The following chapters will illustrate that the emergence of modern
African literature in vernacular languages was closely linked with the
dissemination of Protestantism. It is of the essence of Protestantism, as
founded by Luther, to postulate a direct, personal relationship between
man and his God. The word of God is inscribed in the Holy Scripture.
But each individual is entitled to his own interpretation of this Revela-

tion. The central preoccupation of Protestant missionaries, therefore, was to enable prospective converts to gain a knowledge of the Scriptures, so as to have the basic foundation on which to build up their own relationship with God. Two different ways could conceivably reach that target: either Africans were to be taught the European language so as to gain access to extant versions of the Bible; or the Scripture was to be made available to them in their own languages. It was to this second procedure that Protestant missionaries usually resorted.

While on the whole there was considerable congruence between the national traditions of the colonizers and their religious outlook, one single but exceedingly revealing case shows that religious affiliation was really of primary importance. The tiny kingdom of Lesotho (formerly Basutoland) has proved, in the course of the last hundred years, to be one of the most productive parts of black Africa as far as vernacular creative writing is concerned. Yet, although Basutoland was one of the High Commission Territories under the protection of the British government, literacy and modern education were first introduced there by representatives of the Protestant Missions Evangéliques de Paris during the 1830s. It is certainly significant that they adopted exactly the same educational-linguistic policy as their British colleagues in other parts of Africa, and, although French-speaking, were eager promoters of vernacular writing. One interesting consequence of this is that when Catholic missionaries, mostly French-speaking Canadians, settled in Basutoland, they found that they could not hope for any success in their rivalry with the Protestants unless they too resorted to the same methods: the result is that Lesotho is probably the only country in Africa with a double tradition of vernacular writing, Protestant *and* Catholic.

•   •   •

Since the emergence and growth of vernacular African writing was so intimately bound up with the development of Protestant missionary activity, it is not idle, at this place, to recall that the modern Protestant missionary movement was itself largely an outcome of the fight against the slave trade and slavery and of the opening of Africa to European exploration and enterprise. In 1792, William Carey (1761–1834) issued *An Enquiry into the Obligations of Christianity to Use Means for the Conversion of the Heathen,* an important treatise which testified to an early sense of spiritual duty towards the peoples of what was soon to become the colonial world. Carey was directly responsible for the foundation of the Baptist Missionary Society (1792), the first example of modern missionary enterprise. This was followed, after three years, by the Missionary Society, later to be known as the London Missionary Society (L.M.S.); although it was intended as an interdenominational venture whose purpose was simply to teach the gospel overseas, the main impulse had come from the dissenting churches. In 1796, the Presbyterian Church of Scotland created the Glasgow Missionary Society (G.M.S.), which became active in South Africa in the 1820s. The established Church of England viewed the whole missionary undertaking with misgivings which were not alleviated until the middle of the nineteenth century. Nevertheless, as early as 1799, in spite of the hostility of Anglican bishops, a number of Anglican clergy and lay preachers led by William Wilberforce (1759–1833) founded the Church Missionary Society for Africa and the East (C.M.S.).

Both the L.M.S. and the C.M.S. played an important part in the promotion not only of Christianity, but also of literacy, modern education and creative writing, the former in South and East Africa and Madagascar, the latter chiefly in West and East Africa. The C.M.S. was especially instrumental in bringing about one exceptional development in African literature, for they were in charge of teaching and ecclesiastical duties among the liberated slaves that had settled at Freetown. These came from England, the United States, Canada and the West Indies, and their mother tongue was English. It was through the care of the C.M.S. that that first élites of this Creole community were educated, and they, in turn, were to become responsible for the outburst of English writing in Sierra Leone during the second half of the nineteenth century.[5]

Whereas during the last decade of the eighteenth century the organizational centre of the Protestant missionary movement had been Great Britain, there was considerable co-operation with the Deutsche Christentumsgesellschaft in Basel, which supplied the L.M.S. and the C.M.S. with continental missionaries such as Dr. van der Kemp (1747–1811), who went to South Africa to work among the Xhosa in 1797. This co-operation was by no means discontinued when the Basel Missionary Institute was established in 1815: some of its brightest graduates, such as Koelle, Schön and Krapf, were sent to West and East Africa as members of the C.M.S. and the L.M.S., until the foundation of an independent Basler Evangelische Missionsgesellschaft in 1822. In the middle of the nineteenth century, these German-speaking missionaries contributed greatly to laying the foundations of African linguistics, as exemplified in Karl W. Isenberg's *Dictionary of the Amharic Language* (1842), Jacob F. Schön's *Vocabulary of the Hausa Language* (1843), Julius L. Krapf's *Vocabulary of Six East-African Languages* (1850), or Sigismund W. Koelle's *Polyglotta Africana* (1854).[6]

Meanwhile, Europe's return to peace after the Napoleonic interlude had released tremendous energies for exploration and conquest, both territorial and spiritual. Indeed, a case might be made for the notion that the political scramble for Africa was preceded by a religious scramble, evident in the extraordinary growth of the evangelical missionary movement during the decades following Waterloo. Missionary societies multiplied in Great Britain. They appeared in the United States, in Germany, even in France and later in Scandinavia. While they were much concerned with Asia and the Pacific Ocean, it was undoubtedly in black Africa that their impact was at its deepest and most extensive. It was there, too, that the results of their activities—in terms of the setting up of new literatures—was at its most impressive.

Whilst the encouragement of new literatures was by no means a central preoccupation with the missionaries, it was an almost inevitable consequence or side effect of their educational, proselytizing endeavours. As their main intent was to make the word of God available to their converts in the latter's own languages, the first task of the missionary on reaching hitherto unknown territory, was to familiarize himself with the language of the native inhabitants in order to reduce it to writing. It was this early phase which laid the foundation of African linguistics. But again, to the missionary philology was just a means to an end. His second task was a twofold one: to teach reading and writing to those he hoped to convert, and to procure vernacular translations of scriptural texts. Given the importance of community singing in Protestant liturgy, and the importance of music in African cultural traditions, another urgent task with definite literary overtones was the composition of Christian hymns in the vernacular.

For all this, the missionary-linguist had to rely on local help: he had to be taught as much as he had to teach. Further, he needed reading matter, preferably of an edifying as well as entertaining sort, for his pupils. That is the reason why so many of the vernacular literatures of Africa begin with translations from *The Pilgrim's Progress* or from juvenile adventure stories in English.

At this point, however, a new stage begins. For while the missionary's main efforts were oriented towards the conversion of the "heathens," the demands of the educational process as well as his ingrained, ethnocentred desire to inculcate his own cultural background together with the Christian faith led him to introduce secular reading-matter. Further, his anthropological interest in the populations among whom he was living informed him that they already had a significant patrimony of oral lore, which both he and they, for different reasons, were eager to commit to the permanency of writing. Finally, as a devoted educationist, he could hardly help encouraging the more gifted of his pupils to attempt original composition. That is where modern African literature may truly be said to have begun: with Christian hymns composed by Africans, with recordings of oral lore (especially in the form of traditional stories), with the earliest attempts at original prose composition imitating the kind of stories that the pupils had read at school, either in English or in vernacular versions.

As long as the bulk of the vernacular output consisted of scriptural material, the actual printing was done by the British and Foreign Bible Society, which had been set up in 1804. But as soon as the size of the literate audience justified it, the mission stations brought in their own printing machinery, to issue hymnals, school readers and the local missionary journal. In the course of the 1820s, missionary presses were thus set up by the G.M.S. in South Africa and by the L.M.S. in Madagascar. This early example was followed in many parts of Black Africa throughout the nineteenth century. Material conditions were thus created for the speedy growth of vernacular creative writing and for its dissemination within the fairly narrow limits imposed by the linguistic context. But in Africa as elsewhere freedom of the press simply means freedom for those who own a press. Missionary authorities would be reluctant to print material that did not conform to their own notion of what was good for the community for whose education they felt responsible. As a result one of the masterpieces of modern African literature, Sotho author Thomas Mofolo's *Chaka*, had to wait for about fifteen years until it was eventually printed in 1925 in the face of stiff opposition from at least some of the French missionaries.[7] This was undoubtedly not an isolated occurrence; there were probably many cases in which works of local authorship were held up, or were denied publication altogether, on ideological grounds.

As the century wore on a grievous shift took place in these "ideological" grounds. For in Europe the success of Gobineau's *Essai sur l'inégalité des races humaines* (1853–55) had stimulated the rapid development of a racialism that provided a pseudo-scientific justification for the subsequent expansion of colonialism and imperialism. While the scramble for Africa was in its early stages during the third quarter of the century, many missionaries were affected by this change in the mental climate of Europe. At the same time as the growth in the educational system was fostering a stronger sense of dignity and keener critical attitudes among the African élites, missionary authorities became more and more suspicious not only of any writings that smacked of hostility towards white supremacy, but also of such ethnographical work as could be construed as a vindication of pre-Christian mores and beliefs. The result was that in those areas where missionary influence had been most profound and trusting, such as Sierra Leone or South Africa, a jarring note of distrust crept in during the years that preceded the Berlin Conference. In Sierra Leone, missionary, and soon after administrative, hostility to the anglophone Creole élite of Freetown led to the extinction of a tradition of scholarship that had been developed by such luminaries as Samuel Ajayi Crowther, Africanus Horton and E. W. Blyden.[8] Among the Xhosa of South Africa, on the other hand, the widening gap between black ambitions and missionary imperatives led a fairly large African élite to obtain financial help from liberal-minded whites and to set up their own journal where they could freely voice their grievances until such developments were brought to an end by the superior power of Afrikaner nationalism in the newly-formed Dominion.[9]

In a way, then, the triumph of colonial imperialism, the Berlin Conference, and the European dissemination of racialist attitudes closed the first important phase in the development of vernacular literatures in so far as this development was connected with the evolution of Protestant missionary enterprise. But though the general outline is fairly clear, more research is needed to fill in the details of the picture. Future historians of African literature, following the fruitful example set by general historians of Africa, will do well to scan missionary archives to gain a full picture of missionary attitudes in the particular field of literary history and of the actual effects of such attitudes.

● ● ●

The deterioration in the relationship between the missions and the black élite they had nurtured did not escape the attention of a number of forward-looking observers, who were aware of the need for a thoroughgoing revision of educational policy throughout the African colonies. The first World War created a new climate of opinion, characterized by a strikingly diminished confidence in the universal superiority of western civilization. The humanitarian impulse that underlay the foundation of the League of Nations found expression in the concept of trusteeship. It is also possible that European governments and entrepreneurs found it desirable to be able to rely on a more numerous and better educated élite to help them in their various undertakings. Immediately after the war, the Foreign Missions Conference of North America, the oldest missionary society in the United States, founded in 1810, obtained support from the Phelps-Stokes Fund for a full inquiry into educational systems in Africa. A commission composed of American, British and African educators issued its report, *Education in Africa*, edited by Thomas Jesse Jones, in 1922. In 1923, the trustees of the Phelps-Stokes Fund commissioned a second survey dealing specifically with the eastern part of the continent: the report appeared under the title *Education in East Africa*.

The Phelps-Stokes reports provided comprehensive coverage of all aspects of education in Africa, but they are of special significance for the history of vernacular writing because the commissioners proclaimed their "emphatic belief in the value of the Native languages."[10] They were strongly critical of the linguistic policy that had been pursued by the "Latin" colonizers:

The use of a European Language has been advocated from mixed motives by both Europeans and Natives . . . Fortunately at the present time the only Powers that still maintain this attitude in some of their possessions are the French and the Portuguese. Whatever the motives, whether pride of language, nationality, or even the generous desire to share their language with those whom they control, the policy is unwise and unjust. [11]

While condoning the educational policy that had been maintained by Protestant missionaries, the commissioners went beyond its narrow purpose, i.e. to make the word of God available to the Africans, and defined the importance of the African languages in far more comprehensive terms:

With full appreciation of the European language, the value of the Native tongue is immensely more vital, in that it is one of the chief means of preserving whatever is good in Native customs, ideas and ideals, and thereby preserving what is more important than all else, namely, Native self-respect. All peoples have an inherent right to their own language. It is the means of giving expression to their own personality, however primitive they may be. The processes of education must begin with the characteristics of the people as they are and help them to evolve to the higher levels. No greater injustice can be committed against a people than to deprive them of their own language. [12]

Whether it was because the Phelps-Stokes reports became known throughout western Europe, or because they corresponded to preoccupations that were widespread at the time, the fact remains that "within a short time after the publication of the [first] report, Britain, France and Belgium began issuing policy statements outlining in broad terms the educational policy to be followed in the African territories." [13] The evolution of educational policy in the matter of language use and language teaching simply crystallized and institutionalized the cleavage that has already been observed between the British and "Latin" colonial system. Portuguese authorities apparently remained unaffected and Portuguese educators imperturbably went on disregarding African languages. The French merely reasserted that "the universal use of the French language as the medium of instruction" was a constant principle of their educational policy[14] because French "must gradually become the language of common use to all"[15] throughout French Africa. As to the British government, in 1925 it issued a general policy memorandum entitled *Educational Policy in British Tropical Africa* which specifically declared that "the study of the educational use of the vernaculars is of primary importance."[16] The peculiar case of Belgian Africa will be referred to in the discussion of Kongo literature.

The interest in the study and promotion of African languages now

officially proclaimed by the British authorities was soon to receive concrete implementation. In August 1926, an International Missionary
Conference, held at the Belgian sea-resort of Le Zoute, decided upon
the foundation of an International Institute for African Languages and
Cultures which, as the International African Institute, was soon to become the first really important research centre dealing with Africa. But
the IAI was also concerned with activities of a practical nature. In particular, the discussions of 1926 had shown the need for adequate vernacular literature and in 1930 the IAI launched an international competition for books in African languages. Although the prizes awarded
were not very substantial, this initiative provided powerful encouragement to would-be writers, and initiated creative writing in languages
which had never been used for such purposes before. In the first competition, forty-five manuscripts were submitted in five different languages: Swahili, Hova, Xhosa, Akan and Kongo; and prizes were
awarded to several writers who were to become significant representatives of their national literatures, such as James M. Mbotela in Swahili,
Wast Ravelomoria of Madagascar, Tiyo Soga and S.E.K. Mqhayi in
Xhosa, and J. J. Adaye of the Gold Coast. Different languages were
selected every year, so that in the course of its first four years of existence the IAI competition registered 207 entries in eighteen languages.[17]

In the early 1920s, a group of British missionary societies had formed
an African Literature sub-committee, which published a *Bibliography of
African Christian Literature* (1923). The Le Zoute conference led to the
foundation of an International Committee on Christian Literature for
Africa as a sub-committee of the International Missionary Council.[18] As
its name indicates, this committee was chiefly concerned with the provision of Christian literature, and creative writing was only a minor
preoccupation. Nevertheless, its quarterly bulletin, *Books for Africa*,
which appeared from 1931 to 1963, was extremely useful in disseminating information on African writing and in publicizing the work of
the many periodicals, chiefly teachers' and missionary journals which
sought contributions from Africans. Margaret Wrong was conscious that
such periodicals were "playing an important part in encouraging writing
in the vernaculars, which should bear fruit later in the production of
general literature." In 1950, the Conference of Missionary Societies in
Great Britain and Ireland launched the Margaret Wrong Memorial
Fund Competition, which was organized every year until 1962; unlike
the earlier IAI competitions, interrupted by the war, this was open to
writers using African or European languages. Nevertheless, it provided
valuable encouragement to vernacular writing: the prize-winners included practitioners of Yoruba (F.O. Fagunwa, 1955), Xhosa (Jolobe,
1957), Swahili (Shaaban, 1960), Bemba (Mpashi, 1961) and Hausa
(Abubakar Imam, 1962).

Yet the most fruitful of the developments of the 1930s was the foundation of the Translation Bureau in Northern Nigeria. This was not a purely missionary venture, but a predominantly official initiative. It was designed to supply "literature" in the broadest sense, that is, reading material of a modern kind, to counteract the conservative tendencies of traditional Islamic education. As already recounted, thanks to the efforts of an energetic British officer, Rupert East, it soon developed a sideline in the publication of original creative writing by Hausa authors. Such quick results were by no means achieved by similar institutions which were established in other parts of Nigeria, especially in Ibo and Efik country. They confined themselves to their primary aim, which was to provide vernacular textbooks and translations of European works. Nevertheless, they were aware of the potentialities they opened up for the original, creative use of African languages. Of the Ibo Translation Bureau, for example, it was said at the time that its purpose was "to encourage the Ibo to take an interest and pride in his own language in the hope that eventually his literary powers will be commensurate with his conversational ones which are, indeed, rich."[19]

A similar type of government intervention was evident in the creation of the Inter-Territorial Language (Swahili) Committee in East Africa in 1930. This had wider scope than the Zaria Translation Bureau, as its ultimate purpose was to foster the use of Swahili as a common *lingua franca* for the whole of British East Africa. Nevertheless, one of its central aims was explicitly stated as "giving encouragement and assistance to authors whose native tongue is Swahili."[20] Actually, this body showed little interest in creative writing until the late 1940s, when its dealings with all publishing matters were shifted to the newly created East African Literature Bureau.

These remained exceptions until World War II, although the government of Northern Rhodesia (Zambia) in 1937 set up an African Literature Committee where the government, missions and Africans were represented.[21] But in 1943, the Colonial Office issued a White Paper, *Mass Education in African Society*, which testified to the existence of an acute official awareness that in the passage from the notion of trusteeship to the notion of partnership, a dramatic increase in African literacy was absolutely necessary. Owing to circumstances, this strengthening of educational policy could not have its full effect until a few years after the war, when literature bureaux were set up in many parts of British Africa. Although not all were as active as one might have wished, these new institutions made a decisive contribution to the development of vernacular writing. In a number of cases, they merely provided added impetus for a trend that had been started long ago by Protestant missionaries. But there are several examples where—as in what was known as the Central African Federation (Zambia, Malawi, Rhodesia)—the literature bureaux were really responsible for the birth and early growth of creative writing in African languages.

• • •

These, then, were the main lines of development that characterized the emergence and evolution of such African-language literatures as resulted from the European impact in the British-controlled territories. Some made an early start in the nineteenth century, at the beginning of the modern colonial era. Others did not appear until as late as the mid-twentieth century, when missionary initiative was bolstered by government action. They have received unduly scant attention so far. Swiss scholar Peter Sulzer was the first, outside Africa, to call attention to the amount, the quality and the significance of Bantu-language writing in South Africa.[22]

Ten years later, Janheinz Jahn, by including vernacular works in his pioneering *Bibliography of Neo-African Literature from Africa, America, and the Caribbean* (1965), made it possible to gain a rough idea of their quantitative importance in comparison with African literature in the European languages.[23] Composed in little-known languages, those works suffer from worse neglect than that suffered by Finnish, Dutch or Hungarian literature, for few of those who can read them have so far received the highly specialized type of education that would enable them to properly study their own literatures, either from a critical or a historical viewpoint, combined with the linguistic competence required to convey their findings in world-wide languages. The works written in English or French by such African scholars as Archibald C. Jordan on Xhosa literature or George Kahari on Shona novelists or Mbelolo ya Mpiku on Kongo poetry are quite exceptional. There is little doubt that the progress of higher education throughout Africa will remedy this situation: a tremendous wealth of information lies hidden in the archives of the missionary societies and of the literature bureaux concerned, waiting for the African scholars that will bring to the task both the tools of their scholarly upbringing and their intimate knowledge of the languages and the societies involved.*

---

* M. A. theses and Ph.D dissertations presented at many American and Canadian universities, and to a lesser degree at British and European institutions, by African scholars in the past decade have seriously begun to address this task. (Ed.)

CHAPTER EIGHT
SOUTHERN AFRICA

1. The Nineteenth Century

As Muslim influence never spread south of the Zambezi river, literacy on the southern subcontinent was introduced by European immigrants, and indigenous creative writing first appeared among the Bantu people that had settled farthest south and was thus first to come in touch with them: the Xhosa branch of the Nguni.[1]

The "modern" literary art of the Xhosa began in fact with Christian oral poetry: under the influence of the L.M.S. missionary Johannes van der Kemp (1747–1811), who reached Xhosa country in 1800, a local convert named Ntsikana (c. 1783–c. 1820) composed a hymn which was preserved orally until it was recorded in 1828 by John Philip of the G.M.S. In the course of the 1820s, the Church of Scotland missionaries established their headquarters at a place which they later called Lovedale,[2] and which was to become the main centre for Christian education and literary production in South Africa. They were responsible for reducing the language to writing and for issuing the first vocabularies and grammars. The publication of parts of the Bible in Xhosa translation, however, was the work of representatives of the Wesleyan Methodist Missionary Society, which had been founded in 1813; the Methodists may also claim priority in printing the first Xhosa journal in the late 1830s, although the earliest evidence of Xhosa authorship appears in the G.M.S. journal *Ikwezi* ("The Morning Star"), which was printed at Lovedale during the mid-1840s. Its contributors were students of the Lovedale school, including the son of the old bard Ntsikana.

The first Xhosa writer of note was Tiyo Soga (1829–1871) who was also the first ordained Bantu minister He was renowned as a priest, an educator, a journalist and a translator. As an authority on the language, he sat on the committee appointed in the late 1860s to revise the Xhosa version of the Bible, and in 1867 the Lovedale Press published his translation of the first part of *The Pilgrim's Progress*. Tiyo Soga's concern with the spreading of Christianity did not prevent him from showing a keen interest in the lore of his own people. Modern

Xhosa literature thus made its first steps in a spirit of harmony between white missionaries and black converts. Tiyo Soga extolled the humaneness of the missionaries and their devotion to the betterment of the black man's fate; this he contrasted with the behaviour of the white settlers whom he rebuked because they "do not like the elevation of the natives, whom they would fain keep down as men- and maid-servants." vants."

This was written in the 1850s, but during the second half of the century, the climate in which Xhosa could be written deteriorated steadily on account of two developments.

First, it would appear that the missionaries were not altogether unaffected by the dissemination of racialist theories and the concomitant hardening of colonial enterprise into stark imperialism. Although it is true that the British authorities often tried to resist the Dutch settlers' attempts at increasing their expansion into black territory, the fact remains that with the last quarter of the century, warlike activities against Africans spread to the borders of Basutoland and to Zululand. This impelled the black intellectuals (at the time, almost solely Xhosa) to heartrending questionings. These were reflected in the Lovedale journal *Isigidimi* ("The Herald"), whose editor was the best-known poet of his generation, William Wellington Gqoba (1840–1888). Gqoba himself tried to vindicate Christianity and modern education in long didactic and allegorical poems in which he played down the wars as mere episodes in an otherwise hopeful interracial dialogue. But other writers were more sceptical. They pointed to the discrepancy between the white man's Christian ideals and his actual behavior. Their outspokenness was not viewed with equanimity by the missionaries, and when Gqoba died, in 1888, *Isigidimi* was allowed to vanish quietly.

In the second place, in spite of the comparatively liberal outlook of the British authorities and of their victories in the Boer wars, it soon became increasingly clear that the union of the South African colonies that was being contemplated during the early years of the twentieth century and which came into being in 1910 was likely to be dominated by the Boer segment of the population which had its own views about white supremacy.

Meanwhile, the Lovedale school had produced a considerable number of Xhosa graduates, who may be regarded as the first black élite in southern Africa. Some of these young intellectuals kept aloof from political problems. One case in point was John Henderson Soga (1859–1941), the son of Tiyo Soga and his Scottish wife. An ordained minister, he followed in the steps of his father, composing a large number of hymns, translating the second part of *The Pilgrim's Progress* (1927), and publishing highly informative works in English on *The South-Eastern Bantu* (1930) and *Amaxhosa Life and Customs* (1931). But Soga was a mulatto and had married a white woman. While he kept aloof from political issues, others of his generation were acutely aware of what was in store for them. They were also conscious of their physical weakness, and they realized that their only hope lay in multitribal unity in political action, and in awakening their peoples to the realities of the situation. With the financial help of enlightened Englishmen in Cape Town and elsewhere in the colony, they created independent Xhosa journals such as *Imvo Zabantsundu* ("Native Opinion," founded 1884). Twenty-five years later they organized the National Convention that gathered in Bloemfontein to meet the threat of a racist constitution for the Union of South Africa.

As a result, the main course of Xhosa literature was temporarily deflected, until the early 1920s, from creative writing towards journalism and polemics. The most important representatives of this activist generation were John Tengo Jabavu (1859–1921), John Knox Bokwe (1855–1922) and Walter Rubusana (1858–1936). Though they all shared a common concern with championing the rights of the black man, Bokwe was also a prolific and gifted hymn writer, while Rubusana was dedicated to his people's folklore and published an important collection of proverbs and praise poems (1906). Rubusana also played an important part in founding the South African Native National Congress (1912) together with intellectuals from other ethnic backgrounds and from a younger generation. In spite of their common struggle against white racialism, they also had their differences, and their quarrels had a share of responsibility in the Congress's failure to achieve its purpose. Nevertheless, the intellectual dynamism caused by the determination to meet the challenge of white supremacy had at least one exceedingly important practical result: this was the foundation of an institution of higher learning, Fort Hare College (1916), which remained open to students of all races and all tribes until it was turned into a purely Xhosa university as part of the reform of "Bantu education" in 1960. This is not the place to expatiate upon the manifold consequences of Fort Hare. But in the field of writing in general and of creative writing in particular, the institution had similar effects to those that Fourah Bay College had had in West Africa, and which Ibadan and Makerere College were to have in Nigeria and East Africa. Educational improvement, better acquaintance with English and other European cultures, the acquisition of more scientific habits of thought, and more systematic awareness of African languages were important factors in the growth and consolidation that were to take place in Bantu-language writing during the 1930s.

•   •   •

The clash between the southward movement of black expansion and the northward drive of white, especially Dutch, settlers looking for new pastures and trying to escape from the British administration in Cape Town, led to much turmoil and inner strife among the black peoples along the Drakensberg. This resulted in the emergence of the Sotho nation, whose Paramount Chief, Moshoeshoe (c. 1786–1870), soon realized the desirability of enlisting the help of white men that might advise him and help him maintain the independence of his kingdom in the face of both black and white encroachments.[3] In 1833, he welcomed three young Frenchmen sent out by the Paris Evangelical Missionary Society, which had been founded in 1822.

Because they were the only Frenchmen to wield any kind of influence in Southern Africa, the P.E.M.S. missionaries had no ulterior national motive in their dealings with Moshoeshoe and the neighbouring populations, whether white or black. Although the new creed and new mores which they were trying to introduce inevitably had a disruptive effect upon Sotho society, they could devote a significant part of their activity to maintaining the autonomy of the small kingdom in the face of its neighbours', and especially the white settlers', greed. They were instrumental in launching and bringing to fruition the protected negotiations which, beginning in the 1840s, ultimately led the British government in 1884 to grant protectorate status to Basutoland. This was of decisive importance for the future of the Sotho nation and its literature: while Lesotho itself, as one of the High Commission Territories, enjoyed a measure of autonomy, it suffered from an increasing degree of economic under-development and a large proportion of its population had to migrate to South Africa. Literature in Southern Sotho thus developed two distinct branches: writers in the homeland could claim a considerable amount of freedom and outspokenness with regard to social and political problems; but writers in the Sotho diaspora were submitted to all the restrictions imposed upon Africans in South Africa.

As soon as they reached the country, the Protestant missionaries reduced the language to writing: as early as 1837, a Sotho catechism was printed in the Cape. They established a fairly comprehensive educational system whose base in Morija fulfilled, for Southern Sotho, the same function as Lovedale did for Xhosa: a Teacher Training College was founded in 1868 and a Bible School in 1882. A printing press had been imported in 1841: it issued the first Sotho version of the New Testament in 1845 and the complete Bible was made available in 1878. A translation of *The Pilgrim's Progress* was published in 1872, so that by the end of the century would-be Sotho writers had at their disposal a literary language and one model of western prose fiction.

By the early 1860s, literacy had spread to such an extent that it justified the launching of a vernacular journal, *Leselinyana la Lesotho* ("The Little Light of Lesotho").[4] It was there that a few literate converts found the opportunity to try their talents. The first of them was Azariele M. Sekese (1849–1930), who contributed numerous papers to *Leselinyana* about Sotho folklore in the last decades of the century; these were published in book form in 1893, under the title, *Mekhoa ea Basotho le maele le litsomo* ("Customs and Proverbs of the Basuto"), the first collection of its kind ever to have been compiled by an African.

What is often called, somewhat hyperbolically, "the golden age" of Southern Sotho literature, occurred at a time when Xhosa writers in South Africa had their intellectual energies diverted to the political problems posed by the constitution of the Union. In the years that preceded the first World War, several writers emerged, one of whom was to reach world fame. This was Thomas Mofolo (1876–1948),[5] whose literary career began with an allegorical novel, *Moeti oa bochabela* ("The Traveller to the East," 1907), which testifies to Bunyan's influence; it had been first printed as a serial in *Leselinyana*. It was probably the success of this book that prompted a much older writer, Everitt Lechesa Segoete (1858–1923), to compose another edifying allegorical novel, *Monono ke moholi, ke mouoane* ("Riches are like mist, vapour," 1910). Mofolo's second novel, *Pitseng* (1910) is of special interest, not only because the writer has given up the allegorical technique, but also because he has one of his main characters spend a part of his life in the Cape Colony. His response to the different, racially mixed but white-dominated society that he finds there anticipates the kind of experience that was later to make vast numbers of Sotho people dependent on the prosperous country surrounding them. The note of independent observation and reflexion creeps in when Mofolo observes that "most white people put God last in everything" in spite of their sanctimonious proclamation; speaking of marriage customs, he claims that "the heathens are telling the truth when they say that the evil influences come from the Whites and come into Lesotho with the Christian converts."

The missionaries must have felt that this kind of criticism was acceptable, since they allowed the book to be printed on their press in Morija. Nevertheless friction had already occurred between them and the budding Sotho intelligentsia: in 1899, a controversy had arisen over the publication in *Leselinyana* of articles dealing with traditional divination: some of the missionaries felt that this sort of thing smacked of an undesirable return to pagan beliefs and customs. They must have sensed that this interest in pre-Christian tradition was something that ought to be stopped before it became too influential. For when Mofolo submitted his third novel, *Chaka*, in 1910, publication was delayed for fifteen years. Actually, *Chaka* is a historical novel dealing with the early nineteenth-century Zulu potentate, who had inflicted untold suffering on the Sotho people.[6] But several of the P.E.M.S. missionaries construed it as an apology for pagan superstitions. Sotho readers were to enjoy and appreciate

Mofolo's mastery of the resources of the language. The western reader
is more likely to admire the tragic insight, the depth of perception, and
the admirable structure of the book, which has been translated into
several European languages.[7] It also inspired a number of African writers using French or English, not least of them Léopold Sédar Senghor.[8]

How the procrastination over the publication affected the Sotho intelligentsia is of course unknown, for those early Sotho authors had no
way of making their voices heard other than through the missionary-
controlled press and journal. It is probably significant that after 1910,
the year which saw the publication of Mofolo's *Pitseng* and of Segoete's
only venture in imaginative writing, the latter devoted his talent to the
composition of religious meditations and other devotional works. So did
Mofolo's contemporary Edward Motsamai (1870–1959), whose sole
contribution to creative writing is *Mehla ea malimo* ("The Days of the
Cannibals," 1912), a collection of short stories inspired by popular
folktales. The most prolific of early Sotho writers, Zakea D. Mangoaela
(1883–1963), wisely followed this innocuous example in *Har'a libatana
le linyamat'sane* ("Among the Animals, Big and Small," 1912), and later
turned to linguistic study and the collection of traditional praise poems.[9]

● ● ●

By the time World War I began, then, creative writing in Sotho had
already reached an apex of a sort, while Xhosa imaginative literature,
which had a slightly longer history, was being inevitably thwarted by the
political preoccupations of the Xhosa élite. A start had also been made
with modern-type composition in Zulu.

The history of the Zulu kingdom and of its relation to the Boer settlers
and the British authorities is a very complex one. Its independence had
been recognized in 1832 and the boundary with Natal had been defined
in 1842. The conquest did not begin until 1887. Most of the early
missionary work among the Zulu was done by representatives of the
Wesleyan Methodist Missionary Society and of the American Board of
Commissioners for Foreign Missions which had been founded in Boston
in 1810; in 1882, however, the Trappist order set up in a Catholic mission, Mariannhill, which was to play some part in the later development
of Zulu literature.

During the late 1850s, the foundations of Zulu linguistics were laid by
scholars of many nationalities: the American Lewis Grout (*Isizulu: A
Grammar of the Zulu Language*, 1859), the Norwegian bishop Hans P.S.
Schreuder (*Grammatik for Zulusproget*, 1850), the Anglican bishop of Natal, John W. Colenso (*Elementary Grammar of the Zulu-Kafir Language*,
1855) and the German Jacob Ludwig Döhne (*Zulu-Kafir Dictionary*,
1857).

The American missionaries were responsible for the first scriptural translations, beginning with Newton Adams's *Extracts from Genesis* (1846) and culminating in the publication of the whole Bible by the American Bible Society in 1883. It is, however, indicative of the lack of agreement amongst missionaries working in this area that several different Zulu versions of Biblical material were prepared; the situation, as C.M. Doke once put it, was, "not one of unanimity between the different missions."[10] This was merely a linguistic reverberation of doctrinal and personal conflicts which compounded the overall antagonism among whites on matters concerning the relations between the races. This quarrelsomeness among Protestant missionaries of different denominations and allegiances probably played a part in a phenomenon which is directly connected with the emergence of modern Zulu literature: the early formation of independent African churches.

In the early years of the twentieth century, one of these was the African Native Baptist Church, "probably an offshoot from the Negro Baptist groups which had begun their work in Natal in 1899, and who, as 'Cushites', practised the new sacrament of footwashing."[11] The most renowned member of the sect was one Isaiah Shembe (*c.* 1870–1935), who was to found his own church shortly before the first World War. The illiterate son of a farm labourer, Shembe was a prophet-like character and a prolific composer of oral hymns, some of which he is alleged to have dictated after his death. Although most of his works, which did not reach print until 1940, were composed after 1920, some of them are dated from the time he came from Zululand to Natal in 1910. While Shembe was a contemporary of the Sotho writer Thomas Mofolo, his works represent, in the history of Zulu literature, the same stage of Christian oral art which was personified by the Xhosa poet Ntsikana almost a century earlier. But while there is no evidence that Ntsikana had any qualms about converting himself to the God of missionary Van der Kemp, Shembe was an eloquent and influential representative of the syncretic trend which was to generate specific forms of Christianity throughout black Africa.

●　●　●

Mofolo and Shembe belonged to a slightly later generation than the Xhosa intellectuals who were fighting a rearguard action against the colour-bar society. Several of their contemporaries played an important part in the growth of vernacular writing in South Africa. Among the Xhosa, the most significant figure was Samuel Edward Krune Mqhayi (1875–1945).[12] Although he assisted Jabavu in the editing of *Imvo Zabantsundu* during the first two decades of the century, he did not play a very active part in the struggle for the franchise. He was equally re-

nowned as a traditional oral bard and as a modern-type creative writer.[13]
His *Ityala lama-wele* ("The Lawsuit of the Twins," 1914) gave a new,
more aggressive, twist to the collective self-discovery which had been a
major source of inspiration for African writers: it was designed to vindicate the rationale of customary judicial procedure as opposed to the
new kind of law which the white authorities were preparing to introduce
into the territories under their administration. A prolific writer, Mqhayi
also composed biographies of the Reverend Bokwe and of the Ghanaian
educationist J.E.K. Aggrey, as well as his own autobiography. Several
collections of poems made him, in the words of Zulu critic B.W. Vilakazi,
"the Father of Xhosa poetry" because of his skill in using the traditional
techniques of the praise poem both for traditional and modern topics.
Perhaps his most ambitious work, however, was an allegorical novel, *U-
Don Jadu* (1929), purporting to describe an ideal, multiracial, South African society. In a way, this utopian tale was already outdated by the time
it reached print, not only because racial discrimination had become
firmly entrenched, but also because younger Xhosa writers had introduced a more realistic type of prose fiction.

Mqhayi did have very clear notions as to what race relations in South
Africa should be; he had an articulate sense of the values of his own
people and of the continued relevance of their customs; he was keenly
aware of the need for intertribal solidarity; although he belonged to a
Christian family and had been educated at Lovedale, he refused a teaching post there; and he was connected with the political struggle through
his activity as an assistant-editor to Jabavu. Nevertheless, he does not
seem to have been much involved in the political struggles that went on
during the first few years of this century. This was not the case with the
other two eminent writers who also belonged to the same generation,
John L. Dube (1870–1946) and Sol T. Plaatje (1876–1932).

Solomon T. Plaatje was a Tswana, born in the Orange Free State. A
gifted child, he went to school at the Pniel Lutheran Mission school and
acquired a remarkable knowledge of both English and Dutch. In 1912,
he was appointed General Secretary of the newly formed South African
Native National Congress and was a member of the deputation that was
sent to London to protest against discriminatory legislation following
the Act of Union. He visited Britain on a second occasion in 1919 and
1920, and it was probably there that he embarked on the writing of
Mhudi, the very first novel to have been composed in English by a black
South African. This remarkable historical novel, which was not printed
until 1930, does not fall within the scope of the present study.[14] But it
is important to note that while experimenting with the English language
and the novel form, Plaatje remained true to the pattern set by Xhosa
writers in the nineteenth century: his interest in innovation went hand
in hand with a deep concern with the language, lore and customs of his

own people: while in London, he compiled *Sechuana Proverbs, with Literal Translations and Their European Equivalents* (London, 1916).

But while doing all in his power to make his people and their history known to the English-speaking reader, Plaatje also endeavoured to promote the use of Tswana for imaginative writing. The history of the study of the Tswana language is a curious one, chiefly owing to peculiarities in the career of the L.M.S. missionary Robert Moffat (1795–1883), who managed to compose a Tswana version of *Luke's Gospel* in 1830, at a time when the language had not even begun to receive the serious kind of philological attention which was to result in the *Grammar of the Sechuana Language* (1838) of Wesleyan missionary James Archbell, the *Etudes sur la langue Séchuana* (1841) of P.M.S. missionary Eugène Casalis and David Livingstone's *Analysis of the Language of the Sechuana* (1858). Tswana thus became the first South African language to boast translations of scriptural material. Moffat saw the complete Tswana Bible through the press in 1857, but by 1848 he had already printed a translation of the *Pilgrim's Progress*. In spite of this early start, the Tswana language was used solely for religious and didactic purposes until Plaatje issued his translation of *The Comedy of Errors* (1930) and of *Julius Caesar* (published posthumously in 1937). Plaatje's example may have contributed to the emergence of substantive creative writing in Tswana in the late 1930s.

John L. Dube (1870–1946)[15] was a Zulu born in Natal; he attended the American Board Mission school in Amanzimtoti, and was later sent to the United States, where he studied at Oberlin College before receiving his theological training at the Union Training Missionary Institute, Brooklyn. He soon achieved considerable fame and respect among black intellectuals as the founder of the first native educational institution in South Africa, the Ohlange Institute (1901), and of the first independent African newspaper in Natal, *Ilanga lase Natal* ("The Natal Sun," 1903). Although educated Xhosas were the main driving force behind the movement for united political action, for resistance to settler domination and for educational improvement, they wisely refrained from claiming the leading positions in the South African Native National Congress: for the sake of all-African solidarity, John Dube became its first president, and Sol Plaatje was elected to the secretaryship. The difficulties faced by the African National Congress caused Dube to withdraw from overt political activity in 1917 and to concentrate on educational and literary matters, emphasizing the need for unity, co-operation and self-reliance among the Bantu-speaking peoples of the Union.

It is probably significant that, in his sole book of prose fiction, Dube, like his contemporaries Thomas Mofolo and Sol T. Plaatje, turned to the historical novel. This, we may surmise, was an oblique and politically innocuous way of conveying the lessons that the past held in store for the present. In *Insila ka Tshaka* (1933), which was to be translated into English as *Jeqe, the Body-servant of King Tshaka* (1951), Dube contrasts the insane cruelty and tribal imperialism characteristic of the reign of Chaka and his successors, with the later career of Jeqe, who marries outside his own tribe, helps his fellow men through his learning in the art of healing, and, at the end, decisively helps the Swazi defeat the Zulu through the enlightened advice he gives them.

2. Bantu Writing Between the Wars

While Mqhayi was, as it were, a professional literary man in both the oral and the written fields, for Dube and Plaatje literature was only a by-product of a determination to help their people which had vainly tried to find an outlet in political action: once the failure of the African National Congress became obvious they turned to journalism, educational work, translation and creative writing as a slower, more circuitous, but ultimately, as they presumably hoped, more thorough and efficient way, of improving the lot of South Africa's oppressed black majority, by strengthening awareness of and pride in, their own cultural identity.

Two major factors contributed to shaping the orientations of their successors during the period between the two world wars, which coincided with a decisive turn in the general evolution of South African society.

The first factor was the rise to power of the Afrikaner segment of the population and the gradual tightening of policies of segregation. During the first two decades of the century, the Union had been controlled largely by the British-owned mining industry. It was the very growth of industry and the resulting process of urbanization that prompted the Boer element to improve their status. They turned away from their traditional pastoral way of life through better education. They made use of their demographic superiority over the British in order to fight on two fronts: against the power of British capitalism, and against black competition for unskilled and semi-skilled jobs. The double threat cemented Afrikaner unity and led to the victory of the Nationalist party led by General Hertzog in 1924. Though Afrikaner control was by no means as absolute as it was to become in 1948, the new generation of black writers that came to the fore in the early 1920s were deeply convinced of the uselessness, in any short-term view, of armed resistance; protest writing of the kind that had cautiously emerged on the eve of the Berlin conference and had also been practised at times by Mqhayi, was out of the question. While they drew much of their inspiration from the plight of the urban proletariat which had been growing rapidly in the new industrial cities, their Christian training together with a fear of political repression, drove them away from any sort of social analysis in terms of economic forces, and to emphasize the moral responsibility of the individual.

The second factor was the development of education. Admittedly, the educational policy of the Nationalist government aimed chiefly at providing "facilities for industrial and vocational training for whites . . . in an effort to equip poor whites (most of them Afrikaners) with the skills required of them in a modernizing society."[16] As to so-called "Bantu education," it was still mostly in the hands of Christian missionaries of various denominations, often earnestly working to improve the black man's position. While Fort Hare College was fostering the development of a highly educated élite, a few members of which, like the Xhosa novelist A.C. Jordan and the Zulu poet B.W. Vilakazi, were able to graduate at the University of South Africa, a steady growth of literacy led to an increased demand for vernacular reading matter. Mission schools generally did their best to maintain decent academic standards; while the more important local languages were the medium of instruction in the lower grades, English was taught with considerable efficiency: this was later to make possible the emergence of black writing in English on a truly significant scale. Further, "since education for various racial groups was not differentiated, interchange of children was possible . . . Certain schools helped to fuse together people of different languages and customs . . . Most conspicuously, the University College of Fort Hare drew students from all over southern Africa."[17] In 1936, one official report noted that "There still exists opposition to the education of the Native on the grounds that (a) it makes him lazy and unfit for manual work; (b) it makes him 'cheeky' and less docile as a servant; (c) it estranges him from his own people and often leads him to despise his own culture."[18] Translated into slightly different terms, this suggests that education for Africans at the time, such as it was, tended to foster among its graduates a sense of their own dignity, a desire to improve their social status, a determination to overcome the tribal rivalries of earlier times and to become integrated into the new industrial and urban society, and a definite interest in intellectual pursuits.

● ● ●

Southern Sotho literature failed at first to follow this general pattern. Although Lesotho was not part of the Union and thus largely escaped the pressures of segregatory policies, the printing history of Mofolo's *Chaka* shows that many of the P.M.S. missionaries were dismayed at the prospects opened up by independent creative writing: for a while, the Morija press concentrated on publishing devotional works. Further, a severe drought in 1923–24, followed by the world economic depression,

considerably lessened missionary revenue with dire consequences both
for general education and for literary publication. Only one writer of
note emerged during the early 1930s: David Cranmer Theko Bereng
(b. 1900), whose *Lithothokiso tsa Moshoeshoe le tse ling* ("Poems in Praise of
King Moshoeshoe", 1931), are composed in the style of traditional
praise poetry. This trend was later pursued by George Lerotholi, who
composed praise poems in honour of Chief Seeiso Griffith (1940) and
of King Moshoeshoe II (1954). Intimations of renewal appeared when
the Morija press issued Twentyman M. Mofokeng's *Sek'ona sa joala*
("A calabash of beer," 1939), the first formal drama in Southern Sotho,
which deals with the tensions that the modern way of life generates
between old and new.

Another element of diversification intervened, however, with the sudden growth of the Catholic mission that had been founded in 1862. For
a long time, the Catholic missionaries did little to foster the development
of creative writing. But at the beginning of World War II, they seemed
to realize that imaginative fiction could be of considerable help in their
rivalry against the Protestants. The first result was a novel by Albert
Nqheku (b. 1912), *Lilahloane*, an unabashed piece of propaganda for the
Catholic church against both Protestantism and, to a lesser extent, Com-
munism!

•   •   •

Among the Xhosa, while Mqhayi was composing his allegorical novel
U-Don Jadu, a group of younger writers had introduced a measure of
"realism" into Xhosa prose fiction. They included Henry Masila Ndawo
(1883–1949), Enoch Sillinga Guma (1896–1918), Guybon B. Sinxo
(1902–1962), and the first Xhosa woman writer, L. Kakaza. Wheras
Ndawo's fiction was still strongly influenced by the allegorical technique
of *The Pilgrim's Progress*, it is likely that his younger contemporaries were
better acquainted with the English novel of the nineteenth century. Together, they created the basic pattern of the urban novel, which was to
become a *cliché* in South African vernacular prose fiction and drama, for
it appeared as the most appropriate manner of conveying the sorry
plight of millions of black men and women driven from their ancestral
lands and compelled to seek precarious livelihoods as low-paid unskilled
workers in the industrial city slums.

Conditions inside South Africa were not conducive to sophisticated
adult writing, especially as the main outlet for vernacular works was as
reading material for school children. Most of the writers have been
mission-educated teachers, bent on promoting the less palatable among
the Christian virtues, such as forbearance in the face of injustice and
persecution. The Jim-goes-to-Jo'burg theme was a stock situation. Char-

acters were either entirely bad or entirely good, and the ultimate ground of authorial appraisal was the most conventional criterion of morality. The most popular of those slight novels was Guma's *U-Nomalizo* (1918), which was later translated into English as *Nomalizo, or the Things of This Life are Sheer Vanity* (London, 1928), so that it might be used in mission schools all over Africa. It was also translated into Swahili and Ewe. In retrospect, the preoccupation of Guma and his contemporaries with the evils of a society that was enmeshed in a rapid, pitiless process of industrialization now seems very natural, and such mild strictures on the organization of South African society as are contained in their novels sound innocuous enough. Nevertheless, their often gruesome depiction of the disintegration of family life and of the moral decay wrought by the sheer misery of life in the slums was frowned upon even by those missionaries who had done most for the promotion of Bantu writing: the Rev. R.H.W. Shepherd, of the Lovedale press, could not help pointing out that Sinxo exhibited an objectionable tendency "to depict town life with its undesirable features"!

On a definitely higher level of artistic achievement, however, Xhosa writing between the wars was dominated by two important figures, both of whom were Fort Hare graduates: the Rev. J.J.R. Jolobe (1902–1976) and Dr. Archibald C. Jordan (1906–1968).

Jolobe[19] began his literary career at an early age, with a nondescript little tale, *U-Zagula* (1923), to which he had been inspired by the example of Guma. But it was only after gaining a proper knowledge of the Xhosa language in all its purity that he acquired his reputation, primarily as a poet, with *Umyezo* (1936), a collection in which he gave vent to his Christian feelings and at the same time introduced into Xhosa poetry the lyrical description of nature, a characteristic that was absent from the tradition of praise-poetry as practised by oral bards and adapted in writing by Mqhayi. Yet, tradition was not banished from Jolobe's inspiration, and one of his best pieces in the volume is *U-Thuthula* (1936), a short epic romance recounting the internecine rivalries that had contributed to the undoing of the Xhosa in the early nineteenth century. When he published this own English version of *Thuthula* (London, 1938), it became obvious that English influences had been at work, and that the poem was "closely modelled on the narrative blank verse of Tennyson."[20]

Apart from his activity as a translator and an essayist (*Amavo*, 1940), Jolobe later in life contributed to Xhosa drama with *AmaThunzi obomi* ("The shadows of Life," 1957), which takes up the favourite theme of the prose fiction of the 1920s; he also wrote, *Elundini loThukela* ("On the horizon of the Thukela valley," 1959), a historical narrative which takes its place in the tradition inaugurated in Sotho by Mofolo's *Chaka*.

The finest achievement in Xhosa prose fiction so far, however, was not due to Jolobe but to his contemporary Archibald C. Jordan (1906–

1968),[21] whose *Ingqumbo yeminyanya* ("The Wrath of the Ancestors,"
1940) departs from the superficial moralizing of most earlier Xhosa novels in order to provide in-depth imaginative handling of two major problems which African societies and individuals have to face as a result of
the penetration of western ideas and ways of life: the antinomy of modern education versus traditional beliefs and mores, and the equally
preoccupying contradiction between old customs based on polygamy
and the new trend towards individual love and a Christian conception of
marriage. It is also characteristic of Jordan's originality that he located
the action of his novel in a tribal milien, not in the city slums as was
usual, and that he selected, as his main protagonist, an educated tribal
chief instead of relying on the stock characters of the priest and the
school teacher.

In the early 1960s, Jordan went into exile as so many of the black
intellectuals of the country had done or were about to do. Although this
meant that he no longer had any outlet for creative writing in his own
language, his deep concern with Xhosa literature took on a new form,
and he developed his earlier research into the beginnings of Xhosa writing in *Towards an African Literature: The Emergence of Literary Form in
Xhosa* (Berkeley, 1973), by far the best scholarly study of the birth of
written literature in any of the vernacular languages of Africa.

●   ●   ●

Creative literature in Zulu may be said to have begun in
1933, when John L. Dube published the first Zulu novel. Yet the main
impetus to Zulu literature was provided by younger men, contemporaries of Sinxo, Jolobe and Jordan. Curiously enough, although Zululand
had been subjected to British influence and control at a comparatively
late date and after prolonged resistance which was forcibly crushed in
1906, the first piece of prose fiction to be printed in English by a black
writer in the Union was a novella, ambitiously entitled *An African Tragedy*
(1928), by the Zulu author R.R.R. Dhlomo (1901–1971).[22] This, like
Sinxo's Xhosa novels, gave a sombre picture of African life in the city
slums; but it was also highly critical of such traditional customs as the
bride-price. Perhaps because of Dube's example, Dhlomo's further
writing was entirely in Zulu, and consisted in historical novels about the
leaders who had presided over the rise and decline of Zulu power in the
nineteenth century: *U-Dingane* (1936), *U-Shaka* (1937), *U-Mpande* (1938),
and later *U-Cetshwayo* (1952) and *U-Dinuzulu* (1968). In the 1940s, he
reverted for a while to his earlier inspiration with *Indlela yababi* ("The
evil way," 1946), a dramatic narrative of life in the African townships
of Johannesburg.

His younger brother, H. I. E. Dhlomo (1903–1956) was also one of the early black South African writers who wrote in English. *The Girl Who Killed to Save* (1936), staging a crisis that almost destroyed the Xhosa nation in 1857, is the first play in English by a black writer. *The Valley of a Thousand Hills* (1941) is a long elegiac narrative in the Victorian-Romantic manner, contrasting the harmony of nature with the cruelty of colonial urban society.[23]

In spite of the historical interest and popular success of these works by Dube and the Dhlomo brothers, the most gifted Zulu writer to emerge prior to the second World War was Benedict W. Vilakazi (1906–1947),[24] a linguist and a keen student of traditional poetry, who, like his Xhosa contemporary Jordan, had graduated at the University of South Africa. The best of his work is contained in two volumes of poetry, *Inkondlo kaZulu* ("Zulu Songs," 1935) and *Amal'ezulu* ("Zuly Horizons," 1945), where after experimenting none too successfully with European poetic forms, he returned to the traditional manner of oral art which he applied to modern topics, including a moving and justly renowned poem about the plight of the black miners.

Vilakazi also brought a noteworthy contribution to the development of the novel in Zulu. For at the time when Dube and Dhlomo were initiating the historical novel in Zulu, Vilakazi published *Noma Nini* ("For ever," 1935), which, although it takes place in the late nineteenth century, was the first Zulu novel to deal with the moral and psychological problems involved in the inner clash between the new Christian ideals of conduct and the old "pagan" mores. In this, and in Vilakazi's other two novels, *UDingiswayo kaJobe* ("Dingiswayo, Son of Jobe," 1939) and *Nje nempela* ("Truly, Indeed," 1949), the Zulu critic J.S.M. Khumalo has recently objected to faulty character depiction and plot construction.[25] But although it may be true to claim that the flow of the narrative is encumbered by an undue amount of historical and anthropological information, it is also quite possible that to the author this was the core of his message, which he tried to convey more attractively and more efficiently by embodying it in some love story derived, perhaps, from fashionable western interest in such matters.

• • •

During the 1930s, several schemes were devised, both in South Africa and internationally, to promote the development of African vernacular writing. From 1930, the International African Institute provided considerable encouragement to both budding and already established writers throughout black Africa. During the same period, the May Esther Bedford competition brought encouragement and rewards, which were by no means negligible though perhaps financially insignificant, to several South African writers. Prizes sometimes went to senior writers who had already enjoyed a measure of recognition in their own milieu: IAI prizes were awarded to Mqhayi and Tiyo Soga in 1930, to C.T. Bereng in 1931 and to Vilakazi in 1932. Likewise, Mqhayi and Jolobe were recipients of May Esther Bedford prizes in 1935 and 1936. But languages that might have been described as minor at the time were by no means neglected. An interesting case is Tswana, which, by 1930, had only produced Plaatje's translation of *The Comedy of Errors* by way of written literature. Tswana was one of the languages selected for the fourth IAI competition in 1933, and the jury gave a consolation prize to Lettle Disang Raditladi (1910–1971), a Lovedale graduate who was at the time studying at Fort Hare. In 1937, however, Raditladi was awarded first prize in the May Esther Bedford competition for his play *Motswasele II*, which was not printed until 1945. According to Afrikaner critic J.W. Snyman, this pioneering play, which deals with dynastic quarrels among the Bakwena of Botswana, shows evidence of Shakespearian and Victorian influence, especially in the many changes of scene, the use of asides and soliloquies, the resorting to a heightened style in key moments in the development of the action, which, however is purely anecdotal and does not derive from moral conflicts between or within the characters.[26] Later in his life, after publishing a love tragedy, *Dinshontsho tsa lorato* ("The many deaths of love," 1956), and a collection of poems, *Sefalana sa menate* ("A barn of pleasant things," 1961), where he tried to introduce rhyme into Tswana poetry, Raditladi reverted to the history of Botswana in another drama dealing with civil strife and struggle for power, this time among the Bamangwato, *Segkoma I* (1967).

Yet, the first original composition to have reached print in the Tswana language was a collection of poems, Sam S. Mafoyane's *Moretlo* ("A cluster of fruits," 1937), which was published by the L.M.S. mission at Tiger Kloof, where the poet had had his early education together with Raditladi. Mafoyane had attended the conference of African authors convened by R.H.W. Shepherd in 1936 along with such established writers as Jolobe, H.I.E. Dhlomo and B.W. Vilakazi, but although his slender volume was fairly popular and went through several editions both in Botswana and in South Africa, he does not seem to have persevered in his literary career.

While modern poetry and drama in Tswana were thus being created by Raditladi and Mafoyane, another author of the same generation initiated the Tswana novel. Like Raditladi, Davidson Pelman Moloto (b. 1910) studied at Fort Hare, where he obtained his B.A. in 1940. He had been educated in English, but he had learned written Tswana by reading the Bible. In 1937 he completed the first novel in Tswana, *Mokwena*, which, according to his latest biographer, was not printed until 1940 "because he could not find a person who could read and correct it."[27]

It is a historical and ethnological novel, where the writer describes the tribal customs of the Bakwena as well as the training and life story of one of their chiefs. In 1938, Moloto started writing his second novel, *Motimedi* (1953); the title is the name of the central character, but also means "hooligan," and the story describes the plight and demoralization of the young Tswana migrants who leave their homelands for the mines, the slums and the jails of Johannesburg.[28]

● ● ●

The IAI competition in 1935 was the occasion for bringing yet another South African language to the sphere of literary activity: Tsonga. The Tsonga people live in southern Mozambique and in northern Transvaal. In the early years of the nineteenth century they were subjected to the Zulu, but after the destruction of the Zulu empire in the middle of the century, their old language came into greater use. Westernizing influences were introduced among them by Swiss missionaries; one of these, H.A. Junod, gave an account of the Tsonga in *The Life of a South African Tribe*, which was published originally in French in 1898. According to Monica Wilson, it is "the first detailed study of an African people" and "an anthropological classic."[29] Junod was also responsible for two works in Tsonga that were published considerably later: a collection of Tsonga poetry (1940), and a biography of an African minister, John Mboweni (1958). By the mid-1930s, however, only two Tsonga books were in existence: the Bible and a reader prepared by the Swiss missionaries.[30]

The first creative work of Tsonga authorship ever to reach print was therefore *Sasavona*, a short novel which was published by the Swiss Mission Press in Johannesburg in 1938 after gaining an award in the IAI competition. The author, Daniel Cornel Marivate (b. 1897), had studied at Lovedale and was at the time principal of the Swiss Mission school of Valdezia.[31] *Sasavona* is an edifying tale of a kind that, in other South African languages, had by then become almost traditional: as the author's son, Cornelius T.D. Marivate, a lecturer in Tsonga at the University of South Africa, was later to put it, the title heroine "is described as an irresponsible woman who is unable to manage her family in a proper way." Her fate is contrasted with that of a friend of hers, who achieves a modicum of prosperity after accepting the Christian faith. The reviewer concludes by introducing an interesting distinction which was probably not in the mind of the author: "it seems the writer was trying to show how one (a Bantu) could benefit by incorporating Western ways of life into one's life, but *on the contrary*, the writer ended by advocating Christianity" (my italics).[32]

Sasavona was to remain Marivate's sole venture in creative writing,

although he composed both words and music for a number of hymns
that appear in the Swiss Mission hymnal. In the ensuing years he turned
to the ministry, being ordained in 1956, and later became a member of
the Tsonga Language Committee and of the Bureau of Tsonga Literature and Culture which fell under the so-called Department of Bantu
Education. *Sasavona* likewise remained the only modern-type literary
work in Tsonga until the explosion of vernacular writing that was to
take place after the war.

• • •

While these developments were going on in what was then the Union
of South Africa, the vast territories to the north, later (1954–1963) to
be briefly grouped as the Federation of Rhodesia and Nyasaland,
proved sigularly barren of any literate activity. However profitable the
rule of the British South Africa Company may have been to Cecil
Rhodes and to British business, it was certainly not conducive to any
sort of cultural development and emancipation for the local population.
But even before the Company formally took over the administration of
what was then Rhodesia in 1904, the early missionaries had had to face
tremendous hardships and difficulties, partly as a result of the fierce
independence that characterized African societies on both banks of the
Zambezi.

The situation was different in the area of Lake Nyasa (now Lake
Malawi). The existence of the lake was revealed to the western world in
1859 by David Livingstone, who immediately set out to spread Christianity, western civilization, and British influence in this region, which,
at the time, was being exploited by Swahili slave-traders from the coast
and Portuguese merchants from Mozambique.[33] Around 1875, a number of mission stations were set up, chiefly by the (Anglican) Universities
Mission to Central Africa, the Free Church of Scotland and the Established Church of Scotland. Later in the century, these were joined by
the Dutch Reformed Church (1889) and other, smaller Protestant missionary societies. Permanent Catholic missions did not come to Malawi
until the twentieth century.

It has been pointed out that throughout the colonial period Nyasaland
remained a "rather sleepy backwater" because "it had no valuable min-
erals and consequently little industrial development and few European
immigrants."[34] The British South Africa Company did not really try
to bring the territory under its control; the country was granted protectorate status under a system of direct rule in 1891, and the main
purpose of European intervention was to propagate the Christian faith
and to counteract the slave trade carried on from Zanzibar. This is

probably the central reason why "among the slave-raided tribes of Malawi, the Nyanja, Tonga and Tumbuka, the . . . missions were more successful (than, say, among the Ndebele of Southern Rhodesia), for Christian teaching could more easily be grafted on to societies which did not stress military virtues and raiding, but wished to live at peace with their neighbours." As a result of this peculiar situation and of the country's British-protected status, there is probably some truth in the claim which is sometimes made that "in the early years of European rule African education was more advanced than it was in Southern Rhodesia": the Free Church of Scotland mission school, at Livingstonia, for example, "was a great educational centre by 1900 providing primary education and vocational courses and sending out trained teachers to staff the increasing number of small village schools"; "the full primary course lasted ten years, two years longer than in Southern Rhodesian schools." "In 1930 it was estimated that only 6 per cent of the school population had reached the stage of learning English, [but] bright pupils who managed to stay the course to the upper standards found places in the boarding schools at the larger missions. They might then train as teachers or medical orderlies or find comparatively good jobs in government service."

Although the languages of Malawi do not seem to have received anything like the scholarly attention that was devoted to South African languages, by the time the first World War broke out the New Testament was available in several dialects of Nyanja, in Tonga, in Yao and in Tumbuka. Indeed, the Bible had already been translated into Chewa-Nyanja in 1897 by the Reverend Robert Blake of the Dutch Reformed Church Mission.[35] This missionary society was to play a significant part in the emergence of vernacular literature: as early as 1910, a conference held at its headquarters in Mvera passed "ambitious resolutions" towards "working out a publication programme." While these and later similar resolutions failed to bear the fruit that was expected of them because, as one D.R.C.M. member was later to put it, "no Mission or group of Missions has ever had the service of a full-time, literature missionary,"[36] the missionaries were responsible for providing a unified form of Nyanja which could be understood by speakers of different dialects, and the complete Bible was issued in Union Nyanja in 1922. This was the foundation of literary Nyanja, which is the medium used by most Malawi writers nowadays.

Indigenous authorship, however, did not make a start in Nyanja but in Yao: the first local writer on the record was Yohanna Barnaba Abdallah, who was no Malawian, but originated from neighbouring Mozambique; he became a teacher in 1888, and the first priest to be ordained in the diocese of Nyasaland in 1898. While carrying out his priestly activities, he wrote *Chiikala cha Wayao* ("The Olden Times of the

Yao"), an English translation of which was published locally as *The Yaos* (Zomba, 1919).[37]

The early 1930s were a period of considerable progress in the Protectorate as indirect rule was substituted for direct rule in 1933. Literate Africans began to press for better and higher education, and in 1937 the Protestant missions agreed to build a secondary school which was opened in Blantyre in 1939. African influence in local church life, which had declined after the first World War, made considerable progress not only with the appointment of Africans as church leaders in the established missions, but also with the emergence of independent churches such as the Eklesia Lanangwa, whose founder, Charles Chinula, an ordained minister (1925) of the Anglican church, is said to have translated *The Pilgrim's Progress* into Tumbuka as well as composing hymns in that language.[38] The decade saw the rebirth of the national feeling that had prompted the Chilembwe rising in 1915: it is significant that an account of that rebellion was written down in the early 1930s, in idiosyncratic but perfectly understandable English, by George Simeon Mwase (*c.* 1800–1962).[39] The growth of local African associations was ultimately to lead to the foundation of the Nyasaland African Congress in 1944. In 1932, Nyanja was one of the languages selected for the third competition of the International African Institute, and the first prize was awarded to a prose narrative entitled *Mbiri ya Nthondo* ("Story of Nthondo"), by Samuel Yosia Ntara (b. 1905).[40]

A teacher educated in the schools of the Dutch Reformed Church Mission, Ntara had originally composed this fictional biography of an African during the early decades of the colonial regime in the Chewa dialect of Nyanja, before re-writing it in Union Nyanja for the competition. *Nthondo* was first printed on the mission press (Nkhoma, 1933); an English translation by T. Cullen Young was soon published by the Religious Tract Society (London, 1934), with a foreword by no less a scientist than Julian Huxley, who emphasized the "new insight" it would give its readers into "African anthropology, African psychology, African native problems." *Nthondo* was the first piece of written fiction to be produced in British central Africa, and the importance of Ntara for the foundation of Malawi's modern literature can thus be equated with that of Mqhayi for Xhosa, Mofolo for Southern Sotho and Dube for Zulu. Following the example set by R.R.R. Dhlomo in Zulu, Ntara then chose to turn his attention to the history of his own people. After much research, he published *Mbiri ya Achewa* ("History of the Chewa," 1944), which is very popular in Malawi and has gone through several editions.

Returning to biographical fiction, Ntara then wrote *Nchowa* (London, 1949) which tells the story of an African woman and should thus be viewed as a counterpart to *Nthondo*. At the same time, combining the two trends in his earlier writing, he produced an account of the life and times of *Mnyamboza* (Nkhoma, 1949), which appeared almost simultaneously in an English version by T. Cullen Young, bearing the more explicit title *Headman's Enterprise: An Unexpected Page in Central African History* (London, 1949). This fictionalized biography of a Chewa chieftain, who lived from 1830 to 1926 and proved to be an exceptionally innovative leader, has been characterized by B. Pachai as "excellent history, giving an account of a headman's reaction to the forces around him, the forces of Islam, the forces of Christianity, the forces of the white man's administration," and the forces of hostile tribes. What is more important, as the translator pointed out, the story of Mnyamboza peremptorily belied—as did that of Chaka, and as many West African novels in English were to do during the 1950s and after—the widespread prejudice that "individualism, initiative and experimentation are impossible" in the "tribal" societies of Africa.

3. Post-War Developments

The key to the evolution of South African society, and consequently of South African literature, in the last few decades is to be found in the victory of Dr. Malan's Nationalist Party in the 1948 general election. This gave absolute constitutional power to the Afrikaner section of the population, which had been struggling hard for half a century both to wrench control from the British element and to consolidate the total predominance of whites over non-whites. The ruthless, systematic implementation of *apartheid* policy was to have momentous, although exceedingly ambiguous, consequences for the future of black writing.

A major point is that the Bantu Education Act of 1953 put into practice the most basic recommendation of the Commission on Native Education set up in 1949, namely that "all education, except in the case of a foreign language, should be through the medium of the mother tongue for the first eight school years and [that] mother-tongue instruction should gradually be extended upwards to secondary schools and training institutions."[41] The rationale behind this measure was that "the Bantu child" should not be taught more English or Afrikaans than was necessary "to follow oral or written instructions and to carry on a simple conversation with Europeans about his work and other subjects of common interest."[42] But although the real purpose of this aspect of the Act was to achieve a definite lowering of overall educational standards by confining the black child to the limits of his tribal outlook, on the other hand, a fast-growing market was created, almost overnight, for vernacular literary productions—a decisive change, indeed, from the days in 1942 when an educational authority could observe that "the

stimulation of Native authors has now come to the position when more
material is being offered than the market can assimilate."[43]

The immediate consequences of the protection awarded by the new
official policy to vernacular writing were that a number of second-rate
elder writers at last found an outlet for their works; that younger authors, whose talent was not always obvious, started producing a considerable supply of poetry, drama and prose fiction in the three languages
which already had a long-established tradition of imaginative writing;
and that the other four officially recognized Bantu languages—Tswana,
Tsonga, Venda and Pedi or Northern Sotho—were able to start a written
tradition of their own. This trend was of course re-inforced in 1959
when the government passed two acts which purported to reorganize
(in fact, which tribalized) the whole system of higher education. The
University College of Fort Hare Transfer Act turned an institution
which had been a meeting place for all races and peoples, into a Xhosa
University. As to the Extension of University Education Act, while eliminating black students from the previously open universities, it provided
for the opening of a number of tribal institutions that were to be established, in compliance with a 1954 declaration of Dr. Verwoerd, "as far
as possible in the Native Reserves."[44] The University College of the
North, which serves the Sotho-Tsonga-Venda group, was opened in
1959 as was the University of Zululand, which caters for the needs of
Zulu and Swazi students. But the predominance of vernacular languages
was bound to have other, less palatable, consequences.

The evolution of education for Africans up to 1953 had created the
conditions for the emergence of black writing in English on a significant
scale. This development, which had been initiated by Plaatje, the
Dhlomo brothers and others, gathered momentum when a new generation of writers, born in the 1920s, came to the fore, beginning with
Peter Abrahams's *Mine Boy* (1946). But it was not to reach its apex until
the early sixties, when the brutality of the regime, made glaringly obvious in the Sharpeville massacre of March 1960, created a state of
unbearable inner tension, which such gifted authors as Alex La Guma,
Bloke Modisane, Nat Nakasa and a few others, brought to the attention
of the outside world through the medium of creative writing. Harsh
repressive policies led to their being banned and jailed, or seeking the
safety of exile.

As to vernacular writing, the greater part of its audience is made up
of schoolchildren and semi-literate adults. This situation in itself is not
conducive to the elaboration of mature, sophisticated literature of the
kind that had been contemplated by Dhlomo and attempted by such as
Jordan or Vilakazi. But this intrinsic limitation is further compounded
by the watchfulness and comprehensiveness of an alert system of censorship. The nefarious activities of the Censorship Board were codified

in 1963, in the Publications and Entertainment Act, and exercized with increased thoroughness by the Publications Control Board that was then created. Its terms of reference are so all-embracing that no writer can possibly permit himself to deal with either the principles or the realities of South African society in a spirit of serious, not to mention critical, analysis.

• • •

At first sight, the above remarks may not seem to apply to the literature of Basutoland, a High Commission Territory which became the independent kingdom of Lesotho in 1966. Indeed, after its golden age in the early years of the century, and a deep lull between the two world wars, it gathered new momentum in the early 1940s when the emergence of militant Catholic writing prompted the Protestant missionaries to resume publication of imaginative literature. Both denominations thus fostered a new generation of writers who could afford to be rather outspoken about conditions in South Africa, where a large proportion of the country's male population has to seek a livelihood. This was first visible in *Arola naheng ea Maburu* ("Arola among the Boers", 1942), by Albert Nqheku (b. 1912). Yet, Lesotho is a poor, weak enclave inside South Africa, and neither the authorities, nor the authors themselves, nor the missionaries who print their works, can find it wise to go too far in twisting the lion's tail: Lesotho writers prefer to cling to such unobjectionable themes as the glorious past of the nation (the days of Moshoeshoe are still a fountainhead of inspiration), the clash between the old and the educated young within village communities, and the moral evils that await the Sotho migrant in the big South African cities where he must go to try to escape from the poverty of his own country.

The most important change that has affected Lesotho literature in the last decades is of a formal order: drama, which was initiated by T.M. Mofokeng in 1939, was practised in the 1940s by more gifted writers such as Bennett M. Khaketla (b. 1913) and Jac. G. Mocoancoeng. Much writing has been done for the stage since, as several poets and novelists have also tried their hand at drama. It includes historical plays denouncing the traditional evils of witchcraft and polygamy, and psychological plays such as *Boiphetetso* ("Revenge", 1962) and *Ba ntena ba nteka* ("They bore and attract me", 1965), where Mallane Libakeng Maile (b. 1895) discussed "the social problems connected with extra-marital relationships between men and women—married and unmarried ones."[45]

For a long time, Lesotho poetry was dominated by the prestige of traditional praise poetry, whose techniques had been applied in encomiastic works about the country's new rulers by D.C.T. Bereng and more recently, George Lerotholi. A new note was sounded in the nature poetry of Adam J. Selane in *Letlotlo la Mosotho* ("The walking-stick of the Mosotho", 1942), but Selane was not a native speaker of the language.[46] Poetry on a variety of subjects was attempted by Khaketla, who advocated adapting the rhymes and rhythms of English poetry, and especially by Kemuel E. Ntsane (b. 1920), who is chiefly renowned for his satirical outlook.[47]

It should be obvious that the course of Lesotho literature was influenced in many ways by the vicinity of South Africa, the huge number of Sotho migrant workers there, and the symbiosis between them and the population in the homeland. Students of literature in Southern Sotho never attempt to distinguish between those writers that are citizens of Lesotho and those that were born and are living in South Africa. The fact is that the consequences of government policy in the Republic have worked towards a measure of unification and homogenization. This sounds all the more paradoxical as one of the first effects of the Bantu Education Act 1953 was to bar Lesotho students from attending the South African institutions where they had hitherto been in the habit of gaining a modicum of higher education. The ban lost its *raison d'être* in 1959 with the foundation of the University of the North, which is presumably attended by a number of students from Lesotho, even though the Pius XII University College (which had been set up by the Catholic Fathers in 1945 in a place called Roma) was changed into the University of Botswana, Lesotho and Swaziland in 1964.

Meanwhile, however, it was hardly to be expected that writers in Lesotho should be able to resist the allurements of the enormous potential market that had been created by the South African emphasis on the teaching of vernacular languages. Whereas the early works of such Lesotho authors as Maile, Ntsane, Khaketla and others had been printed on the Protestant press at Morija or the Catholic press at Mazenod, their later works were issued by South African publishers in Johannesburg, Pretoria, Cape Town or Bloemfontein: the same motivation was here at work that has prompted the francophone writers of Africa to seek publication in Paris and the anglophone writers in London or New York. It is also partly in order to attain this purpose that Lesotho authors have proved willing to meet the demands of South African censorship in spite of the theoretically independent status of their own country.

At the same time, a new stream of writing emerged as the Sotho community in the towns and rural areas of South Africa, especially in the Orange Free State, began to produce its own writers. A case in point is Attwell Sidwell Mopeli-Paulus who was born in the O.F.S. in 1913 and is thus a contemporary of Khaketla. His first collection of poetry, *Ho tsamaea ke ho bona* ("To travel is to see," 1945), was printed in Morija, but his subsequent writings, mostly slender pieces of prose fiction, appeared in South Africa. Further, the type of education that he had received in Natal and at the University of the Witwatersrand enabled him to do some English writing of his own and to produce two bulky novels, *Blanket Boy's Moon* (1953) and *Turn to the Dark* (1956) in collaboration with native speakers of English. The most gifted writer in Southern Sotho after Mofolo was Sophonia M. Mofokeng (1923–1957), who, like A.C. Jordan in Xhosa and B.W. Vilakazi in Zulu, was one of the first vernacular authors to have benefited by a full university education up to Ph. D. level. His play, *Senkatana* (1952), based on a Sotho folktale which the writer twisted into an allegory of Christ, the short stories gathered in *Leetong* ("On the way," 1954), and the essays published posthumously under the title *Pelong ya ka* ("In My Heart," 1961), testify to his outstanding abilities: his premature death was a major loss to Sotho Literature.

In the Republic as in Lesotho, Sotho novelists have produced a large number of edifying tales dealing with the humdrum themes that appear suitable for the moral education of the young. It is therefore not surprising that local critics should attach more attention to poetry, not only by Lesotho writers like Ntsane and Khaketla, but also by those who came from South Africa, such as James Jantjies Moiloa (b. 1916) and Ephraim A.S. Lesoro (b. 1929).[48] While duly noting that the range of topics has widened considerably since the days when praise-poetry reigned supreme, commentators tend to focus their observations on the poet's command of the language and on the relevance or otherwise of the innovations introduced under the influence of English poetry.

In 1968, B.T. Leshoai (b. 1921) who came from the Orange Free State and had taken his B.A. at Fort Hare in 1957, published *Masilo's Adventures and Other Stories* and a play entitled *The Wake*, which was printed in *New Writing from Zambia*. It seemed as if this might be the harbinger of a new Sotho literature in English of the kind initiated by Mopeli-Paulus. But given the present linguistic conditions in African education, there is little hope that this expectation will materialize in the foreseeable future.

●   ●   ●

Xhosa literature is the oldest in Southern Africa, and the conditions created by the linguistic terms of the Bantu Education Act at first let to a rapid increase in the literary output. A few writers of the older generation at last had their works published in book form: this is equally true of R.M. Tshaka (b. 1904), whose collection of poetry, *Iintsika zentlambo ye-Tyhume* ("The pillars of the Tyumie valley," 1957), is largely imitative of earlier pioneers,[49] of Godfrey Mzamane (b. 1909),[50] whose sole novel, *Izinto zodidi* ("Important things," 1959), has ranked him among the best three or four Xhosa novelists, and of President

Mthetho Ntloko (b. 1914), who wrote some poetry before turning to the
stage in 1961. But the main achievement of the new generation resided
in the development of Xhosa drama.

It is true that the first play of any genuine value was a late work of
J.J.R. Jolobe, *Amathunzi obomi* ("The Shadows of Life," 1958). But this
had been anticipated by Mafuya Mbidlana's *Zangen'iinkomo* ("The Cattle Come In" 1954), a rather mediocre play dramatizing a theme which
is a commonplace in African-language writing, the abuses of the bride-
price. And in the 1920s, Guybon B. Sinxo had composed under the title
Imfene KaDebeza ("Debeza's Baboon") a few school-plays that had fallen
into oblivion until they were reprinted in 1960. This rescue was one of
the effects of the new interest that was prompting several of the younger
authors to write for the stage. Their plays are inevitably moralizing and
often melodramatic. They are usually defective in character depiction
and the handling of the plot. Nevertheless, some critical recognition was
awarded to those of Aaron M. Mmango (b. 1925) and of M.A.P. Ngani
(b. 1932). There is more originality in *U-Manfene* (1962), where the Rev.
L.M. Mbulawa "depicts the intrigue that takes place when a minister of
religion is unwillingly transferred from one circuit to another."[51] But
according to critic S.Z. Qangule, the best Xhosa drama so far is Witness
K. Tamsanqa's *Buzani kubawo* ("Ask my father," 1958), even though
it is based once more on the old conflict between traditional and modern
outlooks.

Tamsanqa, however, is better known as one of the more skilful practitioners of narrative prose fiction, which grew considerably in the late
1950s and early 1960s. This was apparently the result of a definite
change in the tastes of Xhosa readers. Already in 1954, according to the
testimony of R.H.W. Shepherd, fiction, which in earlier days had
seemed to African readers a waste of time, was "the type of literature
most sought after" by African students at the Lovedale library. "This
swing over, he added, may be partly due to the fact that in no African
language has the novel found so prominent a place as in Xhosa."[52]
Unfortunately, it seems that the Xhosa novel, which had made a promising start soon after the first World War, has regressed rather than
progressed since the publication of Jordan's masterpiece in 1940.
Whereas early novelists such as Ndawo and Sinxo had paid great attention to the major social phenomenon of their time, the migration of vast
numbers of tribesmen to the evils and dangers of city slums, S.Z. Qangule notes that most Xhosa works of the latest period, whether novels
or plays, "have in the main a rural setting. This, he goes on, comes as
no surprise since the vast majority of the 2,300,000 Xhosa still live in
rural areas." But it also makes for escapist writing with regard to the
central issues of the black experience in South Africa. Nor do the novelists appear to aim at any imaginative exploration of the rationale of

the traditional life which is their favourite field. One exception, perhaps, is a novel by D.M. Jongilanga, *Ukuqhawuka kwembeloko* ("The snapping of the skin," 1960) which roundly condemns both the father who is intent on getting a brideprice for his daughter in complete disregard of her feelings, and the girl who, after killing her husband, goes to live with the man she loves in equally complete disregard of her father's will and Christian morality. A considerable proportion of Xhosa novels are obviously calculated to denigrate such aspects of customary life as witchcraft and the brideprice. A very common technique, which is ex-emplified in Mzamane's novel, is what might be called the parallel-lives device, where the fate of a thoroughly evil character who plods his way to deserved ruin is crudely contrasted with that of an immaculately blameless character who rightly obtains the material rewards that seem to go with the practice of Christian virtues. This rudimentary pattern is also at work in E.S.M. Dlova's *Umvuzo wesono* ("The wages of sin," 1954) and in W.K. Tamsanqa's *Inzala kaMlungisi* ("The children of Mlungisi," 1954). In compliance with the desire of the apartheid policy makers to confine Africans to their "tribal lands," when not required as cheap manpower in the industrial cities, Xhosa novelists uniformly present city life in the most unfavourable light: an obvious example is *Umntu akanambulelo* ("A person has no gratitude," 1959), by Bertrand M. Bomela (b. 1928). The notion that destitution in the townships leads to crime and murder is once more belaboured in K.S. Bongela's *Alit-shoni Lingenanbaba* ("The sun never sets but something new occurs," 1971).[53]

Absorption in traditional life is especially conspicuous in recent Xhosa poetry, something that is evident in the work of such young authors as L.M.S. Ngcwabe, L.T. Manyase and Michael Huna. They seem to be wholly taken up with narrative and descriptive poetry about the more bucolic aspects of life in the countryside. In 1968, Z.S. Qangule,[54] who teaches Xhosa at the University of South Africa, could not but complain that, "Taken as a whole, it may be said that Xhosa poetry has not as yet produced a person comparable to Vilakazi." This is ascribed to the fact that "Xhosa poets do not seem to try to understand the tragic side of life." Qangule himself did his best to fill this gap in *Intshuntshe* ("A Spear," 1970),[55] where he described poetry as "the messenger of ideas dancing in the courtyard of experience," and J.V. Cantrell has ap-provingly noted the "sound philosophy" in some of the poems, where "the contradictions and compensations of life are finely balanced one against another." Qangule's sense of tragedy finds more adequate expression in his novel *Izagweba* ("Fighting Sticks," 1972)[56] where an African Romeo and Juliet see their love thwarted by hostility between their parents, who are divided into fanatic traditionalists and equally fanatic adherents of modernization; although the young people manage to have their way, they have been unconsciously poisoned by the quarrels between their parents, and this drives them to ultimate estrangement. Obviously, Qangule departs from the usual crude moral outlook and shows deeper insight into the psychological consequences of acculturation: there is little doubt that he is one of the best hopes for the immediate future of Xhosa literature.

•   •   •

Although the Zulu novel did not appear until the 1930s, the 1950s saw the emergence of a gifted novelist in the person of C.L.S. Nyembezi (b. 1919) who obtained an M.A. degree at the University of the Witwatersrand in 1954. The three novels he wrote during that decade— *Mntanami ! Mntanami !* ("My Child! My Child!", 1950), *Ubudoda abukhulelwa* ("A man must control his strength," 1953) and *InKinsela yase Mgungundlovu* ("The squire from Pietermaritzburg," 1961)—are exceptional in African-language writing for the skilful portrayal of the characters. While they do not overstep the limitations imposed by censorship, Nyembezi, who was head of the department of Bantu languages at Fort Hare, resigned in 1959 in protest against the educational policies of the government. His career as a novelist came to an end at the same time, and he henceforth devoted his talent to translating such works as Alan Paton's *Cry, the Beloved Country* into Zulu, and to publishing several anthologies of Zulu poetry, modern and traditional.

Throughout the 1960s, Nyembezi was thus instrumental in fostering the growth of modern Zulu poetry and the emergence of a number of younger poets such as E.E.N.T. Mkhize (b. 1931) and O.E. Nxumalo (b. 1938). But in Zulu writing as in Xhosa and Southern Sotho, the most remarkable post-war innovation was the rapid growth of drama. Actually, the first written drama in Zulu was *UGubudele namazimuzimu* ("Gubudele and the cannibals," 1941), which had earned its author, Nimrod Ndebele (b. 1913) first prize in the May Esther Bedford competition for 1937. But Ndebele's example found no imitators until Leonard L.J. Mncwango (b. 1926) started a successful career as a dramatist with *Mhla iyokwendela egodini* ("The day of going down in the grave," 1951). He in turn was followed in the 1960s by several of his contemporaries, such as Bethuel Blose Ndelu (b. 1927), whose *Mageba lazihlonza* ("I swear by Mageba," 1962) is a historical drama dealing with a dynastic quarrel.[57]

The most widely practised genre, however, remains the novel. *Uvalo lwezinhlonzi* ("His frowns struck terror," 1957) by Jordan K. Ngubane (b. 1919) is a satire on traditional marriage customs; but it is also a historical novel dealing with the conquest of Zululand in the early years of this century and expressing some bitterness at the destruction of Zulu culture, which may be the reason why it was banned for several years in 1962 while the author, who had been assistant editor of *Ilanga lase Natal*, and who had worked closely with Chief Albert Luthuli, was seeking shelter in Swaziland. Like Peter Abrahams and Ezekiel Mphahlele before him, like other Zulu intellectuals such as Mazisi Kunene and Lewis Nkosi, Ngubane in 1967 resigned himself to seek both the safety and alienation of exile in the West, and migrated to the United States. While teaching at Howard University and lecturing on *apartheid,* he turned to English for his next novel, *Ushaba* (1974), which he chose to describe as an *umlando*, i.e., the form of narrative "which the Zulus developed over thousands of years" as a vehicle "for developing the collective wisdom or strength of the family, the clan or the nation," that must control the communal life of the society. In fact, the element of fable is minimal and there is little room for character delineation of the traditional western type. Ngubane is not concerned with individuals, but with the fate of the black community as a totality. He envisions the freeing of the black man from white oppression through the simple device of withdrawing his labor, an essential pillar of the unparalleled prosperity enjoyed by the white ruling minority. *Ushaba,* the title of which signifies the chaotic order imposed by *apartheid,* is one of the most frightening pieces of writing to have been produced by black South Africa. The plight of the black man had been depicted by many black writers, but also by several white writers such as Alan Paton and Nadine Gordimer, and even by Afrikaner authors like André Brink or Breyten Breytenbach. But Ngubane's inspiration is fed by the wells of hatred which Afrikanerdom's ruthless policy of *apartheid* has generated; he has nothing but contempt for what he regards as the ineffectual hypocrisy of the British liberals; unlike the English fiction produced by African writers during the 1950's, the emphasis is not on pathos and hope, but on a fierce determination to come to a confrontation that will give the white man his deserved reward by eliminating him from South Africa altogether.

While Ngubane was thus lost to Zulu-language writing, the decades following the Bantu Education Act saw the appearance of several considerably more prolific, though less "objectionable," authors such as Kenneth Bhengu, who specializes in historical fiction although his latest novel, *Ubogawula Ubheka* (1968) is a story of love and murder set in the present day. Another popular writer is Moses J. Ncgobo (b. 1928), whose first novel *Inkungu maZulu* ("Watch out, Zulus," 1957) won prizes awarded by the Afrikaanse Pers-Boekhandel and by the South African Academy for Arts and Sciences. It is also noteworthy that some Zulu poets have recently turned their talent to the writing of prose fiction. One example is *Ngisinga empumalanga* ("I scan the East," 1969), where O.E.H. Nxumalo tries to strike an imaginative balance between the losses and gains involved in cultural change.

Whereas the greater part of Xhosa writing has a rural setting, modern Zulu literature has its own characteristics. Inevitably, most works, whether novels, short stories or plays, have an edifying end in view. A frequent target is permissiveness in modern education, due to the breakdown of family discipline and to parental impotence and/or indifference in a city environment. On the other hand traditional life is frequently criticised for its brutal authoritarianism, its inhuman customs in connection with marriage and the bride price, and its crude superstitions culminating in widespread use of witchcraft. These are fairly common topics in black South African writing generally. But Zulu literature seems to have two distinguishing features in its choice of themes. One is that the past greatness of the Zulu nation has remained a constant source of inspiration for many of the writers; it is noticeable that the intertribal outlook to which black intellectuals aspire recently found expression in Ngcobo's *Ukufika kosuku* (1969), which narrates a well known incident in the nineteenth-century history of the Xhosa people. Further, the theme of self-help and self-reliance, which was tirelessly preached by J.L. Dube, has left abundant traces in the many success stories describing how virtue and hard work lead to prosperity.

Zulu literature does not seem to have suffered the same lull that has affected Xhosa writing in recent years.[58] In this respect, one of the most prolific among Zulu writers is D.B.Z. Ntuli (b. 1940), who was one the first B.A. graduates of the University of Zululand and is now a language assistant at the University of South Africa in Pretoria.[59] Since his first novel, *UBheka* (1961), he has published two collections of poetry, two volumes of short stories, another novel, *Ngiyoze ngimthole* ("I shall find him," 1970), and *Indandatho yesithembiso* ("The engagement ring," 1971), the first radio play by a black author in South Africa. Unlike Xhosa, then, Zulu has in some ways profited by the new possibilities opened up by the linguistic-educational policy that is a logical consequence of *apartheid*. Whether this increase in quantity has also led to qualitative improvement can only be assessed by native speakers of the language. Unfortunately, the level of literary criticism has become markedly lower since the days when new books were regularly reviewed by competent scholars in *Bantu* (later *African*) *Studies* or in *South African Outlook*. Whereas later South African critics in the Republic show an increasing tendency to base their judgments on formal criteria, it should be recorded that one Zulu writer in exile, Mazisi Raymond Kunene (b. 1930) has voiced a wholesale dismissal of the recent vernacular output which, he claims, "deals with factual situations without drawing any significant conclusions," asserting further that "never in our entire history has literature been so childish, so trite, so aimless."[60] In 1959, Kunene left for exile as another gifted Zulu writer, Lewis Nkosi (b. 1935), was to do in 1961. Nkosi subsquently turned to English and published one play, *The Rhythm of Violence* (1969), and a volume of critical essays, *Home and Exile* (1969). Kunene went on writing in Zulu, composing plays, lyrical poems, and an epic, which cannot, of course, be printed in the original language outside the Republic. He has, therefore, been compelled to produce an English version of his *Zulu Poems* (1970), which give evidence to his considerable talent and striking originality in their use of traditional Zulu concepts and imagery. They also illustrate the tragic plight of the vernacular writer in South Africa, who is barred from using his own natural medium if he refuses to comply with the demands of the police state.

• • •

Of the nearly two million Tswana speakers, a large proportion live in the Republic of South Africa, especially in the Transvaal. Modern Tswana literature,[61] initiated by Plaatje's Shakespeare translations, arose in the 1940s simultaneously in Botswana, with L.D. Raditladi, and in South Africa, with D.P. Moloto. These were followed by Michael O. Seboni (b. 1912), who was born in Botswana, but had his education in South Africa, where he earned his Ph. D. degree in 1958. His first book was a short novel, *Rammone wa Kgalagadi* ("Rammone of Kgalagadi," 1947) whose title character is an ambitious Tswana herdboy who leaves his country for the mines of Johannesburg, refuses to comply with his people's expectation that he marry his cousin, manages to get enough education to matriculate at Fort Hare and eventually becomes a teacher. Turning then to the kind of inspiration that had animated Moloto in *Mokwena,* Seboni gave brief, slighty fictionalized accounts of two Tswana chiefs in *Kgosi Sebele II* (1956) and *Kgosi Isang Pilane* (1961). Apart from these heavily didactic prose writings, his main contribution is to be found in his translations of Shakespeare's *Merchant of Venice* and *Henry IV*.

The last of the elder writers whose work contributed to the formation of Tswana literature is Samson A. Moroke (b. 1912), an ordained Methodist minister from the Transvaal.[62] His first novel, *Sephaphati* (1959) tells the edifying story of a young man who leaves his home for a carefree life in the city: poor characterization goes hand in hand with endless sermonizing, thus setting the tone for all of Moroke's later works, which include two further novels, one volume of poetry, two plays and one collection of short stories, all published in the 1960s.

It was indeed in the 1960s that modern Tswana literature really started blossoming, thanks mainly to an active group of schoolteachers from the Transvaal. According to A.T. Malepe, the best of them is D.P.S. Monyaise (b.1921), whose four novels are said to be "of a high standard," although "his style is so involved that some of his readers

find it difficult to understand his works."[63] To the critic, it is of course
all-important that pioneers of the Tswana novel should handle the language properly. But there also seems to be a significant evolution in the
author's choice of topics. Whereas his first three novels—*Omphile umphi
Modise* (1960), *Marara* ("Creepers," 1961) and *Ngaka, mosadi mooka*
("The doctor and the nurse," 1965)— "depict the sordid side of life"
in the African "locations" of Johannesburg, his later works are indicative of a withdrawal towards tradition, as in *Bobosi kupe* ("Chieftainship
is sacred," 1967), or towards fatalistic phantasy: Monyaise's latest
novel, *Go sa baori* ("Those who sit near the fire get burned," 1970)
"relates a vision the author had while lying unconscious in hospital after
being attacked on his way to a bioscope with a friend;" according to
Malepe, the literal translation of the title is "those who sit by the fire,
burn," or, more generally, "no plan can succeed against the wishes of
the gods or ancestral spirits."[64]

In the mid-1960s, a new generation of writers came to the fore. Their
main representative is Joseph M. Ntsime (b. 1930),[65] whose father vainly
tried to force him to study for the ministry, and whose brother-in-law
was a well-known witch-doctor in his native village. His reading of
Shakespeare during his years of training as a teacher, and the example
of Raditladi, prompted him to write for the stage. His first attempt was
a light comedy, *Pelo e ja serati* ("A loving heart knows no bounds,"
1965), where a chief tries to prevent his son from marrying the girl he
loves, but ultimately gives his consent. Ntsime then turned to his own
experiences as a youth: *Kobo ntsho* ("The black robe," 1968) dramatizes
his relationship with his father, and *Pelo e ntsho* ("A black heart," 1972)
is yet another indictment of witchcraft, a recurrent theme in vernacular
writing: it had just inspired Cornelius Morake in his story *Merwalo a wa*
("Burdens are falling," 1971).[66]

● ● ●

More then ten years had elapsed since the publication of Marivate's
Sasavona when two further works of creative writing in Tsonga were
issued, in 1949, by the Swiss Mission Press, the only printer of Tsonga
works until commercial publishers took over in the late 1950s.[67] One
was a thirty-page prose story, *Murhandziwani*, by Samuel J. Baloyi (b.
1914), who introduced the otherwise familiar Jim-goes-to-Jo'burg motif
into Tsonga writing. A few years later, Baloyi provided a Tsonga prose
version of *Julius Caesar* (1957) and inaugurated original Tsonga drama
with *Xaka* (1958), a lengthy historical play on Chaka, the nineteenth-
century Zulu conqueror. Baloyi seems to have given up imaginative
writing; in 1953 he had translated Booker T. Washington's autobiography, *Up from Slavery*. In the early 1960s, he was asked to re-write

Rivoningo emunyameni ("Light in darkness," 1950), the Rev. Cuendet's account of the activities of the Swiss Mission in South Africa, the language of which left much to be desired; when this revised version appeared under the title of *Rhuma mina* ("Send me," 1965), it was strongly criticized by C.T.D. Marivate on the grounds that the author had "omitted or avoided mentioning the names of the European missionaries concerned."

The other Tsonga work printed in 1949 was a collection of poems, *Swiphato swa xitsonga*, ("Tsonga poems"), by Etienne P. Ndhambi (b.1914).[68] In the early 1950s, Ndhambi produced a prose story, *Mambuxu*, which is very similar in its theme and brevity to Baloyi's "novelette" of 1949. Like the latter, Ndhambi then vanished from the scene of original creative writing; he is now chiefly known as the author of various language and hygiene manuals, of a collection of Tsonga poems for children, and of some occasional poems, one of which won first prize in a praise poem competition organized for the centenary of the University of South Africa.

Obviously Baloyi and Ndhambi had been composing poetry, drama and fiction as a matter of duty and devotion to their own language. The same must be said of Hudson W.E. Ntsanwisi (b. 1920), a teacher with a B.A. degree from Fort Hare (1946), who now teaches at the University College of the North. Like his elders, he gave himself to imaginative writing only during the first years of his career with two short novels, *Masungi, m'fana ka Maxele* ("Msungi, son of Maxele," 1954), which is concerned with the frustrations arising from the clash of cultures, and *Mahlasela-hundza* ("The warriors," 1957), which is autobiographical in character.

It was in the late 1960s and early 1970s that modern Tsonga literature began to gather momentum with the publication of about a dozen volumes in the span of just a few years. These included collections of poems which are either in the traditional praise-poem style, or else betray the influence of romantic and Victorian poetry in natural description and edifying meditation. There were also a few novels, distinguished from their predecessors by being bulkier, but otherwise dealing with the same trite, uplifting themes: F.A. Thuketana's *Xisomisana* (1968) takes more than two hundred pages to illustrate the evils of witchcraft and the advantages of the Christian faith; in a more than commonly plotless "story," *Xikotikoti wa Matshotsho* (1970), the first Tsonga woman novelist, M.A. Mahuhushi, purports to demonstrate that virtue and education lead to prosperity. She was not the first woman writer in the language, however, for a collection of folktales, *Swa rivala a swi heli* ("There are many happenings in the life of today," 1967) had previously been published by Natala Sumbane, who came from the Tsonga of Mozambique, and who had had a collection of stories printed in

German under the title *Lichter im Dunkeln* (Zürich, 1950).

From this fairly nondescript group, two authors emerge, and they have shown more than a passing interest in creative writing. B.K.M. Mtombeni (b. 1926)[69] is obviously interested in experiment. His first imaginative work was a play, *Malangavi ya mbilu* ("Flames of the heart," 1966) portraying the painful consequences of philandering.[70] Next came *Mibya ya nyekanyeka* ("The straps of the baby-sling are loose," 1967), a novel which seemed to start according to the familiar parallel-lives pattern; an unexpected twist occurs, however, when the "good son," who has become a minister of religion, gets involved in an immorality case and commits suicide, whereas the "bad son" becomes "a useful man in the community."[71] While the author manages to show, as one critic has put it "the social changes and maladjustments which result when Bantu people come to live together in the townships," in this case Soweto, it also contains a warning against premature judgments based on a character's external conformity or otherwise to accepted standards of conduct. Mtombeni also experimented with the short story as distinct from the folktale, and obtained several prizes at a festival in 1971 for various pieces of short fiction which were later gathered and published under the title *Ndzhaka ya vusiwana* ("Heirloom from squalor," 1973).

Mtombeni is one of the very few vernacular writers of South Africa who is not a member of the teaching profession. This is not the case with Eric M. Nkondo (b. 1930),[72] who was appointed to head a newly-founded secondary school in Soweto in the early 1970s. As a writer, however, Nkondo is as much of an experimenter as Mtombeni. His literary career began with two volumes of poetry, *Nthavele ya miehleketi* ("The spring of thought") and *Emahosi* ("At the back of the hut"), both of them printed in 1969. While, according to C.T.D. Marivate, "he departed from the praise poem style and writes subjectively," his poetry, written in free verse divided into stanzas of varying length, is characterized by more vivid imagery and greater depth than is common in modern Tsonga poetry. He then produced what has been described as "the best novel in Tsonga" so far, *Tinhlolo ti be mitsatsu* ("The divine bones have erred," 1973), which "depicts the conflict between the Christian faith and traditional customs," and where, thanks to his study of sociology, "he ably portrays the set-up and the functioning of an extended family." At the same time, he ventured into writing for the stage, and his play *Muhlupeki mgwanasi* obtained first prize in the playwriting competition organized in 1973 as part of the centenary celebrations of the University of South Africa.

•   •   •

While creative writing in Tsonga had made its beginning, however

humble, prior to the second World War, modern literature in Northern
Sotho—a language which is also known as Pedi and which is spoken by
about 1.2 million people in the northern Transvaal—did not make a
start until the early years of the war itself. Nevertheless, there had been
a certain amount of authorship on the part of native Pedi speakers for
several decades.[73] While the first collection of Pedi folktales, *Puku e xo
kopantsoexo xo eona ditaba tsa mehuta-huta* ("A book of miscellanies,"
1893), had presumably been collected by the Berlin Lutheran missionaries who did a great deal to further the language, it is on record that C.
Knothe, G. Trümpelmann and H. Kuschke, whose labours resulted in
the publication of the first Pedi Bible in 1904 or 1905,[74] had received
expert help from one of the first Northern Sotho ministers, the Rev.
Abraham Serote (1865–1930), who was also known as a hymn writer.

Indeed, the first full-size book by a native speaker was a biographical
account of Serote, by Epafras M. Ramaila (1897–1962); it was published
in 1935 by the Literature Commission of the Berlin Mission in Transvaal. Ramaila, who had qualified as a teacher in 1915 and was ordained
as a Lutheran minister in 1944, remained until his death the editor of
Mogwara wa babaso ("A friend of the black people"), the newspaper of
the mission. Apart from his teaching and clerical duties, his main interest remained in history until the early 1950s, when he published two
volumes of short stories, *Molomatsebe* (1951) and *Taukobong* (1954), and
a novel, *Tsakata* (1953), in which the writer's didactic purpose is enlivened by a rich vein of humour.[75]

Yet, Ramaila should by no means be regarded as the founder of
Northern Sotho prose fiction. As P.C. Mokgokong has pointed out,
"during the early forties a conscientious attempt at authorship was made
by writers mainly from the Northern Transvaal, such as M.M. Sehlodimela [in *Mělēlwa*, 1940], Moses J.S. Madiba [b. 1909; in *Tsiri*, 1942]
and A. Phalane [in *Motangtang*, 1943], who popularized the 'makgoweng
motif,' i.e. the theme that portrays a youth from the Bantu homelands
who decides to try his luck in the cities, where he is subjected to all kinds
of bad influences and ends up by becoming bad himself."[76] It was
during the same period that the first drama in Northern Sotho, *Maa-
berone* (1940), was written by one of the German missionaries, G.H.
Franz.[77] This example was immediately followed by Elias K.K. Matlala
in *Tshukudu* ("The Rhinoceros," 1941), a verse tragedy based on the
Samson and Delilah story and incorporating praise poems of the author's clan. The decade also saw the appearance of a historical play by
Matlala, *Serogole I* (1948), and of a collection of didatic poems, *Bala o
tsebě* ("Read, so that you may know," 1948), by Sehlodimela.

But, as Mokgokong further notes, "it was only in the fifties and early
sixties that young and enthusiastic writers mainly from Sekhukhuneland
and adjoining areas . . . departed from the theme of urbanization and

detribalization, and crystallized their own culture in their works." In fact, Northern Sotho has since produced more novels and plays than other South African languages. But Mokgokong, who is one of the most articulate among contemporary critics, does not make exaggerated claims on behalf of this comparatively large output: "The majority of novels and novelettes produced by Bantu writers are but a concatenation of events from which a moral is learnt;" the majority of writers are "only superficial" and very few of them "attempt to probe beneath the surface of life;" as to plays, "most of them are of no literary merit" because "many writers are hampered by their ignorance of the require-ments of a drama" and "regard characters speaking their lines as suf-ficient prerequisite for writing a play."

The most influential writer to emerge in the 1960s was Oliver K. Matsepe (1932–1974),[78] whose untimely death was a major loss for Northern Sotho literature. He left behind eight novels, three of which were published posthumously, and six volumes of poetry which, besides the usual lyrical poems, include Shakespearean sonnets and some of the epic verse tales which seem to be a peculiar feature of contemporary Pedi literature. All of Matsepe's novels portray "various facets of tra-ditional tribal life," with special emphasis on the problems of leader-ship and chieftainship, and on "the dissensions and discords among his people: conflicts which occur as a result of the neglect of traditional values which every member of society must uphold." Matsepe thus tried to rejuvenate the themes of the pioneers and to foster a reappraisal of traditional life as a suitable topic for prose fiction.

With his third novel, *Megokgo ya bjoko* ("The harvest of thought," 1969), Matsepe set out to instill modern narrative techniques into North-ern Sotho prose fiction:[79] the story has a complex organization, and is conveyed through the mediation of a narrator who is in a state of almost Brechtian *Verfremdung* with regard to his tale; Afrikaner critic P.S. Gro-enewald does not hesitate to mention Joyce, Döblin and Faulkner in connection with this book. Matsepe's talent for working out the com-plexities of a problematic situation arising in traditional society was fur-ther exemplified in *Letsofalela* ("An unending problem," 1972), which is remarkable for its masterly use of irony.[80]

It is not surprising that Matsepe, with his exceptional inventiveness in devising fascinating cases in the application of customary law, com-bined with his mastery of the language and the sophistication of his narrative technique, should have exerted considerable influence upon his contemporaries. The first female writer in Northern Sotho, Maggie Rammala (b. 1924), after first writing a short novel based on a facile Jekyll-and-Hyde story, *Lukas Motsheletshele* (1963), published a three-act play, *Rangwane ke go paletse* ("Uncle, I have beaten you," 1971), which "depicts a conflict over chieftainship" between an uncle and his nephew;

as in Matsepe's novel, the witchdoctor plays an important part in one of the character's attempts to frame a solution by means outside customary law.[81] And S.P.P. Mminele (b. 1937) introduces a new twist in *Ngwana wa mobu* ("Child of the soil," 1967) where he castigates the xenophobia which is as much inherent in the tribal outlook as is the tradition of hospitality.[82]

Matsepe's example also helped popularize a genre which had been successfully practised by Jolobe in Xhosa, the epic tale in verse. M. Fela's *Sebilwane* (1961) is a case in point, and it seems to have influenced a recent 50-page poem which obtained greater acclaim, *Ga se ya lesaka le* ("It is not this kraal," 1973) by Herbert M.L. Lentsoane (b. 1946). This is a very pathetic story in which a man who has failed in the city comes back to his homeland, marries a widow and, in the cruel extravagance of his male chauvinism, pours scorn and insults upon the latter's child. The main theme of the story is the contrast between the man's male chauvinism and his educated step-daughter, who displays a mixture of rational tolerance and Christian charity; the man commits suicide on the date that she, now a trained nurse, marries a medical doctor.[83]

• • •

The Venda language is spoken by less than half a million people in the north-eastern Transvaal. Its first appearance in print was an elementary 80-page school-reader issued by the Berlin Missionary Society in 1899.[84] For more than half a century, it was to be used solely by missionaries of the Berlin Lutheran Church, especially of the Schwellnus family. In 1913, Th. Schwellnus issued another primer and a collection of Venda folktales. The ensuing decades were chiefly marked by the tireless activity of P.E. Schwellnus: he was responsible for publishing a Venda version of the *Gospels* (1920), to which the *Acts of the Apostles* and the *Psalms* were later added, until the complete Venda Bible appeared in 1936; and he later prepared several series of school-readers: these, according to R. Sh. Dau, "contain a pure form of Venda which sets an admirable standard form of the language." Dau adds that the same cannot be said of the first readers prepared by a Venda author, P.R. Ngwana, in 1958-59. It is probably indicative of Venda backwardness in education and literacy that *The Pilgrim's Progress* was not translated until 1960, and again by a white missionary, E. D. Giesekke.

Meanwhile, however, a few essays dealing with the history, legends, customs and language of the Venda had appeared in 1940 under the sponsorship of the Pretoria government: they were included in an official publication about *The Copper Miners of Musina and The Early History of the Zoutpansberg*. The authors—S.M. Dzivhani, M.M. Motenda and E. Mudau—were presumably teachers who warmed to their task and, in the main, used the language well. In 1941, P.E. Schwellnus edited *Mudededzi II*, a collection of "essays, folk-tales, historical narrations, and a hundred proberbs all contributed by different writers most of whom are Venda." These, however, remained shortlived experiments in native authorship and until the late 1950s, the most important work in the language was G.P. Lestrade's *Some Venda Folk-Tales* (1949), a collection of seventeen traditional stories with English translation. In his introduction, Lestrade acknowledged the help he had received from a local teacher, W.M.D. Phophi, who was later to publish *Phusuphusu dza Dzimauli* ("Civil strike at Dzimauli," 1956), a historical account of his own tribe.

Modern Venda literature was inaugurated in the mid-1950s, when three authors, all of them originating from the Sibasa district, published their first-books almost simultaneously, laying the foundations for the Venda novel and Venda drama.

In 1954, Titus N. Maumela (b. 1924)[85] wrote the first Venda "novel", *Elelwani* ("Remember"), a 60-page story dealing with one of the many conflicts that are likely to arise when personal feeling interferes with tribal marriage customs; the book ends with love's ultimate triumph. Thereafter, Maumela published several short novels, usually based on the clash between tradition and innovation: *VhaVenda vho-Matsivha* ("The Venerable Matsivha," 1958) narrates the trials of a conservative old Venda who refuses the benefits of modern medicine and enters into conflict with the new-fangled ideas of his son. *Zwa mulovha zwi a fhela* ("The past comes to an end," 1963) is directed against witchcraft and polygamy. *Maele we vho-Mathavha* ("Maele, son of Mathavha," 1966) purports to show the need for family discipline and a modern education. In *Musandiwa na khotsi vho-Liwaga* ("Musandiwa and her father Liwalaga," 1968), the title heroine manages to get training as a nurse in spite of her conservative father's opposition; but her difficulties have hardened her character, and she never becomes popular with her patients.

In 1957, Maumela had become the founder of Venda drama with *Tshililo*, which handles the same topic as his first novel, but gives the victory to tribal custom. He did not return to drama until 1974, when he published simultaneously two rather different plays: *Vhuhosi a vhu thetshelwi* ("Chieftainship must not be challenged") dramatizes the unseating of an acting-chief become dictator; *A hu bebwi mbilu* ("Not the heart is begotten") centres once more on generations in conflict.

In the wake of Maumela's early work, E.S. Madima (b. 1922)[86] published his first short novel, *A si ene* ("It is not him," 1955) where he describes how a pair of lovers rush to their ruin on the Rand and in Pretoria.[87] Almost twenty years after this first Venda attempt at depicting the evils of city life, Madima wrote *Maduvha ha fani* ("The days are not the same," 1971), an edifying success story of the common type. His next work was *Ndi vhidza nnyi* ("Whom shall I tell?"), a collection of poems which contains a number of children's songs, some nature poetry, and historical poems of a more traditional character. He also contributed to the development of Venda drama with an unsuccessful play, *Hu na savhadina* ("Beware of Savhadina," 1974).

Another attempt at diversifying the themes of incipient Venda fiction was *Nungo nzi mulomoni* ("Strength is in the mouth," 1958), where P.S.M. Masekela reverses the Jim-goes-to-Jo'burg (in Venda, the *marhuwani*) motif: his hero is a young teacher, born in Sophiatown (Johannesburg), who leaves the city to work and live among his own people. This threadbare topic was to be handled in its pure form in the mid-sixties by W.D. Makamu in *Nyabele muthia-vivho*, ("Nyabele, the jealous one") and to recur once more, some ten years later, in *Tibu ndi khali* ("You cannot tell what is in another man's heart," 1976) by U.M. Ramaite.

It was also in 1958 that M.E.R. Mathivha (b. 1921),[88] who was later to head the Department of Venda at the University of the North, published *Tsha ri vhone* ("Let us see") a 36-page story focusing on the conflict of generations; it is of some interest to note that Dau, while criticising the writer's use of "bombastic and pompous language," also observes that the story is marred by the author's "bias against the Venda proper, and his inclination towards glorifying the Lemba element who live among the Venda." Mathivha was later to bring his own contribution to the drama with *Mabalanganye* (1963), yet another dynastic play, whose title character is "a prince who wishes to wrench away the reins of power from the reigning chief by foul methods," which predictably include witchcraft.

Most of this pioneering Venda fiction and drama is obviously designed by school-teachers for school-children. This is also true of the very small amount of modern poetry that has been produced so far. The initiator in this respect was P.H. Nenzhelele, whose first collection appeared in 1958. Little improvement was brought by a younger writer, R.R. Matshili (b. 1933),[89] whose poems in *Zwiala zwa Venda* ("Medals of Vendaland," 1967), are chiefly about the natural attractions of Vendaland. He later wrote a novel, *Ndo lata* ("I have turned a new leaf," 1971), whose *makhuwani* hero ultimately turns to Christianity as a relief from the brutality of urban life. Nevertheless, it seems that some hope for renewal can be entertained with the publication of *Tsiko-Tshiphiri* ("Secret creation," 1971) by W.M.R. Sigwavhulimu (b. 1937),[90] who, according to Venda critic T.W. Muloiwa, "differs from the earlier poets in that his poems are devoid of any trace of traditional poetry, and, unlike the earlier poets, he does not preach. To him poetry is the most intense and concentrated form of communication," with the result that his anthology has "immensely improved modern Venda poetry."

4. Malawi, Zambia, Zimbabwe

Samuel Yosiah Ntara had been the first writer ever to reach print in the three territories under British control in the basin of the Zambesi. He was a product of the Dutch Reformed Church and had received decisive encouragement from the IAI competition. Yet, this promising beginning had no follow-up for some twenty years, and when vernacular creative writing arose in the 1950s it was as a result of a process that was entirely different from whatever had taken place in neighbouring South Africa.

Although they were to be brought together into a single federation for a brief period, the three territories differed greatly in their history, and in their colonial status. Nyasaland had been opened up to European penetration in the middle of the nineteenth century by David Livingstone and other Scottish missionaries; it was given protectorate status in 1891. Both Southern and Northern Rhodesia were conquered by Cecil Rhodes in the 1890s, and were administered by his British South Africa Company until 1923. When the Company's rule came to an end new constitutions had to be drawn up: Southern Rhodesia was formally annexed as a colony of Great Britain, and, following a referendum conducted among her sizeable white minority, she was immediately given responsible government under the Crown with a legislative assembly of thirty elected members. Northern Rhodesia, on the other hand, "became a British Protectorate with a typical Crown colony type of government":[91] her legislative council consisted of nine official members, and five unofficial members representing settler interests. In 1945, a Central African Council composed of the governors of the three countries was formed. This was a prelude to the constitution of the Federation of Rhodesia and Nyasaland (1953) which was achieved in the face of stiff African opposition, whereas the Southern Rhodesian whites accepted Nyasaland as the price for gaining control of mineral-rich Northern Rhodesia. Widespread black protest broke out at the end of the decade, led by Hastings Kamuzu Banda in Nyasaland and by Kenneth Kaunda in Northern Rhodesia. In 1964, both Malawi and Zambia became sovereign states. After the failure of protracted negotiations with the British government, Rhodesia made her Unilateral Declaration of Independence (UDI) in 1965, with the white minority in complete control.

• • •

By the time Malawi's Ntara had gained a measure of local fame, a new development occurred in Northern Rhodesia which, in retrospect, appears to have been important for the emergence of vernacular literature in both Northern Rhodesia and Nyasaland. In 1937, the Government of Northern Rhodesia set up an African Literature Committee which was jointly administered by representatives of the Government, the missions, and literate Africans.[92]

Like the Zaria Literature Bureau that had been created in Nigeria a couple of years earlier, this testified to official approval of and support for the intensive campaign for literacy emanating from missionary, educational, and scholarly circles in the early 1930s. During the first years of its existence, the Committee was very active: it prepared a programme of publications in the four official vernaculars of the country; it drafted plans for a publications bureau, which had to be postponed because of the war; it held a literary competition for African authors and received thirteen manuscripts.[93]

Of course, the Committee was not primarily concerned with the promotion of imaginative self-expression, but rather with the provision of educational reading-matter, textbooks, and handbooks, and translations of English classics. Nevertheless, the yearly competitions provided real encouragement to African authorship: the entries for 1946 were in English and in nine local languages, including Bemba, Lozi and Tumbuka; according to the Committee's report, "the largest number dealt with tribal history, customs and proverbs, the next largest group dealt with the modern world and public utilities";[94] second prize went to a narrative in English, *The Lonely Village,* by Andreya Sylvester Masiye (b. 1922): it was printed in London in 1951, and its author was later to become known for further works both in English and in Nyanja. By the late 1940s, a Literature Bureau had been set up under the Education Office on the recommendation of the African Literature Committee.

Meanwhile, in both missionary and government circles, interest in vernacular literature, had been reawakened in Nyasaland. In the years following the end of the war, the Nyasaland Christian Council appointed a Literature Committee which was backed by the International Committee of Literature for Africa: it started a series of Africa Home Library translations, and it organized a competition for biographies of Christian African leaders by African authors. In the late 1940s, a Nyasaland Book Committee was appointed by the government. It was soon felt that co-operation with Northern Rhodesia should become "more formal and thereby more effective", and in 1948, the Literature Bureau of Northern Rhodesia officially became the joint Northern Rhodesia and Nyasaland Publications Bureau, which was to split apart after independence.[95]

As Nyanja is spoken by about 1.7 million people, not only in Malawi but also in eastern Zambia, it is not surprising that the very first piece of imaginative writing to be issued under the imprint of the joint Bureau should have been a 46-page "novelette" in Nyanja, *Nthano ya Tione* ("The story of Tione", 1947), by Ned B. Linje. Very soon, however,

British and South African publishers became interested in the potential
market for reading-matter in Nyanja, and many Bureau publications
were issued in association with such foreign firms as Macmillan, Longman, or even Shuter and Shooter in Durban, while the Oxford University Press printed *Ukawamba* ("Resentment", 1953), a novel by Lester
L. Nkomba (b. *c.* 1926). Nyanja writing gathered considerable momentum in the 1960s, both before and after independence. Most of the
Bureau's publications, in Nyanja, or indeed in any other local languages, consist of very short pieces of prose fiction running from 25 to
50 pages. Designed chiefly for school-reading, they carry such unso-
phisticated titles as *Nkhani za Aonenji* ("The story of Aonenji", 1959)
or *Mbala imodzi yacifundo* ("A generous thief", 1963), both by P. P.
Litete (b. 1928), who later produced a story of love and marriage, *Mkwa-
tibwi Wokhumudwa* (1965). One of the more prolific writers is J. W.
Gwengwe (b. 1930), a school-teacher who was appointed publications
secretary after independence. While most of these slender pamphlets
merely aim at telling a pleasant or thrilling adventure story, some of
them seem to be beginning to tackle the larger issues: *Chakudza* (1965),
by Z. P. Kamende (b. 1929) deals with the generation gap between a
traditional old man and his modern grandchildren. Whereas no poetry
appears to have been printed in Nyanja so far, some attempts at playwriting were made, most notably by S. A. Paliani with *Sewero la mlandu
wa nkhanga* (" The guinea-fowl play", 1952) and by C. C. J. Chipinga
with *Atambwali sametana* ("Cockerels never give each other a haircut",
1961).

Due to the vagaries of frontiers drawn to suit the interests of the
colonizers without regard to the population concerned, there is also a
sizeable minority of Nyanja speakers in Zambia, which has produced
two Nyanja writers. Andreya S. Masiye (b. 1922), who had initiated
Zambian creative writing in English in 1951, later turned to his native
language with a collection of short stories, *Tsoka ndi mwai* ("From sadness
to happiness," 1962), before reverting to English in his novel *Before
Dawn* (1970) which deals with cultural conflicts in a traditional village in
Eastern Zambia. Another Nyanja writer who appeared in Zambia in the
sixties is Jacob Nkosini Zulu (b. 1937) with two "novelettes", *Zomfula
nkazi wacimaso-maso* ("The girl who was never satisfied ", 1961), and
Cibwana ndi ukwati ("A teenage marriage", 1962).

It is surely significant that Daniel P. Kunene, in perhaps the most important essay written concerning mother-tongue literature from Zambia
and Malawi, should have selected four Nyanja writers from Malawi as
prominent examples of what he takes to be the major defect of much
vernacular writing: the fact that it usually appears as an exercise in self-
devaluation. In such stories as A. Mondiwa's *Mfumu Chilembwe* ("Chief
Chilembwe", 1951), Josiah Phiri's *Kalenga ndi mzace* ("Kalenga and his

friend", 1957), Henry Kadondo's *Mtima wa Mfumu Kalanzi* ("The heart of chief Kalanzi", 1958) and Andrew Dani Mvula's *Cosadziwa, mwana wosamvera* ("Cosadziwa, the disobedient child", 1962), Kunene vigorously denounces the sycophantic attitudes towards the white man, his power, his technology and his religion, the ritualistic, unquestioning acceptance of Christianity, and a mixture of self-abasement and inconsistency in their descriptions of African beliefs and mores.[96]

The first book of indigenous authorship in Tumbuka—a language spoken in northern Malawi, but also in eastern Zambia—seems to have been A. D. Mbeba's *Ku Harare* ("Journey to Southern Rhodesia", 1950), which was printed by the United Society for Christian Literature. In 1957, the Northern Rhodesia and Nyasaland Publications Bureau issued the first piece of creative prose fiction in Tumbuka, a 12-page story entitled *Mankhwala pa nchito* ("Medicine at work") by Desmond Dudwa Phiri (b. 1931). Although a few other Tumbuka writers have emerged since then, Phiri remained the most prolific representative of the language in creative writing until 1968, when he turned to English. The late sixties were the time when Malawi literature in English came to the fore with such novelists as Aubrey Kachingwe (b. 1926), David Rubadiri (b. 1930) and Legson Kayira (b. *c.* 1940). Phiri joined their ranks with a play, *The Chief's Bride* (1968), which had first been performed two years earlier in Dar es. Salaam, where the author worked as a civil servant. Tumbuka writing is also represented by one Zambian author, L. K. H. Goma with *Ngoza na Kasiwa* ("Ngoza and Kasiwa", 1962).

But Zambia is a country of over fifty languages. Besides Nyanja and Tumbuka, small-scale beginnings were made in several very minor languages. Creative writing in Luvale was started in 1955 with brief stories by John O. Chikasa and K. J. Manuele; in Tonga with M. C. Mainza's *Kabuca uleta tunji* ("Every day brings something new", 1956); and in Lenje with Stephen Luwisha's *Mukulilacoolwe* ("You have survived by luck", 1962). It is worth noting that Kunene gives special praise to Tonga novelist L. M. Mwinga's *Nyoko ngumwi* ("You have only one mother", 1967), a quest story which he compares most favourably with Mofolo's *Moeti wa bochabela* because "Mofolo's belief in the Christian God represents a separation from his origins and thus makes him a preacher who sermonizes to convert the unconverted, whereas Mwinga's belief in the Ancestral Spirits, being a revalidation of a faith which is taken for granted, demands of him no such sermonizing."

Yet the two major languages in Zambia are those of the people that had wielded substantial power before they were overcome by the British conquerors: the Bemba of northeastern Zambia and the Lozi of western Zambia. As noted by Daniel P. Kunene, modern Bemba writing was inaugurated by Stephen A. Mpashi with *Cekesoni aingila ubusoja* ("Jackson becomes a soldier", 1960), a story that extended to 100 pages. This was accompanied in the late fifties and early sixties by several shorter narratives, as well as collections of folktales and proverbs and even—a rather rare occurrence throughout the then Federation—a volume of poetry, *Amalango* ("Poems", 1962), in joint authorship with Joseph Musapu. Two of Mpashi's novels have been singled out by Kunene as belonging to the relatively small category of African language works that do have "very high quality": *Uwakwensho bushiku* ("He who leads you through the night", 1955) is "the story of a man who clears his prospective brother-in-law from a charge of murder"; greater topical interest attached to *Uwauma nafyala* ("He who beats his mother-in-law", 1955), "the time setting of which " Kunene also states,"is the period just before the creation of the Federation of the Rhodesias and Nyasaland, showing popular African opposition to the idea of federation, and an atmosphere of mutual suspicion and distrust owing to the existence of informers."[97] As the most prolific writer in Zambia, Mpashi was called upon to head the Zambia Publications Bureau soon after independence. Among the Bemba novels that have appeared since, *Sheli* (1961), by W. B. Chilangwa, is a humorous story about the picaresque adventures of a boisterous young man who disguises himself as a girl until finally his own uncle falls in love with him. And Kunene has some praise for "a passionate love story" told by Edward Kabonga in *Ako usuulile* ("He whom you despise", 1968).

Lozi writing began in 1954 with *Liswanelo za luna kwa lifolofolo* ("How not to treat animals") by M. M. Sakubita (b. *c.* 1930), soon followed by a collection of poems, *Lifasi la luna fasi la Bulozi* ("Barotseland, our native land", 1956) by E. N. Kamitondo, and the first play in Lozi, *Milelo ya lifolofolo* ("The animals' plans", 1957), by Kwalombota Mulonda. Kopanu Mushashu's *Muloi wa Mbeta* ("The queen of Mbeta", 1957), "a legend created by the author around an island on the Zambezi river", deserved to be listed by Kunene among the half dozen Zambian novelettes worthy of serious consideration and went through two further editions over the next ten years. The most important writer of Lozi origin is Fwanyanga Matale Mulikita (b. 1928), even though he has only published one short tale in his own language, *Batili ki mwanaka* ("No, this is my child", 1958), turning later to English for his play *Shaka Zulu* (1967).

In the late 1960s, two important events affected the course of Zambian literature. In 1967, the work of the Publications Bureau was taken over by the National Educational Company of Zambia (NECZAM), which was established as a subsidiary of the Kenneth Kaunda Foundation "to act as the Foundation's publishing arm in its commitment to Zambianise the production and distribution of educational books." Professional help and advice was initially provided by Macmillan, who held a minority interest in the company until the latter was entirely controlled by the

Foundation in 1974.[98] NECZAM published in ten languages, and although some two thirds of its 100 new titles each year were concerned with primary education, its general list included a sizeable proportion of prose fiction, drama and poetry. There is little doubt that this provided a great boost to literary production in Zambian languages, which had already reached significant proportions. On this local output, however, very little information is available to the outsider. The economic crisis of the mid-seventies plunged NECZAM into deep financial trouble resulting in an inevitable curtailing of its publication programme, especially for such books as do not have a specific educational purpose. Indeed, after August 1975, and for a long period, no further books were published by NECZAM, "for the simple reason that printers had refused to undertake new work, or in some cases to supply completed work, until outstanding debts had been honoured."[99]

Among their last publications in 1975 were several "novelettes" in Bemba— *Nkobekela tecupo* ("Betrothal is not a guarantee of marriage") by R. M. Kambole, and *Noko nkalolakaya nalyo,* which has been described as a tragic revenge story, by R. M. Kapindula—and in Nyanja: A. U. Mwale's *Cimwendom'mphako* ("A big leg in a branch of the tree"), and D. M. Thunde's humorous novel *Kamtigidi.*

Meanwhile, in Zambia as in Malawi, a new trend was making rapid headway, as writers increasingly turned to English, which provided a more efficient channel of communication with the outside world. A. S. Masiye's example in *The Lonely Village* (1951) thus came to fruition when other vernacular writers adopted English. This should probably be viewed as part of an official policy designed to overcome the tremendous problems inherent in a multilingual state by spreading knowledge of English generally: in 1965, the Zambian government decided to adopt English as the medium of instruction in all primary schools to replace the seven officially approved local languages that had been in use so far.[100]

But literary conversion to English was also a manner of emulating a movement initiated in the mid-1960s by a new generation of Zambian authors: in 1964, the self-styled "New Writers Group" launched a literary magazine, *New Writing from Zambia.* At that time, South African writer Ezekiel Mphlahlele, who had done so much for the promotion of English writing in Nigeria and in East Africa, was lecturing at the University of Zambia in Lusaka, and he was undoubtedly influential in fostering the creation of the Mphala Creative Society, whose own literary and cultural magazine, *The Jewel of Africa,* circulated its first issue in 1968. It was probably as part of this general trend that older vernacular authors resorted to English: it was in English that Lozi writer Mulikita wrote his play *Shaka Zulu* (1967) and his collection of short stories, *A Point of No Return* (1968); Nyanja writer Masiye reverted to English in

his novel *Before Dawn* (1970) and in his play, *The Land of Kazembe* (1973);
and it was in English that Bemba writer Stephen Mpashi wrote his biography of the Zambian President's wife, *Betty Kaunda* (1968). At the same
time, there emerged a pleiad of younger authors whose chosen medium
is English, and who found a ready outlet in the literary magazines and
through NECZAM. It can be safely assumed that their ultimate purpose
is to reach an international audience through publication in London,
something already achieved by Dominic Mulaisho (b. 1933) with his
novel *The Tongue of the Dumb* (1971).

In 1971, Jahn's *Bibliography of Creative African Writing* could list 49
titles for Zambia and 35 for Malawi, all but half a dozen of which were
in indigenous languages. Since then, the proportions have been changing fast; inevitably, English writing gains far more attention, scholarly,
and otherwise, than does vernacular writing.[101]

No balanced picture can be obtained of the literary history and the
literary situation in those two countries until writing in their indigenous
tongues has been studied and discussed with far greater care than has
been done so far.

• • •

As was the case throughout the British Empire, the two main languages of Zimbabwe were reduced to writing by Protestant missionaries
at an early stage in the colonization process. The European conquest
did not begin until the last few decades of the nineteenth century, but
Matthew's Gospel was translated into Ndebele in 1884, the Shona *New
Testament* was printed in 1907, and an Ndebele version of the *Pilgrim's
Progress* appeared in 1913.[102]

For reasons which have not yet been properly investigated, missionary
enterprise did *not* lead—as it did at the time among the Zulu and, to a
much lesser extent, in Malawi— to the gradual, organic growth of native
authorship. In this country—which from 1924 to 1964 was known as
Southern Rhodesia—as in Zambia, the birth of creative writing in African languages was mainly an outcome of government initiative: swift
advances in education during the first post-war decade had created a
situation which George Kahari has described as "Literacy without Literature." In order to meet the acute need for follow-up reading matter, the Southern Rhodesia African Literature Bureau was established
in 1953, its main objective being not only to "promote the reading
habit", but also to "encourage, assist, and advise local authors" in
Shona and in Ndebele. In the words of George Kahari, "the Literature
Bureau is a government department and it works in close contact with
the Ministry of Education. In this way the Bureau is not only the pro-
moter of the 'liberal arts', but also forms part and parcel of the ed-

ucational system of the country. Books published by the Literature Bureau tend to be widely read by African school children. Because an author is aware of the immaturity of his readers, he is often very explicit in his plot." In Zimbabwe, as in other countries where similar conditions prevail, "the length of the novel has been affected by its reading public. If a novel runs to more than 150 pages, publishing and printing become expensive and the reading public, especially school children, cannot afford to buy it." Nevertheless, the length of novels has increased since the Bureau's first publication in 1957. But most works have an overtly edifying theme: "this moralistic approach, apart from being traditional, appears to be related to the fact that most of these authors, at one time or another, have been trained as teachers."[103] A few of them are Protestant ministers or Roman Catholic priests. Despite its late appearance on the African literary scene, Zimbabwean writing is better known than that of Malawi and Zambia. This is due to a collection of essays, *African Literature in Rhodesia* (1966), edited by the Publications Officer, E. W. Krog, and also to the systematic analytical work undertaken at the Department of African Languages of the University of Zimbabwe (founded in 1957). It is noteworthy that the first book-length monograph on an African language writer to have been published was a study of the Shona novelist Patrick Chakaipa, produced by the previously mentioned Zimbabwean scholar, George Kahari. Ndebele writing is less extensive than Shona, for there are only about 600,000 Ndebele speakers as against 3.5 million for Shona; further, Ndebele is closely related to Zulu, and Zulu was the medium of instruction in the schools of Matabeleland until 1968, when it was replaced by Ndebele. Nor has Ndebele writing benefited from the same kind of learned attention that Shona received. From what scant information is available, however, it seems that it shares many of its characteristics with Shona, so that both literatures can be discussed together.

The first piece of imaginative writing issued by the Bureau was a short historical novel, *Feso* (1956), by Shona writer Solomon M. Mutswairo (b. 1924), a Fort Hare graduate.[104] While attending secondary school in Natal in the mid 1940s, Mutswairo had read R. R. R. Dhlomo's Zulu novel *U-Shaka*, which prompted him to compose a similar work in his own language. The action of *Feso* takes place in the eighteenth century and deals with the (probably legendary) invasion of the Vatapa people into the historical Rozwi kindgom which had destroyed the power of the Monomotapa empire shortly before 1700.[105] Mutswairo's purpose was simply to experiment with a narrative structure unknown to his own tradition, and to revive, as vividly as he could, the memory of the past of his nation: he had no intention of conveying hidden, subversive meanings. But with the growth of black nationalism in Rhodesia, this story of invasion and oppression appeared as an imaginative correlative to the

colonial situation, and the book itself as "a subtle tract of protest and call
for liberation." Several passages were recited in public gatherings, especially the lament of the vanquished tribe:

How far will the tyrants go?
In every house and every Village
Our people are being pulled out and punished;
In every place and every court
Where they are accused, they are treated like flies,
Killed without reason— without an honest trial.
Today all the wealth of the land has been taken.

Today they are eating all the fat of the land
And we are reduced to eating the pus of our wounds
Today they are as fat as pigs.
And we are lean as diseased dogs.
Today they live in willful freedom,
And we are gagged, strangled with bindings. [106]

In 1964, when the novel went through a second edition, George Kahari
could dryly observe that this poem was "the only politically inspired
praise song ever to be found in a book circulated by a Government
Department."[107] When the Rhodesian authorities at last became aware
of this, they decided to move against this dangerous work which they
had stupidly been unwise enough to publish and no further printing was
allowed nor the use of the text in schools continued."[108]

Soon after the Shona novel had made its appearance, modern Shona
poetry emerged in its turn with the publication, by the London School
of Oriental and African Studies, of *Soko Risina Musoro* ("The Tale without a Head", 1958) by Herbert W. Chitepo (b. 1923), a lawyer who
graduated in Fort Hare and who was later to move to Tanzania. This
symbolic-epic poem in three cantos illustrated, in dignified allusive
verse, the confusion of the thoughtful contemporary African (the Wanderer) in the country's apparently hopeless situation (represented by
drought and famine); observing the divergent paths of those who seek
to preserve the native beliefs and customs (the Councillor) and those
who find spurious happiness in submitting to what they believe to be
the claims of the future (the Rogue), he reaches the fatalistic conclusion
that "we are all wanderers in the land, we follow a new road which has
no parallel in the past for them that go onwards. Let us walk and be
humble in the darkness which is before us whither we go, the darkness
which is behind whence we have come. God alone is the light."[109]

Such fatalistic confidence in the workings of the deity is conspicuously
absent from the work of Wilson Chivaura (1927–1968), several of whose

poems were printed, together with some traditional poetry and a few poems by Mutswairo, in *Madetembedzo* (1969). Chivaura is obsessed with the transitoriness of things and the inevitability of death, and the only relief in his poetry is to be found in the imaginative recreation of an unspoiled, bygone, past.

For several years the official policy of the Central African Federation was one of "partnership" rather than *apartheid*. To many white Rhodesians, partnership" must have been an unnatural notion. To others, it was probably just a useful contrivance to help them weather the winds of change that were sweeping over black Africa. But in the field of poetry at any rate, the ideal of partnership did produce a measure of co-operation between Rhodesian writers, black and white. Though no one would expect the sturdy settlers of Rhodesia to have produced a numerous progeny of delicate Petrarchists, there had been no dearth of poets and versifiers, whose most significant work had been first gathered in J. Snelling's *New Anthology of Rhodesian Verse* (1938). In 1952, the Salisbury Poetry Society, which had been founded two years earlier, started producing its own magazine, *Rhodesian Poetry*. For a long time, contributions all came from white poets. As N. H. Brettell commented in 1961, "A voice one misses is that of the Rhodesian African. To look for English poetry from him yet is perhaps to expect too much." [110] Yet the issue of that year contained one poem by Dumo Ngcwabe who, it must be admitted, had fallen into the trap defined earlier by Norman H. MacKenzie, as producing "verse spiced for the English market with the sounds and sights of Africa—and possessing no solid nourishment." [111] Later issues, however, were to include several Shona poems in the English versions provided by their own authors, such as Henry Pote (b. 1939), who had graduated at the University College of Roma in Basutoland. But it was also in 1964 that two initiatives were taken which, unfortunately, do not seem to have led to any long-term developments. First, a few white Rhodesian poets availed themselves of their international connections to introduce their black colleagues to a wider audience than they could hope to reach in Rhodesia. So it was that Philippa Berlyn published translations of several Shona poems, especially by Gibson Mandishona, in a special Central African issue of *Poet*, a little magazine published in Madras.[112]

The second initiative was the launching of *Two Tone*, "a quarterly of Rhodesian poetry", followed in June 1968 by *Chirimo*, "a thrice yearly review of Rhodesian and international poetry." Both complied with the inflexible rule that poetry magazines are bound to be ephemeral, but they testified to a commendable effort at interracial co-operation, printing both originals and translations of several poems, publicizing Shona poets already established, and introducing an Ndebele poet, Ndabezinhle Sigogo (b. 1932). The same multiracial, multilingual outlook characterized D. E. Finn's anthology *Poetry in Rhodesia–75 Years* (1968).[113]

It was not until 1969 that the Bureau issued the first anthology of Ndebele poetry under the title *Kusile mbongi zohlanga* ("The dawn of Ndebele poets"), although at least one "Ndebele booklet of poems", entitled *Imbongi zalamhla layizolo*, was in existence in the early sixties:[114] it contained some early poems by Ndabaningi Sithole (b. 1920), an ordained priest and already a prominent nationalist leader, who was condemned, in the same year, to six years hard labour.'

While Zimbabwe is rather exceptional among the former members of the Central African Federation in having produced a sizeable amount of modern poetry fully deserving of serious consideration, the most popular genre, in Shona as in Ndebele, is the novel.[115] Its leading—and also, thanks to George Kahari, most widely known—practitioner is Patrick Chakaipa (b. 1932), a Roman Catholic priest, who was to become the first black bishop of Salisbury. Between 1958 and 1968, he wrote five of the twenty-six Shona novels that had appeared by the end of 1971. As Kahari has pointed out, Chakaipa's inspiration passed through three distinct stages which are indicative of the themes and scope of black Rhodesian prose fiction in general. His first two novels take place entirely in pre-colonial Shona society: like Mutswairo's *Feso*, his *Karikoga gumiremiseve* ("Lonesome Karikoga", 1958) blends the fantasy of the folktale tradition with a realistic picture of warfare between Shona and Ndebele; *Pfumo reropa* ("The spear of blood", 1961) depicts the functioning of the old society, with strong emphasis on the ills that can result from a bad chief's abuse and misuse of his sacred power. A second stage is apparent in *Rudo ibofu* ("Love is blind", 1962), which focuses on the antagonism between Christianity and tradition: the heroine has to overcome both her family background and her love for a Christian young man in order to fulfil her true vocation and become a nun. With *Garandichauya* ("I shall return", 1963), and *Dzasukwa Mwana-asina-hembe* ("Dzasukwa Beer-for-Sale", 1968), Chakaipa turned to the problems of modern urban life and the impact of the new money economy on a people used to a subsistence economy: the disappearance of the community sense, the hankering after material rewards, the dissolution of family life, the addiction to greed, sexual promiscuity, prostitution, and alcoholism.

Chakaipa's work thus illustrates the three main categories of the Shona novel, which Kahari has defined in terms of their setting.[116] A number of Rhodesian novels have an entirely rural setting; they often deal with the pre-colonial past which they try to recreate; some of them offer a critical assessment of the traditional way of life. In a second category, the story passes from a rural to an urban setting, thus enabling the writer to bring out the nature of social change due to the effects of rapid urbanization. Finally, the very scope and depth of this process results in an increasing number of tales that take place entirely in an urban setting, mostly throwing into sharp relief, as do South African stories of the same type, the moral and social evils of city life.

The last two categories are obviously particulary suitable for the imaginative handling of cultural interaction, the main theme of most African writing; but in several cases, an attempt is made at reconciling the apparently discordant values of tradition on the one hand, and of education and Christianity on the other. Such an attempt is exemplified in the first "novelette" of Paul Chidyausiku (b. 1927), *Nhoroondo dzoku- wanana* ("The way to get married", 1958), where the author tries to construct an ideal model for a contemporary African courtship. While the starting point is personal feeling of a modern, individualistic type, all negotiations are conducted bgtween the two families in full compliance with African custom, the bride-price (*lobola*) being restored to its original contractual significance. The idealized relationship here described is seen as the result of a balanced syncretic (and probably utopian) combination of strong Christian faith with respect for what is considered reasonable and legitimate in terms of African traditions. It is significant that Chidyausiku gave up this somewhat starry-eyed outlook in his later works. *Nyadzi dzinokunda rufu* ("Death before dishonour", 1962), which Kahari considers his masterpiece. This begins in a rural community from which the hero escapes in order to evade the mockery of his neighbours at his inability to have children: he finds employment in Bulawayo, where he soon becomes a pimp and a murderer. In *Ndak- ambokuyambira* ("I warned you before", 1962)—the first Shona play ever printed, which made him "the father of Shona drama"—Chidyausiku handled the complexities of acculturation in a lighter vein. This comedy is based on "the traditional story involving a man who told his wife a secret, namely that he had killed a man when, in fact, he had killed a goat";[117] but the hero's motives are interesting: in his (modern) desire to become a successful businessman, he finds he has to resort to traditional magic and get hold of a piece of human flesh; however, he is held back by the (traditional) fear of the avenging spirits and the (modern) fear of being arrested by the police; ultimately, he merely decides to test his wife's discretion and finds her wanting. Chidyausiku's latest novel, *Karumekangu* (1970) reverts to the structure of the earlier fiction although the action is mainly set in the towns of Gwelo and Johannesburg; while describing the book as "a study of the behaviour, reaction and adaptation of the urban Shona to their new Western environment", Kahari notes that the author's "prime concern seems to bring back some lost technique of spoken art by evoking a new urban situation in which to demonstrate the possibilities and potentialities of his native language." [118]

Taken as a whole, the novelistic output, both in Shona and Ndebele,

238   SOUTHERN AFRICA

illustrates the degree of confusion and puzzlement that has been created
by the ambiguous impact of the new ways upon traditional beliefs and
values. This is organized around a few major themes that cut across the
division according to settings, because Christianity, modern education,
and the money economy cannot help but make their influence felt even
in the remotest rural areas. One of these basic themes is education, and
the duties and failures of the educated African. Among the earliest
Shona novels, *Nzvengamutsvairo* ("Dodge the broom", 1957), by Bernard T. G. Chidzero (b. 1927), was the first to offer the syncretic kind of
view which Chidyausiku's second novel was to illustrate in the institution of marriage. It has three male characters who represent three aspects of Shona life: one is an opponent of change and tries to maintain
the purity of Shona tradition; another exemplifies the degeneracy of
Shona culture and the evil sides of social change effected through the
worst forms of western materialism and individualism; the third one is
an educated young Christian who manages to combine the good from
both cultures.[119]
    But two years later, another Shona novel, *Kumazivandadzoka* ("Who
goes to a place, perhaps never comes back", 1959) by John Marang-
wanda (b. c. 1922), conveyed a different message, showing education as
an intrinsically disruptive factor of alienation because the educated
young have more knowledge, and therefore enjoy higher status, than
their elders. The notion that education does not necessarily go hand in
hand with moral improvement is exploited in *Ndakaziva haitungarmiri*
("If I had known, I would not have done it", Shona, 1962), where Xav-
ier S. Marimazhira recounts in lurid detail the story of a head teacher
who does not hesitate to resort to forgery, witchcraft and poisoning in
order to capture the woman he loves. And E. M. Ndlovu's *Inhlamvu
zaseNgodlweni* ("The offspring of Ngodlweni", Ndebele, 1959) contains
fierce criticism of African church ministers who patronize witch-doctors
and clandestine drinking saloons (*shebeens*). A peculiar variety of the educational novel is the parallel-lives story, which seems to be proper to
the Ndebele novel perhaps in imitation of Zulu models. The pattern is
based on the contrast between two characters: one is brought up in an
upright family, becomes a bright student, and later a prosperous and
respected member of the community with a strong interest in church
affairs; the other is the very picture of evil: he has been spoiled by a
weak mother, or one who is herself evil; he grows more and more unruly, becomes addicted to such disreputable occupations as card playing,
keeps bad company and turns to heavy drinking until he becomes a full-
grown criminal who ultimately falls into the hands of the police. Various
forms of this pattern appear in *Inhlamvu zase Godlweni* ("The offspring
of Godlweni," 1959) by Elkana M. Ndlovu (b. 1913), in *Uyokhula umfana*
("The boy grows up", 1961) by Amos Mzilethi (b. 1914), and in *Qaphela*

ingane ("Take care of the boy", 1962) by Lassie Ndondo, the first African woman to have a novel published in Rhodesia.

Love, in its connection with sex and marriage, is another theme frequently treated by Rhodesian writers.[120] In *Ndakamuda dakara afa* ("I loved her unto death", Shona, 1960), Kenneth S. Bepswa (b. 1927) completes the model previously presented by Chidyausiku in proposing a picture of true love as "governed by the Christian principles of charity, self-restraint, of forgiveness, sacrifice and unselfishness."[121] Kahari has observed that Bepswa departs from the narrative folk tradition by introducing a measure of realism: "He has done what was not done. Stories of boys and girls in love were not told. Such stories, however, were told if the individuals concerned became husband and wife, in other words, if the husband paid *lobola*. Kissing was almost taboo; it is commonplace in this novel."[122] Bepswa also criticizes such evils as the spreading of female unfaithfulness and of prostitution, and the decay of the *lobola* custom in consequence of the covetousness induced by the new money economy. *Uvusezindala* ("In days gone by", Ndebele, 1958) by David Ndoda (b. 1925) begins in a similar fashion with a critique of *lobola* in its degraded form: the hero of the story migrates in order to earn the exorbitant sum exacted by his prospective father-in-law; during his absence, the latter marries his daughter off to a higher bidder; the result is murder and suicide. Other forms of western individualism are also taken to task: in *Akusoka lingenasici* ("There is no perfection", Ndebele, 1958), Isaac M. Mpofu tells the story of a girl who is the pride of her family because she has attended primary school, but who elopes with a young man, thus inflicting considerable grief upon her parents. Other writers deal with even less savoury aspects of sex, such as jealousy, adultery, and especially the spreading of prostitution in modern cities.

The outlook of most Zimbabwean writers is shaped by their adherence to Christian standards. They often try to sift the two value-systems with which they are faced in order to invent some syncretism that might make the best of both worlds. In cases where no reconciliation is possible, they invariably stand up in favour of the Christian way of life, as in the indictment of polygamy proposed by L. Washington Chapavadza (1926–1964) in *Wechitatu Muzvinaguhwa* ("Two is company, three is none", Shona, 1963), or in the condemnation of the prejudices connected with female sterility in *Gehena harina moto* ("Hell has no fire", Shona, *1965*) by Giles Kuimba (b. 1936). Needless to say, witchcraft is a favourite target. In spite of this, however, several novels are devoted to a reconstruction of the pre-colonial, pre-Christian past. One of the first Ndebele novels, *Umthwakazi* ("The owner of the state", 1957), by Peter S. Mahlangu (b. 1923), is similar to Mutswairo's *Feso*, except that it sticks closer to historical fact in its account of Mzilikazi, a lieutenant of Chaka and the first king of the Ndebele. A major step forward in the revaluation of the

traditional past was accomplished by Emmanual F. Ribeiro (b. 1935) in
Muchadura ("You shall confess", Shona, 1967), which may herald a new
attitude towards traditional beliefs. Like A. C. Jordan's Xhosa masterpiece, *The Wrath of the Ancestors,* Ribeiro's book dramatizes the age-old
African notion that the avenging spirits of the dead ancestors persecute
those who have ill-treated them until they acknowledge their crimes and
atone for their guilt. The novel represents a bold attempt not only to
make literary use of the traditional beliefs that many Africans still cher-
ish, but also to explore their psychological meaning and moral value.

Black Zimbabwean writing is barely two decades old with still a small
number of works. Nevertheless, it provides a fairly complete and complex picture of some of the major preoccupations of the African élite.
To be sure, white minority rule, especially after U.D.I., was not prepared to tolerate overt social and political criticism. The publication of
On Trial for My Country (1967), a historical novel on the Ndebele by
Shona writer Stanlake Samkange (b. 1922), signalled the emergence of
a Zimbabwean literature in exile and in English. African language writers had no outlet outside their own country and, in consequence, were
bound to limit their imaginative inquiries to the moral and psychological
fields, although it may be presumed that they often resorted to the
weapons of the powerless: a subdued irony and a symbolic obliqueness,
which the reader will perceive but which the critic will be wary of discussing openly. As a group, Zimbabwean writers have shown themselves
well aware of the ambiguities of their situation. In 1971, Abraham Kriel
could observe that "novels which deal with traditional circumstances are
usually hopeful in the end, but there is no novel yet which pictures a
muShona as overcoming his problem and settling successfully in the
city."[123]

But while tradition is often idealized in a manner which is both escapist and utopian, writers are not blind to its shortcomings. The most per-
ceptive writers, who are bound to increase in numbers, are deeply conscious that the old culture, whatever its merits, is not likely to be able to
survive unchanged in the modern world. If its values are to be preserved, it must adapt itself to the overpowering novelties introduced by
western "civilization". Yet this western contribution is itself highly ambivalent. Zimbabwean writers seem to think that Christian values can
easily be reconciled with the essentials of older cultural traditions. Modern education for example, whilst it is a source of knowledge and power,
also undermines the hierarchical structure of the African family and in
some cases it tends to alienate the educated class from the popular
masses. Urbanization provides the most thorough antimony to traditional rural life, and the city is consistently described as a privileged
hatching-place for misery, vice and violence, as it is in the considerably
larger literary output of the Republic of South Africa. As the modern

town is also the place where racial inequality and exploitation of cheap
manpower are most clearly in evidence, it is not surprising that Zimbabwean city novels should all culminate in tragic endings for their black
heroes. Whether this will change now that majority rule is established in
Zimbabwe is of course open to question: the way the city novel has developed in such independent countries as Nigeria and Kenya is not encouraging in this respect. At the present stage, however, it is clear that
the Zimbabwean novel proclaims an essentially ethical approach advocating a sense of selflessness and solidarity which is both Christian and
traditional, preaching the puritan gospel of hard work, and encouraging
education. This is the meaning of Mutswairo's second novel, *Murambiwa
Goredema* ("Murambiwa, son of Goredema", 1959), whose hero, after
tragic ordeals in the Salisbury township of Harare, "realizes that knowledge, diligence and money are the three essentials for making progress
in life", returns to the land, "where he tills the soil and cares for his
family", and sees to it that "his son became a learned man, who works
towards the uplift of his own people by teaching them to read and
write."[124]

In its essentials, this was the lesson taught by Goethe in his *Second
Faust.*

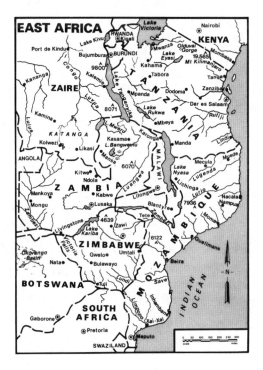

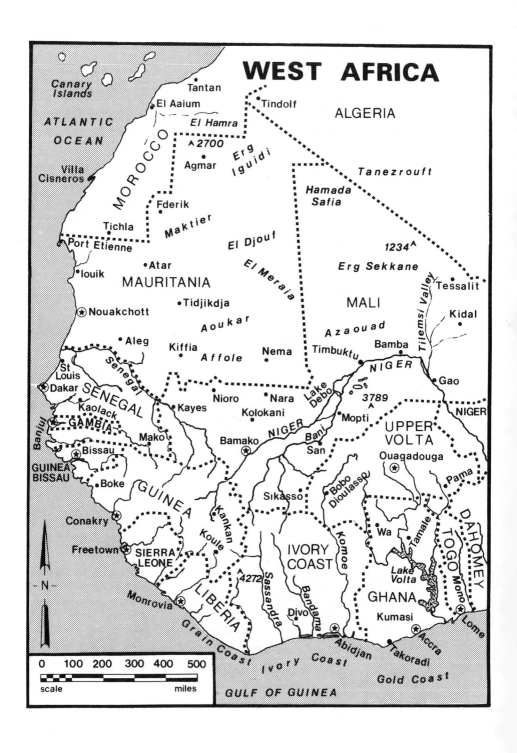

WEST AFRICA

Canary
Islands

ATLANTIC
OCEAN

Tantan

El Aaium

Tindolf

ALGERIA

El Hamra

^2700

MOROCCO

Agmar

Erg
Iguidi

Tanezrouft

Villa
Cisneros

Fderik

Hamada
Safia

Tichla

Maktier

El Djouf

Port Etienne

El Meraia

1234^

Erg Sekkane

Tessalit

louik

Atar

MAURITANIA

MALI

Kidal

Nouakchott

Tidjikdja

Aoukar

Azaouad

Aleg

Kiffia

Affole

Nema

Timbuktu

Bamba

NIGER

Gao

St
Louis

Senegal

Dakar

SENEGAL

Kaolack

Nioro

Kayes

Nara

Kolokani

Lake
Debo

3789
^

Mopti

UPPER
VOLTA

NIGER

Banjul

GAMBIA

Mako

Bamako

NIGER

Bani

San

Ouagadouga

Pama

Bissau

GUINEA
BISSAU

Boke

GUINEA

Sikasso

Bobo
Dioulasso

DAHOMEY

Conakry

Kankan

Komoe

Wa

Tamale

TOGO

Freetown

Koule

SIERRA
LEONE

4272

Sassandra

IVORY
COAST

Lake
Volta

GHANA

Mono

Lome

LIBERIA

Bandama

Divo

Kumasi

Accra

Monrovia

Grain Coast

Abidjan

Takoradi

Ivory Coast

Gold Coast

- N -

GULF OF GUINEA

0 100 200 300 400 500

scale   miles

CHAPTER NINE
WEST AFRICA

1. Sierra Leone and Liberia

African writing in West Africa originated under circumstances that were entirely different from those prevailing in South Africa. Since the early part of the sixteenth century commercial relations connected with the slave trade had existed between Europe and the coast of West Afria. Settlement, such as it was, was limited to a string of forts established along the coast by the various slave-trading nations. The first real settlers from the western world did not arrive until the early years of the nineteenth century: they were blacks, freed slaves brought to Sierra Leone from Britain and Canada and to Liberia from the United States. A number of them had received a modicum of formal schooling; they were Christians; their native language was English.[1]

During the following decades internecine warfare among the Yoruba states provided fresh supplies for the slave trade, which had by now become illegal. The British navy managed to free a number of the slaves. They were then sent to Freetown (Sierra Leone), where they were known as Liberated Africans. The majority of them gratefully adopted both the religion and the language of their "civilized" brethren.

These events had interesting consequences for the literary history of West Africa. Until then, the art of writing had been confined to the Sudanic states of the interior; it had been in Arabic (although, by the early years of the nineteenth century, a beginning had been made with *ajami* literature) and it was Islamic in outlook. However, whereas in South Africa the impact of Europe was leading to the creation of vernacular writing, in West Africa a different trend developed: its starting point was Sierra Leone, and, to a lesser extent, Liberia.[2] Its medium was the English language and its orientation was not imaginative, but didactic. Articulate intellectuals in Sierra Leone and Liberia had no traditional folklore to fall back on but memories of bondage, which, naturally enough, they were keen to forget. They were under the impression that they were the founders of a new order in West Africa, and all their activity was directed towards clarifying and disseminating their notions about the future and the values of the African civilisation which they thought they were heralding. This was the life purpose of such prolific authors as Africanus Horton (1835–1883) in Sierra Leone, of Edward W. Blyden (1832–1912) in Liberia and of a number of lesser luminaries.[3] They had little interest in the tribal cultures in their own countries, although Blyden greatly admired Islamic achievements in Sudanic West Africa. This English writing, which was never more than a trickle in Liberia, died out in Sierra Leone when the growth of British colonialism after the Berlin Conference turned both white missionaries and administrators against the Creole community of Freetown in order to give their solicitude to the "unspoilt" tribes of the interior. By the early years of the twentieth century, a curtain of silence fell over those coastal areas that had been the home of African authorship in West Africa, but its mantle was then taken up by such eminent historians, lawyers, educationists and political writers as Henry Carr (1863–1945) and Herbert Macaulay (1864–1946) in Southern Nigeria, and John Mensah Sarbah (1864–1910), J. E. Casely Hayford (1866–1930) and James Aggrey (1875–1927) in the Gold Coast. As to Sierra Leone and Liberia, they did not emerge on the scene of creative writing in English until after World War II, in the wake of a movement that had just originated in Nigeria.

The language really spoken by the Creoles in Freetown, however, was not standard English but Krio, a creole idiom which is so pervaded with African elements that it is not intelligible to English ears. Although the educated élites used to be contemptuous of Krio, some attempts had been made as early as the nineteenth century, at turning it into a legitimate literary medium, and some verse in Krio appeared in Sierra Leone newspapers.[4] This tradition was taken up again in the 1960s, when Thomas Decker (b. 1916) translated *Julius Caesar* and *As You Like It* into the language.[5] These were performed in 1964, and the *Sierra Leone Language Review* has published a number of Decker's Krio poems since 1965. In the works of such recent writers of English as Julisa Amuda Maddy (b. 1936), Krio now appears frequently as a stylistic device and as a means to establish the social status of the characters.

Nor did genuine African languages fare any better in those two countries (Sierra Leone and Liberia), where English-speaking blacks held social, economic, cultural, and, in varying proportions, political supremacy. J. Gus Liebenow points out that the Americo-Liberian leaders "seemed undisturbed by the fact that . . . the process of expansion created a relationship of political dependency between themselves and the members of more than sixteen tribal groups indigenous to the Liberian hinterland. It was a relationship similar in most respects to that obtaining between whites and Africans in other sectors of the continent. The distinguishing criterion for subordination, however, was not race . . . Rather, the dependency relationship was based upon differences in culture and upon the barriers erected by the Americo-Liberians against either rapid or widespread assimilation of the dominant culture by the tribal people."[6]

Thus exploited, and otherwise left to their own devices, one of these tribal groups initiated a development of remarkable originality. About 1833, a Vai tribesman, Duwalu Bukele (c. 1810–1850), devised a syllabic script whose existence was first reported by agents of the American Board of Foreign Missions in 1834. Bukele claimed that the script had been revealed to him in a dream by "a tall venerable looking white man." It is more likely, however, that the main impetus behind the devising and popularizing of the Vai script was the desire to acquire the power and advantages which were seen to belong to the literate Europeans, Afro-American settlers and Mandingo Muslims with whom the Vai came in contact.[7]

The only work to be written in the Vai script was the short autobiographical and aphoristic *Book of Rora* by one of Bukele's kinsmen, Kali Bara; a translation of it was published in German scholar S. W. Koelle's *Narrative of an Expedition into the Vy country of West Africa* (1849), and the text was printed in Vai script in 1851. Although many Vais learned the script in the course of the nineteenth century, most of the original writing for which it was used has remained in manuscript form and comprises stories and legends and accounts of local history. While agents of the American Episcopal Mission in Cape Mount printed Vai translations of hymns and scriptural material in Roman script, the Vai syllabary was used by Momolu M. Massaquoi in the early years of this century for translating a chapter of St. John's Gospel. Nevertheless, encouragement came from Christian missionaries only, and although knowledge of the indigenous script was widespread among Vai males, scholarly interest in it remained confined to foreign scholars, as the Americo-Liberian ruling class were chiefly bent on preserving their political and cultural, not to mention economic, power monopoly. It was not until President Tubman came to power in 1944 that some half-hearted efforts were made at a so-called "open-door policy," which would allow the interior peoples a semblance of participation in the exercise of power. In the early 1960s, the University of Liberia organized a scheme for the standardization of the Vai script under the direction of Professor Fatima Massaquoi-Fahnbulleh, Director of the African Studies Program, and daughter of Momulu M. Massaquoi.

The Vai script was the first of a number of indigenous graphic systems that were devised along the Guinea coast until the mid-twentieth century, but there does not seem to be any evidence that they have ever been used for purposes other than letter writing and record keeping.

A similar dearth of written production can be observed in the African languages of Sierra Leone, for even after the establishment of a protectorate over the interior, and in spite of the fact that everything was done to prevent Creoles from being active there, whether in education or in the administration, commercial and educational development remained dominated by the Freetown people. In 1921, Kisimi Kamara (*c.* 1890–1962) devised a Mende syllabary,[8] which appears to have achieved a limited degree of popularity during the 1920s and 1930s, being used especially in personal correspondance; "its usage declined rapidly from about 1940 onward, however, with the introduction of the Protectorate Literature Bureau's Mass Literacy campaign, employing the Roman 'Africa' script for the writing of Mende."[9] Meanwhile, Mende had been steadily gaining ground as a *lingua franca*; it is probably understood by about one million people in the southern half of Sierra Leone, and it was used by missionaries for religious and didactic writing.[10] The Protectorate Literature Bureau that was set up in the 1940s had an ambitious programme[11] but it likewise resulted mainly in the production of religious and educational pamphlets. Nevertheless, its report for 1950 mentions that two works of imaginative fiction had been printed in Mende.[12] One of these was a Mende version of Matthew Arnold's story of *Rustum and Zorab,* prepared by E. A. Swari (1950).

As far as the history of creative writing in African languages is concerned, then, the usual consequence of the existence of a black educated élite in Sierra Leone and Liberia was not felt in those two countries: the chief result of this élite's activity was the diffusion of Christianity and literacy in Nigeria, especially in Yorubaland.

2. Nigeria

Among the Liberated Africans of Freetown, there was a fairly large proportion of Yorubas, locally known as Akus. One of these was a young man named Ajayi, who was sold as a slave during the Yoruba wars in 1821. He was set free by a British vessel and sent to Freetown. Baptized under the name of Samuel Crowther, he was among the first graduates of Fourah Bay College (founded in 1827). He was ordained as a minister under the C.M.S. and was sent to Nigeria as a missionary in 1843. The language of the Aku had already received some attention from English missionaries like Henry Townsend.[13] But it was Crowther who was responsible for compiling the first extensive *Vocabulary of the Yoruba Language* (1843) and the first *Yoruba Primer* (1849). It was he who either wrote, checked, or supervised the translation of the Scriptures and he conceived it in such a way that the complete Bible, which was printed as *Bibele mimo* in 1900, "was of a literary order comparable with that of Luther's German translation or the English Authorised Version." Crowther's "influence on subsequent Yoruba literature ... without doubt was overwhelming," for "his choice of a dialect and his selection of idioms and expressions in this dialect, sanctified for the Yoruba reader through his Bible translations and for the linguist through his grammar and dictionary, created standard Yoruba, which has now even affected the spoken language and become so widespread that other dialect forms are rapidly disappearing."[14] Nor was Crowther alone in his devotion to the promotion of Yoruba writing.[15] In 1859, Henry Townsend at Abeokuta launched a fortnightly news-sheet in Yoruba and in English, *Iwe Irohin*, which went through 190 issues until 1867. The growth of literacy, to which the journal's success testified, prompted another missionary, David Hinderer, to produce a translation of Bunyan's *Pilgrim's Progress* (1866), which proved almost as popular as the Bible, and was to exert considerable influence on Yoruba prose fiction in the middle of the twentieth century.[16]

Original Christian composition in Yoruba was first recorded by Henry Townsend during a stay at Otta in 1857. The converts who had gone out to meet him, he wrote in his diary, "sang at my request some of their Christian hymns, words and tunes being of native composition." By 1886, Bishop Crowther could remark that the church of Otta had become well-known for its "native airs," which were composed orally, although Townsend transcribed and edited some of them in the 1850s. According to a prominent Nigerian historian, "credit for this early attempt at evolving Christian hymns in the indigenous musical tradition goes to James White, emigrant catechist at Otta from 1854, ordained 1857, died 1890."[17]

The establishment of the Protectorate of Southern Nigeria at the turn of the century, the creation of an Education department and the promulgation of an education code in 1903, the foundation of the first government secondary school in Lagos in 1911, increased official assistance to mission schools. Last but not least, the influence of Henry Carr (1863–1965), the first Nigerian high official in educational matters,[18] led to the emergency of a literate class and made it imperative to produce reading-matter that was not of an exclusively religious character. During the first two decades of the century, the C.M.S. head-office in Lagos, brought out a series of five Yoruba readers, *Iwe Kike Ekerin Li Ede Yoruba* (1909–1915); these were anthologies containing miscellaneous prose and poetry on a wide variety of subjects; the better pieces were the prose narratives, some of which were taken from traditional oral art, while others were translations from English. More important for the history of modern Yoruba creative writing, however, was the appearance of original Yoruba prose and poetry in the period between the two world wars.

In poetry, the pioneering work seems to have been *Aiye Akamara* ("Human life full of pitfalls," 1921) by Kolawole Ajisafe (1877–1940) of

Abeokuta, a prolific writer, whose works were to include original poems and prose discourses. As the title suggests, his first published poem is a poetic meditation on the vicissitudes of life; one of his last works is *Gbadebo Alake* ("Gbadebo, king of Abeokuta," 1934), a short verse biography of the then recently deceased monarch, containing some outspoken criticism of his policies. A few years later, Adketimkan Obasa (1878–1948), who was the editor of the weekly *Yoruba News,* launched a series of anthologies with *Iwe Kinni Ti Awon Akewi* ("First book of minstrels' utterances," 1927), which was followed by two further volumes in 1934 and 1945. This was published by the "Egbe Agba-O-Tan," a society of well-to-do elderly citizens concerned with the preservation of Yoruba culture. In his preface Obasa claimed that his labours on the work had started as far back as 1886! In spite of his statement that he had merely compiled traditional Yoruba proverbs and other gnomic sayings embodying the wisdom of Yoruba lore, a few of the poems in those anthologies are of his own composition. Yet the most popular of those pioneer poets was a much older man, J. Sobowale Sowande (1858–1936), who wrote under the pseudonym of Sobo Arobiodu. The poems in his *Iwe arofo Orin* ("A book of careful verse," 1929) were composed in the Egba dialect on the pattern of the traditional songs sung in Abeokuta at the festivals of Oro, the god of punishment; but since the author was a Christian, Oro is hardly mentioned and the poems centre on the author's experience of life and on his observations of contemporary events and manners. This, and other poetry by Sowande, have recently been made available in a collected edition.[19]

It was not until the late 1920s that original Yoruba prose fiction of a modern type made its appearance. As in Madagascar, it seems to have begun as a by-product of the lively vernacular press which testified to the efforts of Yoruba writers in those days of fast-spreading literacy. It was then that Isaac B. Thomas, editor of the weekly journal *Akede Eko*, serialized a story in letter form, *Itan Igbesi Aiya Emi Segilola*, which Bamgbose describes as "an autobiographical account of the life of a fictitious prostitute, Segilola, who led a profligate life involving several marriages."[20] This tale, which may have combined influences from Richardson's *Pamela* and Defoe's *Moll Flanders*, must have had some hidden moral purpose in view, for it appeared in book form in 1929, under the imprint of the C.M.S. Bookshop in Lagos. It was soon followed by *Igbehin a dun Omo Orukan* ("The sweet shall succeed the bitter," 1931), by E. Akintunde Akintan (1890–1957), who was the editor of the bilingual weekly *Eleti Ofe*; this novella about an orphan girl who started life unhappily but later married a king and enjoyed a happy family life, exhibits the Victorian morality and the edifying optimism typical of much of the early fiction in African languages prior to the second World War.

Yoruba prose fiction, which had obviously been swayed by the realistic outlook inherent in the western tradition until the end of the nineteenth century, suddenly revealed its original potentialities and reached its maturity on the eve of the second World War, when the C.M.S. book-shop in Lagos issued *Ogboju Ode Ninu Igbo Irunmale* ("The brave hunter in the forest of embodied spirits," 1938) by Daniel Olorunfemi Fa-gunwa (1903–1963), a church primary school headmaster.[21] This is a frame story recounting the adventures of an elderly hunter, Akara-Ogun, in the forest which, in Yoruba folklore, is the seat of all super-natural forces and the abode of trolls, gnomes, ghosts and sundry other uncanny beings. A number of the tales are genuine folk-material; but they are strongly influenced by Western accretions, both religious and literary. The transcendent deity of the Yoruba, Olodumare, becomes identified with the Christian God; several biblical figures intrude into the narrative, as well as allegorical creatures such as Starvation, Peril or Chaos, who are strongly reminiscent of *The Pilgrim's Progress*. Both tra-ditional and Christian attitudes are easily reconciled in the somewhat heavy moralizing tone that pervades the book.

This first work set the pattern for the four "novels" which Fagunwa was to produce from 1945 to 1961. As Bamgbose explains, each of them has an introductory part designed to bring about a meeting between the author and the narrator of the main story. The plot takes the form of a journey, usually a perilous one, which involves the protagonist in a great variety of adventures; it often culminates in a visit to a sage who, in his turn, tells various stories calculated to bring out certain moral values. In a way, then, each of Fagunwa's novels is both a frame story and a quest story, whose obvious structural resemblance to the medieval romances is due, no doubt, to the closeness of both to oral art. As was the case with the many Christian school-teachers who were the founders of modern creative writing in African languages, it was part of Fa-gunwa's purpose to provide school-boys and what literate audience ex-isted among the Yoruba with reading matter exemplifying the mother tongue at its best, thus improving upon the stilted, clumsy, rudimentary style characteristic of text-books produced by Europeans. At the same time, while each of Fagunwa's works is merely a chain of loosely con-nected adventures, he managed to weave into them many of the tales that were part of Yoruba oral lore; but, as Bamgbose has shown, he also derived many incidents from non-Yoruba sources: from Greek litera-ture (Homer's *Odyssey*, Greek myths, and Aesop's fables), from such English works as Marlowe's *Doctor Faustus* and Defoe's *Robinson Crusoe*, from the *Arabian Nights*, and of course from the Bible and *The Pilgrim's Progress*. Bamgbose considers that the stories taken from such foreign sources are seldom properly integrated into the plot, which they serve to embellish in a rather conspicuous way; it is doubtful, however, whether the common Yoruba reader would be aware of this. For all anecdotes and incidents, while being intrinsically exciting as stories, are subservient to the didactic purpose which Fagunwa's writings have in common with the oral tradition as well as with the mainstream of Christian literature. Indeed, a fastidious analyst might think that the moral strain is apt to be marred at times by the inner contradiction so characteristic of western Christianity: Fagunwa's last novel *Adiitu Olodumare* ("The secret of the Almighty," 1961), relates the edifying career of a protagonist whose perseverance enables him to rise from extreme poverty to become the richest man in town; the main story incorporates a number of incidents designed to drive home the evils of money and greed; yet the main reward for the hero's endurance and good nature is wealth!

Bamgbose's strictures are an indication that the time is now ripe for an in-depth critical consideration of Fagunwa. Although his plots may now appear unduly rambling and his moralizing overly obvious and conventional, his success is incontrovertible proof that the Yoruba readership of the day was not much concerned with close-knit structure and coherent narrative organization. To them, fostering moral and societal conformity, both directly, through maxims and proverbs, and indirectly, through parable and allegory, was the fundamental function of the imaginative art. They were further delighted by Fagunwa's mastery of the language and by his skilful rendering of traditional stories; they found his sense of humour, his picturesque imagery and his taste for the weird and the bizarre peculiarly congenial and attractive. His outstanding contribution was to make literate Yorubas fully aware of the value and originality of their traditional legacy. He showed how folktales could be put to legitimate and profitable uses through the medium of the printed word. His influence was decisive upon Tutuola, the first Nigerian writer to achieve world-wide fame,[22] and it is most likely that his example encouraged younger writers such as Wole Soyinka to preserve the specific cultural traditions of the Yoruba and to adapt their ancient myths and beliefs in their own English writings.

The popularity of Fagunwa's first novel was such that those that followed, beginning with *Igbo Olodumare* ("The jungle of the Almighty," 1949), were brought out by the British firm of Nelson. While other British publishers such as Longmans and the University of London Press were becoming interested, a few collections of stories, such as those of Ade J. Aina or Matthias Dada Akerejola, were privately printed in Nigeria in 1950. Official help was also available locally, and in 1953 the Western Region Literature Committee which had been set up in Ibadan in the mid-forties began issuing brief novellas by such writers as Joseph Orogbolo Akinyemi, A.O. Ladeinde and O. Ogunrika, who often imitated Fagunwa's techniques and made considerable use of traditional material with edifying purposes in view. In 1954, the Western Region Literature Committee was superseded by the General Publications Department of the Ministry of Education, also located at Ibadan. These official publishing ventures operated in close association with Yoruba cultural societies such as "Egbe Omo Oduduwa" or "Egbe Ijinle Yoruba", which contributed to the launching of *Olokun*, a journal for the promotion of modern Yoruba literature, in 1957.[23]

In spite of the tremendous success of Fagunwa's fantasy novels, it was at first the more down-to-earth, realistic trend of the early 1930s that was taken up by the new writers encouraged by those initiatives. Of *Ayie Ree!* ("What people do!", 1947) by Adekanmi Oyedele (1900–1957), Babalola says that "it is a clear departure from Fagunwa's trail. It is a realistic novel, a fictitious autobiography, based on the traditional life of the Yoruba people before the coming of the Europeans."[24]

This remained Oyedele's only literary venture, and the rivulet of realism did not become a wider stream until the mid-1950s, with the emergence of Chief Isaac Oluwole Delano (b. 1904), who had obtained an IAI award for a Yoruba version of *Robinson Crusoe* in 1933, and who was already well-known as an officer of the "Egbe Omo Oduduwa". Delano's first work of fiction, *Aiye d'Aiye Oyinbo* ("Changing times, the white man among us," 1955), is a historical novel ranging in time from before the Europeans' arrival in Yorubaland right up to the present. The chief character is the narrator's husband, a village head, who experiences many vicissitudes in the course of the imposition of the British system of indirect rule on the traditional pattern of government. The author skilfully adapts a narrative style fashioned on the characteristic mode of Yoruba elders' delivery of their recollections. Consequently the novel is rich in Yoruba proverbs and idioms and the prose has a dignified, measured tread. The problems raised by the intrusion of the European notion of local government were soon to be handled imaginatively in English by the Ibo writer Chinua Achebe. Delano's next novel, *Lo Ojoun* ("In days of yore," 1963), was another piece of historical fiction, staged in Abeokuta in the 1920s. The central character is a Christian convert, a warrior turned farmer, who tries to steer his rural community through the difficulties of the new era. The novel deals with the problem of drunkenness and the narrative is based on the events which led to the passing of an ordinance to control liquor consumption in Western Nigeria.

Among the elder writers, contemporaries of Fagunwa and Delano, who did not reach print until the late 1950s, mention must be made of Chief Joseph Folohan Odunjo (b. 1904), most of whose work was designed for juvenile readers. In his first printed book, *Agbalowomeeri* (1958), one of the earliest written dramas in Yoruba, the title character is a corrupt chief who is led to an untimely death in the forest of the spirits in punishment for his vices. This play was followed by *Akojono ewi aladun* ("Gathering delicious leaves," 1961), a miscellaneous collection of poems that are mostly didactic; the poetry has the traditional ring of Yoruba poetry with its lofty phrasing and calculated tones. In 1964, Odunjo produced two short novels, *Omo oku orun* ("The deceased woman's daughter") and the story of a boy named *Kuye*, each of which handles the edifying motif of the long ill-treated child whose unflinching courage is ultimately rewarded.

The many initiatives, official and otherwise, for the promotion of Yoruba writing led to the emergence of a younger generation of writers in the mid-1950s. While their elders had been chiefly interested in prose fiction, they made a determined attempt at greater diversification, writing not only novels and novellas, but also poetry and plays. But whereas the work of Delano, and, to a lesser extent, Fagunwa's last novel, evinced a definite tendency towards realistic preoccupation with problems of acculturation, it is noteworthy that some of the younger writers sought their material in their fund of folklore, mythology, history and legend. For example, *Olorun esan* ("God takes vengeance," 1953), by Gabriel Ibitoye Ojo (1925–1962), is a verse rendering of a folk story illustrating the dictum that people reap what they sow. *Ogun Kiriji* ("The Kiriji war"), by Olaya Fagbamigbe (b. 1930), is a poetic account, based on oral sources, of an internecine war that was fought from 1880 to 1893. The Fagunwa vein of fantasy was further exploited by Ogunsina Ogundela (b. 1925), whose two novels—*Ibu Olokun* ("The deeps where Olokun reigns supreme," 1956) and *Ejigbede Lona Tsalu Orun* ("Ejigbede on his way from earth to heaven," 1957)—deal with protagonists journeying from heaven to earth and back, via the oceanic deeps and becoming involved in all sorts of fantastic situations. The same trend reappeared some ten years later, when D.J. Fatanmi (b. 1938) published *Korimale Ninu Igbo Adimula* ("Korimale in Adimula's forest", 1967), yet another sermonizing story about the weird adventures of an enterprising hunter in a ghost-ridden forest.

As to the stream of realism, it was joined by Femi Jeboda (b. 1933), whose full-length novel, *Olowolaiyemo* (1964), won first prize in a competition organized to celebrate Nigeria's attainment of independence 1960. Through the life story of the title character—whose name means Mr. People-rally-round-the-well-to-do-only—Jeboda portrayed the seamier aspects of contemporary life in Yoruba towns. Subsequently, he published an earlier, slighter novella, *Afinju Adaba* ("Mr. Audacious Dove," 1964), which deals with the career and misadventures of a mischievous character in an anecdotal way. The early sixties also saw the launching of detective story writing in Yoruba with *Itan Adegbesan* ("The story of Adegbesan," 1961), by Joseph Akinyele Omoyajowo (b. 1934).

Most of the writers that have been discussed so far belonged to the school-teacher class; their main preoccupation was usually to provide reading-matter for schools, often with a view to perpetuating the spirit of the oral folk legacy. But in the mid-1950s, the need for a more sophisticated approach began to be felt by members of the younger generation who had received higher educational training. In 1954, Adeboye Babalola (b. 1926) published a Yoruba translation of *The Merchant of Venice*. Two years later came his *Pasan sina* ("The whip descends on the wrong person," 1958), which, together with Odunjo's *Agbalowomeeri*, laid the foundations for printed drama in Yoruba. This five-act play focuses on a schoolboy who becomes a masquerader in order to flog his teacher but unfortunately beats the wrong person in execution of his plan. The farcical plot with its moralizing implications still exhibits the characteristics of school drama, but the author has woven a portrayal of the traditional way of life around it. Babalola, who teaches at the University of Lagos, later turned to the scholarly study of oral poetry,[25] but the sixties were to reveal the extraordinary talents of the Yoruba people for drama. This took several forms: the world-renowned Yoruba folk opera will be discussed presently; play-writing in English, most conspicuously illustrated by Wole Soyinka, but also represented by Wale Ogunyemi, Ola Rotimi and others, falls outside the scope of this volume. But in the middle of the decade, Olanipekun Esan (b. 1931), a lecturer in classics at the University of Ibadan, daringly produced Africanized versions of several Greek and Latin works: *Teledalase* ("The Creator's will must prevail," 1965) is a verse rendering of Sophocles' *Oedipus; Orekelewa* ("Beauty Personified," 1965) is a prose comedy based on Plautus' *Mercator*; and *Esin atiroja* ("The tiptoeing war-horse," 1966) dramatizes the Trojan horse story as recounted in Vergil's *Aeneid*.

Meanwhile, the increasing sophistication in Yoruba writing was becoming apparent in the versatile talent of Adebayo Faleti (b.1935), whose chief contribution was to introduce into formal writing the sense of sly humour that is so widespread amongst Africans generally.[26] Faleti's humour was already much in evidence in his long narrative poem, *Eda Ko L'Aropin* ("Never underestimate someone's future achievements," 1956). It also permeated his brief novella *Ogun Awitele* ("A war well-publicized in advance," 1965): the fantastic accounts of the efficacy of Yoruba medicinal and incantatory charms betray a new, mildly satirical, attitude towards traditional lore. But Faleti's first play, *Mwon Ro Pe Were Ni* ("People thought she was mad," 1965), evinced a deepening of his inspiration: the comedy of banter involving drummers, dancers and palm-wine drinkers in a bar is woven into the tragedy of a respected citizen who is condemned for plotting a secret human sacrifice in order to achieve perennial wealth. Faleti then felt ready to attempt full-scale novel writing: *Omo Olokunesin* ("Son of the master of the horse," 1970), is an ambitious historical novel set in the old kingdom of Otu, and dealing with the stratagems used by bands of slaves in the tributary towns to get rid of the Otu ruler's oppressive control. In contrast with the elementary narrative technique hitherto used by most Yoruba authors of modern prose fiction, Faleti knows how to handle and diversify the point of view: the story is recounted by three narrators, each telling a fraction of the tale, before the threads are drawn together in the concluding part, told by the first narrator.

Faleti's versatility is equalled only by that of his contemporary Afolabi Olabimtan (b. 1932), a lecturer in Yoruba at the University of Lagos. His first published work was a short play, *Oluwa L'O M'Ejo Da* ("Only God is a good judge," 1966), where a close-knit plot centreing on a murder is used to depict the disreputable practices among priests of various religions and other professional groups. His realistic novel about a lad nicknamed *Kekere Ekun* ("Leopard Cub," 1967) focuses on a Christian character who marries a second wife; but the main interest of the book resides in the portrayal of many aspects of present-day Yoruba rural life, which appears to be dominated by the antinomy between the requirements of the Christian ethos disseminated through the schools and through the strong corporate life of the church congregation, and the undaunted persistence of traditional institutions like polygamy, religious rites and the popular cult festivals. In *Aadota aforo* ("Fifty poems" 1969,) Olabimtan experimented with western prosodic forms such as rhymed couplets and stanza schemes but at the same time he introduced into vernacular literary poetry a critique of party politics and of slavish imitation of western mores, themes which had featured prominently not only in Nigerian novels written in English since the 1950s, but also in the popular folk-operas. It was perhaps the example of these that prompted Olabimtan to write his second play, *Olaore, afe-tojoye* ("Chief Olaore, king by treachery," 1970), which depicts the fall of good King Obalowo, as a result of an error of judgment he had made; while this is presented as a historical tragedy, the contemporary allusions to Chief Awolowo and the dissensions within his Action Group party are unmistakable to the Yoruba reader.

The growth of formal literary writing in Yoruba thus shows a steady development from folk tale and oral narrative to prose fiction and written drama. In recent years, however, international interest has been drawn to an entirely different development which had been in progress since the mid-1940s: the so-called Yoruba "folk opera".[27]

In Yorubaland as in many parts of Black Africa, the dramatic urge used to find fulfilment in a religious context: during religious festivals, historical events were re-enacted, masquerades were organized to placate the gods and appease the dead. These performances were also an occasion for satire: Joel Adedeji recounts that in the 1920s the king of Oyo banned a travelling theatre troupe, the Apidan Theatre, led by actor-manager Abidogun, because of its irreverent treatment of the

household. Another impulse for theatrical activity was provided by the
missionaries, some of whom turned to medieval dramatic techniques
and favoured the staging of vernacular mystery or miracle plays in order
to familiarize illiterate audiences with the holy story. In the 1930s, according to Ulli Beier, Biblical plays were being performed, especially by
members of break-away African churches; the scriptural texts were handled quite freely, and actors would indulge in the ribald humour so
conspicuous in the mystery cycles of Western Europe.

The secularization of Yoruba drama was pioneered in the mid-1940s
by a teacher and choirmaster, Hubert Ogunde (b. 1916). Ogunde made
his beginnings in 1943, when he had his choristers perform school-plays
adapted from Biblical episodes. In 1944, he founded his Concert Company,[28] which became popular in 1945 with a vernacular play entitled
Strike and Hunger, dramatizing the country-wide strike which broke out
in that year. This operatic play was performed in Lagos, but was soon
banned as provocative by the colonial authorities. In those days, Accra
was still considered the cultural centre of British West Africa, and
Ogunde toured the Gold Coast with great success in 1947 and 1948.
Without relinquishing Biblical inspiration, he africanized his scriptural
subject-matter very freely, and also produced plays based on Yoruba
traditions. Box-office considerations often compelled him to perform
popular musicals designed for sheer entertainment. But in some of his
later plays, he turned back to his earlier social and political inspiration,
his usual target being political corruption and the personal quarrels of
the country's leaders. To this category belong *Yoruba Ronu* ("Let the
Yoruba Think") and *O Tito koro* ("Truth is Bitter"), both of which
respond with pungent satire to political events in Western Nigeria in
1963. The satire of Ogunde's two plays was mainly directed at the greed
and corruption of government circles, which retaliated by banning
Ogunde and his company from performing in Western Nigeria. The
ban was lifted by the military government which took control in January
1966.[29]

Meanwhile, Ogunde's example had been followed by others and, in
the course of the dozen years following World War II, several other
companies, often known as "theatre parties", sprang up in Western
Nigeria. Among the most popular was the Ogunmola Travelling Theatre. It was founded *c*. 1947 by E. Kole Ogunmola (1925–1973), whose
works have many features in common with those of Ogunde: he too
resorted to Biblical material and to Yoruba folklore. But his outlook was
more conspicuously Christian and moralizing, and he had a preference
for social, rather than political, criticism. His best play, *Ife Owo* ("Love
of money", first performed in 1963 and printed in 1965), is a witty
satire of the ambition and foolishness which ruin the happy household
of a wealthy man. But his greatest success was *Omuti*, published in

1967,[30] an operatic Yoruba version of Tutuola's *The Palm-wine Drinkard.*

The theatrical activites of Ogunde, Ogunmola and a few other directors who are also authors, actors and composers became an exceedingly important and characteristic feature of cultural life in Yoruba urban centres. Their works, however, seldom reached print. With their mixture of social satire, slapstick humour and sex appeal, they were conceived primarly as popular entertainment, and usually belonged to show business rather than literature. An important step forward was accomplished in 1961 when a young Yoruba composer, Duro Ladipo (1931–1978),[31] had his *Easter Cantata* performed at All Saints Church in Oshogbo. As Ulli Beier recalled, this "aroused considerable controversy, even in the press, because Ladipo introduced drums into the church. It was as a result of this experience that he began to perform his religious compositions outside the church: in schools, on television and — at the invitation of the Nigerian Arts Council — at the Lagos Museum."

In December 1961 Ladipo and his choir were invited to Ibadan to perform the *Easter Cantata* at the Mbari Club, founded by a group of authors and artists—D.O. Fagunwa amongst them—whose aim was the promotion of the arts. Ladipo decided to create a similar club at Oshogbo. The town already had a theatrical tradition, since Ogunmola had been active there for several years. Ladipo extended his choir into a theatre company. His first play, says Ulli Beier, "did not differ much from the type of play performed by Ogunde and his numerous imitators: [its] plot was much too flimsy to be a worthy vehicle for Ladipo's music". Ladipo then turned for inspiration to the annals of his own people as recorded in the *History of the Yorubas* (1921) to which the Aku schoolteacher and catechist Samuel Johnson (1846-1901) had devoted twenty years of his life. [32] In order to do full justice to those venerable chronicles, he distanced himself from the influence of both church music and the "highlife" music that was popular in the night-clubs of Accra and other important cities in British West Africa. He studied traditional drumming and dance, and delved deeply into classical oral poetry. Ladipo was first attracted to the semi-legendary accounts of the old Yoruba kingdom of Oyo, which had ruled over a mighty empire until it was destroyed by inner dissensions leading to Fulani intervention in the early nineteenth century. The first product of this inspiration, *Oba moro* ("The king catches the ghost", first performed 1962), was little more than a chronicle play, where the historical material is by no means digested into clear dramatic significance. Nevertheless, Ladipo had set up musical drama as a form of art endowed with high seriousness. His best play, *Oba ko so* ("The king did not hang", first performed 1963), dramatizes an episode in the decline of the Oyo empire, when King Shango, deserted by his generals, his people, and even his wife,

was driven to suicide and turned into a god. This was the first Yoruba
opera to gain international acclaim when it was performed at the Berlin
Theatre and Music Festival in 1964, and at the Commonwealth Festival
in Britain in 1965.[33]

With *Oba waja* ("The king is dead," first performed 1964), Ladipo
turned to the recent past and to an incident that actually took place on
the death of the king of Oyo in 1945: the Commander of the King's
House was prevented by the British District Officer from following his
ruler to the grave as custom demands; when the Commander's son, a
trader in Ghana, returned to Oyo, he committed suicide in order to
wash away the stain on the honour of his family. In a way, this story
illustrated one aspect of the familiar theme of the clash of cultures, but
Ladipo turned it into an individual tragedy of compelling power, which
brings out the fundamental antagonism between the individualistic humanitarian values of the West and the heroic demands of traditional
culture.

For *Moremi*,[34] Ladipo turned back to Johnson's *History of the Yorubas*
and to very ancient traditions dealing with semi-mythical times, when
the small Yoruba kingdoms acknowledged the supremacy of Ife, the
earliest of the Yoruba settlements. According to Johnson's account, the
Ife Yorubas were plagued by raids from their Igbo enemies, the original
owners of the land; Moremi, the wife of one of the Ife heroes, promised
the gods to sacrifice her most precious possession if they would permit
her to find out the secrets of the Igbo; she then allowed herself to be
captured by the raiders and because of her beauty she was turned over
to their king: "she became familiar with all their customs", Johnson
says, "and learnt all their secrets; there she also learnt that those who
were such objects of terror to her people were mere men, who covered
themselves from head to foot with *Ekan* grass and bamboo fibres, making them appear extra-human". The Ife people were thus enabled to
fight their enemies successfully with lighted torches. When Moremi returned to the god's sanctuary, she learned that the sacrifice demanded
of her was that of her only son—a favourite motif in warlike societies
and exemplified in the Biblical story of Jephtha and in the Sokame
legend among the Baule of the Ivory Coast. But Ladipo heightened the
tragic stature of the heroine and gave the episode deeper ethical meaning in two ways which were explained by Ulli Beier in his introduction
to *Three Nigerian Plays*. In the drama, Moremi knows from the first that
she will have to sacrifice her son, and she accepts this in order to ensure
the survival of her nation; further, the Igbo raids in the play are the
righteous punishment inflicted upon the Ife, who failed to pacify the
spirits of the land after they had conquered it: the offering of Moremi's
only child is an atonement for this sin of the ancestors, which shall not
be repeated, as the heroine prevents the king of Ife from taking revenge
upon the vanquished Igbo.

The next internationally successful performance of Ladipo's company was *Eda*, a skilful African version of the medieval morality play, *Everyman,* which raises some difficult problems for the historian of Yoruba literature. In his introduction to *Three Nigerian Plays* Ulli Beier claimed that *Eda* was the work of one Obotunde Ijimere, whose *Born with the Fire on His Head* was included in the volume, along with Beier's English adaptation of Ladipo's *Moremi.* Ijimere's name had first appeared in print previously as the author of *The Imprisonment of Obatala and Other Plays*, published in Heinemann's African Writers Series (1966); on the back cover, there was a photograph and a brief notice of a black African, presumably Ijimere himself, who was allegedly born in Western Nigeria in 1930. But Beier's introduction of 1967 revealed that this was only a pen-name. And in 1972, Janheinz Jahn's *Who's Who in African Literature* brought the further revelation that Ijimere was simply a pseudonym for Ulli Beier himself. [35] At any rate, *Eda*, which had been described as "adapted by Duro Ladipo into Yoruba" in the Mbari Mbayo edition issued in Oshogbo in 1965, was republished by the Institute of African Studies at Ibadan in 1970 as an "opera by Duro Ladipo", without any qualifications.

As to "Obotunde Ijimere", he does not fall within the scope of the present study, since no work of his had ever been published in Yoruba, even though Ulli Beier's introduction of 1967 makes the purposefully ambiguous assertion that *"Born with the Fire on his Head* was originally conceived in Yoruba [but] may in fact be more successful as an English verse drama"! In 1963, Ulli Beier became involved with the Lagos "Theatre Express" company, for which "Obotunde Ijimere" wrote several plays in English.

It will best be left to Yoruba historians to decide what place should be ascribed both to Ulli Beier and to "Obotunde Ijimere" in the development of their literature, whether in English, or in their own language. It is likely that this will be done in the not too distant future, for the most original and distinctive feature of the present stage in the evolution of Yoruba culture is the stupendous growth of what may be called, for lack of a better term, "native scholarship". Until the late 1960s, such scant scholarly attention as was accorded to African language writing came from European scholars. The sole exception was South Africa, which had produced such well-trained and well-informed students of her own Bantu literatures as A.C. Jordan and C.L.S. Nyembezi; but the Education Act of 1953 has stifled the growth of this promising development, and there has been a distinct falling off in the quality of scholarly writing by black students of South African literatures. Since independence, there has been a notable growth in the contribution of East African scholars to the study of Swahili literature. But nowhere have historical study and critical evaluation of the literature in the local lan-

guage been pursued with as much zest and efficiency as among the
Yoruba intelligentsia.[36] They have explored their literary patrimony,
both oral and written, with unparalleled thoroughness and enthusiasm
and they have gathered historical facts with unprecedented care and
accuracy. This, incidentally, is the reason why the remaining parts of
this book will appear, unfortunately, so sketchy: apart from Yoruba and
Swahili, and, to a lesser extent, Hausa, information about modern vernacular writing both in West and East Africa is exceedingly limited: it
will be the task of future African scholars to systematically explore this
vast, though still practically virgin, field, to collect all relevant data, and
to organize the results into a coherent account.

● ● ●

While the Hausa community of Northern Nigeria has failed thus far to
make any significant contribution to the English literature of the country,
and while the Yorubas have shown an exceptional degree of creativity in
both African and European languages, the greater part of the literature
produced by the Igbo of South-eastern Nigeria has been in English, beginning with the well-known Onitsha chapbooks of the 1950s. Only extensive historical research will make it possible to account for this intriguing
difference. An early clue was offered more than a hundred years ago by a
famed Sierra Leonean writer of Igbo parentage, James Africanus Horton
(1835–1883), who noted that "The Egboes are considered the most imitative and emulative people of the whole of Western Africa . . . They always
possess a desire of superiority and make attempts to attain it, or excel in
what is praiseworthy". And Horton went on to quote Bishop Crowther,
who wrote scarcely a year after the establishment of a missionary station at
Onitsha in the late 1850s: "From all I could gather by observation, the
Iboes are very emulative. As in other things, so it will be in book learning.
Other towns will not rest satisfied until they have also learned the mystery
of reading and writing, by which their neighbours might surpass them
and put them in the shade."[37]

Bishop Crowther was right . . . up to a point. And he was instrumental
in ensuring partial fulfilment of his own prophecy by producing the
first primer in Igbo in 1857. According to a well-informed Igbo scholar,
this "was more than a linguistic text. It also formed the basic foundation
of Igbo written literature. The extracts it contained became the first
literary creations in the Igbo language".[38] Nevertheless, Paul Hair considers that the pioneer of Igbo literature was Crowther's assistant, J.C.
Taylor, a Sierra Leonean of Igbo origin, who provided the first Gospel
translations in the 1860s. When original Christian composition in the
language began with the publication of a slender collection of *Ibo Hymns*
(1870), it could hardly be said to be of "native authorship" in any strict

sense, for the author, Frederick Weeks Smart, was likewise a Sierra Leonean of Igbo origin. Hair's research gave him "the impression that a mass of Ibo minor literature was published by C.M.S. workers between 1893 and 1914", so that there is some ground for thinking that "there was a time when it seemed that a respectably vigorous Igbo literature was imminent".[39]

One reason why this failed to materialize is the fact that the early linguistic research by Crowther and German missionary-linguist J.F. Schön was thwarted by the baffling variety of Igbo dialects: "This created much difficulty in the work of linguists and was later to result in controversies over orthographies which greatly hampered the growth of Igbo written language and literature."[40] Yet, it is Hair's opinion that this bad start made by linguistic studies cannot be the sole, or even the main, reason for the Igbo's neglect of their own language as a medium for creative writing: at the end of the nineteenth century, he claims, "the Igbo experienced an upsurge of interest in literacy—but it was not a genuine and continuing interest in vernacular literacy. Igbo children, having been taught to read through vernacular primers, were hurried on by their parents to acquire, and to read, English, the language of opportunity; in this way the Igbo gained a position of power in the colonial and post-colonial social and administrative order in Nigeria, but the Igbo language was neglected. It would seem therefore that continuing Igbo lack of interest in the Igbo language is due to the peculiar Igbo environment and psychology, as much as to the failure of generations of linguists to produce an acceptable solution to the dialect problem."

The fact is, as Emenyonu points out, that Crowther's *Primer* "did not seem to have had any effect on other contemporary writers to try to provide something of a literary nature for the Igbo schoolchildren. Publications continued along the traditional grammar books designed to give some assistance to missionaries in their efforts to acquire the Igbo language." The complete Bible was at last translated, and it "was to be a chief influence in Igbo education and literature". "The second stage of missionary activities was devoted to the collection of oral narratives and other oral performances." This resulted in *Akwukwo Ogugu Igbo* ("Igbo Reader", 1927), an enlarged edition of Crowther's primer. "About the same time too, the Methodist Mission translated the *Pilgrim's Progress* into Igbo for use in schools." Likewise, "extracts from such works as *The Arabian Nights, Grimm's Fairy Tales* and *Tales from Shakespeare* were translated into Igbo and used widely in schools".

Actually, genuine "native authorship" was prompted from outside, and modern imaginative writing in Igbo did not make a start until 1932, when it was one of the five languages in the International African Institute competition. Twenty-one Igbo entries were submitted, of which seventeen got some sort of award. The prize winner, Pita Nwana, was a joiner at the Uzuakoli Institute. His *Omenuko* which was first printed in England in 1935, was a slender, 67-page "novelette" but it soon became a favourite with Igbo readers and has often been reprinted since. The story is based on the life of a historical figure, an Igbo chieftain during the early days of British colonization.[41] The hero is a man of overweening ambition who, in his lust for wealth and power, commits a grievous crime against the religion and customs of his village. Instead of seeking pardon and reconciliation, he flees to another town. There, although he achieves some measure of material success and even obtains temporary chieftaincy, he is overcome by a sense of alienation and at last understands, as Nwana puts it, that "no matter how successful a man may be in a foreign land, he cannot fail to realize eventually that there is no place like home". Nwana's tale anticipates in a way the novels that his fellow Igbo Chinua Achebe was later to write in English, for it exemplifies a human conflict between the typically Igbo spirit of self-assertion and the powerful African sense of subvervience to communal values.[42]

In spite of the success of *Omenuko*, Nwana had remarkably few followers, even though a Literature Bureau for Eastern Nigeria was inaugurated in Umuahia in 1949. After one year of activity, its secretary could only complain that "the amount of original work which has found its way to the Bureau for publication has been disappointing"; she commented that "the development of literature is confronted by a number of difficulties, such as diversity of dialect (about which there is tension between one district and another), variety of orthography and script, about which feeling runs so high that most books in the Igbo language have to be published in both the old and the new—a disastrously expensive proposition".[43]

Indeed, according to Emenyonu, it was not until thirty years after *Omenuko* that a second Igbo novel was produced: *Ije Odumodu Jere* ("Odumodu's travels", 1963), by Leopold Bell-Gam. Although the story takes place in the same period as does the earlier book, and in spite of the many similarities between both tales, Bell-Gam has a Christian outlook which is absent from Nwana's novel. Further, he has availed himself of the more cosmopolitan experience made possible by Nigeria's emergence into the modern world. Not only do the hero's adventures carry him to Europe and America, but, as Emenyonu puts it, "the author strives to build his theme into a race issue", although he only succeeds "in making a case for his hero as a Christian": "Odumodu triumphs over the oppressive white race not because he is black but because he is a Christian who practices the teachings of the Bible as well as the Christian doctrines".

Both Nwana's and Bell-Gam's novels illustrated the spirit of enterprise which had long been recognized as characteristic of the Igbo. At the same time, their endings set a pattern which was also characteristic of the Igbo novel in English: it might be called (*pace* Hardy) the return-of-the-native theme.[44] But as far as language is concerned, they failed to stimulate the formation of a significant tradition of vernacular prose fiction. Instead, the Igbo community was the main purveyor of English writing in the 1950s and 1960s, with the Onitsha chapbooks and with such popular novelists as Cyprian Ekwensi, Chinua Achebe, Onuora Nzekwu, Elechi Amadi, Flora Nwapa, and a host of others.[45] Even the nationalistic fervour stirred by the Biafran war does not seem to have led to the production of any worthwhile creative writing in the language.[46] Future historians will probably locate the beginning of real literary development in the mid-seventies, when the Oxford University Press branch in Ibadan and several small publishers in Enugu and Onitsha issued R.M. Ekechukwu's anthology of modern Igbo verse, *Akpa Uche* (1975), E. Obikeh's epic poem, *Eke Une*, the first literary play in Igbo, A.B. Chukuezi's *Udo ka mma*, and several novels, the bulkiest of which was *Isi ekwu dara N'ala* by T.U. Ubesie, who wrote at least four other slighter prose narratives between 1974 and 1976.

•   •   •

Of the various languages spoken in Southern Nigeria besides Yoruba and Igbo, only Efik seems to have given rise to a written art of its own. It is spoken by some three million people of different ethnic groups that live in the Cross River delta in Eastern Nigeria and in the neighboring areas, from Cameroon to the Calabar River. Calabar was an important station for the slave trade and Daryll Ford's *Efik Traders of Old Calabar* (1956) contains the diary, written in pidgin English, of Antera Duke, an Efik slave-trading chief and a member of "the literate conservative merchant oligarchy" that emerged in Calabar at the end of the eighteenth century.[47] This is probably the first important document written in some sort of English by an African on African soil.

In 1846, the United Presbyterian Church of Scotland sent a mission to Calabar under the leadership of Hope Masterton Waddell, whose staff was a Christian Negro group from Jamaica.[48] One of the first tasks of the mission was to embark on what Nigerian scholar Adeboye Babalola calls "a well-planned study of the Efik language";[49] Waddell himself produced the first Efik vocabulary (1846) and the first reader (1847) which were printed on the Old Calabar Mission Press. [50] Scriptural texts were issued with relentless zeal, beginning with William Anderson's version of *Jonah* (1850). A great many Efik proverbs were included in Richard F. Burton's *Wit and Wisdom from West Africa* (London, 1865) and *The Pilgrim's Progress* was made available in Efik in 1868.

Efik authorship, however, was slow to make a start. In fact, in the Niger delta as at other points along the Guinea coast, one of the first original effects of literacy was to act as an incentive for the invention of indigenous scripts. In the early years of the twentieth century, some records were made by members of the Ekpe society in the secret Nsibidi script.[51] In 1936, another alphabet was developed, Oberi Okaime; but this was not a new script: it was never used for transcribing the Efik tongue, but members of a local syncretic church, the Christian Spirit Movement, used it for religious writings in their own "revealed" language.[52]

Here as in many other parts of black Africa, the literary awakening of the written art was stimulated by official initiative. After an Efik-Ibibio literary competition was held in 1933,[53] two writers of unequal stature emerged simultaneously. In his novel *Mutanda oyom Namondo* ("Mudanda in search of Namondo", 1935), E.E. Nkana, says Babalola, "makes the gods and goddesses of traditional belief come alive in the adventures of a king, Mutanda, who went in quest of his lost son, Namondo". Although the Yoruba critic states that this "fascinating novel" made the author's name "a household world among the Efik-speaking peoples", Nkana seems to have given up creative writing altogether.[54]

This was not so with E.N. Amaku, who was born at the turn of the century.[55] A devoted school teacher and a prolific writer, he entered the literary field in 1935 with *Ufök-uto-ikö-Efik* ("The house of poems in Efik") and *Kini kini*, both of which were printed on the press of the Hope Waddell Training Institute. They were followed by a collection of religious poems, *Equaro* (1938). In 1937, Amaku had entered the eighth IAI competition with a story, *Abasi Ekpenyön* , which later formed the last volume in a series of school readers in six books, *Edikot nwed mbuk* (1935–1953), designed to depict Efik culture in all its variety and to convey to Efik children the animal lore of their legacy of oral tradition. In 1945, an Efik Translation Bureau was founded in Calabar,[56] and Amaku contributed several didactic pamphlets to its list of publications.

Amaku remained the sole standard-bearer of Efik writing until 1952, when the first two plays —*Unam öbön enyene kpa öbön* ("The royal meat must belong to the king") by E.E. Okon and *Sidibe* by Ernest A. Edyan—were printed in a single volume. Of these two playwrights, only the latter achieved a measure of popularity. *Sidibe* was performed by the Calabar Cultural Association at Ibadan in 1958.[57] In Babalola's judgment, his best play is *Asibong Edem*, "a tragedy depicting historical events in the political and social life of the great prince Asibong Edem of old Calabar. It portrays vividly various aspects of Efik life and culture, ranging from the luxurious life of the princes in the royal court to the commoners' hard life on the plantations; from the influence of the diviners to the absolute power of the Ekpe secret society. The play depicts how, "in spite of the apparently harmonious blending of the plans of the deities with those of human beings, the gods can thwart at will a man's ambition to become a king even on the eve of the man's coronation".

Among contributors to Efik poetry, such as John I. Ikpeme and Efiom Efana Ita, who emerged in the late 1950s, Babalola singles out Elizabeth E. Asibong, "whose poems are broadcast daily from Calabar over the network of the Nigerian Broadcasting Corporation. Her most popular work is an epic poem composed in 1956 to commemorate the visit of Queen Elizabeth II in Calabar." She reached print with *Hogan Kid Bassey-Eren owo akan eren owo* ("A man who conquers a man", 1957).

As to the probable future of Efik literature, Babalola, writing in 1971, put great hope in "the creation of the South-Eastern State of Nigeria": this, he expects, should lay stronger emphasis "in the schools curricula on the study of Efik, which now serves as the main vehicle of communication among the various ethnic groups of the State." Such a measure should in turn "lead to a rapid development of Efik literature through the exertions of budding writers who—so Babalola claims—evidently abound among the new generation".

Idoma, one of Nigeria's numerous minor languages, is spoken along the banks of the Benue River. It did not produce any creative writing until the late 1960s when Samson O.O. Amali (b. 1947) had his first plays published in mimeographed form at the Institute of African Studies of the University of Ibadan. As informant for Idoma at the Institute, he was the first member of his people to study his own language academically, doing so with the help of the works of R.C. Abraham's.[58] As an undergraduate student, he had been a prolific contributor of poems and essays in English to the *International School Magazine*, but he had always shown intense devotion to the oral lore of his native culture. His work with Professor R.G. Armstrong consisted mainly in collecting a large corpus of Idoma oral tradition, poetry and folktales, some of which have been published with accompanying gramophone records and English translations. This research supplied him with a wealth of material for undertaking vernacular creative writing of his own. While there is some exaggeration in Armstrong's generalization that Amali was "the first Nigerian poet to compose directly in his own language on the basis of a competent, scholarly knowledge of that language",[59] he was certainly the pioneer of Idoma written art. His major contribution is in the field of drama. After a school play in English, *The Downfall of Ogbuu* (composed and performed 1963, mimeographed 1968), he produced *Onugbo MeOko* ("Onugbo and Oko", mimeographed 1968, printed 1972), which deals with the rivalry between two brothers, the elder of whom is jealous of the other's hunting prowess. As Armstrong put it in his Introduction, this is the author's own "poetic and dramatic version of an Idoma traditional, ancestral story", which he re-interpreted so as to "relate it to certain themes of modern life and to adapt it to the needs of the stage. Perhaps the most significant feature of the play resides in the depiction of customary judicial procedure as administered by the elders."

As early as 1966, Amali had published, in the *International School Magazine*, a poem entitled "Coup d'Etat in Nigeria", which showed that he did not wish to remain entrenched in the ivory tower of linguistic and folklore studies. This was reprinted with a French translation in *L'Afrique Actuelle* (1967). The Nigerian crisis of January 1966 and the events leading up to it provided the subject-matter for *Aootilei* ("The Leaders", 1972), a patriotic play where the characters' speeches are "a development from traditional Idoma oratory and chant, as it may be heard in the great public inquests, the poetic chants of the alekwu and ancestral masks, and in public debate", in a fascinating adaptation of the time-honoured devices of oral art to a contemporary topic.

Meanwhile, Amali never stopped composing poetry, both in English[60] and in his native tongue. Several Idoma poems appeared, with their English translations, in *Selected Poems* (1968) and in *Worlds Within Worlds and Other Poems* (1970).

Whatever fate the future may hold in store for the incipient Idoma literature, the very existence of Amali's mother-tongue poems and plays, shows that scholarly research on African languages, coming after the missionaries' educational enterprise and the official support provided by the literature bureaux, can play its part in the emergence and development of modern vernacular writing. This had already been demonstrated in 1964 when Professor Wolf Leslau published *Shinega's Village*: the book had originally been composed in Chaha by Ethiopian writer Sahle Sellassie Berhane Mariam. But the Chaha text never reached print and the author has since relinquished his own language to produce several novels in English. Amali's case is different. Though he may have been prompted in part by his, and Armstrong's, desire to provide linguistic and anthropological documents in Idoma, it is clear that, unlike Sahle Sellassie, Amali is now aiming to lay the foundations of a modern literature in his own language. In this, he has received welcome help from the Ibadan Institute of African Studies, whose "Bilingual Literary Works" series, inaugurated by the publication of several Yoruba operas, now seems bound to stimulate creative writing in other Nigerian languages.

3. Ghana

Statistics published in 1969 [61] show that, out of the nineteen Ghanaian languages that had produced printed material, only five account for the bulk of such creative writing as has been issued so far (Ga: 36 books; Akuapem Twi: 33; Ewe: 15; Asante Twi: 12; and Fante: 10), with Nzema (5 books) and Dangme (3 books) coming far behind. To the Akan group belong Fante, Twi (with its two dialects, Asante-Twi and Akuapem-Twi) and Nzema. Twi and Fante are spoken over the greater part of southern Ghana; there are about one million native speakers of Ewe, who live mainly in south-eastern Ghana and in Togo; Ga, which is closely related to Dangme, has the advantage of being spoken in the area where Accra is situated. The growth of vernacular writing, however, was by no means commensurate with the relative importance of those languages, and the accidents of history are largely responsible for the divergences in the literary fate of Ghanaian languages. [62]

•   •   •

By the early decades of the nineteenth century, the Fante kingdom had already had fairly close trade relations with the western world for a long time. The coastline was dotted with a chain of forts and trading stations which were in the hands of the British, the Dutch and the Danes. Commerce had fostered the rise of a prosperous merchant class, who enjoyed British support in their determination to keep their powerful Asante neighbours to the north away from the profitable European trade. In 1835, shortly before the British government assumed direct responsibility for the administration of the forts and, implicitly, for the protection of the Fante kingdom, the Wesleyan Missionary Society began operations which were soon to be vigorously pursued under the direction of a British mulatto, Thomas Birch Freeman. It has been noted by a historian of the Presbyterian church that the Wesleyans "began their work at Cape Coast and although they were active in rural areas their main strategy was invariably to settle first in the large urban centres"; they were thus in close touch with the new, modernizing, politically conscious merchant class, whose young people "preferred the Wesleyan schools because of their emphasis on the English language in contrast with the emphasis on the vernacular in the Basel Mission schools".[63] By the time the Fante confederation was constituted in 1868, as a reaction to the steady and disquieting growth of British power and control, Wesleyan educational policy, which was soon to culminate in the foundation of a famous secondary school for the Fante bourgeoisie at Mfantsipim in 1876, combined with the influence of such Sierra Leonean thinkers as Africanus Horton, had created a small but articulate and energetic intellectual class, whose linguistic medium was English. It made its voice heard through the Cape Coast newspapers and through the books of a number of young British-educated Fante lawyers and educationalists, such as John Mensah Sarbah (1864–1910), J.E. Casely Hayford (1866-1930), and James Aggrey (1875–1927).[64]

While these circumstances account for the fact that early Ghanaian writing, which was mainly of a didactic and political nature, originated among Fante authors writing in English, the Methodist Missionaries did not relinquish their usual linguistic tasks altogether. As early as 1860, one of the first Fante primers had been published by Timothy Laing and W.A. Hanson, both of them natives of Ghana.[65] During the late nineteenth century an African Wesleyan minister, A. W. Parker, produced a Fante version of two gospels. In 1886 a Fante version of *The Pilgrim's Progress* was produced by his colleague Jacob Benjamin Anaman.

Original writing in Fante, however, did not make a start until yet another Wesleyan minister, who was at one time headmaster of Mfantsipim, Gaddiel Robert Acquaah (*c.* 1884–1954), had a collection of hymns printed locally in 1929. His literary career had begun in 1920 with an English rendering of *Fante Classical Poems*; his interest in traditional culture remained conspicuous in the folk-tales recorded in *Ababaawa na atwer* ("The Maid and the toad", 1932), in *Mfantse mbebusem* ("Fante proverbs", 1940) and in *Mfantse amambra* ("Fante customs", 1947). A tireless writer, he contributed to the Fante translation of the Bible, he wrote a biography of Wesley, and he helped edit various Fante readers, grammars and textbooks for school use. His original poetry was gathered in *Akyekyewere* ("Songs of comfort", n.d.). Acquaah remained an isolated figure until the early 1930s, when Fante became, with Twi, Ga and Ewe, one of the four local languages selected for the West African School Certificate.[66] This encouraged the development of an educated Fante readership whose needs were catered for by a weekly secular newspaper printed in Cape Coast, *Amansuon* (1943–*c.* 1960), and by a few early samples of modern vernacular prose fiction such as Henry James Martin's *Ekumfi Benada* ("The great Tuesday of the Ekumfi people", 1936) and J.E.K. Korsah's *Kweku a oridzi ne drew* ("Kweku is enjoying himself", 1937).

When the Vernacular Literature Bureau was established in 1951, Fante was one of the nine languages selected for promotion, although with meagre results in the sphere of creative writing. Between the foundation of the Bureau and Ghana's accession to independence in 1957, only a handful of works of prose fiction were published in that language. The bulk of Fante writing remained devoted to the description of customs and the recording of folk-tales and proverbs. A few "novelettes" were produced by two authors who achieved some prominence after independence, when the institution was given its present name of Bureau of Ghana Languages. They were Samuel Koli Otoo (b. 1908), who produced a number of slender stories, and J.A. Annobil (b. 1911), whose activity, however, remained chiefly connected with the Methodist Book Depot in Cape Coast. The policy of the Bureau led to a large growth in Fante authorship with *Akan Awensem* ("Akan poems", 1964) by a younger writer, Winful E. Archie (b. 1922); a collection of folktales, *Ndzemba ahyese* (1963) by Daniel K. Abbiw (b. 1915), who was also responsible for a Fante version of some tales by Tolstoy (1961); and *Obaatan Kesewa* (1967), a story by Efua Theodora Sutherland (b. 1924), who is better known for her contributions to Ghanaian drama of the early 1960s, both in Fante and in English. Perhaps the most significant Fante writer to have reached print after independence was Kobena Gyate Akwa, who also signed himself Joseph Ghartey (1911–1967):[67] he had been producing stories and plays for the Ghana Broadcasting Company ever since its inception in 1937; one of the most successful of them, *Twer Nyame* ("The flower-basket") was printed in 1959, and two further plays of his were issued posthumously by the Bureau of Ghana Languages in *Aso awar nye ni* (1971).

• • •

In 1828, German-speaking missionaries of the Basler Evangelische Missionsgesellschaft, in connection with Danish trading interests in the Christiansborg area, began operations in the Twi-speaking territories.[68] After a few difficult years on the coast, they moved inland to Akropong where they established a school in 1843 and a catechists' training college in 1848.[69] In contrast with the Wesleyans, "the Basel Committee insisted that, at all costs, the African was to hear the Gospel, to read the Bible, and worship and be taught in his own tongue. Johannes Gottlieb Christaller was commissioned by the Home Board to devote himself solely to the Twi language, the most widely-spoken in the Gold Coast . . . Six years after his arrival in Akropong, in 1859, Christaller was able to publish the four Gospels and the Acts, and "cater for school and worship needs in the shape of Bible portions, hymns and catechetical passages". Christaller's Twi Bible was printed in 1870–71, his Grammar in 1875 and his Dictionary in 1881, so that it has been possible to claim that his work "raised the Twi language to a literary level and provided the basis of all later work in the language".[70] As early as 1883, the mission launched a periodical, *The Christian Messenger* ,which was mostly in Twi, and which was continued intermittently until 1933.[71] A translation of *The Pilgrim's Progress*, the work of the Rev. David Asante, was printed in Basel in 1885. And original composition made an early start with *Bere Adu*! ("Now is the time!", 1913), a collection of twenty-five short stories by J.J. Adaye. Though nothing is known of this early author's biography, he achieved some fame with a collection of proverbs (1934, reprinted 1947), and a later scholar, C.A. Akrofi, edited another collection of his short stories in 1948. This intense activity led to the Akuapem-Twi dialect assuming a position of literary priority and pre-eminence, despite the fact that it is spoken only in a small part of southern Ghana, whereas Asante-Twi, which can boast a far larger number of speakers in central Ghana, remained neglected for many decades.

As a result of the defeat of the Germans in West Africa, the work of the Basel Mission was taken over in 1917 by Presbyterian missionaries of the United Free Church of Scotland, under whose auspices the linguistic and educational work was continued by one of Christaller's disciples, Clement Anderson Akrofi (1901–1967). After Christaller, no one did more than Akrofi for the serious study of the Twi language and lore, with his Twi grammar (*Twi Kasa Mmara*, 1937), his *Twi Spelling Book* (1938), and his *Twi Mmebusem: Twi Proverbs, with English Translations and Comments* (1958), all of them composed at a time in the history of Ghana "when the road to recognition as a scholar lay in the ability with which one was able to handle European languages".[72] Nor was he alone in this, for other members of his generation showed a deep interest in their own culture, as is obvious in several bulky works on Twi, and more generally Akan, culture and customs, such as *Akanfoo amammere* (1950) *Kotonkrowi* (1964) and *Tete Akorae* (1970) by Bennett Smith Akuffo (b. 1902), or *Twifo amamuisem* (1951) by Safori Fianko (b. 1895).

There were others among Akrofi's contemporaries who made a decisive contribution to creative writing in Akuapem-Twi by initiating formal drama in the language. In 1935, the Scottish Book Depot in Accra published *Nana Agyeman hwehwe* ("In search of Nana Agyeman") by Emmanuel J. Osew (b. 1900). This play in verse was followed some twenty years later by *Asantehene Osee Tutu* (1955), a historical drama on the famous Osei Tutu, the eighteenth century founder of the Asante empire. Osew's example was soon followed by another graduate of the Basel Mission schools, who was to play an important role in the history of Ghana: Joseph Boakye Danquah (1895–1965), whose vernacular drama *Nyankonsem (Fables of the Celestial)* was published in 1941. The career of Danquah, who had obtained a Ph.D. at the University of London in 1927, signalled the coalescence of several trends that had been developing separately in Ghana. As a highly-trained Twi intellectual, he was able to share in the leadership role which had formerly been the preserve of English-oriented Fante Methodists. His first printed book had been *Akan Law and Customs* (1928). Writing both in Akwapem-Twi and in English, he became "the self-appointed interpreter of Western tradition and thought to the traditional élite, and he also sought to clarify traditional customs and problems to the rising generation of young men".[73] He was also responsible for suggesting that the name of the Gold Coast should be changed to Ghana. As one of the founders of the United Gold Coast Convention in 1947, he was regarded as the most prominent politician in the country until the advent of Kwame Nkrumah and his more radical Convention People's Party. After independence, he was one of the leaders of the opposition and was put in jail, where he died. It is worth recalling that Danquah also contributed to Ghanaian drama in English with *The Third Woman* (1943).

Sound foundations had thus been laid for Akuapem-Twi writing long before official encouragement was given to the vernacular languages. Nevertheless, educational development and the foundation of the Vernacular Literature Bureau made it possible for some elder writers to have their works published. This was the case with the stories of A.P.A. Martinson (b. 1900), *Adowa dwontofo* ("Adowa, the singer", 1964) and *Afoofi bere nhoma* (1966). But an impressive number of new authors also came to the fore. Many of them wrote for the stage, following in the wake of Osew and Danquah. They include E.O. Koranteng (b. 1915) with *Mpuaasa ntiamoa* ("A man with three tufts of hair", 1950) and *Osabarima* ("The warrior", 1961), E.N. Safo with *Afrakoma* (1954), and J. Yeboa Dankwa with *Okanni ba* (1966). But the greater part of creative writing in Akuapem-Twi consists of brief novelettes which are often based on traditional folk-stories. This genre which, in Ghana as in most parts of Africa, is mainly designed for school use, is represented by D. Offei Darko's *Obra ye bona* ("Life is a battle", 1968); by Edwin Efa, A.V.N. Amarteifio, whose *Bediako* (1962) is also available in an English translation (1964), and Lawrence D. Apraku, who, after two vernacular stories, wrote *A Prince of the Akans* (1964) in English. A.A. Opoku (b. 1912), who was educated at Aprokong although he was born in Asante province, tried his hand at several genres: after *Odehuro* ("Shouting the yam", 1953), a play about the traditional yam festival, he published a short novel, *Mo Ahenewa* ("Well-done, king's offspring", 1961), and, later, a small collection of poems, *Mese wo amen* (1971).

In the nineteenth century, Akuapem was only a distant province of the mighty Asante empire that had its capital, Kumasi, in Central Ghana. Being situated nearer to the coastline, it proved more accessible to the literacy campaigns of the Basel missionaries: hence the early emergence of its dialect as a literary language. The empire itself, or rather what remained of it after a long process of decline, did not come under British control until 1897, when Prempe, the last Asante emperor, was arrested and exiled. Early attempts to start mission work in 1881 had been nullified by the last Ashanti wars. The expulsion of the Basel missionaries in 1917 did nothing to accelerate the growth of literacy, a prerequisite for the emergence of the written art. Nevertheless, the bulk of the Twi-speaking community doggedly refused to accept Akuapem-Twi as its literary language, so that in the early 1950s, both Akuapem-Twi and Asante-Twi were selected for promotion by the Vernacular Literature Bureau, thus recognizing the existence and validity of an independent literature which had just been created in Asante-Twi. [74]

The founder of Asante-Twi literature was J.H. Kwabena Nketia (b. 1921), a musicologist of international repute, who, although he had been educated in Akropong, wrote the first printed works in his own dialect. His first story, *Semode* ("Pleasant news", 1936), followed by a collection of folktales, *Akanfoo anansesem nghoma* (1949), a play, *Ananwoma* (1951), a short story, *Kwabena Amoa* (1952) and a collection of poems, *Anwonsem 1944–1949* (1952), can be said to have laid the foundation of Asante-Twi literature, which developed with great rapidity, while Nketia devoted more and more of his attention to the scholarly study of traditional oral art and music, not from a narrowly Asante angle, but as samples of the wider Akan culture.

Among the earliest practitioner of Asante-Twi was Robert Asare Tabi (*c*. 1910–1958) who began with a biography of *Ohene Khama* (1949), after which he provided a Twi version of an English translation of some tales by Tolstoy, *Ayesem mmiensa bi* (1952), as a model for the writing of short prose fiction. In 1953, he published an account of traditional festival customs, *Odwiratwa*, and *Aka m'ani* ("I would just watch"), a short play about a trader who is driven to ruin by drunkenness and other vices. After his untimely death, the Bureau of Ghana Languages issued another play of his, *Me nko me yam* ("My own stomach only", 1960), which dramatizes a folktale of the spider cycle, and *Ohia nhye da* ("Poverty comes unexpectedly", 1962), a short historical novel set in the 1880s when cocoa cultivation was introduced into the Gold Coast.

The early 1950s saw the appearance in print of a considerably older writer, Thomas Yao Kani (1877–1962),[75] who had already gained a considerable local reputation as a traditional story-teller and a music lover. His first publication was a collection of folk stories humorously entitled *Asikayo, Akanfoo nnuane titire ne abasem* ("The main concerns of the Akan are money-making and story-telling", 1950). This was followed by several other similar collections and a number of vernacular pamphlets dealing with the Asante language and folk riddles, or more generally with Akan culture.

When the Vernacular Literature Bureau was founded in 1951, Tabi was appointed editor for Asante-Twi until 1956. From 1960 to 1964, this post was occupied by his contemporary Andrew Christian Denteh (b. 1913). Like most vernacular writers of the pioneering generations, Denteh was primarily interested in the preservation of oral lore: his *Agyaa Ananse* ("Father Spider", 1964) is a folktale of the spider cycle, and his *Akwasi Mahuw* (1964) is a biographical story describing traditional Asante life and clan disputes in the eighteenth century. Denteh is not a prolific writer: his most important literary achievement is perhaps the launching, in 1968, of *Odawuru*, a high-quality Akan journal that is concerned with modern and traditional literature, ethnography and history.

Most writers of Asante-Twi who emerged during the 1950s and early 1960s proved to be interested exclusively in the recording of oral lore, especially tales and proverbs, but a turning point seemed to occur around 1965: a new form of prose fiction began to gain the upper hand with the publication of a half dozen so-called novels, which were really short stories extended to 30–60 pages. The trend had been anticipated by Joseph Oduro with *Seantee: A novel in Asante-Twi* (1958), an edifying 42-page narrative recounting how an overly pampered child eventually grows up to be a hardened criminal. Michael Boateng Amanfo, who had begun with *Akan ayesem mmienu bi* ("Two Akan folktales", 1960), later produced two "novels", *Se ebewie* ("How will it end?", 1964), and *Mehunie a anka* (" 'Had I known' is always too late", 1967). Of the authors of prose fiction who emerged in the late sixties and early seventies, mention must be made of E.M. Opong: after *Asem-se-be* (1966), a collection of stories designed to illustrate traditional proverbs, he turned to straight narrative with *Kwabena Gyam* (1967), and later brought his contribution to the developing corpus of Asante-Twi drama with his play *Apene: baabiara nye* (1969). The example set by Nketia and Tabi in this respect had already been followed by another dramatist, Kwabu Adom-Ampofo, with the two plays issued as *So mu yie* (1967). As to poetry, its only notable representative among the younger generation is Joseph Kwasi Brantuo with *Asetena mu Awonsem. Poems of Everyday Life, with English translation* (1964); Brantuo has been a frequent contributor to *Odawuru*.

● ● ●

East of the Volta River, several dialects of Ewe are spoken by about two million people living in south-eastern Ghana, southern Togo, and Benin (formerly Dahomey). Although it is reported that a catechism was produced in Spanish and in one of the Ewe dialects in the seventeenth century,[76] Christianity and literacy were introduced there in 1853 by representatives of the Norddeutsche Missionsgesellschaft, also known as Bremen Mission. They settled in an area where the main dialect was Anlo, which therefore became the basis for literary Ewe.[77] It has been claimed that the first school-reader was composed in 1848, but it never reached print. The foundation for Ewe writing was laid by Bernard Schlegal (d. 1859), in his *Schlüssel zur Ewe-Sprache* (Stuttgart), which was accompanied by a selection of proverbs and fables. Schlegel was also responsible for Ewe versions of several scriptural texts, which were published posthumously.

German missionary activity gained in efficiency when the greater part of Eweland became a German colony under the name of Togo in 1884. Scientific work on the Ewe language was considerably amplified thanks to Diedrich Westermann (1876–1956). Although Westermann could claim in 1905 that "the influence of the mission had elevated Ewe to the status of a written language and had already created a sizeable amount of literature",[78] this should be taken to refer only to scriptural and didactic material produced mainly by the missionaries themselves. They must have had literate local assistants trained in the school which had been founded in 1863, but the emergence of original writing in Ewe was probably thwarted by the fact that, from the early years of the twentieth century, the German administration laid increasing emphasis on the spreading of the German language, a trend which was strengthened by the creation of a number of *Reichsschulen*. In fact, no evidence, has come to light of any imaginative work of African authorship being composed in Ewe during the German regime, if we except Andreas Aku's Ewe version of *The Pilgrim's Progress* (Bremen, 1906).

Nevertheless, Ewe remained the chief medium of instruction at primary school level. At the turn of the century, the missionaries even launched two monthly journals, the Catholic *Mia holo* ("Our friend", founded 1894) and the Protestant *Nutifafa na mi* ("The Messenger of peace", founded 1903). According to Petr Zima, "although primarily functional religious publications, both early missionary periodicals in Ewe also served as a basis for the first attempts to write at all in Ewe. [They] provided the first forum for initial attempts to translate short stories, excerpts from world literature and for the writing of short original stories in Ewe. Oral poetry and other forms of oral literature, collected by expatriate or Ewe teachers and missionaries, were also recorded and published." But normal development of Ewe writing was slowed down by the vicissitudes to which the course of history submitted Eweland as a result of the first World War. The Germans were defeated as early as 1914. Togo was submitted to joint Anglo-French occupation until the end of the war, after which the western part was annexed to the Gold Coast and the eastern part remained under French administration as a League of Nations mandate. This split had far-reaching consequences for the literary history of Ewe. Eastern Togoland became subjected to the principles that determined cultural and educational policy throughout French Africa. As early as 1921, Governor General Merlin had declared that "L'enseignement se propose avant tout de répandre dans la masse la langue française afin de fixer la nationalité." A decree of 1924 stipulated that "Le francais est seul en usage dans les écoles. Il est interdit aux maîtres de se servir avec les élèves des idiomes du pays."[79] In 1956, a report to the United Nations repeated that "il apparaît de plus en plus, à la lumière de l'expérience, que seule la langue francaise reste le véhicule indispensable à la formation culturelle approfondie de la population togolaise".[80] All official support was thus withdrawn from vernacular teaching, which became confined to religious education. The departure of the German missionaries left Ewe protestants in French Togoland to their own devices until 1931, when some help became available from the Société des Missions Evangéliques de Paris. But in spite of the fact that *Mia holo* had always been published in Lomé, and that publication of the protestant journal was shifted from Bremen to Lomé in 1925, the contribution of French Togoland to the growth of Ewe literature remained negligible when compared with the fast increasing output in that part of the country that had been annexed to the Gold Coast.

For under the British administration, the activities of the German missionaries were taken over by the United Free Church of Scotland, and the study of vernacular languages remained essential in the educational system. When Ewe was one of the five African languages selected for the third IAI competition in 1932, first prize went to *Toko atolia* ("The fifth landing-stage"), a play by Ferdinand Kwasi Fiawoo (1891–1969), who can be regarded as the initiator of original indigenous authorship in the language.[81] Fiawoo was a member of the African Methodist Episcopal Zion Church, which had been founded in 1898 by a black American Wesleyan minister. He wrote his play while studying at the Johnson C. Smith University in North Carolina for a B.A. in philosophy. The plot deals with the themes of marriage and good conduct in general. It is built on the pattern typical of many African folktales and early written works, with two contrasted characters illustrating the duality of good and evil. The story revolves around two young suitors wooing a girl named Fudzikomele; the girl's parents favour Aghebada, the villain of the play; in order to avoid this marriage, Fudzikomele flees from home. She is captured by a white slave-trader, and Aghebada and his virtuous rival Fumasi go out to rescue her; whereas the former soon returns with a false story of her death, Kumasi manages to bring her back and obtains parental permission to marry her. Meanwhile, Aghebada pursues his criminal career and is condemned to being buried up to his neck in the sand at the fifth landing stage along the river, there to await his deserved fate. But the chivalrous Kumasi is seized with pity, releases him and helps him leave the country. Aghebada repents and changes his name to Ameghedzy, "Done with evil". While much of the dramatic interest resides in the portrayal of traditional mores and customary judicial institutions, the play is obviously critical of tribal society: the first part undermines the tradition of parental authority through the picture of the blindness of Fudzikomele's parents and of their cruelty to their daughter. The second part contains an implicit indictment of the severity of customary law.

In later years, Fiawoo wrote two other plays which remained unprinted for a long time.[82] The title of *Tuinese* is the name of the central character, but it also means "Make an appeal to the Creator" as an arbiter for justice. As the writer explains in his preface, the play derives from an ancient Ewe custom according to which "the person who told a lie to the detriment of another was punished by the victim who committed suicide as an appeal to God". Side by side with this traditional element, the play has a secondary theme which is concerned with the advocacy of Christian education for women. The original manuscript, composed in 1945, was destroyed when the author's house was burnt down in 1953; as re-written in 1958, it is a drama in blank verse which is divided into three acts and seven scenes. Each scene begins with a Shakespearean sonnet recited by a chorus. In his preface, the author makes the point that the play complies with classical prescriptions respecting the unities of time, place and action. Fiawoo's third and last play, *Fia yi dziehe* ("Fia's Upland Journey", composed 1959) is likewise a historical drama describing the workings of traditional custom: it focuses on the condemnation (the upland journey) of a tribal ruler (the Fia).

Fiawoo's pioneering play was so successful with Ewe audiences (and once it was made locally available, to readers as well) that a fairly large crop of vernacular authors emerged in the years following the second World War. Their task was greatly facilitated by the fact that the British publishers Longmans and Macmillan became interested in the potentialities of the market for Ewe writing. The creation of the Vernacular Literature Bureau in 1951 further boosted literary production in the language. The most popular genre at first was short prose fiction, which took several distinct forms. It is noteworthy that the recording of oral tales represents a smaller proportion of Ewe writing than in a number of other African languages. Although the very first book-length production of indigenous authorship—*Mise gli loo* ("Once upon a time", 1934) by P.M. Desewu (b. 1909)—belonged to this genre, and although school-readers are apt to contain a number of folk stories, the only writers who achieved some fame in this respect were E.K. Amegashie (d. 1949) with his collection *Vovogi* ("Leisure time", 1947), and the first Ewe woman writer, Lily Baëta with *Da to gli nam* ("Tell me a story, mother", 1952). In fact, several of the writers who made their beginning in the late 1940s and early 1950s learned their craft by translating excerpts from some masterpieces of English and world literature. C.A.R. Necku (b. 1909) adapted the first two parts of *Gulliver's Travels* (1943) and a number of Grimm's *Tales* (1943). H.K.B. Setsoafia (b. 1914) translated Shakespeare's *Julius Caesar* (1950), and later told Chaucer's story of Griselda in Ewe verse (1954). The Rev. L.G. Baëta provided vernacular versions of Lamb's *Tales from Shakespeare* (1954 and 1959) and of some stories of Tolstoy (1956). C.K. Nyomi even wrote an Ewe adaptation (1950) of Enoch Guma's *Unomalizo*, based on a Twi version of the English translation! At the same time, however, those early writers born under the German regime contributed to the growth of original composition with a number of short stories and simple "novelettes" shaped on the familiar pattern of the fictional biography. One of the earliest examples of the latter was Amegashie's *Togbi Mawuena II* ("Chief Mawuena II", 1947). P.M. Desewu then published a collection of short stories, *Le nye adaba te* ("As I saw it", 1948). G.K. Tsekpo (1890-1974), a prolific writer of didactic works and of short stories such as *Keto na se* ("Open your ears and listen", 1953), also wrote three novelettes whose didactic purpose is thinly disguised under fictional appearances: *Tsa kpo* ("Travel and learn", 1953), *Be engu kpo* ("Think of it", 1960), and *Minya zozo* ("Be careful", 1959). *Sagbadre* ("The swallow", 1940), by Israel Kafu Hoh (b. 1912), recounts an episode in the nineteenth-century conflicts between the Anlo and the Danes; Hoh was later to turn to the stage with a school-play in English, *Prodigal Brothers* (1967), and a vernacular drama, *Srokuda* ("Fear death", 1969), which deals with an orphan girl abused by a wealthy merchant. E.T. Adiku (b. 1912) began with a collection of short stories, *Nufiame nutinyawo* ("Didactic tales", 1949), which was followed by a kind of ethnographical novelette, *Bumekpo* ("Let us think together", 1959).

Ewe writing grew at such a rapid pace during the 1940s and the 1950s that by the time Ghana and Togo gained their independence in 1957, German linguist Ursula Hintze could claim that more books and articles had been written in and about the Ewe language than in and about Igbo or even Yoruba, even though Ewe is spoken by far fewer people than the two Nigerian languages.[83] Nor did the rate of growth abate after independence, as a new generation of younger authors born after the first World War came to the fore while their elders were still very much active. The first piece of prose fiction that with its 139 pages could genuinely be called a novel had been produced by Sam Obianim (b. 1920) in 1949: under the title *Amegbetsa alo Agbezuge fe nutinya* ("Man, or the adventures of Agbezuge"), it recounts the odyssey of a young man during the wars between Ewe and Asante. Obianim next offered a female counterpart to this with *De menye de* ("If I had known", 1954), which deals with the sorry fate of a girl who rejects parental control in order to lead a life of debauchery. This highly edifying theme recurs in a much slighter work, *Nya zozo* ("Be cautious", 1961) by E.Y. Dogoe, one of the writers who kept turning out novelettes in the old manner. But in the main, Obianim's contemporaries and juniors did not hesitate to embark upon more substantial works. F.K. Nyaku (b. 1924), who had translated a biography of Aggrey (1953), wrote *Kofi Nyameko nutinya* ("The life of Kofi Nyameko", 1955) and *Amedzro etolia* ("The third stranger", 1973): in both novels, families broken up by slander and intrigue are restored to harmony and prosperity through Christianity and education. K. Ayena's *Asi tsu atoawo* ("The five rivals", 1969) is about a woman's infidelity and salvation; Kodjo Ayeke's *Hlobiabia* ("Revenge", 1973) in the same manner shows how an unhappy young man who had started his life in a spirit of revenge, later repents and becomes a useful citizen. Ewe prose fiction remained strongly influenced by the heavy moralizing sense which is characteristic both of traditional culture and of Christian ethics, until Y. Seth Akafia (b. 1940) published *Ku le xome* ("Death at home", 1970), a detective story which Amegbleame regards as the first Ewe novel to show a degree of sophistication. The diversification of Ewe prose fiction is further evidenced in V.K.A. Glapke's *Adela megbloa wo kata o . . .* ("The hunger does not tell everything", 1973), which bears some resemblance to the Yoruba tales of Fagunwa and Tutuola in its manner of exploiting the resources of fantasy and the supernatural.

Fiawoo's plays, which had inaugurated Ewe imaginative literature, had been chiefly devoted to the representation of traditional life and customs on stage. In spite of their local success, no further drama was printed until well after the achievement of independence. One exception was C.K. Nyomi's *Wodzi Xola na mi* ("The Saviour was born for us", 1945), a Christmas play of the kind that Christian missionaries had been trying to promote throughout Africa for a long time. Ten years later, Bidi H.K. Setsoafia (b. 1914), who had gained some experience in playwriting by translating Shakespeare's *Julius Caesar* (1950) had his *Mede ablotsi dela* ("I married a 'been-to' ", 1956) published by the Literature Bureau. Although this comedy of manners, which exploits the opposition between the snobbery of the younger generation and the religious fanaticism of their devout elders, was sufficiently popular to be reprinted in 1964, no new play appeared in Ewe until Setsoafia's next experiment, *Togbui Kpeglo II* ("King Kpeglo II", 1968). This was a political tragedy cautiously set in the colonial period: its protagonist is a fictional chieftain whose abuses drive the population to rebellion and ultimately lead to his committing suicide. S.Y. Kwamuar's *Ewo moya na Fiaga Agokoli* ("King Agokoli was surprised", 1969) likewise deals with the effect upon the Ewe people in a remote, though not entirely mythical, past of the arbitrariness and cruelty of one of their early rulers. It is not surprising that these two plays, written during a period of political upheaval that saw in Ghana the eviction of Nkrumah in 1966, and in Togo the assassination of Sylvanus Olympio in 1963 and the military take-over of 1967, should be mainly concerned with the uses and abuses of power, as were many of the early classical tragedies of Western Europe in the Renaissance, when playwrights used the stage as a medium to admonish the emerging monarchs and to warn them against the dangers of misrule and oppression. [84]

In spite of the abundance and liveliness of Ewe oral poetry, very little written poetry has been produced so far, even though some Ewe writers composed tales in verse. The reason is presumably that traditional poetry is closely allied to music, which is left aside in the written art.[85] Indeed, it was not until the early 1970s that a significant amount of Ewe poetry did reach print. As Amegbleame rightly points out,[86] the very titles of the three collections he discusses make it clear that, to Ewe people, "la poésie est la fille de la musique et l'une ne peut être conçue sans l'autre": in 1964, the Rev. K.R. Nuatsuako published *Hakpanyawo* ("Words for songs") which was sufficiently successful to be reprinted in Accra in 1967. In 1970, there appeared a bulky collection, *Henowo fe gbe* ("Voice of the singers") by Israel K. Hoh, G.W.K. Kwasi Kuma (b. 1931) and R.K. Kiya-Hinidza (b. 1944). In 1973, L.K.M. Seshie edited *Akpalu fe hawo* ("The songs of Akpalu"): Akpalu (1895-1974) was a renowned, non-literate, oral bard. These collections, which are bulkier, and therefore costlier, than most books and pamphlets printed in Ewe, were a promising novelty, for they demonstrated the richness and variety that provides the inspiration for Ewe poetry, as well as the diverse and exacting linguistic skills which the Ewe poet is called upon to demonstrate.

But the most startling development to have occurred in recent years is the emergence of Togolese authors writing in Ewe. It is true that the vernacular had remained in written use among religious circles, both Protestant and Catholic, even under the French regime. But it is also true that for more than a dozen years after independence, the Togolese authorities showed little desire to promote the national language. Nevertheless, the need to counter French cultural imperialism made itself felt as early as 1962, when the Ministry of Education created the Ewe Academy, whose leadership was almost entirely in the hands of Protestant ministers and Catholic priests. It was not until 1969 that the five-year plan for the period 1971-1975 made provisions for the introduction of Togolese languages into the school curriculum. While full implementation of these objectives is still far away, university lecturers and students in Lomé created the Ewe Club, an informal association whose journal *Togo Gedzedze* ("Light on Togo") was launched in December 1973. The first literary fruit of this newly-opened area of recruitment was a play, *Kpoli Dzogbe alo Gbe Medzi* ("Kpoli Dzogbe or Gbe Medzi") by S.K. Anika (b. 1954). It was performed in Lomé in September 1973, and published in mimeographed form by the Université du Bénin in 1974. Following in the wake of the Ghanaian Ewe playwrights who had attempted to recapture something of Ewe precolonial identity, Anika turned for his inspiration to a legend connected with the oracular cult of Fa, which is widely spread not only among the Ewe of Ghana and Togo, but also among the Yoruba of Nigeria and the Fon of Dahomey.

● ● ●

Some Ghanaian scholars have been known to reflect wistfully on the "South African miracle" and the interest in vernacular language study and literary creativity it generated. They complained that "the impetus given to the study of Ghanaian languages by the Christian missions seems to have been lost with the passing of the control of schools into the hands of the Government".[87] The fact remains, nevertheless, that there has been continuity in progress since the early 1930s, when four vernacular African languages (Twi, Ga, Ewe and Fante) were selected to be taught in schools: in the early 1950s, the Vernacular Literature Bureau recognized the distinction between Akwapem-Twi and Asante-Twi, and selected four more languages for promotion: Adangme, Nzema, Kassem and Dagbani. And by the late 1960s, the Bureau of Ghana Languages had issued pamphlets and books in nineteen local languages.

In most of the minor and minority languages, these publications include no works of creative writing, although five pieces of prose fiction had been produced in Nzema since the language was first put to imaginative use in print in two stories by Arthur Kolora Mensah: *Bedie me nwora ko o!* ("Listen to my story", 1953) and *Egya Awienze* ("Mr. Awienze", 1954); not until a dozen years later did the next Nzema literary work appear: this was a collection of poetry by Francis Couloo Ainooson, *Nyanza aloma* ("The Nyanza bird", 1967). It was during the same period that Rudolph Philippe Djabanor published two short pieces of prose fiction in Adangme, *Nilemi he sane kome* ("Some stories about wisdom", 1951) and *Mamle Dole* ("Mamle, the beautiful lady", 1953); here again, several years elapsed before another imaginative work appeared in the language: John N. Nanor's *Ebe he kake* ("It's so everywhere", 1967). An interesting exception to this not very exhilarating pattern is Ga.

That Ga is a minority language is fairly obvious, although the figures given for the number of Ga speakers fluctuates widely according to the sources.[88] Nevertheless, statistics issued by the Bureau of Ghana Languages show that Ga outstrips all other Ghanaian languages in the production of prose fiction. This is due to two historical factors. When the first German missionaries reached the Gold Coast in 1826, they settled in a coastal area under Danish administration which was in the territory of the Ga. Until they moved to a healthier place in the interior, they were unaware that Twi was a far more important and widespread language, and they choose Ga as the medium of instruction. An auxiliary consideration was adduced in 1858 by one of the missionaries who claimed that preference went to Ga because of "the moral and political supremacy of the Ga proper over the Adangme and other tribes around".[89] Thus it came about that Ga, as Heine puts it, "in spite of its limited number of users, boasts of a rich literature, amongst which there is a Bible translation".[90] For lack of reliable information, it can be assumed that this "rich literature" for a long time consisted of religious and educational works only.

The second important factor is that Accra, Ghana's capital city, is situated in the Ga-Adangme area, where missionary activity had given Ga undisputed educational priority. It has been pointed out that "by 1945, there were four times as many Adangme speakers as there were Ga speakers; yet Ga has served schools in the Ga and Andangme areas prior to that date and ever since". [91] It is no doubt to this strong urban foundation that the growth of modern writing in Ga is to be ascribed. For Accra grew rapidly with the remarkable demographic expansion that took place in many African cities in the post-war years. It is no coincidence that the first modern works in Ga appeared during the 1950s. They did not comprise more than a few pieces of short prose fiction, one of which, however—Nicholas Akrong Odoi's *Gbomo ke wala* ("Man and life", 1953)—proved highly popular since it was reprinted five times in ten years. As was the case with Nzema and Adangme, it was in the 1960s that the Bureau of Ghana languages began to show active interest in Ga creative writing, and published such longer works as *Ganyobi* ("The Ga child", 1961) by E.A.W. Engmann, *Gbotsui mli gbome* ("The man in the anthill", 1964) by E. Lamte-Lawson, and *Otswa te otswa ohienaa* ("You have singed your own beard", 1966), a play by Albert A. Amartey.

CHAPTER TEN
WEST CENTRAL AFRICA

As Africa was moving towards independence in the late 1950s, a huge segment of the continent between Nigeria to the West, Uganda and Tanzania to the East, Zambia and Namibia to the South, had been for a long time in the hands of the French (Congo, Gabon, Cameroon, Tchad, and the Central African Republic), of the Portuguese (Angola), the Spaniards (Equatorial Guinea) and the Belgians (Zaïre, Rwanda, Burundi). The French, the Spaniards and the Portuguese, unwitting inheritors of the Roman tradition of cultural imperialism, paid no attention, or showed downright hostility, to the African languages which they truly regarded as "vernacular" in the etymological sense of the word, i.e., fit only for uncivilized slaves. Educational policy was characterized by a paternalistic form of intellectual colonialism which aimed at full integration of a tiny élite into the metropolitan culture. No official support could be given towards the encouragement of imaginative writing in African languages. Belgian policy led to similar results, though from slightly different motives. Educational policy in the Belgian Congo was shaped to meet the requirements of the administration, the Catholic Church and the large companies, all of whom were likely to consider with extreme suspicion the very notion of a black élite. Teaching was in the hands of Catholic missionaries. Although Belgian missionaries and administrators were active in the study of the local languages and oral lore, they failed to make any serious attempts at promoting native authorship. Such African-language writing as appeared in this art of Africa resulted from the sporadic and often very transient influence exerted by a few protestant missionary societies.

1. Cameroon

In the early years of the nineteenth century, the momentum of the Fulani *jihad* had carried Islamic influence to its easternmost point, Adamawa, which was later to become part of colonial Cameroon. The European conquerors and the Christian missionaries, German and French alike, exerted little influence upon Adamawa, whose *ajami* literature (see above, pp. 48–52) remained, throughout the nineteenth and part of the twentieth centuries, the only written form of the literary art in Cameroon.

The Christian impact began to make itself felt when Alfred Saker of the Baptist Mission came over from the off-shore island of Fernando Po and settled among the Duala people of southern Cameroon in 1845.[1] He devoted a considerable part of his activity to the study of the local language (*Grammatical Elements of the Dualla Language with a vocabulary compiled for the use of missionaries and teachers*, 1855), and to the translation of the Bible. His version of *Matthew* (1848) was followed by a number of other scriptural texts, until the whole Bible was set up in print in 1872. It is to him that Duala owes the distinction of being "the third Bantu language into which the whole *Bible* was translated".[2]

In 1884, after German merchants had successfully competed for trade against the British, and German explorers and agents had established German influence in the interior, Germany declared a protectorate over the Cameroon area, which was later extended to Lake Chad, thus encompassing Adamawa. The Baptist missionaries accordingly decided to move from Cameroon to the Congo. In 1885, a continental missionary conference held in Bremen asked the Basler Evangelische Missionsgesellschaft to take over.[3] The first Basel missionaries reached Duala in 1895. Although the Duala did not number more than twenty to thirty thousand, their trade contacts with the Europeans had given them a position of power over the peoples of the interior and their language became a *lingua franca*. The missionaries made it the medium of school and religious instruction, so that Duala developed from a trading language into a school and church language.[4] While Saker's life work was being carried on by such Basel missionaries as T.H. Christaller with his *Handbuch der Duala-Sprache* (Basel, 1892) and H. Seidel's *Duala-Sprache in Kamerun:Systematisches Wörterverzeichnis und Einführung in die Grammatik* (Heidelberg, 1904), indigenous authorship began with Yoshua Dibundu, with a collection of hymns entitled *Besesedi ba Yehowa* ("Praises of Jehovah", 1896). A vernacular journal, *Elolombe ya Kamerun* ("The sun of Cameroon") and a monthly, *Mulee Ngea*, were launched in 1903.[5] One of the first Cameroonian ministers, Josef Ekolo, who was to be ordained in 1912, wrote an account of his stay in Europe, but the original version does not seem ever to have reached print : it appeared in a German translation, *Wie ein Schwarzer das Land der Weiszen ansieht* (Basel, 1908).

That Duala failed to develop into a full-fledged literary language is due to a combination of three historical factors. First, at grassroots level its status as the *lingua franca* of Cameroonian trade had always been challenged by pidgin English, which "ousted Duala to an increasing extent and became the language of the market place and plantations".[6] Second, in the early years of the twentieth century, it became the German administration's official policy to train élites in the German language. This led to a local *Kulturkampf* with the Basel missionaries, and to the ephemeral emergence of a Cameroonian literature in German, whose main representative was Duala Misipo (b.1901). Finally, as a result of the capture of Duala by French and British troops in 1914, the greater part of Cameroon was administered by the French under a League of Nations mandate. By 1917, the last Basel missionary, who happened to be an Australian, had been expelled and the Basel stations were taken over by the Société des Missions Evangéliques. The well-known principles of French educational and cultural policy were applied with as much consistency as was deemed feasible in a mandate territory: Cameroon became one of the most productive areas in the field of creative writing in French, boasting such talented pioneers as Mongo Beti and Ferdinand Oyono.

This, however, was not the end of Duala as a literary language. The impetus provided by the Protestant missionaries had some important consequences. A Duala monthly, *Dikalo* ("The Message") was launched in 1928. A beginning was made with secular writing in 1930, when Isaac Moumé Etia (1889-1939) published *Ikolo a bulu na bulu bo*, a selection of tales from the *Arabian Nights*, and his bilingual, French-Duala, collection, *Les Fables de Douala*. From such scant information as is available, it seems that the most prolific exponent of Duala writing was Martin Itondo, who emerged in 1933 with *Neketi na mongo* ("Spears and arrows"). He then collaborated with Paul Helmlinger to produce *Minia na bedemo basu* ("Our proverbs and customs", 1934), which was soon followed by *Kyango ma Mandesi Bell* (1938), a biographical account of a Duala chieftain of the period of the European conquest. On the eve of independence, Itondo had also published a collection of hymns, *Myende na Yesaya* (1954) and, with Munz Dibundu and Paul Helmlinger, another book in Duala, *Nimele bolo* ("Push the canoe"). In 1960, a new type of inspiration found expression in Duala with the nationalistic poems gathered by Epanya Yondo Elolonge (b. 1930) in his bilingual, Duala-French collection *Kamerun! Kamerun!*, which was published by Présence Africaine in Paris.

•   •   •

Halfway between Duala and Adamawa lies the country of the Bamum, which the Germans reached at the turn of the century. It was there that Sultan Njoya (*c*. 1880-1933) created one of those indigenous scripts

which were invented in imitation of European writing at various points
along the Guinea coast. Through Hausa traders and contacts of a more
bellicose nature with the Fulani emirates of Adamawa, the Bamum knew
of the existence of writing and of manuscripts in the Arabic script. Njoya
noticed that the Europeans too used writing, although of a different
kind. He realized the advantages inherent in this manner of commu-
nicating over long distances, but at the same time he shrewdly perceived
that using his own language would ensure greater secrecy in his correspondence with his emissaries to the German authorities. During the
first five years of the century, he ordered some of his councillors to
create an ideographic script, which went through many successive
changes until, by 1918, the hundreds of original signs had been greatly
simplified and reduced in number to give them phonetic significance.[7]
The script, which was taught to dignitaries and their children, was
chiefly used for conveying messages and for the recording of accounts
and archives. It was also employed, under Njoya's personal supervision,
for the writing of a 548-page manuscript on the history and customs of
the Bamum.[8]

But Njoya was jealous of some the neighbouring potentates who had
a secret language, understood by the ruling class and completely esoteric
to the common people; this is not an uncommon occurrence in black
Africa, where secret languages are often the last vestige of the language
once spoken by conquerors who, in the course of generations, have
adopted the language of the vanquished for day-to-day usage. Njoya
decided to fabricate his own secret language. In 1912, he learned from
a missionary of the Basel mission a number of German, French and
English words to which he ascribed entirely arbitrary meanings, mixing
them with Bamum words, also distorted from their normal sense, in
order to create his personal vocabulary. By 1918, a considerable part
of the *History and Customs of the Bamum* had been translated into this
language by a large number of copyists.

Nor did Njoya's inordinate inventiveness stop there. For after successfully resisting the inroads of Muslim Fulani, the Bamum found
themselves under strong pressure to adopt Christianity. Njoya, who had
become converted to Islam in 1917, had powerful objections to this,
rooted in his unwillingness to abandon polygamy. In order to evade the
rival demands of Islam and Christianity, he founded a religion of his
own, which he claimed, in the hope of satisfying everyone, was a reconciliation of both. The tenets of this new religion were recorded in the
Bamum language and script in 1916–17; they show that while Christian
elements were largely overshadowed by Islamic influence, liberal quotations from the Koran and the Bible are added to frequent reminiscences from the Bamum's original animistic faith.[9]

According to the Cameroonian scholar Martin Z. Njeuma, "The writ-

ing spead quickly and became taught in several schools throughout Bamum. This made it possible for written records to be kept and for once
oral accounts to be documented. Many of the accounts about the history
of Bamum in the European administrative records have largely been
translations of earlier indigenous records in the Bamum script."[10]
There is no evidence that the script was ever used for creative purposes.

• • •

Several other Cameroonian languages have been reduced to writing
since the beginning of the colonial process. By the late 1960s scriptural
material was available in more than fifteen local languages and dialects.[11]
But the only one for which there is serious evidence that it was used for
literary purposes is Bulu, which is spoken in an area between Duala and
the Gabon border. Christianity was introduced there as early as 1871
by representatives of the American Presbyterian Missionary Board
which had been active in Central Africa since its foundation in 1837.
Several schools had been established prior to the German defeat, and
it is presumably the fact that Cameroon was granted mandate status
instead of becoming a colony that made it possible for the American
missionaries to carry on their work unhampered. They had installed a
printing press at Elat in 1914 and a teacher training college was founded
near Ebolowa in 1922. Their efficiency was such that according to Catholic historian Engelbert Mveng, "American Protestantism was long regarded as the natural religion of the Bulu"![12]
    This, however, does not seem to have led to any significant amount
of native authorship. In fact, the earliest Bulu piece of prose fiction on
the record is Jean L. Medu Njemba's *Nganga kôn* ("The white ghost",
1939). The title, which connotes the ideas of ghost and albino, refers to
the white man; this is the only work of genuine prose fiction written in
Bulu. It depicts the life of the tribe at the time when the first Europeans
reached their country. It is so popular that several of its characters have
been integrated into the local folklore and are frequently represented
in painted frescoes on Bulu houses. Some ten years later, the Presbyterian Mission press at Ebolowa published *Dulu bon be Afri Kara* ("The
journey of the children of Afri Kara", 1948), by Ondoua Engutu (b.
1929), a school teacher who had graduated from the Presbyterian Training College. Engutu (whose name is wrongly printed as Engute on the
title page) did not set out to write fiction, but to save from oblivion the
historical legends connected with the origins and migrations of the Fang
people of Cameroon and Gabon: Afri Kara is the father of all Africans;
he was a descendant of Hamata, the father of all mankind. When Afri
Kara's family was attacked by red-skinned people (who, the author sug-

gests, may have been Arabs), they fled in different directions and his sons became the ancestors of the various tribes in the area. Engutu's book is as popular as Medu Njemba's and was reprinted in 1954 and 1956. Equal success went to the Bulu version of *The Pilgrim's Progress*, which first appeared at some unspecified date and went through a third printing in 1956.[13]

Although Cameroon is distinguished from the other African countries that were once part of the French empire in having a tradition of vernacular writing in three local languages, prospects for the future are not very bright. The reason for this can be found in French linguist Pierre Alexandre's terse summary of the prevailing attitude towards problems of language use: "The official languages are English (West Cameroon) and French (East Cameroon), on an equal footing at the federal level (but with a *de facto* predominance of French). The school system supports, for the most part, the French colonial tradition, with a European language used as a medium from the start. There are a few literacy classes in some of the vernaculars, organized by the Christian missions without any official recognition. Since independence there have been heated discussions among the intelligentsia between cultural nationalists who favour a wider use of the vernaculars, and unificationists, who fear that this would consolidate tribal consciousness and be detrimental to nation building. The federal government—and its French technical advisers—support the latter view."[14]

2. Belgian Africa: Kongo and Kinyarwanda

Towards the end of the year 1482, a Portuguese sailor, Diego Câo, discovered the estuary of a large river which he called *Zaire*, after the local words *maia nzadi*, meaning "river".[15] In fact, he had reached the mighty Kongo state, which was to trade with Portugal during the ensuing decades, and soon to contribute appreciably to supplying the slave trade. The Kongo kingdom covered a vast area that is now divided among several countries: part of Congo, Cabinda, western Zaïre and north-western Angola. Relations were friendly at first. During the last few years of the fifteenth century, a Kongo embassy was sent to Lisbon; King Nzinga Kuwu was baptized as Joâo I; the royal family and most of the nobility became Christians as well. Missionaries built a school in 1504. In 1506, after some disturbances, King Affonso succeeded to the throne. Sons of the Kongo ruling class were sent to Lisbon for training. A few of them studied in Rome and became ordained priests. For a variety of reasons, relations turned sour during the last few years of the reign of Affonso who died in the 1540s, and under his successors, all of whom bore Christian names.

By 1514, however, there were some literate Kongo young men, who served as *amanuenses* to the monarchs. The letters exchanged between the Kongo court and Portugal throughout the sixteenth century are the earliest documents written by Africans in any European language,[16] but neither the Catholic missionaries nor the Portuguese authorities paid any attention to the local language until the first quarter of the seventeenth century. It is reported that the first missionaries to have learned Kongo were two Jesuit fathers who reached the country in 1619.[17] One of them, Mattheus Cardoso (1574–1625), was responsible for the publication in Lisbon of the first book in Kongo to have been preserved: *Doutrina Christâa . . . na lingoa do Reyno de Congo* (1624).[18] This was a Portuguese catechism with interlinear Kongo translation, designed for Christians in Kongo and for Kongo slaves brought to the plantations on the island of Sâo Tomé. But the most important work on the language was done by Italian Capuchins, who undertook to revitalize the mission work in 1641, when King Garcia II came to the throne. They were taught Kongo by Abbé Emmanuel Roboredo (d. 1666), the son of a Portuguese gentleman and of a local lady of the royal family; he was ordained into the Capuchin order in 1652. This linguistic study resulted in what C.M. Doke calls "the first known grammar of an African language". Under a somewhat unwieldy title—*Regulae quaedam pro difficillimi Congensium idiomatis faciliori captu ad grammaticae normam redactae* (1659)—it was a 98-page description of Kongo by Giacinto Brusciotto (1601–1659). According to Van Bulck, this pioneering work sank into oblivion for more than two hundred years, until renewed European interest in Africa led to its being translated into English (London, 1882) and Portuguese (Luanda, 1886).

• • •

In 1885, the Berlin conference divided the land of the Kongo into three parts which were apportioned to France, Portugal and the Belgian king Leopold II. Given the principles of French and Portuguese cultural and educational policy, it was not to be expected that much attention would be paid to the scientific study of the language in Angola and in Congo, let alone that efforts would be made towards the promotion of vernacular writing. But the portion that had been allotted to King Leopold, the Congo Free State, had a special status. It had at any rate already been visited, since 1879, by representatives of the Livingstone Inland Mission which had just been created by the British Baptist Missionary Society. These missionaries immediately set out to reduce Kongo to writing, compiling a vocabulary, a grammar and an early reader, *Nsamu Wambote* ("Good news"). In 1884, the year before the Berlin Conference reached its conclusion, the British Baptists were joined by

Swedish members of the Svenska Missionförbundet, which had been founded in 1878, and of the American Baptist Foreign Mission Society, who had already built a school (1882) at Mukimbungu, halfway between Kinshasa and the estuary. This school can rightly be regarded as the cradle of modern Kongo literature, which made swift progress during the last two decades of the nineteenth century.[19]

In the initial stages the Protestant missionaries played their usual seminal role as linguists and translators: William Holman Bentley, of the Baptist Mission, produced his *Dictionary and Grammar of the Kongo Language* (1888). Swedish missionary Nils Westlind published a translation of the *New Testament* (1891). The whole Bible, completed by another Swede, K.E. Lamann, became available in 1905. They received valuable help from African assistants,[20] some of whom were responsible for initiating authorship in the Kongo language, which found a ready outlet in *Minsamu Miayenge* ("Peace Messages"), a monthly journal launched in 1892. It was here that one of the three Kongo versions of *The Pilgrim's Progress*[21] was printed serially in 1898; it was published in book form in 1912. It was probably the reading of Bunyan's masterpiece which prompted such early Kongo writers as Abeli Kiananwa to Christianize the habit of ascribing prophetic value to dreams, and to create a new poetic genre, the *ngozi* ("dream"), which interprets dreams as allegorical visions. In the main, however, Kongo poets adapted traditional genres to Christian purposes and produced hymns to the glory of Christ, using concepts, terms and poetic forms that were readily accessible to their audience. Many of the more than four hundred hymns gathered in *Minkunga Miayenge* ("Peace songs", 1887) were the work of catechists such as Abeli Kiananwa, D. Makosi and E. Nkadi. Others, like Pauli Dikoko or Davidi Malangidila were more interested in the folktale, which they submitted, to use Zairian scholar Mbelolo ya Mpiku's graphic image, to a process of "embezzlement", arranging the stories so as to give them a Christian meaning.

After this early flowering, which was also reflected in several didactic works jointly written by English, Swedish and American missionaries and their disciples, a decline seems to have occurred in the production of Kongo writing. Further research will probably make it possible to decide whether increasing competition from the Catholic missionaries, brought in with Leopold II's support after 1885, the transfer of sovereignty to the Belgian state on the king's death in 1909 and the effects of the first World War and other circumstances played any significant part in this decline. It seems, however, that the Protestant missionaries in Kongo, like their colleagues in Lesotho, felt that a new stage had been reached in their appointed task, and that the time had come to concentrate on doctrinal teaching and Biblical commentary; on the other hand, the new generation of catechists tended to show more radical hostility towards what they regarded as pagan traditions—an attitude which was to contribute to the reaction of syncretic movements in the early post-war years.

• • •

The revival which occurred in the late 1920s was no longer connected with Mukimbungu, but with developments at a station that had been created by American and English Baptists at Kimpese in 1908. The mission included the Kongo Evangelical Training Institute, whose name was to be changed to Ecole de Pasteurs et d'Instituteurs in 1933. Kongo remained the medium of instruction until 1948, when its place was taken by French because the missions received government subsidies and had to submit to official school inspection. The Kimpese staff included an American medical doctor, Catherine L. Mabie (b. 1872), who was selected in 1926 to represent the Conseil Protestant du Congo at the conference convened in Le Zoute (Belgium) by the International Missionary Council. She was very much impressed by the emphasis laid on the paramount importance of promoting the vernacular languages. On her return to Kimpese, she started composing Kongo textbooks on hygiene and childcare. In this she was helped by Timoteo Vingadio, who had been one of the first pupils to matriculate at Kimpese.[22] In 1928, they jointly published two books: *Nsamu wa Nsau Kuluso* was a Kongo version of *Robinson Crusoe; Nsweswe Ansusu Antembe ye ngana zankala* ("The little white hen and other tales") contained some poems composed in the traditional manner, stories adopted from non-African works, and a number of folktales which were not diverted from their original significance.

The example of Catherine Mabie and Timoteo Vingadio acted as an incentive for a new generation of Kongo-language writers, all of whom had been trained at Kimpese. Inevitably, hymn-writing remained the primary activity of such poet-composers as Miguel Nekaka, who won the prize for Kongo writing in the first IAI competition in 1930, Samuel A. Nsimba (d. 1948), Remy Malutama (1920–1956) and several others, whose works appear in an enlarged hymnal, *Minkunga mia kintwadi* ("Songs of unity", 1956), so entitled because it was designed for use in all Protestant denominations and communities. The collection also included a number of the Mukimbungu poems, so that it is possible to observe that the later-hymn writers tended to produce poetry of a more intellectual character, less closely modelled on the traditional oral art and more definitely influenced by western church music.

With regard to prose fiction, a collection of tales interspersed with poems was published jointly by Jackson Ngangu and American missionary Mary Bonar under the title *Tangeno nsamu* ("Read the tales", 1944).

The most important event of the 1940s was the emergence of the novel. Apart from the translations of *The Pilgrim's Progress* and of *Robinson Crusoe*, a powerful incentive had come from Swedish missionary John Petterson's three-volume novel, *Nsamu a Mpanzu* ("The life of Mpanzu", 1935–1938), a didactic story recounting the childhood and adolescence of the mission-trained protagonist, his six years' travels in Kongo territory and among the other peoples of the then Belgian Congo, the book closing on Mpanzu's preparations for a trip to Belgium after an old sailor has given him full particulars about life in Western Europe.

The first genuine Kongo novelist, however, was A. Emile Disengomoka (1915–1965)[23] who was also the first Kimpese graduate to complete his studies in a Belgian teacher-training college. Although he was chiefly active as a writer of hymns and essays, his most original contribution to Kongo literature was *Kwenkwenda. Klisto yovo kanda* ("Where shall I go? To Christ or to the clan?"), which was printed some time during the war. Through the story of Kwenkwenda, a young man educated in a mission school, who is called upon to head his clan, Disengomoka, appears to be the first Zairian writer to have shown himself fully and explicitly aware of the implications of the coming together of African and European cultures. But the ideology of negritude, which was in the making in Paris, had not yet percolated to Central Africa, and the writer's viewpoint remains fundamentally Christian as the hero tries to achieve some sort of synthesis, basically by sifting what is good and what is evil by Christian standards in the values and mores of his own society.

It was probably the success of *Kwenkwenda* which prompted Disengomoka's contemporary Jacques N. Bahele (b. 1911) to the writing of *Kinzonzi ye ntekelo andi Makundu* ("Kinzonzi and his grandson Makundu", 1948) which lays considerably stronger emphasis on the importance and validity of traditional culture. Kinzonzi is a leading member of his tribe, and he takes care to inculcate the ancestral outlook to his mission-trained adolescent grandson. The old world view is expressed in a large number of proverbs, which Makundu devotedly records without trying, as the Mukimbungu catechists had done, to "embezzle" them to the benefit of Christianity. An ordained minister and head of a mission station, Bahele has done important research on his people's oral lore, and has gathered a number of traditional stories in *Bingana bia nsi a Kongo* ("Tales from the Kongo country", 1953).

It was also during the 1930s that a new trend appeared which was not derived from missionary teaching and example, but from a messianic movement prompted by an acute sense that the European brand of Christianity was ill-adapted to African culture. Its leader, Simon Kimbangu (1889–1951), was arrested a few months after he had proclaimed his message in 1921; he was exiled to far away Katanga (now Shaba), where he died thirty years later.[24] Although many of his disciples were likewise arrested and exiled, persecution gave rise to a stream of esoteric underground poetry where the unorthodox beliefs and feelings of the faithful were disguised in a way that only the initiated could understand: Kimbangu was "he" or "the old man", the missionaries and the colonial authorities were "they" or "the accusers", Kimbangu's village was "there" or "the New Jerusalem". Most of these early hymns were transmitted orally. They exhibited an interesting mixture of determination and bitterness.

•   •   •

By the time war came to a close, however, Kimbanguism had become firmly rooted in Kinshasa. Kimbangu's disciples became more hopeful for his return, and even after his death in Katanga, their claim for official recognition became increasingly outspoken, until on the eve of independence, the colonial administration rescinded the ban on Kimbangu's church. This evolution was reflected in the hymns composed in the 1950s, and the coming of independence was triumphantly celebrated by Kimbanguist poets, for whom religious freedom and political emancipation were one and the same thing. According to Mbelolo, the literature produced by Kimbangu's followers is "one of the most precious treasures of Kongo culture".

The nationalistic trend in Kimbangu's movement was not unconnected with a wider *crise de conscience* which crystallized in the mid-1950s around the ABAKO (*Alliance des Bakongo*), an allegedly "cultural" organization which swiftly developed into a political party when the colonial authorities allowed overt political activity in 1956. The ABAKO contributed to the growth and diversification of Kongo literature through its newspaper, *Kongo dia Ngunga* ("Kongo of the bell", founded 1954), so entitled, presumably, as a token of modernity, and as a reference to the Christian habit of summoning congregations by means of bells rather than the traditional tomtoms. This title, however, was soon found objectionable and the paper was renamed *Kongo Dieto* ("Our Kongo"): combining tribal pride with political expediency, its contributors turned traditional proverbs into political slogans; they recorded and printed traditional tales which they "embezzled" in a new direction, giving them militant political significance. Some, like Raphaël Batsikama, composed poems that played skilfully upon the ambiguities inherent in the fact that the vast, multitribal country had been named after the huge river which reaches the ocean in Kongo territory. As political activity became increasingly important, the proportion of creative writing receded in *Kongo Dieto*, but in 1960 Batsikama founded *Ngonge Kongo: Carnets d'Histoire et de Littérature Kongo*, which was printed largely in French, but which helped spread many works of Kongo oral art, such as songs, proverbs and riddles.

Meanwhile, the protestant missions had become aware of the need to provide better printing and publishing facilities so as to encourage the kind of writing that they desired to foster. Several printing presses had operated in the Lower Congo area since the end of the nineteenth century. To facilitate distribution, the Union Mission Bookshop was established at Léopoldville (now Kinshasa) in 1935 under the joint sponsorship of the Congo Protestant Council and the British and Foreign Bible Society. Its chief aim was to provide a depository and distributing centre for Bibles and Christian literature for Belgian Congo and some adjacent regions. Towards the end of the second World War, it was realized that new provisions had to be made in the publishing field, and the Léopoldville bookshop was reorganized with a printing department added to the importing and distributing service. This was LECO (Librairie Evangélique du Congo), which became operational in 1948 and soon published books and periodicals in more than twenty languages.[25] Kongo was bound to loom prominently among these.

At the same time, however, African clergymen were increasingly losing their monopoly over mission-sponsored creative writing, even though the majority of the new authors had of course received part at least of their education in missionary schools: several of them, like Lucien Fwasi and Noé Diawaku (b. 1932) were author-composers, whose hymns appeared in *Minkunga mia Kintwadi*; the former later composed hymns for the Kimbanguist Church. But the most prominent of the writers who emerged after the war was André Ndomikolay Massaki (b. 1923), who came from Angola to settle in Kinshasa, where he edited a Protestant Kongo journal, *Sikama* ("Awakening", founded 1958). His chief contribution to imaginative literature in the language is *Mwen'Ansiona*("The orphan",1960), first published serially as *Nsamu a Nsiamindele* ("The life of Nsiamindele") in *Sikama* (1959). This short, largely autobiographical novel gives a rather unfavourable picture of conditions in Portuguese Angola; it also deals with such topics as the Christian struggle against witchcraft and traditional marriage customs.[26] In 1963, Massaki started editing *Moyo* ("Salvation"), a bi-lingual, Kikongo–Kituba, monthly.[27] Only one member of this generation is an ordained minister: H. Antoine Wantwadi, whose novel *Niklisto mu Kongo dia Kimpwanza* ("The Christian in independent Congo", 1965) recounts the life story of Matumwene, whose sufferings at the hands of the colonial administration prompt him to the conclusion that it is his moral duty as a Christian to join the struggle for independence; when this is finally obtained, he enters into active politics and, as elected assistant-mayor of his township, he starts a new fight against corruption in favour of administrative and social reform.

The most prolific Kongo writer in independent Zaire is A. Fikiau kia Bunseki (b. 1934), whose works are issued in mimeographed form so as to be more readily available to the slender resources of the average Kongo reader. He wrote a large number of didactic pamphlets dealing with such varied fields as the Kongo language, Kongo anthropology, political science, and even algebra. In 1964, he left Kinshasa and returned to his place of origin, where he founded an institution known as *Skûlu kia Minsoniki* (Authors' School) and *Kikîmba kia Kôngo* (Kongo Academy), whose purpose it is to encourage both research and authorship in Kongo and in other Zairian languages such as Lingala, Swahili and Tshiluba. His chief contribution to imaginative writing is *Dingo-Dingo* ("The cycle of life", 1966), a collection of seven long poems which successfully convey the Kongo *Weltanschauung* through systematic use of popular formulas, proverbs, songs and other techniques characteristic of Kongo oral art.

An important outlet for Kongo writing disappeared in 1973, when the Zairian government banned all missionary periodicals as part of a policy designed to strengthen its control over the press and other media. Another aspect of Zairian policy is a determination to bolster national unity by spreading Lingala, which used to be the *lingua franca* of the armed forces under Belgian rule and which is now the language of the political and administrative leadership. It is, therefore, quite possible that the short-term future may see Kongo lose its literary predominance among Zairian languages, and that official support may lead to the emergence of creative writing in Lingala.[28]

Although Protestant missionaries of many denominations and nationalities were active throughout the Belgian Kongo, their influence could not compare with that of the Catholic Church, which had the enormous advantage of working in close co-operation with the colonial administration. The distinguishing feature of Belgian Catholic enterprise was the deep interest shown by missionaries in the study of African cultures, languages and folklore. This had no parallel either in French or in Portuguese Africa. In this respect, the scientific contribution of the Belgian Catholic missionaries is truly on a par with that of Protestant missionaries in British Africa. But although the Catholic missions did publish a number of vernacular journals such as *Ntentembo eto* ("Our guiding star", 1901) or *Kukiele* ("Dawn comes", 1929) in Kongo, and many others in a variety of languages, and while Belgian scholars were responsible for the recording and publishing of a tremendous amount of oral art, this did not lead—for reasons which have not yet been properly investigated—to the emergence of any new form of literature worth mentioning, even in such widely spoken languages as Luba, Lingala, or Ngwana, the local version of Swahili. The only exception in Belgian Africa is Kinyarwanda.

Rwanda and Burundi had been part of German East Africa until they were allocated to Belgium under a League of Nations mandate after the first World War.[29] Though modern development, including the establishment of schools, had been started under German rule, much of the early linguistic research was effected by Belgian members of the order of the White Fathers, which had been founded in the late 1860s by Cardinal Lavigerie, archbishop of Algiers, originally in order to penetrate Algeria and the Sahara. Even during the German regime F. Dufays had published a German Kinya-wanda dictionary in Trier (1913). He was followed in the early 1920s by P. Schumacher, and by E. Hurel, whose *Manuel de langue Kinyarwanda* and *Grammaire Kinyarwanda* were printed in Algiers in 1921.[30] As was usual in Catholic mission territory, vernacular literary production was limited to translations of the New Testament and of the catechism.

At the time of the second World War, however, scholarly attention was called to the very elaborate body of oral Rwanda poetry, whose three main genres, the pastoral, the heroic and the dynastic, have since been thoroughly studied by Belgian and Rwanda scholars.[31] Foremost among the latter was Alexis Kagame (b. 1912), who was ordained to the Catholic priesthood in 1941 and obtained his Ph. D. at the Pontifical Gregorian University in Rome in 1955 with a dissertation entitled *La Philosophie Bantu-Rwandaise de l'Etre* (Brussels, 1956).[32] As early as 1936, while a seminary student in Kabgayi he had started researching the history of the Rwanda kingdom as recorded by traditional bards. The *mwami* (king) of the day, Mutara III, set up a fund for the publication of the vast amount of material that was thus collected. While the greater part of Kagame's scholarly writings were issued in French, his vernacular works appeared under the imprint of a firm that was variously known as "Editions Royales" and "Editions Morales". A large proportion of this consists in valuable collections of traditional poetry designed to clarify the past history of Rwanda. The first was *Inganji Karinga* ("The victorious royal drum", 1943).[33]

Before the second World War Kagame had been appointed editor of *Kinyamateka* ("The Herald"), a post which he held from 1938 to 1952. In addition, he had entered the field of creative writing with *Matabaro Ajya Iburayi* ("Matabaro leaves for Europe"), a "novelette" describing the experience of a Rwanda child in Europe. The various episodes were published serially in *Ikinyamateka Tshy' Abana* ("The Children's Journal", 1938–1939). They do not seem ever to have been printed in book form. This was to remain Kagame's sole venture into imaginative prose, for at the same time as he was pursuing his research into oral traditions, he started composing poetry of his own: *Umwaduko w'Abazungu muli Afrika yo hagati* ("The arrival of the Europeans in Central Africa", 1947) is a historical poem extolling the civilizing mission of Leopold II and

Cardinal Lavigerie. *Icara nkumare irungu* ("Sit down and let me entertain you", 1947) is a collection of paradoxically humorous poems, some by Kagame, others of unknown popular authorship, dealing with a famine that had ravaged the country in 1943: they may be said to have resulted from a response to natural calamities similar to that which prompted Boccaccio to the writing of the *Decameron* at the time of the plague in Florence. Kagame's keen sense of humour was further exemplified in *Indyohesha-birayi* ("The seasoner of potatoes", 1949), which has been described as a satirical-gastronomical poem on pork, and in *Iyo wiliwo nta rungu* ("How to spend the day pleasantly", 1949), a collection of traditional humorous poems, some of which date back to the eighteenth century.

By the late 1940s, however, Kagame had begun to turn away from this type of inspiration which had provided light relief from his scholarly pursuits, and he published the first part of a three-volume didactic-epic poem in 31 cantos, *Isoko y'Amajyambere* ("Sources of Progress", 1949–1951) which recounts the growth of Christianity in Rwanda. More importantly, a start was made with the publication of the great creative work of his life, *Umulirimbyi wa Nyili-Ibiremwa* ("The singer of the Lord of Creation"), where he was to recount, in traditional verse, the religious history of mankind from Creation to the present day. This immense narrative poem of more than 35,000 lines, divided into 18 parts and 150 cantos, had been conceived in 1941; it took Kagame twenty-five years to complete it. Only the first two parts have been published thus far in their entirety (1950 and 1953), although several brief sections of the rest appeared in local journals in the late 1960s. Kagame's own French version of the first two parts appeared in Brussels as *La Divine pastorale* (1952) and *La Naissance de l'univers* (1955).

Kagame, who had thus been the initiator of indigenous authorship in Rwanda, also remained its sole representative for more than a quarter century. His deep attachment to his country's traditions and the high level of education he had been able to obtain had combined to turn Rwanda into a quite exceptional case in the history of African-language literature. But Kagame's loneliness was an indication that a new, and less ambitious, beginning had to be made if Rwanda writing was to experience the slow continuous growth which had characterized the other written literatures of the continent. This is what occurred in Kigali in the early 1970s, when a Catholic organization, Caritas Rwanda, started publishing a series of unpretentious little books bearing the imprint "Éditions Rwandaises." This was an opportunity to print a few of the many plays that have been written in Rwanda. One of the most prolific among budding playwrights is Calixte Kamugunga, a teacher of mathematics whose *Impundu kwa makuba* ("Happiness after trial", 1970) tells the comforting story of an unemployed accountant who is about to lose his *fiancée* to a prosperous-looking clerk; the latter, however, is a thief and when he is jailed, the hero gets his job. Another play by the same writer, *Mafene ngiye mu mugi* ("Mafene, I am going to town", 1972) is a Rwanda version of the Jim-goes-to-Jo'burg story: the hero has to become a thief in order to survive in the city; but the play has a hopeful ending as the protagonist returns to his village, there to work in a peasant co-operative. In a modest way, this was a fruitful year for Rwanda literature, for it also saw the publication of *Ibereho Nkindi* ("Stay alive, Nkindi"), by François Byuma (b. 1952), who later had many poems both in French and in Kinyarwanda printed in such local journals as *La Source* and *Le Diapason*; he is also the author of some unpublished prose fiction in his own language.

It was also in 1972 that the Editions Rwandaises issued *Nta byera* ("Nothing can be spotless"), a collection of short stories by Rwanda's first woman writer, Victoire Nsanzubuhoro. Next came *Umusilimu* (1973), a verse narrative where Laurent Kamali (b. 1950) handled what had been Okot p'Bitek's favourite theme in neighbouring Uganda: the satire of the Europeanized African. Another verse narrative was *Aho mbikenge* ("I knew it", 1973), in which Jean-Chrysostome Nsabimana (b. 1946) recounted the breakdown of his own engagement! The "Editions Rwandaises" then turned back to the theatre with *Mbese Uwera uralizwa n'iki?* ("Why are you crying, Uwera?", 1974), where Edwalidi Rutesiya (b. 1950) inveighs against the abuses of parental authority in matters of love and marriage, especially when it is associated with superstitious beliefs and subjection to witchcraft. After a slight 26-page story by Lieutenant-colonel Epimaque Ruhashya, *Umugore gito* ("The greedy woman", 1976), the firm issued nothing beyond a three-act play, *Ni jye mwiza* ("I am the prettiest", 1977) by Evariste Nsabimana (b. 1949), who has written a number of other plays, and Innocent Bahinyuza's *Umubyeyi w'imbabazi*, a collection of ten long poems, some of which had appeared in the two local literary journals in the early seventies.

This was the end of the Editions Rwandaises: in spite of its nearly five million inhabitants and the efforts of the government to promote the spreading of literacy, Rwanda with its gross domestic product of $66 per capita is simply too poor to provide a market for imaginative writing, however cheaply it may be printed.

CHAPTER ELEVEN
EAST AFRICA

The most important single feature in the literary landscape of East Africa is the preponderance of Swahili, due to the seniority and prestige of written works in the language, its association with Islam, the power of the Swahili-speaking slave-traders of Arab stock, the official support given it by colonial administrations for their convenience, and the further support which it has received from independent governments in their attempt to use it as an instrument for Africanization and national integration. The course of Swahili literary history has been described at some length in Chapter V; what is in need of emphasis at the present stage is the fact that for a variety of reasons, the growth of Swahili did arouse a measure of resistance.

It has been pointed out that "in its ethnic composition, East Africa is characterized by its large number of small tribes : 120 in Tanzania, 31 in Uganda, and 27 in Kenya. Many of these tribes number only 150,000 to 200,000, and the only groups which reach anything like the size of the Ashanti, the Igbo or the Yoruba are the Kikuyu speakers [in Kenya] or the Ganda [in Uganda], reckoned at about two million people each." There is thus a *prima facie* case for the notion that only these two were in a position to resist the encroachment of Swahili : the smaller groups recognized the need for an inter-tribal medium of communication, but the spread of Swahili met with resistance from the larger ethnic groups.[1]

Originally, hostility to Swahili was bolstered among the inland populations by memories of the hated slave trade. In many cases, this attitude was further stimulated by the Christian missionaries, who resented official colonial policy on the Swahili language because Swahili was closely connected with the progress of Islam. During the German Colonial Congress in 1905, Julius Richter, a missionary, pointed out "that Islam was victorious wherever the languages that carried it were spreading, and that in order to check its advance, it was necessary first to prohibit Swahili as a government language."[2]

Two further points are of some importance as well. One is that Swahili did not penetrate into Uganda and the interior of Tanzania until the middle of the nineteenth century and was thus unable to grow as powerful roots there as it did in the immediate vicinity of the coastal area. Secondly, while Swahili can easily be learned by Bantu speakers as a *lingua franca*, it is an utterly foreign language to such speakers of non-Bantu languages as the Luo and the northern tribes of Uganda, and Kenya.

The tangled interplay of these various factors accounts for the differences that are observable in the output of creative work in Swahili in the three countries that were once part of British East Africa. Tanzania is now the main source of Swahili writing even though there were abortive attempts between the second World War and independence to promote some of the local indigenous languages.[3] On the other hand, although coastal Arabs did gain some influence in Uganda during the second half of the nineteenth century, the country has hardly produced any creative writing in Swahili.

The case of Kenya is different again. Its islands and coastal strip include part of the homeland of Swahili, and it has become the country's official second language. But this has proved a bone of contention between the two major ethnic groups: the Bantu-speaking Kikuyu and the Nilotic Luo. Even among the Kikuyu, as Whiteley noted in 1956, "indifference or antagonism to Swahili was from the 1930s coupled with advocacy of the vernacular, and was associated with the establishment of the Independent Schools, but this was an unusually vehement reaction and part of a much wider rejection of all things introduced by or associated with Europeans." In the course of the following decades, the presence of a fairly large settler population in Kikuyu country, where the capital was also located, led to an increasing valuation of English as a means for promotion and an alternative *lingua franca*: in the mid-1950s, a report of the East African Royal Commission observed that people of all levels of education regarded English as the "gate of entry to a new world." According to Whiteley, this phenomenon "suggests that no large body of people [in Kenya] has yet attained wealth or prosperity within the traditional framework of peasant or large-scale cultivation of cash crops, as has occurred in Buganda, where, it would seem, the proportionate prestige value of English is less." Since independence, the second major factor in the literary make-up of East Arica has been the explosive growth of English writing in Kenya, much of which is produced by Kikuyu authors.

With Swahili enjoying a monopoly of official support in Tanzania and English fast becoming the main cultural medium, and an effective means of communication between different ethnic groups in Kenya, it is surprising that the only other language to have produced a sizeable amount of writing in East Africa should be Ganda.

1. Uganda

Ganda is a Bantu language spoken by more than one million people in Buganda, formerly a comparatively powerful and highly centralized kingdom which had established its control over such weaker neighbouring states as Bunyoro, Ankole and Busoga by the time the British explorer John Hanning Speke (1827–1864), in his search for the sources of the river Nile, reached their capital on the banks of Lake Victoria in 1862. Of more far-reaching significance however, was Stanley's visit to the Kabaka (king) Mutesa I's court in 1875, for he sent a famous letter to the *Daily Telegraph* calling for missionaries to introduce Christianity to the Baganda. In 1876, missionaries were already on the spot, having come from two directions: a small group of Cardinal Lavigerie's Catholic White Fathers, and a few Anglican representatives of the Church Missionary Society. This is not the place, however, to recount the quarrels and intrigues that erupted between the white priests, or to dwell upon the persecutions to which both European and African Christians were submitted in the early 1880s, under Mutesa's successor, Mwanga II.

These unsavoury events did not slow down the pace of Christianization or the growth of literacy. Already by 1880 Alexander M. Mackay (d. 1890), a young Scottish engineer who was the leader of the Protestant missionaries, had reduced the language to writing. He "had printed lesson sheets on his little printing press from wooden types he had cut with his own hands, had translated the Ten Commandments, some Psalms, and had begun a version of St Matthew's Gospel".[4] Simultaneously, C.T. Wilson had produced his *Outline Grammar of the Luganda Language* (1882). *The New Testament* (1893) and the complete *Bible* (1896) were mainly the work of another C.M.S. missionary, G.L. Pilkington (d. 1897), who received valuable help from a Ganda Christian trained by Mackay, Henry Wright Duta.[5] In 1912, Ganda became the official language of Buganda.

Although, significantly, the early Christians in Buganda were called "readers", writing by Bugandans did not make a start in the manner that had been usual in black Africa. In many cases, the first converts, who were also the first writers, had come from the lower classes, or from oppressed minority groups, who found in Christianity and literacy a hope for future happiness, a prospect of advancement in the new colonial world that was taking shape, and a means of gaining status in their own eyes and in the eyes of society. But in Buganda, the ruling class became aware of the need for change at an exceptionally early stage. The disturbances that took place in the 1880s resulted largely from the puzzlement and the ensuing revulsion provoked by the network of rivalries that set one against another not only the Christian Europeans and the Muslim Arabs, but also the Christian sects and the representatives of the three European powers (Britain, France and Germany). In 1890, however, the Heligoland Treaty assigned Buganda to British control; a Protectorate was declared in 1894; in 1898, King Mwanga was deported to the Seychelles islands "because of his opposition to Christian and Moslem encroachments, as well as the British imperial designs";[6] real power passed to the hands of the man who had been Mwanga's prime minister (*Katikiro*) since 1889, Apolo (later Sir Apolo) Kagwa.

Apolo Kagwa (1865–1927) had been baptized by the C.M.S. in the mid-1880s, during the period of persecution. He held his post until 1926, but in his early manhood, he had acquired a passion for writing which, as Taban lo Liyong rightly claims, "was unique in his time"— unique that is, for a member of the traditional ruling classes. His intense literary activity during the first decade of the twentieth century makes him the founder of modern Ganda writing. Although as a Christian convert he was "particularly severe on any signs of survival of pagan belief",[7] his literary output was entirely dedicated to the recording of the history, customs and lore of the Ganda people. After *Entala za Buganda* ("The wars of Buganda", 1894), he published his best-known work, *Basekabaka be Buganda* ("The kings of Buganda", 1901), which purports to be an account of the history of the Ganda kingdom; a revised edition dealing with the royal houses of the neighbouring kingdoms as well was printed in London by the Sheldon Press in 1927; it was later translated into English as *The Kings of Buganda* (Nairobi, 1971). Other aspects of Ganda culture were dealt with in *Ekitabo kye empisa za Buganda* ("The book of the traditions and customs of the Baganda", 1905), a translation of which, *The Customs of the Baganda*, was published in New York in 1934, and *Ekitabo ky' edika bya Abaganda* ("The books of the clans of the Baganda", 1908). His last book was *Engero za Buganda* ("Uganda folklore stories", 1927), parts of which were translated in *The Tales of Sir Apolo. Uganda Folklore and Proverbs* (London, 1934).

In 1902, Apolo Kagwa was invited to attend the coronation of King Edward VII as official representative of the Protectorate. He was accompanied by his secretary, Ham Mukasa (1871–1956).[8] The latter, who had first learned to read and write Arabic from Muslim religious texts, had been converted to Christianity soon after the persecutions; he was also one of the first in Buganda to have learned English. He was already known as the author of a Ganda commentary on St. Matthew's Gospel, which was said to have had "a good sale", whatever that might mean, by the Rev.

Ernest Millar, who accompanied both men to England as interpreter and guide. During their journey, Kagwa and Mukasa kept a diary from which the latter composed a fascinating account of their experiences and observations. I have found no evidence that the Ganda version ever reached print, but the book was immediately translated into English by Millar as *Uganda's Katikiro in England* (London, 1904); it was reprinted in New York in 1971, and later edited anew by Uganda writer Taban lo Liyong (London, 1975). Mukasa was to write one more book, *Simuda Nyuma* ("Go forward", 1934), which deals with the recent history of Buganda and contains reminiscences of the reigns of Mutesa I and Mwanga II. As one of the most prominent county chiefs, he became a member of the Buganda Parliament (*Lukiko*) from which he resigned in 1941, in protest against the remarriage, contrary to custom, of the *Kabaka's* widow to a commoner.[9]

After this early flowering, there was a slowing-down in Ganda writing, due perhaps to British attempts at spreading Swahili as an official language throughout Uganda. These efforts met with fierce resistance from the Ganda, and the *kabaka* himself wrote in the *Uganda News* of 22 February 1929, that he was "entirely opposed to any arrangements which would in any way facilitate the ultimate adoption of [Swahili] as the Official Native Language of the Baganda in place of, or at the expense of, their own language."[10] In leading circles, English was widely felt to be a better choice as a second language, and from that date, says Whiteley, "there was no further question of Swahili participating in Uganda's linguistic discussion, though its use . . . persisted and flourished on the football field and in various other situations where use of English or Luganda was neither desirable nor possible"! Indeed the next contributor to Ganda writing was none other than the king himself, Sir Daudi Chwa II (1897-1939), with two volumes of memoirs: *Lwaki Sir Apolo Kagwa yawumula* ("Why Sir Apolo Kagwa retired"), printed in Nairobi, is a collection of letters and records of conversations; *Okuwumula kwa Stanislas Mugwanya* ("The retirement of Stanislas Mugwanya"), printed in Uganda, deals with the man who had been appointed second regent on the king's ascent to the throne, and who had held the post of Chief Justice of Buganda, "the highest position to which a Catholic could aspire".[11] Daudi Chwa was also responsible for a locally printed pamphlet in English, *Education, Civilization and Foreignization in Buganda* (1935), where he wrote about principles that were designed to promote the modernization of his country while shunning subservience to European imperialism.

Most of the Ganda works of the 1930s belong to the same type of writing. The doings of the Chief Justice were once more the subject of Joseph Musanje's *Olugendo lwa Stanislas Mugwanya nu Bulaya ne mu nsi Entukuvu* ("The journey of Stanislas Mugwanya in Europe and in the

Holy Land"). The White Fathers' Printing Press produced *Magezi ntakke*, yet another book about Ganda history and customs, by J.T.K. Ssazabalangira, and yet another travelogue, John Nsubuga's *Omuganda mu Bulaya* ("A Muganda in Europe"). The Gambuze Press, which had printed Daudi Chwa's little book on Mugwanya now issued a brief collection of English essays about *The Life and Work of Canon Apolo Kivebulaya*, a Ganda pioneer missionary who has a special place in the history of Christian missions because he went to work among the Congo pygmies: "His greatest achievement was the translation of St Mark's Gospel, apparently from the Lunyoro version, into the pygmy language; using his work, linguistic science was at last able to answer the question whether the pygmies had a language of their own."[12]

Although by the time the second World War broke out Ganda writing had been in existence for about half a century, the output remained slender, and very limited in scope. According to Snoxall, two major handicaps had prevented its growth: one was the failure of the French Catholic White Fathers and the British Protestant Church Missionary Society to agree on a single method for spelling the language. This had meant that "the publications of the mission presses have been confined to works produced by members of their own denomination only, and authors have perforce resorted to the local presses with their often inferior and broken type, which has adversely affected the appearance of the printed work. A further contributory cause to the comparative lack of vernacular literature, is the expense involved in publishing editions for a very limited public, and it is in this respect mainly that the local printing presses have performed such a valuable task for they have enabled authors to publish works which the larger and more modern presses would have considered not worth accepting." To this it must be added, however, that such writing as did reach print emanated from the ruling caste and was confined to their preoccupations and interests, which had little to do with imaginative literature.

It is true that Ganda had seemed to join the general pattern in 1932, when several Ganda authors were awarded prizes in the second IAI competition. One of these was Eridadi M.K. Mulira, a teacher and journalist who, twenty years later, was to found the Uganda National Congress. This has been described as "a national political party", "the first political group in Uganda, organized on a basis other than ethnicity".[13] As a party of all races and peoples, the UNC was a failure but it paved the way for Milton Obote's Uganda People's Congress so that Mulira can be regarded as a precursor, within Buganda, of a conscious reaction against the limitations of Ganda nationalism, which had been carefully nurtured and exacerbated by most previous writing. Thus absorbed in politics, Mulira's imaginative abilities did not reach print until 1968, with the publication of a brief tale, *Teefe*.

After the IAI competition's failure to stimulate a different kind of writing in Ganda, a new beginning was made in 1954, when another teacher, Michael Bazze Nsimbi (b. 1910), was awarded the Margaret Wrong Prize Medal for a monograph on Ganda place names. The creation of the East African Literature Bureau after the war made it possible for Nsimbi to publish several pieces of narrative fiction for juvenile readers: *Muddu awulira* ("The obedient servant", 1953), *Kitagenda ne Kagenda* ("Kitagenda and Katenga", 1960), *Kagenda ne banne* ("Kakenda and his friends", 1961), and *Kagenda ne banne bakola ki?* ("What has become of Kagenda and his friends?", 1962). In 1968, Nsombi was appointed vernacular language advisor to the Uganda Publishing House, which issued Mulira's *Teefe*. By that time, however, two further developments had taken place in Ganda writing, both represented in the activities of two writers: Edward E.N. Kawere and Y.B. Lubambula. In 1954, the former had published *Zinunula omunaku* ("They buy a poor man"), his first novel, which was followed by a detective story, *Nketta mu bizinga* ("A spy on the island", 1960) and by a collection of poetry for children's use, *Ebitontome eby'amakulu* ("Didactic poems", 1963). But written poetry had first been illustrated by *Ennyimba ezimu* ("Some songs", 1958), by Lubumbula, who then turned to prose fiction with a "novella" intriguingly entitled *Zikusooka. Olugero lwa dereeva omwati-ikirivu* ("All is well that ends well. The story of a famous car driver", 1969).

Prose fiction seemed bound to grow faster than poetry, for the early 1960s saw the appearance of several "novels", all of them composed with a juvenile audience in mind: Jackson Kaswa produced *Omuganda n'enswa* ("The Muganda and the white ants", 1960) and *Omunaku kaama* ("A poor man is like a wild yam", 1960). Next came Christopher G. Kiwanuka Musisi with a detective novel entitled *Kikonyogo* ("Unexpected luck", 1961) and Binsangawano with *Bonna baasumagira* ("Were they all fooled?", 1962). All these books were published by the EALB in association with such British publishers as Macmillan, Longmans, Nelson and the Oxford University Press. Most of them were recommended for primary school reading, but when Marshall Idi Amin Dada came to power in 1971, a second phase in the history of Ganda writing came to an end, without being allowed to explore and exploit its potentialities.

• • •

By the time European explorers reached Lake Victoria, Buganda was the dominant power because it was the most politically advanced state in the area; it remained so under the protectorate and after Uganda obtained her independence in 1962, until the coup engineered by Mil-

ton Obote in 1966. Even in precolonial days, then, Buganda had a tradition of superiority. From a linguistic and political point of view, the
population of Uganda fell into two groups: the Bantu-speaking peoples
in the southern part of the country comprised the kingdoms of Bunyoro, Toro and Ankole, and the less centralized chiefdoms of Busoga;
their languages are closely similar to Ganda. The Nilotic and Nilo-Hamitic peoples to the north, such as the Acoli and the Karimojong, spoke
utterly different languages; they had no centralized form of government
and were considered backward by their southern neighbours. The British protectorate originally established over Buganda in 1894 and trans-
formed to include Kenya in 1895, was extended to Toro in 1900, Ankole in 1901 and Bunyoro in 1903. It later came to cover Acoli and the
other northern territories as well, until the whole of Uganda was amalgam-
ated into a political entity within its present borders.[14]

Buganda's superior power led to continued advance in educational,
and consequently literary, matters: "Both the Catholic and Protestant
missionaries who arrived in 1870 were forbidden to leave the Kampala
area where Mutesa I's capital was situated, and so Buganda got an
educational head-start. The first secondary schools were set up in this
region; Buganda had the highest rate of secondary school and university
educated citizens in Uganda in the years before independence."[15] To
this should be added that the first institution of higher learning, catering
for the whole of East Africa, Makekere College, was established near
Buganda's capital in 1939. As a result, little attention was paid to the other
languages of Uganda, especially as text-books in the Ganda language could
be used throughout the Bantu-speaking areas. An *Elementary Lunyoro Grammar*, dealing with the Toro dialect of Nyoro, was published by B.H.E.
Maddox in 1902; the Nyoro New Testament was available in 1905 and the
complete Bible in 1912; but there is no trace of any subsequent indigenous
literary activity, either in Nyoro or in the other languages of Uganda, until
the middle of the twentieth century.

The emergence of Uganda writing in non-Ganda languages was the,
perhaps slightly unexpected, result of the foundation of the East African
Literature Bureau.[16] In 1945, the East African Governors' Conference
appointed an English writer living in Kenya, Elspeth Huxley, to submit
proposals for the provision of reading material for the rapidly increasing demand from literate Africans. As a result of her report, the EALB
was established in 1948 under the administration of the East African
High Commission. However, in 1947, the then manager of the C.M.S.
Bookshop in Nairobi, Charles Richards, had been appointed adviser to
the East African governments on literature for Africans. In a memorandum entitled *A Proposed Literature Organization for East Africa*, he advised,
as John Ndegwa recounts, "that in the first instance publishing should
be in Swahili and Luganda and that as soon as orthographies were

agreed on, this should be extended to Gang-Dho-luo and Kikuyu."
This, almost inevitably, meant endorsing the existing literary hierarchy
of East African languages, but, Ndegwa goes on, "as it happens, developments were too quick for this recommendation to be followed and publications were in many more languages right from the onset."[17] A
glance at the early catalogues of the EALB and of the British publishers
who were often working in association with the Bureau shows that the
vast majority of these publications were primers, school readers, and
textbooks of various kinds—essential for teaching purposes. Besides, as
Granston was to put it as late as 1960, "most modern African readers of
Swahili and vernacular books are mainly interested in practical subjects.
This limits the number of imaginative works by African authors that can
be published, but there are already signs of a growing interest in reading
for pleasure."

Swahili received pride of place in the publication programme of
the EALB, but one of the earliest works of creative writing to be
issued by the Bureau under its usual imprint, the Eagle Press, was a
novel in the Acoli dialect of Luo: *Lak tar miyo kinyero wi lobo* ("You
have white teeth, then laugh", 1953) by Okot p'Bitek (b. 1931).[18]
This is the familiar story of an Acoli boy who has to go away to work
in Kampala in order to earn the enormous amount of money which
is claimed as a bride price for the girl he wants to marry. He fails to
raise the sum, has his meagre property stolen from him, and must
walk home as poor and miserable as ever. This sort of tale exploits
one of the best-documented social phenomena that resulted from
the introduction of a money economy into African societies. But the
distinguishing feature of Okot's novel is that the hero's pathetic
odyssey is above all a pretext for satirical commentary. After this,
Okot composed a lengthy poem in rhymed verse, *War pa Lawino*
("Song of Lawino"), a first version of which was rejected by publishers, probably, Heron suggests, "because of its forthrightness in
sexual matters." Undaunted, Okot reworked and expanded his
poem from a thirty-page manuscript to more than 100 pages. At the
same time, he turned it into English: the latter appeared in 1966,
while the vernacular version, which had been completed at the same
time, was not printed until 1969. By that time, Okot's outspokenness
and his sarcastic comments aimed at Uganda politicians had caused
him to be dismissed from his post as Director of the Uganda Cultural Centre; he then found employment at the University of
Nairobi. He has been living in exile ever since and has turned to
English as his sole medium for literary expression. The publication
of *Song of Lawino* however, established his position as the most gifted
writer to have emerged in East Africa after Kenya's Njugi wa
Thiong'o.

Ngugi himself had been a student at Makerere College, which was the cradle of English writing throughout East Africa. Indeed, the inter-territorial college, and especially its English department, remained for several years the most productive centre for English writing; its literary magazine, *Penpoint*, was launched in 1958; an important Conference of African Writers of English Expression was held there in 1962, and in 1965 David Cook published *Origin East Africa: A Makerere Anthology*. Much of this output, however, had come from Kenyan students, and in the course of the early sixties, Uganda's place in this respect was grad-ually taken over by Kenya. Although after independence imaginative writing in English grew appreciably, not only with Okot's poetry, but also with the novels of Okello Oculi, Robert Serumaga and Eneriko Seruma, not to mention the prolific talent of another Luo writer, Taban lo Liyong, the most significant literary event of the 1960s was the first appearance of creative work in several of the country's languages. A second Luo writer, J.P. Ocitti, emerged with *Lacan ma kwo pe kinyero* ("Every dog has its day", 1961), and especially *Acam, towa* (1970), a novel depicting married life in an Acoli village; the protagonist is notable for his laziness, drunkenness and gluttony. In 1963, modern fiction in Nyoro-Toro began with *Ha munwa gw'ekituuro* ("At the point of death"), a "novelette" by Timothy B. Bazarrabusa (1912–1966), Uganda's first High Commissioner in London, with E.D. Kagoro's *Mainaro omusuma kakingo* ("Mainaro, the great thief") soon followed by his *Kalyaki na Marunga* ("Kalyaki and Marunga", 1964), and with a collection of tales, *Kibbaate kya Kaseegu n'enganikyo* ("Kibbaate, son of Kaseegu, and other stories"), by L.T. Rubongonya, who also gathered some information about the language and lore of Bunyoro in *Linda engeso n'orulimi rw'ihanga* ("The customs and language of the coun-try"). The first book in Runyankore had been published in 1955 by EALB; it was an account of traditional history entitled *Abagabe b'Ankole* ("The kings of Ankole") by A.G. Katate and L. Kamungungunu. In 1966, Y. Ntungweriisho provided a highly condensed adaptation of Washington Irving's *Rip van Winkle*, and the following year, the EALB issued *Kizegi n'abantu bamwo* ("Kizegi and his people") by P. Ngolo-koza.

There is little doubt that these writings were prompted to some extent by the growing self-confidence felt by the non-Ganda population of Uganda as a result of the policy of the country's first prime minister, Sir Milton Obote, himself a Lango, who was determined to undermine the predominance of Buganda in the federal structure of Uganda. The inevitable clash between Obote and Mutesa II, *kabaka* of Buganda who was at the same time the President of Uganda, broke out early in 1966: Obote assumed presidential powers and the king escaped to England. Some admittedly minor after-effects of these events were soon felt in the literary field, for a Milton Obote Foundation was immediately set up in Kampala, under whose imprint several books in non-Ganda languages were issued. These included Bazarrabusa's third published work of fiction, *Obu ndikura tindifa* ("I will never die", 1966) in Nyoro-Toro, a novelette by Wilson Ogwal-Otim, *Ojuc angwec kwan* ("Ojuk the runaway", 1966), published in Luo with an English translation, and the very first book printed in Soga, E.J. Lyavala-Lwanga's *Endheso dh' Abasoga* ("Tales of the Basoga", 1967).

2. Kenya

Although classical Swahili literature originated and flourished on islands and coastal areas that are now part of the Republic of Kenya, the latter's contribution to the recent development of Swahili creative writing cannot bear comparison with that of Tanzania. In Tanzania, Swahili has acquired the status of a national language. Consequently, no official support or financial encouragement is given to the vernacular languages spoken by the 120 small tribes that constitute the inland population of the country.

An entirely different linguistic situation prevails in Kenya, whose ethnic groups are both fewer and larger: with 2.2 million people, the Kikuyu make up 20 per cent of the population; there are more than 1.2 million Kamba people; and Luo is a Nilotic language which is spoken by over 1.5 million, not only in Kenya, but also in Uganda and Tanzania. The Richards Memorandum of 1947 showed that while immediate growth was contemplated for Swahili and Ganda, short-term forecasts included the emergence of the written art in Luo and Kikuyu. This was a legitimate expectation, for several Kenya languages, especially among those belonging to the Bantu group, had been reduced to writing. Already in the nineteenth century, Kamba had been one of the languages considered in Johann Ludwig Krapf's *Vocabulary of Six East-African Languages* (1851); and after J.T. Last's little *Grammar of the Kamba Language* (1885), the first scholarly study had been E. Brutzer's *Handbuch der Kambasprache* (1906). The study of Kikuyu was started at the beginning of the century with A.W. McGregor's *English-Kikuyu Vocabulary* (1904) and *A Grammar of the Kikuyu Language* (1905); interest in the language was expressed in rather unprecedented form in an *Italian-Kikuyu Dictionary* published by the Italian Mission in British East Africa, and even a *Lexicon Latinum-Kikuyense* (1931) issued by the Catholic Mission at Nyeri![19] Even such a minor language as Taita had been studied in J.A. Wray's *An Elementary Introduction to the Taita Language* (1894), while the Catholic missionary A. Héméry had published in Zanzibar a *Vocabulary of French-Swahili-Taita* (1901).[20] The *New Testament* had been printed in Kamba (1920) and in Kikuyu (1926); and if the Kikuyu Bible was not available until 1951, Jomo Kenyatta had edited a vernacular nationalist journal, *Muigwithania*, from 1928 to 1930.[21] From its inception then, the EALB gave considerable attention not only to the two established languages, Swahili and Ganda, but also to a number of lesser languages spoken in Uganda and in Kenya. And so did the British publishers who were active in East Africa, sometimes in close association with EALB. Throughout the 1950s and the 1960s, a considerable amount of school material was thus printed in a variety of Kenyan languages : not only Kikuyu, Kamba and various dialects of Luo, but also Luyia, Meru, Masai, Taita, Kalenjin and Pokot.

These publications consisted essentially of language-teaching material, elementary readers and didactic works on such topics as agriculture, commerce and hygiene. The nearest approach to imaginative literature was to be found in upper-grade primary-school readers which consisted of abridged adaptations of western fiction or collections of traditional tales. In the first category are a Kikuyu version of *Robinson Crusoe*, which went through a second edition in 1958, and adaptations of *The Pilgrim's Progress* not only in Kikuyu (2nd ed., 1968) but also in Kalenjin. As to writing by Africans, this concentrated on the recording of folkstories, which were supposed to provide suitable reading matter for children while helping them, as did the study of their own languages, keep in touch with traditional culture. As early as 1951, EALB issued S. Malo's *Sigend Luo mu duogo chuny* ("Merry Luo stories"). Kamba was illustrated in *Mutunga na ngewa yake* ("Mutunga and his story", 1954) by John S. Mbiti (b. 1931), whose later work, entirely in English, comprises a volume of poetry, *Poems of Nature and Faith* (1969), and several important books dealing with African religions. After independence, further Kamba stories were collected by Thomas M. Ngotho in *Kutheea kuma yayayani* ("From the sky", 1962), *Mithimukyo na ngewa ingi* ("Mithimukyo and other tales", 1962), and *Kimena kya nzou na Mbui* ("The enmity between the elephant and the goat") which went through a third printing in 1966. Pokot, a minor Nilo-Hamitic language of northern Kenya, was represented by Annette Totty's *Kikorum cho pu Pokot* ("Ten Pokot short stories", 1963). In the mid-1960s, J.M. Mshila authored *Mashomo ga kadadu* ("Folk tales of the Wadewida") in Taita. A few other vernacular authors dealt with the history and customs of their people : they include D.N. Michuki's *Bururi wa Embu* ("History of the Embu people", 1962) in Kikuyu and Daniel M. Wako's *Akabaluyia bemumbo* ("Customs of the Luyia people"), which had its fourth edition in 1965.

The reason why vernacular writing (as distinguished from Swahili) failed to reach beyond this very elementary stage in Kenya and has not produced any creative work that could bear comparison with Okot p'Bitek's poetry and prose in Acoli, is to be found in the peculiar history of the country. Living alongside the so-called "White High-lands", which were originally part of their own homeland, and around the outskirts of Nairobi, it was the Kikuyu who "felt the racial, economic and political tensions in their severest forms": they became the dominant ethnic group in Kenya, not only in terms of numbers, but also because they were "the most advanced tribe, with more educated members and a higher degree of political consciousness".[22] The first organized protest movement in East Africa was the Kikuyu Central Association (founded 1922) of which Jomo Kenyatta soon became secretary-general. It was the Kikuyu who "started their own school system, partly because of a shortage of schools for Africans, but also in order to combat the teaching of the missionary schools on such subjects as polygamy and circumcision".[23] They were also the first to recognize the advantage to be gained by adopting English rather than Swahili as a *lingua franca*. They formed an important and active segment of the population at Makerere College. The first book written by a Kikuyu to attract world-wide attention was Jomo Kenyatta's *Facing Mount Kenya* (1938). When the East African authorities undertook to promote vernacular languages in the 1950s, the more highly educated among Kikuyu intellectuals kept conspicuously aloof. Instead, they launched two varieties of writing in English: autobiographical accounts, often based on the traumatic experiences of the Mau Mau rebellion and its bloody repression, include *Land of Sunshine* (1958) by Muga Gicaru (b. 1920), *Mau Mau Detainee* (1963) by Josiah Mwangi Kariuki (b. 1929), and *Child of Two Worlds* (1964) by Mugo Gatheru (b. 1925). At the same time, James Ngugi (b. 1938), then a student at Makerere, was initiating East African drama in English with *The Black Hermit* (first performed 1962, published 1968); his first two novels, *Weep Not, Child* (1964) and *The River Between* (1965), were shortly to establish him as one of Africa's most talented writers. In the late 1960s, further Kikuyu novelists such as Charity Waciuma, John Karobi, Godwin Wachira and Stephen Ngubiah built on the foundations laid by Ngugi; they were soon joined by authors from other ethnic groups.

• • •

This book is not concerned with African literature in European languages. But it seems relevant to inquire whether the fantastic growth of English writing in Kenya since independence should be regarded as a passing phenomenon that is likely to fade out before the obvious advantages and facilities of writing in the author's and readers' mother tongues. The answer to this question is, of course, dependent upon the linguistic policy built into the educational system: the whole of the last part of this book should have made it clear that where a vernacular literature did develop, it was because the early missionary teachers had found it advisable to use the local language as a medium of instruction.

In this respect, the trend in Kenya today is distinctly unfavourable to the promotion of African languages. The official attitude was defined as follows by the Kenya Education Commission in 1964 : "The vernacular languages are essential languages of verbal communication . . . We apprehend, therefore, that the vernaculars will continue to serve their historic role of providing a means of domestic verbal communication. We see no case for assigning to them a role for which they are ill adapted, namely the role of educational medium in the critical years of schooling."[24] Not everybody is in favour of confining the vernaculars to "domestic verbal communication." At the first East African Conference on Language and Linguistics which was held in December 1968, Arthur Bagunywa, a member of the Uganda inspectorate, pointed out that "the question of providing incentives for learning a chosen vernacular should be the ultimate responsibility of national governments. Once there is a commitment and desire to see the rural community play an active part in local government it is hoped that language policies will gradually take a clear-cut and logical course of development in full recognition of certain selected African Vernaculars."[25] This, we must note, is a Ugandan viewpoint.

But in Kenya, as was pointed out by Eddah Gachukia of the University College, Nairobi, things were moving in an entirely different direction. "Since independence," there has been a growing trend towards the use of English as the medium of instruction. Today, about 60 per cent of the primary schools in Kenya including almost all the schools in the urban areas use English as the medium of instruction from Primary I . . . 25 per cent of the schools use the predominant African Vernacular of the area, or Swahili as the medium of instruction from Primary I to III . . . All schools are expected to use English as a medium of instruction from Primary IV to VII." Wherever and whenever an African language is not the medium of instruction, "the Kenya Primary Syllabus does state clearly that Vernaculars and Swahili, together with other subjects, should be taught in primary schools." Actually, however, "it was found in 1965 that the majority of teachers in the English medium streams had dropped the teaching of vernacular languages and Swahili altogether and were using the time allocated to these subjects for the revision of other subjects."

Gachukia also went into the reasons underlying this growing disaffection towards the vernaculars either as a medium or as a subject : "The use of English as a medium of instruction has often been linked with the quest for political unity in Kenya . . . There was in 1964 and 1965 a reaction against the colonial system of separate tribal and racial institutions. The development of Vernaculars then had undertones of divisionism. This feeling seems to have disappeared to a great extent today." But with political motives fading out, the main reason, in the late 1960s, was of an economic order : "The lack of vernacular newspapers, periodicals and literature is another factor that has hindered any enthusiasm or motivation that could have encouraged the teaching of the vernacular languages. A number of unsuccessful attempts to print periodicals in the Vernaculars have been made, and their failure seems to be mainly due to high costs of printing and publishing. The same problem has been encountered in the process of preparing and publishing readers in the Vernaculars. Whereas it is possible to produce at reasonable cost attractive readers in English for young children, the same exercise becomes expensive in the various Vernaculars. The amount of work involved is greater and the number of potential users smaller."[26]

This is exactly the problem with which the East African Literare Bureau was confronted as defined in its report for the year 1967–68: "Intensive and extensive publicity notwithstanding, we have had a lot difficulties in selling a number of books written in the vernacular. We have, as a result, decided to accept only a limited number of manuscripts which fall under this category and where possible to have them translated either into English or Swahili." In economic terms, this is a typical vicious circle : textbooks and reading material are too expensive to print because the demand, the potential readership, is too small; and the readership cannot be increased because there is no teaching material to spread literacy. Still in purely economic terms, demand can conceivably be primed through government subsidies until vernacular publishing becomes a sound commercial proposition. The problem, however, does not rest with the consumers only : it also has to do with what we might call the intellectual producers of vernacular reading matter. As the EALB report further says, "There is another reason to the Bureau's attitude to vernacular manuscripts besides the limited size of their market, and that is the difficulty of finding the right readers to assess their value. Some of the manuscripts received and published in the past have turned out to be unpopular not so much because they were expensive as because they had little to offer to the readers. The author may have written about his tribe, their customs and tradition or their history, and the customer may be already well versed in all these subjects because his grand-ma, papa or any other relative had already given him the facts. The Bureau will therefore be very cautious in accepting manuscripts of this nature for publication."[27] This allusion to the kind of books that were listed a few pages back makes it clear that a heavy responsibility rests with the writers themselves.

The emergence of vernacular literature in Europe owed much to the talented men who decided to forgo the prestige inherent in Latin and to compose the *Chanson de Roland*, the *Poema de mio Cid*, the *Divina Commedia* in what was then regarded as the proper idiom of unlettered barbarians. This is the dilemma of the African writer today : either he may use a European language and thus gain recognition (and financial reward) from a worldwide audience, but at the risk of cutting himself off from the very roots of all but the most esoteric creative flowering, the common experience of his own society; or he may use his own mother tongue, stoically shun the appeal of the world market, remain one of the inglorious Miltons of the present age, but help his own people's advance into the age of mass literacy, and pave the way for future achievements and renown.

Can it be that there is no way out of this dilemma? Can it be that the written art in sub-Saharan Africa will be addressed only to a necessarily small élite minority of Afro-Saxons—to borrow Ali Mazrui's convenient phrase?[28] Many writers in Renaissance and Classical Europe were equally at east—following the example set by Petrarch—in Latin and in the then humble languages that they had learnt at childhood. How is it, then, that in this transitional period in the long history of black Africa, almost none of her already numerous and well known writers, men of very great ability, should have proved willing, or indeed eager, to put their talent in the service of their own ancestral language *as well*?

Part at least of the answer to this question lies in the fact that no writer can ignore the fact that resorting to the people's language, however desirable an achievement, can be a dangerous occupation in those parts of Africa today where the concepts of freedom, democracy, tolerance have only the slightest hold on the minds of those in power. As this book ends with a chapter on East Africa, the case of Ngugi wa Thiong'o will provide an apposite conclusion.

For nearly twenty years, Ngugi has made his way towards world fame as one of the finest novelists in black Africa, as perhaps the best writer to have come not only from his own country, Kenya, but from the whole of what used to be British East Africa. He achieved this on the basis of his four great novels, culminating in *Petals of Blood* (1977). But, as he explained in the course of an interview, "it was in the course of writing the novel that I came to be more and more disillusioned with the use of foreign languages to express Kenya's soul or to express the social conditions in Kenya." The main reason for this, he commented, was that, "if you learn a people's language and you adopt their culture, you are more likely to see yourself in terms of their world outlook, their aspirations." This led him to the conclusion that it was the task of Kenyan writers to recount their country's history and to formulate her national aspirations "in the various national languages, including the main national language which is Swahili. But all the other national languages, Gikuyu, Luo, Giriama, Kamba, Maasai, are part and parcel of our national culture, and we should express ourselves fully in those national languages instead of expressing ourselves in a foreign language like English", the ultimate purpose being that there should "be a vital relationship between the writer and the mass of Kenyan people."[29]

In compliance with these views, Ngugi wa Thiong'o co-authored with Ngugi wa Mirii (no kin of his), a play written in his own language, Kikuyu, *Ngaahika Ndenda* ("I will marry when I choose to"), which has been described as "the first piece of literature by any major author which tried to interpret for its audience society's workings in one of Kenya's ethnic languages."[30] It deals with the simple, pathetic story of a poor labourer whose wealthy Christian neighbours covet the small plot of land that he owns, in order to build a pesticide factory with the help of foreign capital; they achieve their unholy purpose by playing upon the poor man's and his wife's credulousness: they persuade him to take out a loan against the security of his land, so that he can pay for his own marriage to be "cleansed" in church. When he is unable to refund the money, the bank has his land auctioned off.[31]

The play is hardly more critical of the new African society than is *Petals of Blood*, which had been launched with official support and had obtained tremendous success in Nairobi. *Ngaahika Ndenda* was accordingly licensed to be performed at the Karimithu Community Centre in Limuru, a few miles from Nairobi. It was intended as a purely popular undertaking, being performed not by professional actors and actresses, but by local villagers. As one Nairobi journalist put it, the play attracted "large crowds from Limuru as well as neighbouring areas and Nairobi. The play united families. People saw it and invariably went home and brought their mothers, grandmothers, relatives and children. Children enjoyed it because it taught them something about their history and culture. Some of those who saw the play had not been to a theatre before but they enjoyed the performance because it was relevant to their lives and they could identify with it. They also commented on the authenticity of the play and this showed that it reflected some of their social needs and problems."[32]

But after it had been performed for a few Sundays, its license was abruptly revoked by the district commissionner at Kiumbu on the grounds that it was provocative. On 31 December, 1977, Ngugi was picked up by the police at his home and put in detention under Kenya's security regulations. As an anonymous contribution to *African Perspectives* was to put it two months later, Ngugi's detention "came as a shock because of Kenya's enviable record in this regard. The government has always allowed its intellectuals the freedom to express their criticisms of society as it is presently constituted, and no writer or artist has ever been jailed, with or without trial." Indeed, according to the *Nairobi Times*, "a highranking minister" was at pains to explain "that Ngugi's deten-

tion was a matter of state security and had more to do with his activities
than with his ordinary writing. 'We have not banned his books, have
we?' the minister said."[33]

That of course, is the point. As long as Ngugi, or Kibera or the many
others who were critical of the corruption and exploitation characteristic
of the Kenyatta regime voiced their objections in English novels and
plays which can only be understood by a small number of highly educated people, most of whom belong to the privileged class anyway,
there was obviously no need to ban them, for, as Fibi Munene aptly put
it, "if a play is in English or Kiswahili, it leaves out the majority of the
people in this country." Conditions become vastly different when a
gifted writer manages to phrase his message in the language really spoken by men, so that the majority of the people can grasp what he has
to say. To the powers that be, they become unacceptable when this
message runs counter to the orthodoxy of the system. This was the case
with Ngugi, who declared in his *Weekly Review* interview: "If you see
that you are poor because God has willed it, you are more than likely
to continue to pray to God to right your condition. But if you know that
your poverty is not God-conditioned, but it is socially conditioned, then
you are likely to do something about those social conditions that are
assuring that you be poor."

In Africa as elsewhere, there are few governments—whether they are
white or black does not seem to matter greatly—that want the bulk of
their population to be enlightened about the ideological mechanisms
which ensure the continued subservience of the oppressed and exploited
and the continued prosperity of the powerful and wealthy. There is
nothing new in this confrontation. The case of Ngugi wa Thiong'o—
who was held in detention, without trial for over a year without the
government even bothering to make known the reasons behind this
arrest, his whereabouts unknown—was the clearest demonstration that
creative writing in the peoples' language is not just a harmless educational pastime, but an effective weapon in man's struggle for enlightenment and justice.

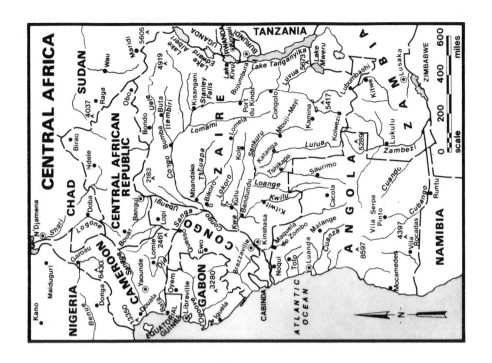

CENTRAL AFRICA

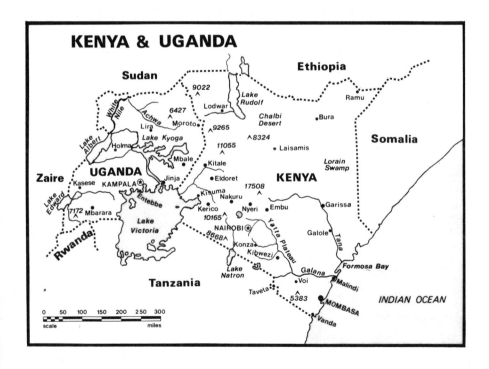

KENYA & UGANDA

NOTES AND REFERENCES

NOTES TO CHAPTER ONE

1 The standard works on the history of Ethiopian literature date from the first decades of this century : Enno Littmann, "Geschichte der äthiopischen Literatur" in C. Brockelmann (ed.), *Geschichte der christlichen Literaturen des Orients* (Leipzig, 1907), pp. 185-270, and Ignazio Guidi, *Storia della letteratura etiopica* (Rome, 1932). The latest and most serviceable account is Enrico Cerulli, *La letteratura etiopica con un saggio sull' Oriente Cristiano* (3rd ed., Florence, 1968). A number of texts are conveniently gathered in Paul E. Huntsberger (comp.), *Highland Mosaic : A Critical Anthology of Ethiopian Literature in English* (Athens, Ohio, 1973), which contains translations of pieces originally written in Ethiopian languages, besides extracts from English works by Ethiopian authors.

2 Y.M. Kobischanow, "The Origins of Ethiopian Literature", in M.A. Korostovtsev (ed.), *Essays on African Culture* (Moscow, 1966), pp. 28-45.

3 G.W. B. Huntingford (ed.), *The Glorious Victories of Amda Seyon, King of Ethiopia* (Oxford, 1965). See also E. Ullendorf's critical review in the *Bulletin of the School for Oriental and African Studies*, XXIX (1966), 600-611.

4 R. Pankhurst (ed.), *The Ethiopian Royal Chronicles* (Addis Ababa-London, 1967), pp. xii-xiii.

5 Enno Littmann, *Die altamharischen Kaiserlieder* (Strassburg, 1914).

6 Donald Levine, *Wax and Gold : Tradition and Innovation in Ethiopian Culture* (Chicago, 1965), p. 8.

7 Lanfranco Ricci, "Le vite di Embaqum e di Yohannes, abbati di Dabra Libanos di Scioa", *Rassegna di studi etiopici*, XIV (1955-58), XXII (1966), 75-102, and XXIII (1967-8), 79-219.

8 For a more detailed account, see Albert S. Gérard, *Four African Literatures* (Berkeley, 1971), pp. 271-386 and especially Thomas Leiper Kane, *Ethiopian Literature in Amharic* (Wiesbaden, 1975).

9 Stephen Wright, *Ethiopian Incunabula from the Collections in the National Library of Ethiopia and the Haile Sellassie I University* (Addis Ababa, 1967).

10 An English version entitled *Tobbya* was published by Tadesse Tamrat in *Ethiopia Observer*, VIII (1964), 242-67.

11 Menghistu Lemma, "Modern Amharic Literature : The Task Ahead", *Voice of Ethiopia*, 19 May 1965.

12 English translation in *Ethiopia Observer*, VII (1964), 321-60.

13 English translation, London, 1970.

14 See on this two articles by David F. Beer: "Ethiopian Literature and Literary Criticism in English : An Annotated Bibliography", *Research in African Literatures*, VI (1975), i, 44-57, and "The Sources and Content of Ethiopian Creative Writing in English", *ibid.*, VIII (1977), i, 99-124.

15 Mäkonnen Endalkachew, *Three Plays : King David the Third, The Voice of Blood, The City of the Poor* (Asmara, n.d.).

16 Kebbede Mikael, *Annibal, tragédie en cinq actes* (Addis Ababa, 1964).

17 See for example Tsegaye's early play, "Tewodros", *Ethiopia Observer*, IX (1966), iii, 211-226.

NOTES TO CHAPTER TWO

1 See especially J. Spencer Trimingham, A *History of Islam in West Africa* (London, 1971); Vincent Monteil, *L'Islam noir* (2nd ed., Paris 1971); Djibril Tamsir Niane, *Le Soudan occidental au temps des grands empires* XIe-XVIe siècles (Paris, 1975).

2 R.A. Nicholson, *A Literary History of the Arabs* (Cambridge, 1969), p. 430. See also P.F. de Morses Farias, "The Almoravids, Some questions concerning the character of the movement during its periods of closest contact with the Western Sudan," *BIFAN*, B, XXIX (1967), 794-878.

3 Thomas Hodgkin, *Nigerian Perspectives : An Historical Anthology* (London, 1969), p. 68.

4 Trimingham, p. 68; Monteil, p. 74.

5 Sékéné Mody Cissoko, "L'intelligentsia de Tombouctou aux XVe et XVIe siècles", *BIFAN*, B, XXXI (1969) iv, 927-952. See also G. Vajda, "Contribution à la connaissance de la littérature arabe en Afrique occidentale," *Journal de la Société des Africanistes*, XX (1950), 229-237; Vincent Monteil, "Les manuscrits historiques arabo-africains", *BI-FAN*, B, XVII (1965), 531-542, XXVIII (1966), 668-675, XXVII (1967), 57-65; René Baesjou, "Over Arabische litteratuur in West-Africa", *Kroniek van Afrika*, XII (1972), iv, 173-186; Sékéné Mody Cissoko, *Tombouctou et l'empire Songhay : Epanouissement du Soudan nigérien aux XVe-XVIe siècles* (Dakar, 1975).

6 A French translation was provided by O. Houdas and M. Delafosse, *Tarikh el-fettach* (Paris, 1913). See also J.O. Hunwick, "Studies in the Ta'rikh al-Fattâsh: Its Authors and Textual History," *Research Bulletin* (Centre of Arabic Documentation, Ibadan), V (1969), 57-65; N. Levtzion, "A Seventeenth-Century Chronicle by Ibn al-Mukhtar : A critical Study of *Ta'rikh al-fattash*." *BSOAS*, XXXIV (1971), iii, 571-593.

7 Trimingham, p. 5.

8 On Ahmad Baba, see *Encyclopedia of Islam*, I (1960), 279-80; J.O. Hunwick, "A New source for the Biography of Ahmad Bâbâ al-Tinbûkti (1556-1627)," *BSOAS*, XXVII (1964), 568-593; *Id.*, "Further Light on Ahmad Bâbâ al Tin-bûkti," *Research Bulletin* (Centre of Arabic Documentation, Ibadan), II (1966), ii, 19-31. On the *Dibaj*, see also A. Cherbonneau, "Essai sur la littérature arabe au Soudan d'après le

Tekmilet ed Dibadj de Ahmed Baba le Tombouctien," *Revue de la Société Archéologique de Constantine*, II (1854-55), 1-42. For a comprehensive compilation of all known data, see Mahmoud A. Zouber, *Ahmad Bâbâ de Tombouctou (1556-1627). Sa vie et son oeuvre* (Paris, 1977).

9 The *Tarikh al-Sudan* was translated into French by O. Houdas (Paris, 1900). See Charles Monteil, "Notes sur le Tarikh es-Soudan", *BIFAN*, B, XXVII (1965), 479-530.

10 Trimingham, p. 5.

11 *Ibid.*, p. 5.

12 *Ibid.*, p. 140.

13 Mervyn Hiskett, "An Islamic Tradition of Reform in the Western Sudan from the Sixteenth to the Eighteenth Century", *BSOAS*, XXV (1962), iii, 577-596. *Habe* is a Fulani word which means "foreigner", "barbarian" : it was applied to the Hausa population.

14 Hodgkin, p. 90.

15 English translation by T.H. Baldwin (Beirut, 1932).

16 Trimingham, p. 133.

17 *Ibid.*, pp. 122-124.

18 Mervyn Hiskett, *A History of Hausa Islamic Verse* (London, 1975), p. 15.

19 A.D.H. Bivar and M. Hiskett, "The Arabic Literature of Nigeria to 1804 : A Provisional Account," *BSOAS*, XXV (1962), i, 104-148. See also Hodgkin, p. 132, and Hiskett, *Hausa Islamic Verse*, pp. 14-15.

20 J.D. Fage, *A History of West Africa* (Cambridge, 1969), p. 33.

21 On this and the foregoing paragraphs, see the article by Bivar and Hiskett referred to in note 19.

22 Hassan Ibrahim Gwarzo, "The theory of Chronograms Expounded by the 18th-Century Astronomer-Mathematician Muhammad b. Muhammad," *Research Bulletin* (Centre of Arabic Documentation, Ibadan), III (1967), 116-123.

23 Hodgkin, however, claims that Jibril was a member of the Fulani élite and belonged to a clan which had originally migrated from Futa Toro (*op. cit.*, p. 35). But according to Hiskett, Jibril was a Tuareg scholar, "connected by marriage to the Fulani family tree" (See *The Sword of Truth*, [London 1973] p. 23).

24 Fage, p. 148.

25 Cf. M. Hiskett, "Material Relating to the State of Learning among the Fulani before Their *Jihad*," *BSOAS*, XIX (1967), iii, 550-578. *Id.*, "An Islamic Tradition of Reform in the Western Sudan from the Sixteenth to the Eighteenth Century," *BSOAS*, XXV (1962), iii, 577-596.

26 M. Hiskett, *The Sword of Truth : The Life and Times of the Shehu Usuman dan Fodio* (London, 1973). On Usman's bibliography, see W.E.N. Kensdale, "Field Notes on the Arabic Literature of the Western Sudan : Shehu Usumanu dan Fodio", *Journal of the Royal Asiatic Society*, 1955, pp. 162-168. See also N. Tapiéro, "Le grand shaykh peul Uthmân ibn Fûdî et certaines sources de son Islâm doctrinal", *Revue des Etudes Islamiques*, XXXI (1963), 49-88.

27 *Sword of Truth*, pp. 118-119.

28 *Ibid.*, p. 52. See I.A.B. Balogun, *A Critical Edition of the* Ihya al-sunna wa ikhmad al-bid'a *of 'Uthman b. Fudi Popularly Known as Usuman dan Fodio*, Ph. D. Thesis (London, 1967).

29 Cf. Ismael Hamet, "Le Nour el-Eulbab de Cheikh Otmane ben Mohammed ben Otmane dit Ibn Foudiou," *Revue Africaine*, XLI (1897), 297-320.

30 Hiskett, *Sword of Truth*, p. 119.

31 *Wird* ("Litany"), transl. *ibid.* p. 66.

32 Hiskett, "*Kitab al-farq* : A work on the Habe Kingdoms attributed to Uthman dan Fodio", *BSOAS*, XXIII (1960) iii, 558-579.

33 *Sword of Truth*, p. 120. Cf. T. Hodgkin *The Radical Tradition in the Literature of Muslim West Africa* (London, 1968).

34 Other works of Usman's are available in English: see H.R. Palmer, "An Early Fulani Conception of Islam," *Journal of the African Society*, XIII (1913-14), 407-414, XIV (1914-15), 53-59, for a translation of *Tanbih al-Ikhwan* ("Warning to the Brethren"); A.D.H. Bivar, "A Manifesto of the Fulani *Jihâd*," *Journal of African History*, II (1961), ii, 235-243 for *Wathigat ahl al-Sudan* ("Document for the Black People"); B.G. Martin, "Unbelief in the Western Sudan : Uthman dan Fodio's *Ta'lim al-ikhwan*", *Middle Eastern Studies*, IV (1967), i, 50-97 ("Instruction of the Brethren").

35 See W.E.N. Kensdale, "Field Notes on the Arabic Literatures of the Western Sudan : Abdullahi dan Fodio", *Journal of the Royal Asiatic Society*, 1956, pp. 78-80.

36 Translation in M. Hiskett, 1957 (see note 25 above).

37 Edited and translated by M.Hiskett (Ibadan, 1963).

38 W.E.N. Kensdale, "Field Notes on the Arabic Literatures of the Western Sudan: Muhammadu Bello", *Journal of the Royal African Society*, 1958, pp. 53-57. See also H.F.C. Smith, "Muhammad Bello, *Amir Almu'ninin*," *Ibadan*, June 1960, pp. 16-19.

39 Quoted in Hodgkin, *Nigerian Perspectives*, p. 220. Said's *History of Sokoto* was first translated into French by O. Houdas in *Tedzkiret en-Nisian* (Paris, 1901). There is also an English translation by C.E.J. Whitting (Kano, n.d.).

40 For a translation see E.J. Arnett, *The rise of the Sokoto Fulani* (Kano, 1922).

41 Hodgkin, p. 198.

42 See D. Denham, H. Clapperton, and W. Oudney, *Narrative of Travels and Discoveries in Northern and Central Africa, in the years 1822, 1823, and 1824* (London, 1826) pp. 171-172.

43 H.F.C. Smith, "Arabic Manuscript Material Bearing on the History of the Western Sudan", *Historical Society of Nigeria, Supplement to News Bulletin*, III (959), iv.

44 Quoted in Hodgkin, *op. cit.*, p. 220-222.

45 Fage, p. 45.

46 Ivor Wilks, *The Northern Factor in Ashanti History* (Legon, 1963); *Id.*, "The growth of Islamic Learning in Ghana", *Journal of the Historical Society of Nigeria*, II (1963), iv, 409-17; Thomas Hodgkin, "The Islamic Literary Tradition in Ghana," in I.M. Lewis (ed.), *Islam in Tropical Africa* (London, 1966), pp. 442-460.

47 Jack Goody, "Restricted Literacy in Northern Ghana" in Jack Goody (ed.), *Literacy in Traditional Societies* (Cambridge, 1968), pp. 198-264.

48 *Ibid.*, pp. 235 and 246.

49 *Ibid.*, p. 214.

50 "The Islamic Literary Tradition in Ghana", p. 454.

51 Goody, *op. cit.*, p. 219.

52 Baesjou, p. 180.

53 Goody, p. 243. On Umar see also H. Sölken, "Zur Biographie des Imam Umaru von Kete-Kratyi", *Africana Marburgensia*, III (1970), ii, 24-30; B.G. Martin "Two Poems by al-Hajj Umar", in J.R. Goody (ed.), *Salaga : The Struggle for Power* (London, 1967).

54 Jack Goody and Ivor Wilks, "Writing in Gonja", in J. Goody (ed.), *Literacy in Traditional Societies*, pp. 241-258.

55 Amar Samb, *Essai sur la contribution du Sénégal à la littérature d'expression arabe* (Dakar, 1972); but see also Paul Marty, *Etudes sur l'Islam au Sénégal* (Paris, 1917).

56 Siré Abbas Soh, *Chroniques du Foûta sénégalais*, transl. by Maurice Delafosse and Henri Gaden (Paris, 1913).

57 Trimingham, p. 161.

58 Lucy C. Behrman, *Muslim Brotherhoods and Politics in Senegal* (Cambridge, Mass., 1970), p. 19. For a history of the Tijani order, see Jamal M. Abun-Nasr, *The Tijaniyya : A Sufi Order in the Modern World* (London, 1965).

59 Trimingham, p. 181.

60 On Umar, see V. Monteil, *L'Islam noir*, pp. 96-102; A. Samb, pp. 41-72; Trimingham, pp. 181-186; Abun-Nasr, pp. 106-128; and especially Fernand Dumont, *L'anti-Sultan ou Al-Haji Omar Tal du Fouta, combattant de la foi (1794-1864)* (Dakar, 1974).

61 Trimingham, p. 163.

62 For an interim bibliography of al-Hajj Umar, see B.G. Martin, "A Mahdist Document from Futa Jallon", *BIFAN*, XXV, B (1963), 47-65.

63 Cf. B.G. Martin, "Notes sur l'origine de la *tariqa* des Tijaniyya et sur les débuts d'al-Hajj Umar", *Revue des Etudes islamiques*, XXXVII (1969), 267-290.

64 Baesjou, p. 180.

65 Trimingham, p. 227.

66 *Ibid.*

67 Samb, pp. 259-301. See also Claudine Gerresch, "Le Livre de Métrique *Mubayyin al-Iskal*, du Cadi Madiakhaté Kala. Introduction historique, traduction et glossaire", *BIFAN*, XXXVI, B (1974), iv, 714-832.

68 Behrman, p. 63. See also Marty, pp. 75-181.

69 Abun-Nasr, pp. 143-145. On the Arabic poetry of Malik Sy and his dynasty, see Samb, pp. 331-398.

70 Samb, pp. 421-482. See also Marty, pp. 223-231; Fernand Dumont, *La Pensée religieuse d'Amadou Bamba, fondateur du mouridisme sénégalais* (Dakar-Abidjan, 1975), and T.B. Kake, *Amadou Bamba, fondateur du mouridisme* (Dakar, 1976).

71 Trimingham, pp. 227-28. On the *Muridiyya*, see Behrman, *op. cit.*; Vincent Monteil, "Une confrérie sénégalaise : les Mourides du Sénégal", *Archives de Sociologie des Religions*, VII, n° 14 (1962), 77-102; Cheikh Tidiane Sy, *La confrérie sénégalaise des Mourides* (Paris, 1969).

72 Dumont, pp. 12-15.

73 Samb, pp. 421-422.

74 *Ibid.*, pp. 452-453.

75 *Ibid.*, pp. 143-144.

76 *Ibid.*, pp. 494-498.

77 *Ibid.*, pp. 484-490.

78 *Ibid.*, pp. 499-503.

79 *Ibid.*, pp. 107-128.

80 A. Samb, "*La vie d'El-Hadji Omar* par Cheikh Moussa Camara", *BIFAN*, B, XXXII (1971), i, 44-56.

81 Samb, 213-235. See also Abun-Nasr, p. 146.

82 *Ibid.*, 235-241.

83 *Ibid.*, 309-330.

84 *Ibid.*, 381-386.

85 *Ibid.*, 140-147.

86 Baesjou, p. 181.

NOTES TO CHAPTER THREE

1 Fulfulde is the name given by some of the Fulani communities to their own language. In order to avoid unnecessary confusion, we shall use the term "Fulani" for both the people and their language, although Fulani groups themselves use a wide variety of words, such Peul, Poular, Fulbe, Fula, etc.

2 Hiskett, *Sword of Truth*, pp. 33-36.

3 *Ibid.*, p. 53.

4 *Ibid.*, p. 54.

5 Trimingham, p. 206.

6 G. Pfeffer, "Poetry and Prose of the Ful'be", *Africa*, XII (1939), 285-307.

7 Pierre Lacroix, *Poésie peule de l'Adamawa* (Paris, 1965).

8 Rupert East, *Stories from Old Adamawa* , (Lagos, 1935).

9 On Fulani poetry in the Futa Jalon, see Gilbert Vieillard, "Poèmes Peuls du Foûta-Djallon", *Bulletin du Comité d'Etudes Historiques et Scientifiques de l'A.O.F.*, XX (1937), iii, 225-269, and "Notes sur les Peuls du Foûta-Djallon", *BIFAN*, II (1940, i-ii, 85-210; Alfa Ibrahima Sow, "Notes sur les procédés poétiques dans la littérature des Peuls du Foûta-Djallon", *Cahiers d'Etudes Africaines*, V (1965), iii, 370-387, *La Femme, la Vache, la Foi. Ecrivains et poètes du Foûta-Djallon* (Paris, 1966), and *Chroniques et récits du Foûta-Djallon* (Paris, 1968); Christiane Seydou, " 'Majjado Alla gaynaali' poème en langue peule du Foûta-Djallon", *Cahiers d'Etudes Africaines* VI (1966), 643-681, "Essai d'étude stylistique de poèmes peuls du Foûta-Djallon", *BIFAN*, B, XXIX (1967), 191-233, "Poésie religieuse au Foûta-Djallon," unpublished seminar paper of the Centre of African Studies, SOAS, University of London, 1968, and "Panorama de la littérature peule", *BIFAN*, B. XXXV (1973), i, 176-217. See also Joseph E. Harris, "Protest and Resistance to the French in Foûta Djallon", *Genève-Afrique*, VIII (1969), i, 3-18.

10 *Le Filon du bonheur éternel*, edited with a French translation by Alfa Ibrahima Sow (Paris, 1971).

11 Quoted in Hollis R. Lynch, *Edward Wilmot Blyden, Pan-Negro Patriot (1832-1912)* (London, 1967), pp. 96-97.

12 For a detailed discussion of a poem by Bouba-Ndiang, see Seydou, "Essai d'étude stylistique . . ."

13 Mohammadou Aliou Tyam, *La vie d'El Hadj Omar*, transl. Henri Gaden (Paris, 1935).

14 Oumar Ba, "Dix-huit poèmes Peul modernes", *Cahier d'Etudes Africaines* , II (1962), iv, 536-550; "Trois poèmes poular", *ibid.*, VII (1968), ii, 318-322.

15 Oumar Ba, *Mon meilleur chef de canton* (Lyon, 1966).

16 Hiskett, *Sword of Truth*, p. 56. For biographical details on some Hausa writers, see Albert S. Gérard, "Biographies of Eleven Nigerian Writers", *Research in African Literatures,* V (1974), ii, 206-212. The most informative work on the subject so far is Mervyn Hiskett, *A History of Hausa Islamic Verse* (London, 1975).

17 Hiskett, *Sword of Truth*, pp. 107-111.

18 Published in *Wak'ok'in wa'azi* (Zaria, 1959). See Hiskett, *Sword of Truth*, p. 178.

19 Hiskett, *History*, pp.28-37.

20 *Ibid.*, pp. 118-130.

21 *Ibid.*, pp.64-72.

22 M. Hiskett, " 'The Song of the Shaihu's Miracles': A Hausa Hagiography from Sokoto", *African Language Studies*, XII (1971), pp. 71-107. See also R.A. Adeleye and F.H. El-Masri, "*Sifo-fin Shehu*: an Autobiography and Character Study of Uthman b. Fudi in Verse", *Research Bulletin* (Centre of Arabic Documentation, Ibadan), II (1966), i, 1-13.

23 Hiskett, *History*, pp. 92-102.

24 *Ibid.*, pp. 73-91.

25 *Ibid.*, p. 103.

26 Don Scharfe and Yahaya Aliyu, "Hausa Poetry", in Ulli Beier (ed.), *Introduction to African Literature* (London, 1964), pp. 34-40.

27 Also named Umaru Salaga by Hiskett and Shehu na Salaga by Scharfe and Aliyu.

28 Hiskett, *History*, p. 105. The Hausa writings of al Hajj Umaru were first revealed by German scholar A. Mischlich, "Ueber die Herkunft der Fulbe", *Mitteilungen des Seminars für orientalische Sprachen*, XXXIV (1932), 183-196. See also Heinz Sölken, "Die Geschichte von Kabi nach Iman Umaru", *Mitteilungen des Instituts für Orientforschung*, VII (1959), i, 123-162; IX (1961), i, 30-99. For detailed analysis of Umaru's Hausa Poetry, see Stanislas Pilaszewicz, " 'The Song of Poverty and of Wealth': A Hausa Poem on Social Problems by Al-Hadji Umaru", *African Bulletin*, n° 21 (1974), 67-115, and " 'The Arrival of the Christians': A Hausa Poem on the Colonial Conquest by Al-Hadji Umaru", *Ibid.*, n° 22 (1975), 55-129.

29 Jack Goody and Ivor Wilks, "Writing in Gonja", in J. Goody (ed.), *Literacy in Traditional Societies* (Cambridge, 1968), pp. 241-261.

30 M. Hiskett, " 'The Song of Bagauda': A Hausa King List and Homily in Verse", *BSOAS*, XXVII (1964), iii, 540-567; XXVIII (1965), i, 112-135; ii, 363-385.

31 For full details, see P.E.H. Hair, *The Early Study of Nigerian Languages* (Cambridge, 1967), pp. 31-68.

32 See N. Skinner, *Hausa Readings : Selections from Edgar's Tatsuniyoyi* (Madison, 1968).

33 V. Klíma, K.F. Růžička, P. Zima, *Black Africa : Literature and Language* (Prague, 1976), p. 171.

34 Rupert E. East, "A First Essay in Imaginative African Literature", *Africa*, IX (1936), iii, 350-357. On these early modern works, see Donald J. Consentino, "An Experiment in Inducing the Novel", *Research in African Literatures*. IX (1978), i, 19-30. More general information about modern Hausa writing will be found in Neil Skinner, "Realism and Fantasy in Hausa Literature", *Review of National Literatures*, II (1971), ii, 167-187, and Adeboye Babalola, "A Survey of Modern Literature in the Yoruba, Efik and Hausa Languages", in Bruce King (ed.), *Introduction to Nigerian Literature* (Lagos, 1971), pp. 50-63. See also Connie L. Stephens, "The Current Status of Hausa Literature", a paper presented at the twentieth meeting of the African Studies Association (Houston, 1977).

35 Neil Skinner, "From Hausa to English : A study in Paraphrase", *Research in African Literatures*, IV (1973), ii, 154-164.

36 English translation by Mervyn Hiskett (London, 1967).

37 Skinner, "Realism and Fantasy."

38 Neil Skinner, "NORLA. An experiment in the Production of Vernacular Literature, 1954-1959", *Revue des Langues Vivantes*, XXXVI (1970), ii, 166-175.

39 Abdulkadir Dangambo, "Nazari a kan *Nagari Na Kowa*", *Harsunan Nijeriya*, IV (1974), 27-36.

40 Skinner, "Realism and Fantasy", p. 181.

41 Hiskett, *History*, p. 151.

42 Neil Skinner, "The Slattern—A Theme of Hausa Poetry", in Veronika Six *et al.* (eds.), *Afrikanische Sprachen und Kulturen—Ein Querschnitt* (Hamburg, 1971), 288-297. *Id.*, "A Hausa Poet in Lighter Vein", *African Language Review*, IX (1970), 163-175.

43 For a detailed discussion of the similarities between the Arabic and Hausa prosodic systems, see M.K.M. Galadanci, "The Poetic Marriage Between Arabic and Hausa", *Harsunan Nijeriya*, V (1975), 1-15.

44 Hiskett, *History*, 193.

45 *Ibid.*, p. 161.

46 Neil Skinner and Kabir Galadanci, "*Wakar Soja*—a Hausa Poem of the Civil War", in W.L. Ballard (ed.), *Essays on African Literature* (Atlanta, 1973), pp. 97-125.

47 *Wakokin Sa'adu Zungur* (Zaria, 1957). These poems have been reprinted with an English translation and a biographical introduction in Dandatti Abdulkadir, *The Poetry, Life and Opinions of Sa'adu Zungur* (Zaria, 1974).

48 Hiskett, *History*, pp. 114-115. For a closer discussion of those two poems, see Dandatti Abdulkadir, "The Role of a Hausa Poet", *Harsunan Nijeriya*, VI (1976), 1-20.

49 Ibid., p. 160. See *Wakokin Mu'azu Hadejia* (Zaria, 1958).

50 D.W. Arnott, "The Song of the Rains, a Hausa Poem by Na'ibi S. Wali", *African Language Studies*, IX (1968), 130-147; A.V. King and M.R. Ibrahim, "*The Song of the Rains*: Metric Values in Performance", *ibid.*, 148-155.

51 Klíma *et al.*, *Black Africa*, p. 174.

52 Neil Skinner, Tom Allen and Charles N. Davis, "Wakar Bushiya: a Hausa satirical poem by Isa Hashim", *Research in African Literatures*, V (1974), ii, 180-193.

53 J.N. Paden, "A Survey of Kano Hausa Poetry", *Kano Studies*, I (1965), 33-39; L. Muhammad, "Comments on John D. Paden's 'A Survey of Kano Hausa Poetry'", *ibid.*, II (1966), 44-52; J.N. Paden, "Letter of Reply to L. Muhammad's Comments on 'Kano Hausa Poetry'", *ibid.*, 53-55.

54 Harry Land, in Colin Legum (ed.), *African Handbook* (Harmondsworth, 1969) p. 305.

55 Skinner, "Realism and Fantasy", pp. 185-186.

56 Trimingham, p. 175.

57 John D. Hargreaves, *West Africa : The Former French States* (Englewood Cliffs, 1967), pp. 65 and 68.

58 See Desmond T. Cole, "The History of African Linguistics to 1945", *Current Trends in Linguistics*, VII (1971), p. 18.

59 Hargreaves, p. 84.

60 *Ibid.*, p. 85.

61 Henri Gaden, "Légendes et coutumes sénégalaises : Cahiers de Yoro Dyâo", *Revue d'Ethnographie et de Sociologie*, III (1912), 119-137, 191-202; R. Rousseau, "Le Sénégal d'autrefois : études sur le Oualo, cahiers de Yoro Dyâo", *Bulletin du Comité d'Etude historique et scientifique de l'A.O.F.*, XIV (1929), 131-211; *id.*, "Le Sénégal d'autrefois : étude sur le Cayor, cahiers de Yoro Dyâo", *ibid.*, XVI (1933), 237-298; *id.* "Le Sénégal d'autrefois : seconde étude sur le Cayor (complément tiré des manuscrits de Yoro Dyâo)", *BIFAN*, B, III-IV (1941-1942), 79-144.

62 Amadou Wade, "Chronique du Wâlo sénégalais (1186?-1855)", in V. Monteil, *Esquisses sénégalaises* (Dakar, 1965), pp. 13-19.

63 Its existence was first revealed to the outside world in Cheikh Anta Diop, *Nations nègres et culture* (Paris, 1954), pp. 345-347, which lists a number of Wolof poets, about whom, however, very little is known.

64 See Pathé Diagne, "Chronique linguistique", *Présence Africaine*, n° 61 (1967), 149-154; A. Samb, "L'influence de l'Islam sur la littérature wolof", *BIFAN*, B. XXX (1968), ii, 628-641.

65 Bassirou Cissé, "Poème de Moussa Ka (1883-1967) : 'Ma dyêma burati . .' ", *BIFAN*, B, XXX (1968), iii, 847-860.

66 Amar Samb, "Jaaraama, Un poème wolof de Moussa Ka", *BIFAN*, B, XXXVI (1974), iii, 592-612.

67 *Id.*, Contribution du Sénégal, pp. 398-407.

69 See on this Ayo Bamgbose (ed.), *Mother Tongue Education. The West African Experience* (London, 1976), pp. 22-23.

NOTES TO CHAPTER FOUR

1 On the history of Madagascar, see Pierre Boiteau, *Madagascar, Contribution à l'histoire de la nation malgache* (Paris, 1958), and Hubert Deschamps, *Histoire de Madagascar* (Paris, 1972, 4th ed.).

2 Etienne de Flacourt, *Histoire de la grande Isle de Madagascar* (Paris, 1661), p. 195.

3 Boiteau, p. 41.

4 G. Mondain, "Note sur les tout premiers débuts de la littérature malgache avant l'arrivée des Européens", *Bulletin de l'Académie Malgache*, n.s. XXVI (1944-45) pp. 43-48, and "Note historique sur les manuscripts arabico-malgaches", *Ibid.*, XXX (1951-52), pp. 161-166. The latest discussion is L. Munthe, "La tradition écrite arabico-malgache: un aperçu sur les manuscripts existants", *BSOAS*, XL (1977), i, 96-109.

5 Deschamps, p. 52.

6 See especially Gabriel Ferrand, *Les Musulmans à Madagascar et aux Iles Comores* (Paris, 1891), I, 101-136, and, for further bibliographical information, the articles and books by G. Ferrand, Gustave Julien and Gustave Mondain, listed in G. Grandidier, *Bibliographie de Madagascar* (Paris, 1905-1935).

7 Maurice Bloch, "Astrology and Writing in Madagascar", in Jack Goody (ed.), *Literacy in Traditional Societies* (Cambridge, 1968), 277-297.

8 E.F. Gautier et H. Froidevaux, "Un manuscrit arabico-malgache sur les campagnes de La Case dans l'Imoro", *Notices et extraits des manuscrits de la Bibliothèque royale*, XXXIX (1909), 31-182.

9 Hugues Berthier, *De l'usage de l'arabico-malgache en Imerina au début du XIXe siècle : Le cahier d'écriture de Ramada I* (Tananarive, 1934).

10 Boiteau, pp. 89, 98-99.

11 James Sibree, *Fifty Years in Madagascar. Personal Experiences of Mission Life and Work* (London, 1924), p. 192.

12 *Ibid.*, p. 288. See also J. Richardson, "Malagasy 'Tonon-kira' and Hymnology", *Antananarivo Annual*, I (1876), 151-163.

13 Boiteau, p. 99.

14 Those documents were printed half a century later in W.E. Cousins, *Malagasy Kabary from the Time of Andrianampoinimerina to 1872* (Tananarive, 1873). For a detailed discussion of the "Merina manuscripts" dealing with historical matter, see Alain Delivré, *L'Histoire des rois de l'Imerina : Interprétation d'une tradition orale* (Paris, 1974), especially pp. 72-94.

15 S. Ayache, *Le manuscrit de Raombana* (Unpubl. diss., Paris, 1970), reviewed in Henri Raharijaona, "Raombana, L'Historien (1809-1855) de S. Ayache", *Bulletin de l'Académie malgache*, L (1974), ii, 45-47. Ayache's dissertation was later published as *Raombana l'historien (1809-1855)* (Antananarivo, 1976).

16 On Rainandriamampondry, see E.-F. Gautier, *Trois héros* (Paris, 1931), pp. 65-139.

17 Bakoly Domenichini-Ramaiaramanana, *Hain-Teny d'autrefois, Haintenin'ny fahiny* (Tananarive, 1968). On this peculiar Malagasy genre, see Jean Paulhan, *Les hain-teny mérinas, poésies populaires malgaches* (Paris, 1913).

18 T. Matthews, *Thirty Years in Madagascar* (New York, 1904), pp. 254-266.

19 On Andrianaivoravelona, see Sibree, *op. cit.*, pp. 220-221 and Berthe Raharijaona, "Une grande figure malgache : Josefa Andrianaivoravelona", *Bulletin de l'Académie malgache*, XLI (1971), ii, 1-3.

20 Claude-Marie Lorin and Albert Rakoto Ratsimamanga, "Littérature malgache", *Histoire des Littératures, Encyclopédie de la Pléiade* (Paris, 1955), I, p. 1456.

21 On this dramatic tradition, see a series of articles contributed by M.-F. Robinary to the *Bulletin de Madagascar* from 1950 to 1953.

22 " 'Her Majesty's, Madagascar", *Antananarivo Annual*, IV (1890), 185-189.

23 Galliéni, *Neuf ans à Madagascar* (Paris, 1908), p. 52, quoted in Boiteau, p. 290.

24 See Alain Spacensky, *Madagascar : Cinquante ans de vie politique, de Ralaimongo à Tsiranana* (Paris, 1970).

25 Information about Malagasy vernacular writers and writing is far from readily available. See especially H. Randzavola, "La Littérature malgache", *Encyclopédie coloniale et maritime : Madagascar-Réunion* (Paris, 1947), II, 219-224, and Charles Rajoelisolo, "L'origine et l'évolution de la poésie contemporaine malgache", *Bulletin de l'Académie Malgache*, n.s. XXXVI (1958), 331-341. Many biographical notices are to be found in Régis Rajemisa-Raolison, *Dictionnaire historique et géographique de Madagascar* (Fianarantsoa, 1966).

26 Sibree, p. 143.

27 *Ibid.*, p. 294.

28 Matthews, pp. 279, 372.

29 Camille de Rauville, "Climat de la vie intellectuelle madécasse", *Encyclopédie Coloniale et Maritime* : *Madagascar-Réunion* (Paris, 1947), II, 225-227.

30 M.-F. Robinary, *Au Seuil de la terre promise* (Tananarive, 1965), pp. 97-98. This autobiographical novel by the first Malagasy poet of French expression, is one of the few sources in French regarding the emergence of modern drama in Madagascar. For more details, see Albert Gérard, "La naissance du théâtre à Madagascar", *Bulletin d'information CEDEV* (Liège), n° 8 (1967), 28-35. This article was translated into English by Anthony Graham-White, "The Birth of Theatre in Madagascar", *Educational Theatre Journal*, XXV (1973), iii, 362-365.

31 Elie-Charles Abraham, "Théâtre malgache", *Tatamo*, n° 1 (1953).

32 Boiteau, pp. 290-298.

33 F. Ranaivo, "Fredy Rajaofera, poète malgache", *Bulletin de l'Académie Malgache*, 46 (1968), 195-203.

34 An idea of the abundance of the Malagasy press can be obtained from Jean-Claude Poitelon, Germaine Razafintsalama and Rasoahanta Randrianarivelo, *Périodiques malgaches de la Bibliothèque nationale* (Paris, 1970).

NOTES TO CHAPTER FIVE

1 For the historical background, see Roland Oliver and Gervase Matthew (eds.), *History of East Africa* (London, 1963). A more specific account can be found in C.S. Nicholls, *The Swahili Coast : Diplomacy and Trade on the East African Littoral, 1798-1956* (London, 1971). See also J. Spencer Trimingham, *Islam in East Africa* (Oxford, 1964). A basic tool for the study of Swahili literature is Marcel van Spaandonck, *Practical and Systematical Swahili Bibliography* (Leiden, 1965). This has been corrected and completed in Alberto Mioni, "La bibliographie de la langue swahili", *Cahiers d'Etudes Africaines*, VII (1967), 485-532. For more up-to-date information, see E.F. Bertoncini, "An Annotated Bibliography of Swahili Novels and Stories Published Between 1960-1975", *Asian and African Studies* (Jerusalem), 13 (1977), 181-91.

2 G.S.P. Freeman-Greville, *East African Coast : Select Documents* (London, 1962), p. 31.

3 Quoted in Lyndon Harries, *Swahili Poetry* (Oxford, 1962), p. 53. The present account of Swahili literature owes much to this highly informative book, henceforth referred to simply as "Harries." It is also greatly indebted to a number of remarks and suggestions kindly supplied by Professor Harries. For a slightly earlier brief survey, see Alfons Loogman, "Barden der ostafrikanischen Küste", *Afrika-heute*, (1961), 274-281. The reader will find more information in Jan Knappert, *Four Centuries of Swahili Verse* (London: Heinemann, 1979), which was published as the present book was already moving to press.

4 See E. Dammann, "Suaheli-Dichtungen des Scheichs Muhammed bin Abubekr bin Omar Kidjumwa Masihii aus Lamu," *Studien zur Auslandskunde. Afrika*, I (1942), ii, 125-196.

5 Harries, pp. 147-8.

6 Wilfred Whiteley, *Swahili, the Rise of a National Language* (London, 1969), p. 18.

"bibliography"

7 Basil Davidson, *East and Central Africa to the Late Nineteenth Century* (London, 1967), p. 132.

8 Jan Knappert, *Traditional Swahili Poetry* (Leiden, 1967), p. 3.

9 The Saiyid family was to play a major part in the development of Swahili literature to the end of the nineteenth century. See Harries, pp. 86 sqq., and R.B. Serjeant, *The Saiyids of Hadramaut* (London, 1957).

10 Jan Knappert, "The Hamziya Deciphered", *African Language Studies*, IX (1968), 52-81. See also M.B. Mkelle, "Hamziyya—the Oldest Swahili Translation", *Kiswahili*, XLVI (1976), 6, 71-75.

11 The poem was first published, with a German translation, in C.G. Büttner and C. Meinhof, "*Chuo cha Herkal*", *Zeitschrift für Kolonialsprachen*, II (1912), 1-36, 108-136, 194-232, 261-296. A more detailed edition, with a Dutch translation, is available in Jan Knappert, *Het epos van Heraklios. Een proeve van Swahili poëzie* (Alkmaar-Leiden, 1958). For a discussion of the Arabic substratum, see Rudi Paret, "Die arabische Quelle der Suaheli-Dichtung *Chuo cha Herkal*", *Zeitschrift für Eingeborenensprachen*, XVII (1927), iv, 241-249, and Martin Abel, *Die Arabische Vorlage des Suaheli-Epos Chuo cha Herkal* (Berlin, 1938).

12 Some of the more important of those "epics" have been collected and translated in J.W.T. Allen, *Tendi. Six Examples of a Swahili Classical Verse Form* (London, 1971).

13 Jan Knappert, "The Utenzi wa Katirifu or Ghazwa ya Sesebani", *Afrika and Übersee*, LII (1969), 81-104, 264-313.

14 A transliteration was first provided in E. Steere, *Swahili Tales as Told by the Natives of Zanzibar* (London, 1870). A better edition is to be found in C. Meinhof, "Das Lied des Liongo", *Zeitschrift für Eingeborenensprachen*, XV (1925), iv, 241-265, and in Alice Werner, "The Swahili Saga of Liongo Fumo", *BSOS*, IV (1926), ii, 247-255. I have used the translation in Harries, pp. 188-192.

15 W. Hichens, *Al-Inkishafi. The Soul's Awakening* (London, 1939). See also R. Allen, "*Inkishafi* A translation from the Swahili", *African Studies*, V (1946), iv, 243-249. The poem is here quoted from the translation in Harries, pp. 90-103.

16 Whiteley, p. 19.

17 W. Hichens, *Diwani ya Muyaka bin Haji Al-Ghassaniy* (Johannesburg, 1940).

18 Harries, p. 2.

19 Whiteley, pp. 19-20.

20 Whiteley, p. 19.

21 Harries, p. 13.

22 Harries, "A Swahili Takhmis", *African Studies*, XI (1952), ii, 59-67. The poem is here quoted from the new translation provided by Harries in *Swahili Poetry*, pp. 202-207.

23 Harries, pp. 226-233.

24 This poem was "the first Miiraji discovered by a European" and "also one of the first Swahili poems ever printed" (J. Knappert, *Traditional Swahili Poetry*, [Leiden, 1967], p. 200 n.) It was edited, with a German translation, in C.G. Büttner, *Anthologie aus der Suaheli Litteratur* (Berlin, 1894). For an English version, see J. Knappert, *Swahili Islamic Poetry* (Leiden, 1971), pp. 242-275. Several other versions are available. The longest one is to be found in Ernst Dammann, *Dichtungen in der Lamu-Mundart des Suaheli* (Hamburg, 1940), pp. 1-72. Parts of another text, whose author (or copyist) names himself Ali wa Salimu, have been edited and translated in J. Knappert, *Traditional Swahili Poetry*, pp. 202-242. For Mohammad Jambein's *Utenzi wa Miiraji*, see below, p. 333, note 56. The latest version seems to have been the one by Juma Mwindadi, was printed in Dar es Salaam in 1951.

25 J.W.T. Allen, *The Swahili and Arabic Manuscripts and Tapes in the Library of the University College, Dar-es-Salaam* (Leiden, 1970).

26 Knappert, *Traditional Swahili Poetry*, p. 202.

27 *Id., Swahili Islamic Poetry*, pp. 227-241.

28 *Id., ibid.*, p. 21.

29 *Harries*, pp. 118-127. The poem was first edited in Alice Werner, "An Alphabetical Acrostic in a Northern Dialect of Swahili", *BSOS*, V (1929), iii, 561-569. For another edition, with German translation, see E. Dammann, *Dichtungen in der Lamu-Mundart des Suaheli* (Hamburg, 1940), pp. 328-334.

30 First edited in E. Dammann, "Eine Suahelidichtung mit alphabetischer Akrostichis", *Mitteilungen der Auslandschochschule an der Universität Berlin*, XLII (1939-40), iii, 72-77. See also L. Harries, "A Poem from Siu from the Swahili-Arabic Text", *BSOAS*, XIII (1950), 759-790. Translation in *Swahili Poetry*, pp. 192-201.

31 This is the date given by Alice Werner, "Utendi wa Ayubu", *BSOS*, I (1921), 297-320, II (1922), 297-320, 347-416. According to J.W.T. Allen, however, this information may well refer "only to the name of the scribe who copied the poem and the date when he did so. It is more likely that it was composed much earlier and the author must be considered unknown" (*Tendi*, p. 370). But the exceptional sophistication in the structure of the poem does not seem to favour the hypothesis of an early composition. Cf. Albert Gérard, "Structure and Values in Three Swahili Epics," *Research in African Literatures*, VII (1976), i, 7-22.

32 Jan Knappert, *Traditional Swahili Poetry. An Investigation into the Concepts of East African Islam as reflected in the Utenzi Literature* (Leiden, 1967), p. 11.

33 This *utendi* was first edited in Sir Mbarak Ali Hinawy, *Al-Akida and Fort Jesus, Mombasa* (London, 1950). It is here quoted from the translation in Harries, pp. 130-143.

34 See most notably R. Coupland, *The Exploitation of East Africa, 1856-1890* (London, 1939).

35 Harries, p. 216.

36 Edited in Mbarak Ali Hinawy, *op. cit.* Translation quoted from Harries, pp. 232-239.

37 Harries, p. 216.

38 Lyndon Harries (ed.), "The *Mzigo Song* by Ali Koti", *Swahili*, XXXV (1965), 47-53.

39 First edited by Alice Werner, "The *Utendi of Mwana Kupona*", *Harvard African Studies*, I (1917), 147-181. Translation in A. Werner and W. Hichens, *The Advice of Mwana Kupona upon the Wifely Duty* (Medstead, 1934). Here quoted in the translation of Harries, pp. 70-87.

40 Harries, p. 86.

41 Some information about this writer is available in E. Dammann, "Die Ocaberlieferung der islamischen Suahelidichtung", *Zeitschrift der deutschen morgenländischen Gesellschaft*, CVIII (1958), i, 42-45.

42 Ernst Dammann, *Dichtungen in der Lamu-Mundart des Suaheli* (Hamburg, 1940), 276-284.

43 Ernst Dammann, "Die paränetische Suaheli-Dichtung *Tabaraka*", *Mitteilungen des Instituts für Orientforschung*, VII (1959-60), 411-432.

44 For a translation of the Arabic prose version of Barzanji's *maulid* which is current on the East Coast, see Jan Knappert, *Swahili Islamic Poetry*, pp. 48-60.Composing poems on the birth of the Prophet in imitation of Barzanji's *maulid* seems to have been a favourite occupation with Swahili writers. Knappert provides text and translation for a "Maulid rhyming in *da*" composed by Mohammed bin Uthman (*ibid.*, pp. 102-131), a Maulid rhyming in *na*, known as *Kitabu Maulidi* (*ibid.*, pp. 276-311), and the *Maulidi ya Jambeni*, composed by Sheikh Muhammad Jambein al-Bakari (*ibid.*, 340-365). As to Sayyid Mansab, he is responsible for two different versions of the same story, a shorter one rhyming in *wa* (*ibid.*, pp. 133-143), and a more elaborate one known as *Maulidi ya Mansabu* (*ibid.*, pp. 312-339 and Harries, pp. 103-119).

45 Whiteley, *Swahili*, p. 23.

46 Hemed Abdallah, *Utenzi wa Seyyidna Huseni bin Ali (The History of Prince Hussein, son of Ali)*, with translation and notes by J.W.T. Allen (Dar es Salaam, 1965).

47 Hamad Abdallah Saidi Abdallah Masudi el Buhry el Hinawy, *Utenzi wa Abdirrahmani na Sufiyani. The History of Abdurrahman and Sufian*, with translation by Roland Allen and notes by J.W.T. Allen (Dar es Salaam, 1961).

48 Ernst Dammann, *Dichtungen in der Lamu-Mundart des Suaheli* (Hamburg, 1940), pp. 141-213.

49 Hemedi bin Abdallah bin Said bin Abdallah bin Masudi al Burhyi, *Utenzi wa vita vya Wadachi Kutamalaki Mrima 1307 A.H. The German conquest of the Swahili coast, 1891 AD.*, with translation and notes by J.W.T. Allen (Dar es Salaam, 1955).

50 A Lorenz and Abdul Karim bin Jamaliddini, "Gedicht vom Majimaji-Aufstand", *Mitteilungen des Seminars für orientalische Sprachen* XXXVI (1933), 227-259. The poem is here quoted from the translation of W.H. Whiteley, *Utenzi wa vita vya Maji-Maji* (Kampala, 1957).

51 See J. Iliffe, *Tanganyika under German Rule*; the quotations are from pp. 194, 198, 195 and 200.

52 Iliffe, p. 25. See also A.R.W. Crosse-Upcott, "The Origin of the Majimaji Revolt", *Man*, LX (1960), 71-73.

53 Whiteley, pp. 58-59. See C. Velten, "Suaheli-Gedichte", *Mitteilungen des Seminars für orientalische Sprachen*, XX (1917), 61-182; XXI (1918), 135-183.

54 See Trimingham, *Islam in East Africa*, p. 46; Oliver and Matthew, *History of East Africa*, p. 146.

55 J. Knappert, *Swahili Islamic Poetry*, pp. 340- 365.

56 J. Knappert (ed.), "Utenzi wa Miiraji. The Ascension of the prophet Mohammed, by Sh. Moh. Jambein", *Afrika and Übersee*, XLVIII (1964), 241-274.

57 Kijumwa's adherence to Christianity is mentioned in E. Dammann, "German Contributions to Swahili Studies in Recent Decades", *Bulletin of the East African Swahili Committee*, No. 26 (1956), p. 13.

58 E. Dammann, "Suaheli-Dichtungen des Scheichs Muhammed bin Abubekr bin Omar Kidjumwa Masihii aus Lamu", *Studien zur Auslandkunde : Afrika*, (1942), ii, 125-196.

59 See above, pp. 94-5.

60 Haji Chum and H.E. Lambert, *Utenzi wa vita vya Uhud. The Epic of the Battle of Uhud* (Dar es Salaam, 1962). In the following discussion, I owe my thanks to Professor Bernth Lindfors for permission to make use of material published in *Research in African Literatures*, VII (1976), i, 7-22.

61 R.A. Nicholson, *A Literary History of the Arabs* (Cambridge, 1969), p. 175.

62 Whiteley, p. 65.

63 Abdullah bin Hemed bin Ali Liajjemi, *Habari za Wakilindi* (Dar es Salaam, 1957). See A.B. Hellier, "Swahili Prose Literature", *Bantu Studies*, XIV (1940), 247-257.

64 S.A. Strong (ed.), "The Arabic Chronicle of Kilwa", *Journal of the Royal Asiatic Society*, (1895), pp. 385-430.

65 M. Guillain, *Documents sur l'histoire, la géographie et la commerce de l'Afrique orientale*, 3 vol. (Paris, 1856).

66 A. Werner (ed. and transl.), "Chronicle of Pate", *Journal of the African Society*, XIV (1914), 148-161, and XV (1915), 278-297. See also M. Heepe, "Suaheli-Chronik von Pate", *Mitteilungen des Seminars für orientalische Sprachen*, XXXI (1928), 145-192.

67 W. Hichens and Shaaibu Faraji bin Hamed al-Bakariy al-Lamuy, "Khabar al-Lamu. A Chronicle of Lamu", *Bantu Studies*, I (1938), 1-33.

68 Hemedi bin Abdullah of Dargube, Tangata, "A History of Africa", transl. by E.C. Baker, *Tanganyika Notes and Records* n° 32 (1952), 65-82.

69 For works issued in Moscow and Peking, see especially Alberto Mioni's supplement to Van Spaandonck's Bibliography mentioned in note 1 above.

70 Whiteley, p. 67.

71 For a brief assessment of the history and work of the Committee, see Whiteley, pp. 80-96.

72 On those events, see Oliver and Matthew, p. 245.

73 Janheinz Jahn, *A History of Neo-African Literature* (London, 1968), p. 89. In the original German, Jahn uses the term "Zöglingsliteratur", *Geschichte der neoafrikanischen Literatur* (Düsseldorf, *1966*), pp. 252-253.

74 Micere Githae Mugo, "Gerishon Ngugi, Peninah Muhando and Ebrahim Hussein : Plays in Swahili", *African Literature Today*, 8 (1976), 137-141.

75 Jan Knappert, "Notes on Swahili Literature", *African Language Studies*, VII (1966), 126-159. On Abdullah Saleh Farsy, see especially pp. 146-148.

76 The works of Abdullah Saleh Farsy are listed in Mioni's supplement to Van Spaan-donck's *Bibliography* (see note 1 above).

77 Whiteley, p. 10. For Shaaban Robert's bibliography see J.W.T. Allen, "The Complete Works of the Late Shaaban Robert, M.B.E.", *Swahili* XXXIII (1963), ii, 128-142.

78 For a more balanced appraisal, see Lyndon Harries, "Tale from Tanga : A Literary Beginning", *East Africa Journal* III (1966), ii, 4-6, and "Shaaban Robert : Man of Letters", *Présence Africaine* N° 93 (1975), 394-199; the following paragraphs owe much to these two essays; see also M.M. Mulokozi, "Two Utopias : A Comparative Exami-nation of William Morris's *News from Nowhere* and Shaaban Robert's *Siku ya Watengi wote*", *Umma*, V (1975), 134-58. For a detailed Marxist discussion of Shaaban's prose, see Rainer Arnold, *Afrikanische Literatur und nationale Befreiung. Menschenbild und Ge-sellschaftskonzeption im Prosawerk Shaaban Roberts* (Berlin, 1977).

79 First printed in *Pambo la Lugha*; quoted from the translation in Harries, pp. 160-171.

80 Shaaban Robert, *Kielezo cha Insha* ("Explanation of the essay", Johannesburg, 1954). Translation in L. Harries, "Swahili Literature in the National Context", *Review of National Literatures*, II (1971), ii, p. 47.

81 Harries, "Tale from Tanga : A Literary Beginning."

82 Shaaban Robert, *Marudi Mema na Omar Khayyam* (London, 1952).

83 See preceeding note. A brief review, by D.V. Perrott, appeared in *Swahili*, n° 23 (June 1953), 78-80.

84 See Jan Knappert's review in *Journal of African History* X (1969), ii, 341-342.

85 Lyndon Harries, "Swahili Literature in the National Context." See also : Jurgen Sachs, "Swahili-Lieder aus Sansibar", *Mitteilungen des Instituts für Orientforschung*, XII (1966), 221-240, and A.A. Suleiman, "The Swahili Singing Star, Siti Binti Saad, and the *Tarab* Tradition in Zanzibar", *Swahili*, XXXIX (1969), 87-90. *Taarab* is the local name for singing groups that organize dances and sing-song concerts, especially in Zanzibar and Mombasa. See Jan Knappert, "Swahili Tarabu Songs", *Afrika und Über-see*, LX (1977), iii, 116-55.

86 Shaaban Robert, *Maisha Yangu* (London, 1949), and *Maisha Yangu na Baada ya Miaka Hamsini* (London, 1966). For a somewhat cryptic discussion of this autobiography, see Rajmund Ohly, "The Morphology of Shaaban Robert's *Maisha Yangu na Baada ya Miaka Hamsini* (A Study of Structural Poetics)", *Africana Bulletin*, N° 13 (1970), 9-23.

87 H. Brode, "Autobiographie des Arabers Schech Hamed bin Muhammed el Murjebi, genannt Tippu Tip", *Mitteilungen des Seminars für Orientalische Sprachen* , V (1902), 175-277 and VI (1903), 1-55; W.H. Whiteley, "Maisha ya Hamed bin Muhammed el Murjebi yaani Tippu Tip", Supplement to the *Journal of the East African Swahili Committee*, XXVIII (1958), ii and XXIX (1959), i; Fr. Bontinck, *L'Autobiographie de Hamed ben Mohammed el-Murjebi Tippo Tip (ca. 1840-1905)* (Brussels, 1974).

88 Cf. *Swahili*, XXXVI (1966), i.

89 Sheikh Amri Abedi, *Sheria za kutunga mashairi na diwani ya Amri* ("The Rules of Poetic Composition and the Poems of Amri", Kampala, 1954).

90 L. Harries, "Swahili Literature in the National Context", p. 61.

91 See Jan Knappert, "The first Christian *Utenzi* : A New Development in Swahili Literature", *Afrika aud Übersee*, XLVII (1964), iii/iv, 221-232.

92 "Ukumbysho wa Marehemu Sheikh Mathias E. Mnyampala" (Memorial to the late Sheikh M.E.M.), *Swahili*, XXXIX (1969), 2-10, translated in L. Harries, "Swahili literature in the National Context", p. 56. For further considerations on Mnyampala's late poetry, see also L. Harries, "Poetry and Politics in Tanzania", *Ba-Shiru*, 4 (1972), 52-54. Mnyampala's political inspiration is especially conspicuous in his *Waadhi wa ushairi* ("Discourse on poetry", 1965).

93 Carol Eastman, "The Emergence of an African Regional Literature : Swahili", *African Studies Review*, XX (1977), ii, 53-61.

94 Harries, "Tale from Tanga : A Literary Beginning."

95 Whiteley, p. 67.

96 *Poems from Kenya. Gnomic verses in Swahili by Ahmad Nassir bin Juma Bhalo*, translated and edited by Lyndon Harries (Madison, 1966). Ahmad Nassir also authored or copied an epic poem on the story of the Fall, *Utenzi Wa Maisha ya Nabii Adamu*, which was published in Jan Knappert, *Four Swahili Epics* (Leiden, 1964), pp. 59-89.

97 Hasani bin Ismail, *The Medicine Man. Swifa ya Nguvumali*. Ed. and tr. Peter Lienhardt (Oxford, 1968).

98 Whiteley, p. 99.

99 L. Harries, "Poetry and Politics in Tanzania." See also M.M. Mulokozi, "Revolution and Reaction in Swahili Poetry", *Umma*, IV (1974), 118-38.

100 As reported by Harries, *ibid*. On this type of poetry, which often consists of dialogue verse, written to be read aloud, or even "performed", see J.S.M. Mwangomango, "Ngonjera na Ushairi", *Kiswahili,* XLI (1971), ii, 67-72, and Abdulazi Y. Lodhi, Ahmed S. Faris and Mohammed Y. Lodhi, *Swahili Poetry : A Guide for Beginners* (Uppsala, 1975).

101 On another novel by the same writer, *Alipanda upepo na kuvuna tufani* ("Who sows the wind reaps the tempest", 1969), see a brief review in Anton Vorbichler, "Neuere Swahili-Literatur", *Afrika und Übersee*, LVII (1973), i, 50-52.

102 On this author see (or rather hear) "Conversations with African Writer Euphrase Kezilahabi", tape n° 5 issued by the African Field Service in Washington.

103 Eastman, "Emergence of an African Regional Literature." On early theatrical activites in Tanzania, see E.N. Hussein, "An Annotated Bibliography of Swahili Theatre", *Swahili*, XXXIX (1969), iii, 49-60. This section on the latest Swahili drama is indebted to Micere Githae Mugo, "Gerishon Ngugi, Peninah Muhando and Ebrahim Hussein : Plays in Swahili", *African Literature Today*, n° 8 (1976), 137-141 and to L.A. Mbughuni, "Old and New Drama from East Africa" *Ibid.*, 85-98.

104 An English version of *Kinjeketile* was published in 1970. Hussein's main source is *not* Abdul Karim bin Jamaliddini's *utenzi*, but some of the testimonies collected in C.G.K. Gwassa and John Iliffe (eds.), *Records of the Maji Maji Rising* (Nairobi, n.d. [1969]).

104 An early version, which was apparently composed when the poet was about sixteen, was published by Jan Knappert in *Swahili*, XXXIV (1964), i. The Knappert quote, however comes from the review by Ohly mentioned in note 106.

106 R. Ohly, "A Review of *Utenzi wa Maisha ya Adamu na Hawaa*", *Kiswahili*, XLII, ii/ XLIII, i (March 1973), 123-125. Additional information in "Conversations with African Writer Abdilatif Abdalla", tape n° 19 of the African Field Service.

107 J. Knappert, "The Appreciation of Swahili Poetry", quoted in Ohly, *loc. cit.*, p. 124.

108 In this respect, interesting indications can be found in Ahmed Mgeni, "Appointments with Cupid", *Kiswahili*, XLII, ii, XLIII, i (March 1973), 126-133, a review article on a collection of short stories (*Mapenzi ni Kikohozi*) issued by Longman. Another popular Longman series, "Hadithi za Kusisimua" ("Exciting Stories", 1968-1971), is discussed in some detail in Carolyn A. Parker and Douglas Kavigha, "Hadithi za Kusisimua, Crime and Passion in Swahili Literature", Paper presented at the 20th meeting of the African Studies Association (Houston, 1977).

109 M.M. Mulokozi in his review of Abdilatif's *Sauti ya Dhiki*, *Umma*, IV (1974),i, 58-62.

110 See also Rajmund Ohly's review in *Kiswahili* , XLIV (1974), ii, 82-91.

111 See on this Farouk M. Topan, "Modern Swahili Poetry", *BSOAS*, XXXVII (1974), i, 175-187. Topan provides a detailed analysis of three poems by Euphrase Kezilahabi, Ebrahim Hussein and Crispin Hauli. He mentions two "forthcoming" collections : Kezilahabi's *Kichomi*, and Hauli's *Maishairi tasa*. See also, by the same writer, "Swahili literature plays major social role", *Africa Report*, XXI (1971), ii, 28-30.

112 S.Chiraghdin (ed.), *Malenga wa Mvita* (Nairobi, 1971), p. 14, quoted in Topan, *loc. cit.*, p. 176.

NOTES TO CHAPTER SIX

1 J. Spencer Trimingham, *Islam in East Africa* (Oxford, 1964), p. 61.

2 I.M. Lewis, "Literacy in a Nomadic Society : The Somali Case", in Jack Goody (ed.), *Literacy in Traditional Societies* (Cambridge, 1968), pp. 265-276.

3 The main source of information concerning Somali literature is B.W. Andrzejewski and I.M. Lewis, *Somali Poetry. An Introduction* (Oxford, 1964), from which all the poems quoted in this chapter are derived. On Raage Ugaas, see pp. 64-66, and B.W. Andrzejewski and Musa H.I. Galaal, "The Art of the Verbal Message in Somali Society", in J. Lukas (ed.), *Neue afrikanistische Studien* (Hamburg, 1966), pp. 29-39. Some factual information about Somali writers is also to be gleaned from Andrzejewski's notices in D.R. Dudley and D.M. Lang (eds.), *The Penguin Companion to Literature : 4. Classical and Byzantine, Oriental and African* (Harmondsworth, 1969).

4 The present-day Majerteyn province is a large and barren area, but it has proved singularly productive as far as poetry is concerned, many examples of which are to be found in Enrico Cerulli's essay on "La poesia dei Somali", *Somalia, scritti vari editi ed inediti*, III (Rome, 1964), 1-40.

5 I.M. Lewis, *The Modern History of Somaliland* (London, 1965).

6 On the Mullah, see especially Robert L. Hess, "The Poor Man of God—Mohammed Abdullah Hassan", in Norman R. Bennett (ed.), *Leadership in East Africa : Six Political Biographies* (Boston, 1968), pp. 63-108.

7 Enrico Cerulli, *Somalia I* (Rome, 1957), p. 156. Cerulli's chapter on Muhammad b. Abdullah Hassan al-Mahdi was first printed in *The Encyclopedia of Islam*, IV, 667-668.

8 See B.W. Andrzejewski and Musa H.I. Galaal, "A Somali poetic combat", *Journal of African Languages*, II (1963), i.

9 Andrzejewski and Lewis, pp. 56-57, 134-137.

10 Andrzejewski and Galaal, ii.

11 Andrzejewski and Lewis, pp. 58, 114-134.

12 This poem was edited in Enrico Cerulli, *Somali III*, pp. 12-18.

13 I.M. Lewis, "Sufism in Somaliland : A Study in Tribal Islam - I", *BSOAS*, XVII (1955), 591-602. On Awes, see Cerulli, *Somalia I* (Rome, 1957), 187-188 and *Somalia III*, 117-138. One of Awes's best-known *qasidas* was edited, with an Italian translation, in M.M. Moreno, *Il somalo della Somalia* (Rome, 1955), 364-367.

14 On Ali Maye, see Lewis, "Sufism in Somaliland", and especially Cerulli, *Somalia I*, 196-197.

15 Andrzejewski and Lewis, pp. 57, 102-104. See also, by the same authors, " 'An Elder's Reproof to his Wife' by Abdullahi Muusa", in Alan Loma and Raoul Abdul (eds.), *3,000 Years of Black Poetry* (New York, 1970), pp. 57-59.

16 *Ibid.*, pp. 56, 104-109.

17 One of his poems is translated in Margaret Laurence (ed.), *A Tree for Poverty : Somali Poetry and Prose* (Nairobi, 1954). See Mahamed Farah Abdillahi and B.W. Andrzejewski,

"The Life of Ilmi Bowndheri, a Somali Oral Poet Who is Said to Have Died of Love", *Journal of the Folklore Institute*, IV (1967), 191-206.

18 B.W. Andrzejewski, "The *Roobdoon* of Sheikh Aqib Abdullah Jama : A Somali Prayer for Rains", *African Language Studies*, XI (1970), 20-34.

19 Andrzejewski, "The *Roobdoon* of Sheikh Aqib", pp. 21-22.

20 Andrzejewski and Lewis, pp. 150-151.

21 The most informative discussion of Somali writing in Arabic is E. Cerulli, "Note sul movimento musulmano nella Somalia", *Rivista degli Studi Orientali*, X (1923), i, 1-36, reprinted in *Somalia I*, pp. 177-210 (see especially pp. 187-189 and 196-199). For a brief summary in English, see *ibid.*, p. 150.

22 Lewis, "Sufism in Somaliland — I", p. 595.

23 I.M. Lewis, *The Modern History of Somaliland*, pp. 131-2.

24 This refers to broadcasts from Cairo, London and Moscow, which, Andrzejewski says, "all vie in their desire to please the public by maintaining high aesthetic standards and avoiding unnecessary loan-words."

25 B.W. Andrzejewski, "The role of broadcasting in the adaptation of the Somali language to modern needs", in W.H. Whiteley (ed.) *Language Use and Social Change. Problems of Multilingualism with Special Reference to Eastern Africa* (London, 1971), pp. 262-273.

26 For a detailed discussion, see John W. Johnson, *Heellooy Heelleellooy : The Development of the Genre Heello in Modern Somali Poetry* (Bloomington, 1972).

27 Andrzejewski and Lewis, *Somali Poetry*, p. 51.

28 *Ibid.*, pp. 146-152.

29 See John W. Johnson, "A bibliography of the Somali language and literature", *African Language Review*, VIII (1969), 279-297. This was later updated in John W. Johnson, "Research in Somali Folklore", *Research in African Literatures*, IV (1973) i, 51-61. See also Andrzejewski, "The *Roobdoon* of Sheikh Aqib."

30 B.W. Andrzejewski, "The veneration of Sufi saints in Somali literature", *African Language Studies*, XV (1974), 15-53.

31 I.M. Lewis, "Literacy in a Nomadic Society", p. 168. See also E. Cerulli, "Tentativo indigeno di formare un alfabeto somalo", *Oriente Moderno*, XII (1932), iv, 212-213; and Mario Marino, "L'alfabeto 'osmania' in Somalia", *Rassegna di Studi Etiopici*, X (1951), 108-121.

32 I.M. Lewis, "The Gadabuursi Somali Script", *BSOAS*, XXI (1958), i, 134-156.

33 Cerulli, *Somalia III*, pp. 138-139.

34 M.H.I. Galaal, "Arabic Script for Somali", *Islamic Quarterly*, I (1954), ii, 114-118.

35 Andrzejewski, "The role of broadcasting", p. 271. On the history and diversity of

education in Somali territories, see I.M. Lewis, *The Modern History of Somaliland*, pp. 97, 102, 133, 136, 140 and 148-149.

36 Andrzejewski and Lewis, *Somali Poetry*, p. 39.

37 See B.W. Andrzejewski, "The *Roobdoon of Sheikh Aqib.*"

38 For general background information, see J. Contini, "The Somalis : A Nation of Poets in Search of an Alphabet", in Helen Kitchen (ed.), *A Handbook of African Affairs* (New York, 1964), 301-311. A more detailed account is available in B.W. Andrzejewski, "The Introduction of a National Orthography for Somali", *African Language Studies*, XV (1974), 199-203. On the preliminary discussions, see especially M. Pirone, "La lingua somala e i suoi problemi", *Africa* (Rome), XXII (1967), ii, 198-209, and B.W. Andrzejewski, S. Strelcyn and J. Tubiana, "Somalia : The Writing of Somali", in *Somaliya : Antologia Storico-Culturale* (Mogadishu, 1969), pp. 1-19.

39 B.W. Andrzejewski, "The Somali Academy of Culture", *IAI Bulletin* (Supplement to *Africa*, XLVII (1977), i, p. 7.

40 On this recent writing, see B.W. Andrzejewski, "The Rise of Written Somali Literature", *African Research and Documentation*, n° 8/9 (1975), 7-14.

41 For an extensive discussion—in Russian, with an English summary—of this book, see A.K. Zholkovsky, "Somaliiski rasskaz *Ispuitanie proritsatelya* (Opuit porozhdayushchego opisaniya)", *Narody Azii i Afriki*, VII (1970), 104-115, 252-253.

42 For a discussion of Somali drama, see B.W. Andrzejewski's Introduction to Hassan Sheikh Mumin, *Leopard Among the Women : Shabeelnaagood : A Somali Play* (London, 1974).

43 On those two plays, see the section on "Oral drama" in B.W. Andrzejewski, "The veneration of Sufi saints in Somali literature", *African Language Studies*, XV (1974), pp. 29-30.

44 John W. Johnson, *Heellooy Heelleellooy*, p.ix.

45 Andrzejewski, "The Rise of Written Somali Literature." This article is, so far, the only source of information in English on the subject. The account was later updated in B. W. Andrzejewski, "Five years of Written Somali : A Report on Progress and Prospects," *IAI Bulletin* (Supplement to *Africa*, XLVII (1977), iv, 4-5), which does not mention any further creative writing.

NOTES TO CHAPTER SEVEN

1 Gerald Moser, *Essays in Portuguese African Literature* (University Park, Pa., 1970).

2 Janheinz Jahn, "Modern African Literature : Bibliographical Spectrum", *Review of National Literatures*, II (1971), ii, 224-242.

3 Janheinz Jahn and Claus Peter Dressler, *Bibliography of Creative African Writing* (Nendeln, Liechtenstein, 1971).

4 A Gérard, "La politique coloniale et la formation des littératures vernaculares en Afrique britannique", *Commonwealth*, I (1974-75), 3-10.

5 On the writing produced by this black population whose mother-tongue was English, see notably R.W. July, *The Origins of Modern African Thought* (London, 1968).

6 For detailed information concerning the history of the study of African, especially Bantu, languages, see C.M. Doke, "Early Bantu Literature : The Age of Brusciotto", *Bantu Studies*, IX (1935), ii, 87-114; *Id.*, "Bantu Language Pioneers of the Nineteenth Century", *Bantu Studies*, XIV (1940), iii, 207-246; *Id.*, *Bantu : Modern Grammatical, Phonetical and Lexicographical Studies since 1860* (London, 1945, rptd. 1967); C.M. Doke and D.T. Cole, *Contributions to the History of Bantu Linguistics* (Johannesburg, 1961); Desmond T.Cole, "The History of African Linguistics to 1945", *Current Trends in Linguistics* VII (1971), 1-29. Of considerable relevance to the history of early writing in African languages is C.M. Doke, "Scripture Translation into Bantu Languages", *African Studies*, XVII (1958), 82-99. Unfortunately, no one has ever bothered to provide a bibliography of the numerous African-language versions of that seminal work, Bunyan's *Pilgrim's Progress*.

7 For a detailed account of the *Chaka* business, see Albert S. Gérard, *Four African Literatures* (Berkeley, 1971), pp. 127-131.

8 Christopher Fyfe, *Sierra Leone Inheritance*, pp. 311-12. A. Gérard, "Contribution de la Sierra Leone à la littérature ouest-africaine de langue anglaise", *Commonwealth*.

9 Gérard, *Four African Literatures*, pp. 41-51.

10 L.J. Lewis (ed.) *Phelps-Stokes Reports on Education in Africa* (abridged) (London, 1962), p. 65.

11 *Ibid.*, p. 64.

12 *Ibid.*, p. 63.

13 L. Gray Cowan, James O'Connell, David G. Scanlon (eds.), *Education and Nation-Building in Africa* (New York, 1965), p. 6.

14 *Ibid.*, p. 8.

15 *Ibid.*, p. 55, quoting the *Instructions relatives à l'application de la circulaire du 8 mai 1925 . . . réorganisant l'enseignement en Afrique Equatoriale Française* (Brazzaville, 1926).

16 Quoted *ibid.*, p. 49.

17 Lists were published in the journal of the Institute, *Africa*, IV (1931), iii, 352, VI (1933), i, 102, VI (1933), iv 483, VII (1934), iii, 375, IX (1936), i, 109, X (1937), i, 111, XI (1938), i, 94, XI (1938), iv, 499, and XII (1939), iv, 472. On the early activities of the Institute, see Edwin W. Smith, "The Story of the Institute : A Survey of Seven Years", *Africa* VII (1934), 1-27.

18 Margaret Wrong, *Africa and the Making of Books, Being a Survey of Africa's Need of Literature* (London, 1930).

19 "Vernacular Text-Book Committee and Translation Bureaux in Nigeria", *Oversea Education*, III (1931), i, p. 32.

20 Wilfred Whiteley, *Swahili. The Rise of a National Language* (London, 1969), p. 83.

21 "African Literature Committee, Northern Rhodesia", *Books for Africa*, IX (1939), iii, 45-46.

22 Peter Sulzer, *Schwarze Intelligenz : Ein literarisch-politischer Streifzug durch Südafrika* (Zürich, 1955).

23 Biographical information about many of the writers mentioned in the third part of this book is readily available in Janheinz Jahn, *Who's Who in African Literature* (Tübingen, 1972) and in Donald E. Herdeck, *African Authors. A Companion to Black African Writing 1300-1973* (Washington, 1973).

NOTES TO CHAPTER EIGHT

1 For historical background information on South Africa, the most reliable source is Monica Wilson and Leonard Thompson (eds.), *The Oxford History of South Africa*, 2 vols. (Oxford, 1969 and 1971). For a detailed survey of creative writing in the three main Bantu languages of South Africa (Xhosa, Southern Sotho and Zulu), the reader is referred to my *Four African Literatures* (Berkeley, 1971). In order to avoid needless overlapping and redundancy, the present chapter attempts to offer a synchronous survey of the written art not only in the seven officially recognized vernacular languages of the Republic, but also of creative writing in Zambia, Malawi and Zimbabwe. For reasons of space, any such bibliographical references are given as are not to be found in my earlier book. The most valuable first-hand account of early Xhosa literature is A.C. Jordan, *Towards an African Literature. The Emergence of Literary Form in Xhosa* (Berkeley, 1973). See also Gideon Lebakeng Mangoaela, "Vernacular writing in Southern Africa : A Brief Introduction," in Donald E. Herdeck, *African Authors. A Companion to Black African Writing 1300-1973* (Washington, 1973), p. 491-496; B.E.N. Mahlasela, *A General Survey of Xhosa Literature from its Early Beginnings in the 1800s to the Present* (Grahamstown, 1973); and several short essays in a special Xhosa literature issue of *South African Outlook*, n° 103 (1973).

2 R.H.W. Shepherd, *Lovedale, South Africa, 1824-1955*, (Lovedale 1971).

3 Leonard Thompson, *Survival in Two Worlds : Moshoeshoe of Lesotho, 1786-1870* (Oxford, 1975).

4 D.P. Kunene, "*Leselinyana la Lesotho* and Sotho Historiography," *History in Africa*, IV (1977), 149-61.

5 The latest brief biography of the Sotho writer is C.F. Swaenepoel, "Thomas Mofolo", *Limi*, III (1975), i, 4-6. For a stylistic discussion, see Daniel P. Kunene, "Towards an Aesthetic of Lesotho Prose", *Dalhousie Review*, LIII (1973-1974), 701-719.

6 The latest translation to date is the Afrikaans version of C.F. Swaenepoel, *Tjhaka* (Cape Town, Tafelberg, 1974).

7 Recent studies on *Chaka* include C.F. Swanepoel, "Oor die interpretasie van *Tjhaka*",

Limi, III (1975), i, 64-80, and Chidi Ikonne, "Purpose versus plot : The Double Vision of Thomas Mofolo's Narrator", in Christopher Heywood (ed.), *Aspects of South African Literature* (London, 1976), pp. 54-65.

8 For comparative discussions of the Chaka theme, see E. Rattunde, "Die Gestalt des Chaka in der 'littérature néo-africaine d'expression française'", *Romanische Forschungen*, LXXXII (1970), 320-344; Kolawole Ogungbesan, "A King for All Seasons : Chaka", *Présence Africaine*, n° 88 (1973) 197-217; Dorothy S. Blair, "The Shaka Theme in Dramatic Literature in French from West Africa", *African Studies*, XXXIII (1974), iii, 113-141; Nyembwe Tshikumambila, "Le personnage de Chaka : du portrait épique de Mofolo au mythe poétique de L.S. Senghor", *Zaïr-Afrique*, n° 87 (1974), 405-420; Ayi Kwei Armah, "Chaka", *Black World*, XXIV (1975), iv, 51-52, 84-90; and especially Donald Burness, *Shaka, King of the Zulus, in African Literature* (Washington, 1976).

9 J.R. Masiea, "The symbolical element as found in Mangwaela's collection of the war praise-poems", *Limi*, n° 12 (1971), 66-86.

10 Doke, "Scripture Translation into Bantu Languages", p. 89.

11 G. Bengt Sundkler, *Bantu Prophets in South Africa* (London 1948), p. 50. Patricia E. Scott, *Samuel Edward Krune Mqhayi, 1875-1945 : A Bibliographic Survey*, and *Id.* (ed.) *Mqhayi in Translation : A Short Autobiography of Samuel Krune Mqhayi* (Grahamstown, 1976); Jeff Opland, "Two Unpublished Poems by S.E.K. Mqhayi", *Research in African Literatures*, VIII (1977), i, 27-53. See also a special Mqhayi issue of *South African Outlook*, n° 109 (1975).

12 S.C. Satyo, "S.E.K. Mqhayi", *Limi*, II (1974), ii, 1-2.

13 On this subject, see J. Opland, "Imbongi Nezibongo : the Xhosa tribal poet and the contemporary poetic tradition", *PMLA*, XC (1975), ii, 185-208.

14 *Mhudi* has been reprinted (Johannesburg, 1975) with an introduction by Tim Couzens. For critical discussions, see Tim Couzens, "The Dark Side of the World : Sol Plaatje's *Mhudi*", *English Studies in Africa*, XIV (1971), ii, 187-203, and "Sol T. Plaatje's *Mhudi*", *Journal of Commonwealth Literature*, VIII (1973), i, 1-19; Stephen Gray, "Sources of the First Black South African Novel in English : Solomon Plaatje's Use of Shakespeare and Bunyan in *Mhudi*", *Munger Africana Library Notes*, n° 37 (1976), 6-28. In recent years, John L. Comaroff discovered and edited *The Boer War Diary of Sol T. Plaatje* (London, 1973).

15 D.B. Ntuli, "J.L. Dube", *Limi*, II (1974), ii, 3-4.

16 *Oxford History of South Africa*, II, p. 223.

17 *Ibid.*, p. 78.

18 *Ibid.*, p. 223.

19 B.E.N. Mahlasela, *Jolobe, Xhosa Poet and Writer* (Grahmstown, 1973); Patricia E. Scott, *James James Ranisi Jolobe : An Annotated Bibliography* (Grahamstown, 1973). See also Anon., "J.J. Jolobe", *Limi*, V (1977), 7-8.

20 John Reed and Clive Wake (eds.), *A Book of African Verse* (London, 1964), p. 3.

21 Z.S. Qangule, "A.C. Jordan", *Limi*, II (1974), i, 1-2.

22 See special R.R.R. Dhlomo issue of *English in Africa*, II (1975), i.

23 A large number of other writings by H.I.E. Dhlomo have been discovered and will soon be edited by Tim Couzens. See also N.W. Visser, "H.I.E. Dhlomo (1903-1956) : The Re-emergence of an African Writer", *English in Africa*, I (1974), ii, 1-10; H.I.E. Dhlomo is further considered in a sensitive essay by Maria K. Mootry, "Literature and Resistance in South Africa : Two Zulu Poets", *African Literature Today*, VI (1973), 112-119, which also deals with the poetry of B.W. Vilakazi.

24 D.B.Z. Ntuli, "B.W. Vilakazi", *Limi*, II (1974), i, 3-4. For an English translation of a representative selection of Vilakazi's poem, see *Zulu Horizons* (Johannesburg, 1973).

25 J.S.M. Khumalo, "Plot and Character in Vilakazi's Novels", *Limi*, n° 14 (June 1972), 1-22.

26 J.W. Snyman, " 'n Bespreking van *Motwasele II*", *Limi*, n° 12 (June 1971), 60-55. On Tswana writing, see Anon., "Bibliography of Tswana", *South African Outlook*, LXXVI (1946), p. 132, and A.T. Malepe, "A Brief Survey of Modern Literature in the South African Bantu Languages : Tswana", *Limi*, n° 6 (June 1968), 68-75.

27 A.T. Malepe, "D.P. Moloto", *Limi*, II (1974), ii, 8-9.

28 J.W. Snyman, "Die Roman *Motimedi*", *Limi*, II (1974), i, 77-80.

29 *Oxford History of South Africa*, I, 1976.

30 See L.A. Nel (comp.), *Bibliography of the Bantu Languages in the Republic of South Africa : VI Tsonga* (Pretoria, 1963), and C.T.D. Marivate, "A Brief Survey of Modern Literature in the South African Bantu Languages : Tsonga", *Limi* n° 6 (1968), 35-44.

31 Some information is to be gained from a complacently patronizing anonymous article entitled "The Meritorious Marivates", *Bantu*, XIX (1972), iii, 10-15.

32 Marivate, *loc. cit.*, p. 38. Mention should be made at this point of the abortive attempts made in the 1930s towards the formation of a written art in two dialects that are so closely related to Tsonga as to be mutually intelligible : Ronga and Tswa. They are spoken by populations living in the south of Mozambique, but literacy was brought to them by Protestant missionaries who availed themselves of printing facilities in South Africa. According to A.A. Jacques, the differences in writing between them "are very largely artificial and due to the direction given by the various Missions to the literary development of each of these dialects." The Bible was printed in Ronga and in Tswa in 1903, and the Swiss Mission in South Africa produced a Ronga version of *The Pilgrim's Progress* in 1916. By 1930, however, publication in the Ronga dialect had stopped "owing to the policy of the Portuguese authorities which discourage the use of the vernacular." (Jacques). As regards Tswa, on the contrary, indigenous author-ship was for some unknown reason encouraged until the late 1930s. "The first books to be published in Tswa were printed on a small mission press near Inhambane in the years 1885 to 1890, but it was not until twenty-five years later that much literary activity took place" (Persson). Between 1931 and 1940, collections of proverbs, riddles, fables, and legends by such writers as Aron S. Mukhombo, N.J. Mbanje and Elias S. Mucambe, were published at the Central Mission Press in the Transvaal under the

sponsorship of the Methodist Episcopal Mission. It is of interest to note that the first—
and apparently only—novel in Tswa, *Landikezani ni bapsali bakwe* ("Landikezani and his
parents"), was published around 1940 by Elias S. Mucambe. This fairly bulky 140-
page piece of prose fiction does not seem ever to have received serious attention, and
Tswa literature was thus still-born, presumably for the same reason that settled the
fate of Ronga literature. For bibliographical information, see A.A. Jacques, "A survey
of Shangana-Tsonga, Ronga and Tswa literature", *Bantu Studies*, XIV (1940), iii, 260-
270, and J.A. Persson (comp.), "A Tswa Bibliography", *South African Outlook*, LXXVI
(1946), p. 10.

33 For historical background information, see P.E.N. Tindall, *History of Central Africa*
   (London, 1968) and Bridglal Pachai, *Malawi : The History of the Nation* (London, 1973).

34 Quotations in this paragraph are from Tindall, pp. 245, 213, and 255-6.

35 Pachai, p. 32.

36 J.L. Pretorious, "A Short Report of the Literature Situation in Nyasaland", *Books for
   Africa*, XVIII (1948), iii, 37-38.

37 Some information on Abdallah and early unpublished Malawi writings can be found
   in Pachai, *op. cit.*, pp. 53 and 202, and Robert I. Rotberg (ed.), *Strike a Blow and Die*
   (Cambridge, Mass., 1967), p. 9. *The Yaos : Chiikala cha Wayao*, arranged, edited and
   translated by Meredith Sanderson, has now been reprinted with an introduction by
   Edward A. Alpers (London, 1973).

38 Pachai, p. 211.

39 The Mwase typescript, composed in 1931-32, has been edited by Robert I. Rotberg,
   Strike a Blow and Die. A Narrative of Race Ralations in Colonial Africa (1967).

40 B. Pachai, "Samuel Josiah Ntara, Writer and Historian", *Society of Malawi Journal*,
   XXI (1968), ii, 60 ff. On the development of Nyanja into a *lingua franca* and the
   vicissitudes of its various dialects, among them Cewa, see Bernd Heine, *Status and use
   of African Lingua Francas* (Munich, 1970), pp. 60-62. Bibliographical infomation is available in S.M. Made, R. Jackson and M.V.B. Mangoche Mbewe (comps.), *100 Years of
   Chichewa in Writing, 1875-1975* (Zomba, 1976). For a translation of Ntara's *Mbira Ya
   Achewa*, see Beatrix Heintze (ed.), *The History of the Chewa* (Wiesbaden, 1973).

41 *Oxford History of South Africa*, II, p. 225.

42 *Report of the Commission on Native Education*, 1949-1951, quoted *ibid*.

43 C.M. Doke, "The Native Languages of South Africa", *African Studies*, I, (1942), 136-
   141.

44 Quoted in Brian Bunting, *The Rise of the South African Reich* (Harmondsorth, 1964), p.
   217.

45 J.M. Lenake, "A Brief Survey of Modern Literature in the South African Bantu Languages : Southern Sotho", *Limi*, n° 6 (June 1968), 75-81.

46 *Ibid.*, pp. 79-80.

47 J.M. Lenake, "K.E. Ntsane", *Limi*, II (1974), i, 8-9.

48 See especially A.J. Moloi, "The Germination of Southern Sotho Poetry." *Limi*, n° 8 (June 1969), 28-59. For biographical information, see J.M. Lenake, "J.J. Moloi", *Limi*, VI (1978), 1-3.

49 Z.S. Qangule, "A Study of Tshaka's poem 'Igqili'", *Limi*, I (1973), ii, 1-22.

50 See anonymous biographical notice in *Limi*, V (1977), 9-10.

51 S.Z. Gangule, "A Brief Survey of Modern Literature in the South African Bantu Languages : Xhosa", *Limi*, n° 6 (June 1968), p. 22.

52 R.H.W. Shepherd, "Recent Trends in South African Vernacular Literature", *African World* (March 1955), pp. 7-8.

53 Brief review by S.C. Satyo in *Limi*, II (1974), ii, 79-80.

54 See Anon, "Unisa Language Assistants", *Bantu*, XIX (1972), viii, 24-26.

55 See brief review by J.V. Cantrell in *Limi*, n° 14 (June 1972) pp. 54-55.

56 Brief review by S.C. Satyo in *Limi*, II (1974), ii, 78-79.

57 H.C. Groenewald, "Struktuurbeskrywing van die historiese drama in Zulu", *Limi*, V (1977), 48-59.

58 Brief reviews of recent literary production in Zulu can be found in *Limi*, n° 10 (June 1970), 8-10, n° 14 (June 1972), 55-57, and II (1974), ii, 80-82.

59 See Anon, "Unisa Language Assistants", *Bantu* , XIX (1972), viii, 24-26.

60 From an anonymously printed report, "Literature and Resistance in South Africa", *Afro-Asian Writings*, I (1968), ii/iii, 88-95.

61 For information about recent Tswana writing, see A.T. Malepe, "A Brief survey of Modern Literature in the South African Bantu Languages : Tswana", *Limi*, n° 6 (June 1968), 68-75, and the same critic's short reviews in *Limi*, n° 10 (June 1970), 18-19; n° 14 (June 1972), p. 62; and II (1974), ii, 83-84.

62 A.T. Malepe, "S.A. Moroke", *Limi* VI (1978), 4-5.

63 A.T. Malepe, "D.P.S. Monyaise", *Limi*, II (1974), i, 7-8.

64 *Limi*, n° 14 (June 1972), p. 62.

65 A.T. Malepe, "J.M. Ntsime", *Limi*, III (1975), i, 1-2.

66 *Limi*, n° 14 (June 1972), p. 62.

67 For information about Tsonga writing, see C.T.D. Marivate, "A Brief Survey of Modern Literature in the South African Bantu Languages : Tsonga", *Limi*, n° 6 (June 1968), pp. 36-44, and the same critic's short reviews in *Limi*, n° 10 (June 1970), 11-16; n° 14 (June 1972), 57-59; III (1975), ii, 71-73.

68 C.D.T. Marivate, "E.P. Ndhambi", *Limi*, III (1975), ii, 1-2 where the author's birth-date is erroneously given as 1913.

69 C.D.T. Marivate, "B.K.M. Mtombeni", *Limi*, II (1974), i, 4-5.

70 C.D.T. Marivate, "Review of the patterned language as used by B.K.M. Mtombeni in his Tsonga play : *Malangavi ya Mbilu*", *Limi*, n° 10 (June 1970), 42-46.

71 N.J. Shipalana, "B.K.M. Mtombeni's *Mibya ya Nyekanyeka*"; *Limi*, n° 10 (June 1970), 30-41. See also Charlotte Nkondo, "The titles of four Tsonga literary works", *Limi*, IV (1976), 71-78.

72 C.D.T. Marivate, "E.M. Nkondo", *Limi*, II (1974), ii, 4-5.

73 See Anon., "Bibliography of literature in Northern Sotho", *South African Outlook*, LXXVI (1946), p. 178; P.C. Mokgokong, "A Brief Survey of Modern Literature in the South African Bantu Languages : Northern Sotho", *Limi*, n° 6 (June 1968), 60-68, and the brief reviews contributed by the same critic to *Limi* n° 10 (June 1970), 14-16; n° 14 (June 1972), 60-62; II (1974), ii, 62-63; and V (1977), 75-79.

74 Doke, "Scripture Translation. . . ", p. 99.

75 P.C. Mokgokong, "Humor in some works of Ramaila", *Limi*, ñ 10 (June 1970), 47-50. A biographical notice of Ramaila is to be found in T.D.M. Skota (ed. and comp.), *The African Yearly Register*, 3rd ed. (Johannesburg, 196-), pp. 54-56.

76 To the three writers mentioned by Mokgokong should be added J.I. Serote's *Molato* ("Guilt", 1943). On those early writers, see the relevant section in G.L. Letele, "Some recent literary publications in languages of the Sotho group", *African Studies*, III (1944), 161-171.

77 Franz's play contains a number of lyrics, one of which has been discussed in P.S. Groenewald, "Moeder is dood—'n metriese en 'n literêre ontleding van die gedig 'Gê ke le luwa Tukatole'", *Limi*, n° 14 (June 1972), 23-31.

78 P.C. Mokgokong, "O.K. Matsepe", *Limi*, II (1974), ii 6-8.

79 P.S. Groenewald, " 'n Voorstudie tot O.K. Matsepe se *Megokgo ya Bjoko* (1969) : die vervreemding van die vertellerkarakter", *Limi*, I (1973), ii, 23-58.

80 P.S. Groenewald, "O.K. Matsepe : By die verskyning van *Letsofalela*, 1972," *Limi*, III (1975), i, 47-63.

81 P.C. Mokgokong, "M.M. Ramala", *Limi*, II (1974), i, 6-7.

82 For competent discussions of Northern Sotho writing, see the various essays in Afri-kaans by P.S. Groenewald : "Karakters en karaktertekening in Noord-Sotho", *Limi*, IV (1975), ii, 48-61; "Moses Bopape en Stephen Ratlabala, *Ithute Direto*", *Studies in Bantoetale* I/II (1974-1975), 1-17; "D.G. Palaki Tsebe *Noto-ya-masogana* 'Lesibana' ", *ibid.*, 18-57; "Die Ontwikkeling van die Noord-Sotho-verhaalkunst", *ibid*; III (1976), i, 1-12; "Die Moraalstorie", *ibid.*, 13-38; "Die betekenis van die moderne Noord-Sotholetterkunde", *ibid*, IV (1977), i, 1-18, and "Die speurverhaal", *ibid.*, 19-45.

83 C.K. Nchabeleng, "H.M.L. Lentsoane", *Limi*, IV (1976), 5-11. In the early fifties, Nchabeleng (b. 1936) himself published several works of creative writing in Northern Sotho : his play, *Sealogana* (1971), a novel, *Masela wa Thabanaswana* (1972), and a collection of short stories, *Magalagapa a tau* (1976). See S.M. Serudu, "C.K.D. Nchabeleng," *Limi*, VI (1978), 6-11.

84 See L.A. Nel (comp.), *Bibliography of the Bantu Languages in the Republic of South Africa. VII. Venda* (Pretoria, 1964); R. Sh. Dau, "A Brief Survey of Modern Literature in the SouthAfrican Bantu Languages : Venda", *Limi*, n° 6 (June 1968), 44-60. See also brief reviews in *Limi*, n° 14 (June 1972), 59-60, and V (1977), 80-81.

85 T.N. Makuya, "T.N. Maumela", *Limi*, II (1974), i, 5-6.

86 T.W. Muloiwa, "E.S. Madima", Limi, III (1975), ii, 3-4.

87 T.N.N. Makuya, "Characterisation in novels", *Limi*, II (1974), i, 41-44.

88 T.N. Makuya, "M.E.R. Mathivha", *Limi*, II (1974), ii, 5-6.

89 T.W. Muloiwa, "R.R. Matshili", *Limi*, III, (1975), ii, 2-3.

90 T.W. Muloiwa, "W.M.R. Sigwayhulimu", *Limi*, IV (1976), 3-4.

91 Tindall, *op. cit.*, p. 267.

92 Anon., "African Literature Committee, Northern Rhodesia", *Books for Africa*, IX (1939), iii, 45-46.

93 See anonymous "Report, 1940" in *Books for Africa*, XI (1941), i, pp. 5-6

94 Anon., "African Literature Committee, Northern Rhodesia, *Books for Africa*, XVIII (1948), i, 8-9.

95 See J.L. Pretorius, "A Short Report of the Literature Situation in Nyasaland", *Books for Africa*, XVIII (1948), 37-38, and G.H. Wilson, "The Northern Rhodesia-Nyasaland Joint Publications Bureau, *Africa*, XX (1950), i, 60-69. For later developments see Steve S. Mwiyeriwa, "Printing Presses and Publishing Houses in Malawi", *African Book Publishing Record*, IV (1978), ii, 87-97

96 Daniel P. Kunene, "African Vernacular Writing—An Essay on Self-Devaluation", *African Social Research*, IX (1970), 639-659.

97 Kunene, *loc.cit.*, p. 640. For a detailed discussion of this novel, see Daniel P. Kunene, "An Analysis of Stephen A. Mpashi's *Uwauma nafyala*", in Bernth Lindfors and Ulla Schild (eds.), *Neo-African Literature and Culture. Essays in Memory of Janheinz Jahn* (Wiesbaden, 1976), pp. 258-266.

98 Anon., "National Educational Company of Zambia Ltd", *African Book Publishing Record*, I (1975), ii, 135-136. See especially Simon D. Allison, "State Participation in Publishing : the Zambian experience", *in* E. Oluwasamni (ed.), *Publishing in Africa in the Seventies* (Ile-Ife, 1975), pp. 59-69.

99 Geoffrey J. Williams, "The Zambian Publishing Scene : A Commentary", *African Book Publishing Record*, III (1977), i, 15-21.

100 Cf. B. McAdam, "The English Medium Scheme in Zambia", *in* T.P. Gorman (ed.), *Language in Education in Eastern Africa* (Nairobi 1970), pp. 37-50.

101 It is highly significant that none of the items on Zambian literature in the *MLA Annual Bibliography* refer to writing in the African languages, whereas a steady growth of interest is observable in the scholarly study of Swahili literature and of vernacular writing in Nigeria and South Africa.

102 G. Fortune, "75 Years of Writing in Shona", *Zambezia*, I (1969), i, 55-67.

103 George Kahari, *The Novels of Patrick Chakaipa* (Salisbury, 1972), pp. 1-10.

104 An English translation of *Feso* is available in D.E. Herdeck, S.M. Mutswaito, *et al.*, *Zimbabwe. Prose and Poetry* (Washington, 1974).

105 On the early history of Mashonaland, see P.E.N. Tindall, *History of Central Africa* (London, 1967), pp. 52-59.

106 *Zimbabwe. Prose and Poetry*, p. 66.

107 G.Kahari, "Oral and Written Literature in Shona : Contrasts and Continuities", *in* G. Fortune (ed.), *African Languages in Schools* (Salisbury, 1964), 97-102.

108 D.E. Herdeck, "Introduction", *Zimbabwe. Prose and Poetry*, pp. 9-12.

109 H.W. Chitepo, *Soko Risina Musoro*, translated and edited with notes by Hazel Carter (London, 1958), p. 42. The poem and its translation have been reprinted in *Zimbabwe*, pp. 233-265. See Christopher Devlin,"A Shona Ecologue," *The Month*, n.s. XXI (1959), iii, 150-157.

110 N.H. Brettell, "Preface", *Rhodesian Poetry*, n° 6 (1961), pp. 5-6.

111 Norman H. Mackenzie, "Preface", *Rhodesian Poetry*, n° 4 (1957).

112 *Poet*, V (1964), i.

113 Modern Shona poetry has been the object of a good deal of learned attention, es-pecially in its connection with traditional oral poetry. See notably G. Mandishona (ed.) "The Trend of the Moderns in Shona Poetry", in G. Fortune, *African Languages in Schools*, pp. 108-112; this essay has been reprinted as "The Trend in Modern Shona Poetry" in E. W. Krog (ed.), *African Literature in Rhodesia* (Gwelo, 1966), pp. 63-69, which also contains analyses of individual Shona poems pp. 164-210. See also C.H. Borland, "The oral and written Culture of the Shona", *Limi*, n° 8 (June 1969), 1-16; M.A. Hamutyinei, "The Revival of Shona Poetry", *Nada*, X (1970), ii, 12-15.

114 This is mentioned in S.J. Nondo, "Ndebele poetry", *in* G. Fortune (ed.), *African Languages in Schools*, pp. 103-107.

115 Much useful information on individual Shona and Ndebele novels is to be found in E.W. Krog (ed.), *African Literature in Rhodesia*, pp. 97-163 (Shona) and 211-236 (Nde-bele). See also Albert S. Gérard, "African Literature in Rhodesia", *Africa Report*, XIII (1968), v, 41-42. A large number of Shona novels are discussed, from the point of view of their ethical and philosophical significance, in Abraham Kriel, *An African Horizon*.

Ideals in Shona Lore and Literature (Cape Town, 1971). See also G.P. Kahari, "Tradition and Innovation in the Shona Novel : Social Change and the Assault on Urban Morals", *Nada* XI (1976), 309-320.

116 George Kahari, *The Imaginative Writings of Paul Chidyausiku* (Gwelo, 1975), p. 17.

117 *Ibid.*, p. 150.

118 *Ibid.*, pp. 132 and 121.

119 G. Kahari, "Tradition and Innovation in Shona Literature : Bernard Chidzero's *Nzvengamutsvairo*", *Revue des Langues Vivantes*, XXXVII (1971), i, 75-80; G. Fortune, "Social Registers in Chidzero's *Nzvengamutsvairo*", *African Studies* XXXII (1973), 99-111.

120 Beat Inauen, "Ehekrisen auf Shona", *Bethlehem*, LXXIV (1969), 217-223.

121 Krog. p. 98.

122 Kahari, "Oral and Written Literature in Shona", *loc. cit.*, p. 101.

123 Kriel, *African Horizon*, p. 236.

124 *Ibid.*, pp. 126-127.

NOTES TO CHAPTER NINE

1 For historical background material, see Christopher Fyfe, *History of Sierra Leone* (London, 1962), Arthur T. Porter, *Creoledom. A Study in the Development of Freetown Society.* (London, 1963), J. Gus Liebenow, *Liberia : The Evolution of Privilege* (Ithaca, 1969), Christopher Clapham, *Liberia and Sierra Leone. An Essay in Comparative Politics* (Cambridge, Eng., 1976).

2 See Albert Gérard, "Contribuição da Serra Leôa na literatura de lingua inglesa da Africa Ocidental," *Africa* (Lisbon), I (1978), i, 89-94.

3 For a thorough study of this nineteenth-century English writing, see Robert W. July, *The Origins of Modern African Thought* (London, 1968).

4 E.D. Jones, "The Potentialities of Krio as a Literary Language", *Sierra Leone Studies*, n.s. IX (1957); *Id*, "Krio in Sierra Leone Journalism", *Sierra Leone Language Review*, III (1964), 24-31; Leo Spitzer, "Creole Attitudes towards Krio", *Sierra Leone Language Review*, v (1966), 39-49.

5 S. Modupe Broderick, "*Julius Caesar* and *Udat Di Kiap Fit* : An Analysis", *Ba Shiru*, Winter 1971, 49-60; "Conversations with African Writer Thomas Decker," tape n° 24 of African Field Service.

6 Liebenow, *Liberia*, pp. 17-18.

7 David Dalby, "A Survey of the Indigenous Scripts of Liberia and Sierra Leone : Vai, Mende, Loma, Kpelle and Bassa", *African Language Studies*, VIII (1967), 3-51. For full

information, see Dalby, "The Indigenous Scripts of West Africa and Suriname : Their Inspiration and Design", *Ibid.*, IX (1968), 156-197; "Further Indigenous Scripts of West Africa : Manding, Wolof and Fula Alphabets and Yoruba 'Holy Writing'", *Ibid.*, X (1969), 161-181; and "The historical problems of indigenous scripts of West Africa and Suriname", in D. Dalby (ed.), *Language and History in Africa* (London, 1970). See also S.E. Holsoe, "An early Vai manuscript from Liberia", *African Languages*, II (1976), 32-59, and, for an account of Islamic influence on Vai writing, Jack Goody, Michael Cole, and Sylvia Scribner, "Writing and Formal Operations : A Case Study among the Vai", *Africa*, XLVII (1977), iii, 289-304.

8 This was first recorded by A.T. Sumner, "Mende Writing", *Sierra Leone Studies*, XVII (1932), 29-33; see also S. Milburn, "Kisi Kamara and the Mende Script", *Sierra Leone Language Review*, III (1964), 20-23.

9 Dalby, "Survey of the Indigenous Scripts. . .", p. 21.

10 Bernd Heine, *Status and Use of African Lingua Francas* (Munich, 1970), p. 145. See P.E.H. Hair, "Bibliography of the Mende Language", *Sierra Leone Language Review*, I (1962), 39-61. Some writing was also done in Susu : P.E.H. Hair, "Susu Studies and Literature, 1799-1965", *Sierra Leone Language Review*, IV (1965), 38-53.

11 Anon., "Mende Literature Programme", *Books for Africa*, XVI (1946), i, 8-10.

12 Anon., "Report from the Protectorate Literature Bureau, Sierra Leone, 1950", *Books for Africa*, XXI (1951), iv, 59-61.

13 For the history of Yoruba language studies, see P.E.H. Hair, *The Early Study of Nigerian Languages* (Cambridge, Eng., 1967), pp. 4-30.

14 *Ibid.*, p. 17.

15 For a general account of Yoruba writing, see Adeboye Babalola and Albert S. Gérard, "A Brief Survey of Creative Writing in Yoruba", *Review of National Literatures*, II (1971), ii, 188-205, and Adeboye Babalola, "A Survey of Modern Literature in the Yoruba, Efik and Hausa Languages", in Bruce King (ed.), *Introduction to Nigerian Literature* (Lagos, 1971), especially pp. 50-54. The present section is heavily indebted to these two essays.

16 Robert Koester, "Bunyan in Yoruba", *Journal of Commonwealth Literature*, VII (1972), ii, p. 156.

17 J.F. Ade Ajayi, *Christian Missions in Nigeria, 1841-1891* (Evanston, 1965), p. 225.

18 On these developments see A. Babs Fafunwa, *History of Education in Nigeria* (London, 1974), pp. 92-99.

19 M. Lijadu (ed.), *Awon arofo orin Sobo Arobiodu* (Lagos, 1974). See Olatunde Olatunji, "Religion in Literature : The Christianity of J.S. Sowande (Sobo Arobiodu", *Orita* (Ibadan), VII (1974), 3-21.

20 Ayo Bamgbose, *The Novels of D.O. Fagunwa* (Benin City, 1974), p. 15.

21 This was later translated by Wole Soyinka as *The Forest of A Thousand Daemons. A*

Hunter's Saga (London, 1968). Excerpts from Fagunwa's works have been translated in *Odù*, IX (1963), *Black Orpheus*, XV (1964) and XIX (1966), and in W. Whiteley (ed.), *A Selection of African Prose*, vol. II (London, 1964). For early critical studies, see A.O. Olubummo; "D.O. Fagunwa : A Yoruba Novelist", *Odù*, IX (1963), 26-39; Ulli Beier, "Fagunwa, a Yoruba Novelist", *Black Orpheus* n° 17 (June 1965), 51-56, reprinted in U. Beier (ed.), *Introduction to African Literature* (London, 1967), pp. 188-195; Afolabi Olabimtan, "Religion as a Theme in Fagunwa's Novels", *Odù*, XI (1975), 101-114. It is noteworthy that Fagunwa is, apart from Hausa poet Sa'adu Zungar, the only vernacular writer in West Africa to whose work a full-scale monograph has been devoted : Ayo Bambgose, *The Novels of D.O. Fagunwa* (Benin, City, 1974).

22 On the triangular relation between Tutuola, Fagunwa and the oral tradition, see E.N. Obiechina, "Transition from Oral to Literary Tradition", *Présence Africaine* , n° 58 (1967), 140-161, and "Amos Tutuola and the Oral Tradition", *Ibid.*, n° 65 (1968), 85-106; Bernth Lindfors, "Amos Tutuola's *The Palm-Wine Drinkard* and Oral Tradition", *Critique*, IX (1968-69), 42-50, and "Amos Tutuola and D.O. Fagunwa", *Journal of Commonwealth Literature*, IX (1970), 57-65; Richard Priebe, "Tutuola, Fagunwa, and Shakespeare", *Ibid.*, VII (1973), i, 110-111; Abiola Irele, "Tradition and the Yoruba Writer: D.O. Fagunwa, Amos Tutuola and Wole Soyinka", *Odù*, XI (1975), 101-114.

23 O. Esan, *"Olokun*, A Yoruba Literary Journal", *Odù*, IX (1963), 38-39.

24 B. King (ed.), *Introduction to Nigerian Literature*, p. 52.

25 S.A. Babalola, *The Content and Form of Yoruba Ijala* (London, 1966).

26 "Independence", an English version of an earlier poem by Faleti, was published in *Black Orpheus*, n° 8 (n.d.), pp. 4-5.

27 The interest of this genre was first recognized and signalled in Ulli Beier, "Yoruba Folk Operas", *African Music Society Journal* I (1964), i, 32-34. Beier returned to the topic in a *Black Orpheus* essay on "Yoruba Theatre" which was reprinted in his *Introduction to African Literature* (London, 1967), pp. 243-254, and in "Saving a Language", *Africa Quarterly*, V (1966), iv, 324-338. By then, Yoruba scholars were beginning to take over. Oladele Taiwo's *An Introduction to West African Literature* (London, 1967) contains valuable information on the subject (pp. 68-71). For a comprehensive early account, see Oyin Ogunba, "Le Théâtre au Nigeria", *Présence Africaine*, n° 58 (1966), 67-90. The most prominent specialist of traditional drama and its relation to both the folk opera and modern stage drama is Joel Adedeji, whose main studies on the subject are : "The Place of Drama in Yoruba Religious Observance", *Odù*, III (1966), i, 88-94; "Form and Function of Satire in Yoruba Drama", *Odù*, IV (1967), i, 61-72; "Oral Tradition and the Contemporary Theater in Nigeria", *Research in African Literatures*, II (1971), 134-149; "The Church and the Emergence of the Nigerian Theatre, 1866-1914", *Journal of the Historical Society of Nigeria*, VI (1971) 25-45; "The Literature of the Yoruba Opera", in W.L. Ballard (ed.), *Essays on African Literature* (Atlanta, 1973), pp. 55-77; "A Profile of Nigerian Theatre 1960-1970", *Nigeria Magazine*, n° 107-109 (1971), 3-14; "Trends in the Content and Form of the Opening Glee in Yoruba Drama", *Research in African Literatures*, IV (1973), 32-47; "Aesthetics of the Yoruba Opera", *Journal of the New African Literature and the Arts*, n° 13/14 (1972), 41-48. See also Adrian A. Roscoe, *Mother is Gold. A Study in West African Literature* (Cambridge, Eng., 1971), pp. 176-200; Anthony Graham-White, "Yoruba Opera : Developing a New Drama for the Nigerian People", *Theatre Quarterly*, XV (1974), 33-41; Oyekan Owomoyela, "Folklore and Yoruba Theatre", in Bernth Lindfors (ed.), *Critical Perspectives on Nigerian Literatures* (Washington, 1976), pp. 27-40.

28 Etienne Bertrand, "Le phénomène 'Ogunde'", *Afrique Littéraire et Artistique,* n° 23 (1972) 72-78; Ebun Clark, "Ogunde Theatre : The Rise of Contemporary Professional Theatre in Nigeria, 1946-72", *Nigeria Magazine,* n° 114 (1974), 3-14, and 24-33; *Id, Ibid,* n° 115-116 (1975), 9-24; *Id,* "Ogunde Theatre : Content and form", *Black Orpheus,* III (1974-1975), ii-iii, 59-85; Bernth Lindfors, "Ogunde on Ogunde : Two Autobiographical Statements", *Educational Theatre Journal,* XXVIII (1976), 239-246; Ngozi Ujoh, "Hubert Ogunde 40 Years on Stage", *Spear* (Lagos), June 1976, 36-38.

29 *Yoruba Ronu* was first printed in 1964. Other Ogunde plays reached print in 1967, in the three volumes of *Aropin n' t' enia* ("Men wish each other short-lived progress") and the two volumes of *Ologbo dudu* ("The black cat").

30 A bilingual version was published by the Institute of African Studies of the University of Ibadan in 1972. See Ulli Beier, "E.K. Ogunmola : A Personal Memoir", in Bernth Lindfors and Ulla Schild (eds.), *Neo-African Literature and Culture* (Wiesbaden, 1976), pp. 111-118.

31 Early reports are : Lyndon Harries, "An Experiment in Drama", *Nigeria Magazine,* n° 89 (June 1966), 157-159, and Herbert L. Shore, "Duro Ladipo, African Original", *Africa Forum* II (1966), i, 107-110. See also Ulli Beier's informative Introduction to *Three Nigerian Plays* (London, 1967).

32 Quite recently, however, Chief Oludare Olajubu has convincingly argued that *Oba Koso* at any rate was more closely indebted to an earlier account which had been written in Yoruba by an Englishman, A.L. Hethersett, and which was printed in *Iwe Kika Ekerin* shortly before the first World War: "The Sources of Duro Lapido's [sic] *Oba Ko So*", *Research in African Literatures,* 9 (1968), iii, 329-62. See also Robert G. Armstrong, "Traditional Poetry in Ladipo's Opera *Oba Ko So,*" *Ibid.,* pp. 363-81.

33 For a convenient selection of British press responses to the play, see Ulli Beier, "The Magic Spell of Duro Ladipo", *Gangan : A Magazine of the Western Nigeria Ministry of Home Affairs and Information,* n° 3 (1970). The play has a complicated printing history. An English version first appeared in Ulli Beier, *Three Yoruba Plays : Oba Koso, Oba Moro, Oba Waja* (Ibadan, 1964). The Institute of African Studies at Ibadan next came up with *Selections from Oba ko so* (1966). In 1968, the Institute issued a bilingual edition, which went through a new, revised and enlarged edition in 1972. Meanwhile, the Lagos branch of Macmillan had made the Yoruba text of the play commercially available in 1970.

34 English version in Ulli Beier (ed.), *Three Nigerian Plays* (London, 1967).

35 This was later confirmed, most authoritatively, in Ulli Beier, *The Return of the Gods : The Sacred Art of Susanne Wenger* (Cambridge, Eng. 1975), p. 20, where the interesting point is made that one of Ladipo's last plays, *Oluweri,* "produced for the fifth Ife Festival of the Arts... was Ladipo's adaptation of Ijimere's *Woyengi.*" See also Charles R. Larson, "Ulli Beier—African Playwright?" *Books Abroad,* XLVI (1972), 393-6.

36 The early growth of this fascinating trend can be traced in Ayo Bamgbose, "Yoruba Studies Today", *Odù,* n.s. 1 (1969), 85-100.

37 J. Africanus B. Horton, *West African Countries and Peoples* (London, 1968) pp. 175 and 182. For a modern elaboration of this observation, see Simon Ottenberg, "Igbo Re-

ceptivity to Change", in W.R. Bascom and M.J. Herskovit (eds.), *Continuity and Change in African Cultures* (Chicago, 1959) pp. 130-143.

38 Ernest N. Emenyonu, "Igbo Literary Backgrounds", *The Conch*, V (1973), 43-60.

39 P.E.H. Hair, *The Early Study of Nigerian Languages*, pp. 98-99.

40 Emenyonu, *loc. cit.*, p. 50

41 See A.E. Afigbo, "Chief Igewbe Odum : the Omenuko of History", *Nigeria Magazine*, n° 90 (Sept. 1966), 222-231.

42 For a detailed discussion of *Omenuko*, see E.N. Emenyonu, "Early Fiction in Igbo", *Research in African Literatures*, IV (1973), i, 7-20.

43 Marjorie Stewart, "The Eastern Nigeria Literature Bureau", *Books for Africa*, XX (1950), iv, 53-54.

44 See Austin J. Shelton's discussion of Ekwensi's *Jagua Nana* in "Le principe cyclique de la personnalité africaine : Le retour à la brousse ou le recul ontologique", *Présence Africaine*, n° 46 (July 1963), 64-77.

45 It is highly revealing that for Austin J. Shelton, "The Articulation of Traditional and Modern in Igbo Literature", *The Conch*, I (1969), i, 30-52, Igbo literature has only two components : oral art and English writing. Vernacular writings are dismissed as "merely printed versions of traditional literary works" and "collections of biographies." Shelton does mention one "novel", *Dimpka*. This is presumably *Dimpka muta igu na ide akwuwko*, an anonymous 24-page booklet issued by the Eastern Education Department (Enugu, 1950).

46 See however, Chike Okonyia, *Igbo Grammar and Composition* (Onitsha, 1962), who claims that "a rudimentary Igbo literature has begun to emerge in recent years. To a great extent it has been sponsored by the spirit of nationalism which preceded the attainment of Nigerian independence" (pp. 3-4).

47 Thomas Hodgkin, *Nigerian Perspectives. An Historical Anthology* (London, 1960), p. 38.

48 John E. Flint, *Nigeria and Ghana* (Englewood Cliffs, 1966), p. 120; Stephen Neill, *A History of Christian Missions* (Harmondsworth, 1964), p. 309.

49 Adeboye Babalola, "A Survey of Modern Literature in the Yoruba, Efik and Hausa Languages" in Bruce King (ed.), *Introduction to Nigerian Literature* (Lagos, 1971), pp. 50-63. This essay contains the only account of Efik writing in existence (pp. 55-57).

50 See A.N. Ekpiken, *A Bibliography of the Efik-Ibibio-Speaking Peoples of the Old Calabar Province of Nigeria 1668-1964* (Ibadan, 1970).

51 This was first noted in J.K. MacGregor, "Some Notes on 'nsibidi' ", *Journal of the Royal Anthropological Institute*, XXXIX (1909), 209-219; Elphinstone Dayrell, "Some 'nsibidi' Signs", *Man*, X (1910), 113-114; *Id.*, "Further Notes on 'nsibidi' Signs with their Meanings from the Ikom districts, Southern Nigeria", *Journal of the Royal Anthropological Institute*, XLI (1911), 521-540.

52 See R.F.G. Adams, "Oberi Okaime : A New African Language and Script", *Africa*, XVII (1947), 24-34; K. Hau, "Oberi Okaime Script, Texts and Counting System", *BIFAN*, B, XXIII (1961), iii, 291-308; David Dalby, "The Indigenous Scripts of West Africa and Surinam : Their Inspiration and Design", *African Language Studies*, IX (1968), 156-197.

53 Anon., "Efik-Ibibio Literary Competition", *Nigerian Teacher*, 1 (1934), iii, 49.

54 An exceptionally unilluminating review by R.F.G. Armstrong appeared in *Nigerian Teacher*, n° 8 (1936), 61-62.

55 Some biographical information on Amaku can be found in Anon., "Still Teaching", *West Africa*, n° 2152 (2 July 1958), p. 653.

56 R.F.G Adams, "Efik Translation Bureau", *Africa* XVI (1946), ii, p. 120.

57 See Moffat Akpan, "Udoma Drama Cup Comes to Calabar", *Hope Waddell Magazine*, N° 17 (July 1958), 23-24 and the *Program and Synopsis for the Play "Sidibe" by Ernest Enyang* issued by the Calabar Cultural Association (Ibadan, 1958).

58 R.C. Abraham was apparently the first scholar interested in the language with *The Principles of Idoma* (London, 1938) and with *The Idoma Language* (1951), which was printed in Oturkpo, Amali's native place, on behalf of the Idoma Native Administration. The first Idoma primer appeared in 1951, and some scriptural material was made available in 1962. See Nduntuei O. Ira, *Bibliography of Nigeria* (London, 1971), pp. 169-170.

59 In his Introduction to Samson O.O. Amali, *Onugbo mlOko* (Ibadan, 1972).

60 For a slight, not very balanced, discussion of Amali's English poetry, see John Mc-Veagh, "Poetry and Mr. Amali", and R.G. Armstrong, "A Rejoinder to McVeagh", *Ibadan*, N° 29 (July 1971), pp. 93-97 and 100. This unfortunate controversy was resumed after several years by John McVeagh and A.W. Thomson in *Ibadan*, n° 30 (1975), 42-44.

61 Efua Sutherland, "Textbooks for the Study of Ghanaian Languages" in J.H. Birnie and G. Ansre (eds.), *The Study of Ghanaian Languages* (Legon, 1969), pp. 25-41.

62 The best survey of Ghanaian vernacular writing is to be found in Petr Zima, "Literatures in West African Languages", in Vladimír Klima, Karel Frantisek Růzicka and Petr Zima, *Black Africa : Literature and Language* (Dordrecht and Prague, 1976), pp. 140-179, especially pp. 152-163. The original Czech version of this book was *Literatura cerné Afriky* (Prague, 1972). The present section is much indebted to this account. For bibliographical information see *Bibliography of Works in Ghana Languages* (Accra, 1967) and Dennis M. Warren (comp.) and Alan R. Taylor (ed.), *The Akan Literature of Ghana : A Bibliography* (Waltham, Mass., 1972).

63 Noel Smith, *The Presbyterian Church of Ghana, 1835-1960* (Accra, 1966), p. 141.

64 On this activity in English, see especially Robert W. July, *The Origins of Modern African Thought* (London, 1968), p. 329.

65 S.K. Otoo, "The growth of Fante Literature", *New Orient Bimonthly*, III (1962), 164-166.

66 See E.O. Apronti and A.C. Denteh, " 'Minority' Languages", in *The Study of Ghanaian Languages*, pp. 18-23.

67 Obituary notice by E. Ofori Akyea in *Okyeame*, IV (1968), i, 120.

68 Neill, *A History of Christian Missions*, p. 307.

69 J.B. Webster and A.A. Boahen, *The Revolutionary Years. West Africa since 1800* (London, 1967), p. 215.

70 Noel Smith, *The Presbyterian Church of Ghana 1835-1960* (Accra 1966), pp. 54-55.

71 See P. Jenkins and Francis Dankwa, "A Forgotten Vernacular Periodical", *Mitteilungen der Basler Afrika Bibliographien*, 9 (1973), 27-33, and H.M.J. Trutenau, "The 'Christian Messenger' and its Successors : A Description of the First Three Series of a Missionary Periodical with Articles in Ghanaian Languages (Twi and Ga)", *ibid.*, pp. 38-53.

72 Obituary notice by Kofi Asare Opoku in *Okyeame*, IV (1968), i, 120-122.

73 Harris W. Mobley, *The Ghanaian Image of the Missionary : An Analysis of the Published Critiques of Christian Missionaries by Ghanaians* (Leiden, 1970).

74 Some information about Asante-Twi writing can be found in Francis Boakye Duah, "Influence of Oral Folklore on Written Literature in Africa South of the Sahara as Exemplified in Ghana", *Universita 17. Listopadu V Praze. Sbornik Studentkych Praci*, I (1971), especially pp. 18-26.

75 See J. Kwasi Brentuo, "A Tribute to Opanin Yao Kani", *Okyeame*, II (1964), i, 67-68.

76 See H. Labouret and F. Rivet, *Le Royaume d'Ardra et son évangélisation au XVIIe siècle* (Paris, 1929) and Diedrich Westermann, *Wöterbuch der Ewe-Sprache* (Berlin, 1954), p. xxiii.

77 Gilbert Ansre, "Language Standardization in Sub-Saharan Africa", *Current Trends in Linguistics*, VII (1971) 680-699. Creative writing in Ewe was first noted in Paul Wiegräbe, "Neuere Literatur in Ewe", *Afrika und Übersee*, XLIV (1960), 132-136. The most readily available account is due to Petr Zima in Vladimir Klíma, *et al.*, *Black Africa : Literature and Languages* (Prague and Dordrecht, 1976), pp. 152-156. Much information is to be found in an unpublished dissertation by Simon Agbeko Amegbleame, *Essai d'analyse d'une production écrite africaine : La Littérature ewe* (Bordeaux, 1975); I am much indebted to this work, a short summary of which was published by the author himself as "Naissance et développement d'un corpus imprimé africain : La littérature éwé", *Afrique Littéraire et Artistique*, n° 39 (1976), 37-42. See also Simon Amegbleame, *Le Livre ewe : Essai de Bibliographie* (Bordeaux, 1975). There are a few discrepancies between this and the data in Suzanne Lafage, "Contribution à un inventaire chronologique des ouvrages entièrement ou partiellement en langue éwé", *Annales de l'Université d'Abidjan*, Série H, *Linguistique*, VII (1974), i, 169-204. For general bibliographical information, see *Id.*, "Contribution à un inventaire chronologique des publications concernant l'aire culturelle éwé", *Ibid.*, VIII (1975), i, 159-189; and K. Zielnica, *Bibliographie der Ewe in West-Afrika* (Vienna, 1976).

79 Quoted in A Moumouni, *L'Education en Afrique* (Paris, 1967), pp. 46 and 55.

80 *Rapport annuel du Gouvernement français à l'Assemblée générale des Nations Unies sur l'administration du Togo placé sous la tutelle de la France. Année 1956*, p. 207, quoted in Amegbleame, *op. cit.*, p. 36.

81 The play caught the attention of Diedrich Westermann and was soon published with a German translation (Berlin, 1937); a few years later, the author provided his own English version (London, 1943). According to Suzanne Lafage, however, both plays had first appeared in 1948 allegedly under the curious imprint of the "Ghana Informations Service"!

82 Ferdinand K. Fiawoo, *Tuinese -Fia yi dziehe. Two plays in Ewe and English*, with a German introduction by H. Jungraithmayr (Marburg an der Lahn, 1973).

83 Ursula Hintze, *Bibliographie der Kwa-Sprachen und der Sprachen der Togo-Restvölker* (Berlin, 1959), p. 93.

84 Simon A. Amegbleame, "Le théâtre dans la littérature éwé," *Afrique Littéraire et Artistique*, n° 51 (1979), 33-41.

85 On Ewe oral poetry, see F. N'Sougan Agblemagnon, *Sociologie des sociétés orales d'Afrique noire* (Paris, 1959), pp. 114-135.

86 Amegbleame, *op. cit.*, p. 122.

87 E.O. Apronti and A.C. Denteh, " 'Minority' Languages."

88 In his paper "Zur Ausbreitung einer westafrikanischen Stammessprache (Das Twi)" published in J. Lukas (ed.), *Afrikanistische Studien* (Berlin, 1955), pp. 220-230, E.L. Rapp considers that Ga "is spoken by somewhat more than 50,000 people as mother tongue and understood by about 100,000 others as lingua franca and school language." But in the 1960 Population Census of Ghana. *Special Report 'E'. Tribes in Ghana* (Accra, 1964), the Ga population is claimed to amount to 236,210.

89 J. Zimmermann, *A Grammatical Sketch of the Ga or Accra Language* (Stuttgart, 1858), p. 863, quoted by Apronti and Denteh, *loc. cit.*, p. 19.

90 Bernd Heine, *Status and Use of African Lingua Francas* (Munich, 1970), p. 144.

91 Apronti and Denteh, *loc. cit.*, p. 19.

NOTES TO CHAPTER TEN

1 See E.B. Underhill, *Alfred Saker. A Biography* (London, 1884).

2 C.M. Doke, "Scripture Translation into Bantu Languages", *African Studies*, XVII (1958), p. 87.

3 Fritz Raaflaub, *Die Schulen der Basler Mission in Kamerun* (Basel, 1948); Erik Halldén, *The Culture Policy of the Basel Mission in the Cameroons, 1886-1905* (Uppsala, 1968).

4 E. Meyer, "Das Problem der Verkehrssprachen von Tropisch Afrika, insb. von Kamerun", *Mitteilungen der geographischen Gesellschaft Hamburg*, XLVIII (1944), 253-288. See also Bernd Heine, *Status and Use of African Lingua Francas*, pp. 125-126.

5 Some information about vernacular writing, especially Duala, is to be found in J.C. Bahoken and Engelbert Atangana, *La politique culturelle en République unie du Cameroun* (Paris, 1975), pp. 59-61. See also Engelbert Mveng, *Histoire du Cameroun* (Paris, 1963), p. 453.

6 Heine, p. 126.

7 The earliest notices of the Bamum script were M. Goehring, "Der König und seine Schrift", and "Die Bamumschrift", *Der Evangelische Heidenbote*, LXXX (1907), 41-42 and 83-86. It received intermittent attention during the ensuing decades and has now been thoroughly discussed in I. Dugast and M.D. Jeffreys, *L'Ecriture des Bamoum sa naissance, son évolution, sa valeur phonétique, son utilisation* (IFAN-Cameroun, 1950) and in the three volumes of A. Schmitt, *Die Bamum-Schrift* (Wiesbaden, 1963).

8 This work, which is of considerable historical and anthropological importance, was translated into French by H. Martin as *Histoire et coutumes des Bamoum* (IFAN-Cameroun, 1952).

9 See Basile-Juléat Fouda, Henry de Julliot and Roger Lagrave, *Littérature camerounaise* (n.p., 1961), pp. 119-127.

10 Martin Z. Njeuma, "The Ancient History of Bamum from its Origin to the Eve of Colonialism", in *Symposium Leo Frobenius* (Cologne, 1974), pp. 249-265.

11 See Jean Fontvieille (Comp), *First International Exhibition of African Books Catalogue* (Yaounde, 1968), pp. 47-49. Also see François Bontinck, *Le catechisme kikongo de 1624: réedition critique* (Brussels, 1978).

12 Mveng, p. 455.

13 Reference in Fontvieille, p. 49. For some information on the other two Bulu works mentioned in this paragraph, see Pierre Alexandre and Jacques Binet, *Le groupe dit Pahouin (Fang–Boulou–Beti)* (Paris, 1958), pp. 124-126; Pierre Alexandre, "Proto-histoire du groupe Beti-Bulu-Fang : essai de synthèser prospore", *Cahiers d'Etudes Africaines*, 5 (1965), 503-60, especially pp. 538 *sqq.*; Brian Weinstein, *Gabon : Nation-Building on the Ogooué* (Cambridge, Mass., 1966), pp. 131-35.

14 Pierre Alexandre, "A Few Observations on Language Use Among Cameroonese *Elite* Families", in W.H. Whiteley (ed.), *Language Use and Social Change*, (London, 1971), pp. 254-261.

15 On this period in the history of the Kongo state, see Willy Bal, *Le Royaume du Congo aux XVe et XVIe siècles*, (Léopoldville-Brussels, 1963), and Jan Vansina, *Kingdoms of the Savanna* (Madison, 1966).

16 The greater part of this correspondence was printed considerably later, in L. da Paivo Manso, *Historia do Congo, Documentos* (Lisbon, 1877). See Gerald M. Moser, *Essays in Portuguese-African Literature* (University Park, Pa., 1969).

17 On the early study of the Kongo language, see C.M. Doke, "Early Bantu Literature : The Age of Brusciotto", *Bantu Studies*, IX (1935), ii, 87-112, and G. van Bulck, *Les recherches linguistiques au Congo belge* (Brussels, 1948), pp. 334-360.

18 There is reliable evidence, however, that an earlier catechism, now lost, was printed in Evora (Portugal) 1556 under the title *Cartilha de Doutrina christâ em lengoa de Congo* (Bal, *op. cit,*, p. 84).

19 This account of Kongo literature is considerably indebted to Mbelolo ya Mpiku, "Introduction à la littérature kikongo", *Research in African Literatures*, III (1972), ii, 117-161. This article, like A.C. Jordan's studies on the emergence of Xhosa writing, is a model of the kind of research that ought to be done on the early history of African-language literatures. For background information on the Protestant missions, see E.N. Braekman, *Histoire du Protestantisme au Congo* (Brussels, 1961).

20 For information on one of these, sometimes known as M.D. Nlemvo Don Zoao, see Francois Bontinck, "Donzwau M.D. Nlemvo (c. 1871-1938)", *Revue Africaine de Théologie*, II (1978), iii, 5-32.

21 It was done by Ruth Waldfridsson under the title *Ngiendolo ankwa klisto*. The Religious Tract Society later published two other versions of Bunyan's book : one by H. Ross Philips, *Vit'Avevela* (1906), and the other by Thomas Lewis, *Ngyend'a Mundutianzila* (no date given). A fourth translation, prepared by Carl Palmkvist, appeared in 1930.

22 Albert Gérard, "Aux sources de la littérature congolaise : Timoteo Vingadio," *Cahiers Congolais de la Recherche et du Développement*, XIII (1970), i, 57-62. See Catherine Mable, *Congo Cameos* (Philadelphia, 1953).

23 See André Mlassaki, *A.E. Disengomoka. Zingu kiandi : 1915-1965* (Kinshasa 1968). This biographical account, originally published in Kongo, has been translated into Lingala and Kituba.

24 One of the earliest Kimbanguist writings is the prophet's autobiography, which he dictated to his disciples in 1921; this was recently translated and printed in P. Raymaekers, *Histoire de Simon Kimbangu, prophète, d'après les écrivains Nfinangani et Nzungu* (Kinshasa, 1971). For further information on Kimbanguist doctrines and writings, see E. Anderson, *Messianic Popular Movements in the Lower Congo* (Uppsala, 1958), John M. Janzen and Wyatt MacGaffey, *An Anthology of Kongo Religion,* (Lawrence, 1954), Marie-Louise Martin, *Kimbangu. An African Prophet and His Church* (Oxford, 1975), W. Ustdorf, *Afrikanische Initiative : Das aktive Leiden des Propheten Simon Kimbangu* (Bern, 1975). Though it is the most important of the Kongo syncretic churches, Kimbangu's is not the only one, whether in Zaïre or in the adjacent French and Portuguese territories. In most cases, their hymnals exist only in typed or mimeographed form. According to information conveyed by Mbelolo ya Mpiku, special mention should be made of the Church of the Holy Ghost in Africa, which was founded by Esaïe Masamba. The latter was exiled in 1935 and died in 1964. He is the author of a 500-page prophetic book relating his "vision", *Ngunza wasimpama mu dikawa kwa Nzambi andi* ("The prophet's loyalty to God's message"), of which three typed copies only are in existence. His disciples are responsible for two hymnals : *Minkunga mia Kimpeve* ("Songs of the Spirit", Nzieta, 1965) is mimeographed, but *Nkunga mia Dibundu dia Mpeve Yanlongo mu Afelika* ("Songs of the Church of the Holy Ghost in Africa") was printed in Kinshasa in 1966. A highly original feature of those hymns is that many of them were composed by women.

25 George W. Carpenter, "LECO : La Librairie Evangélique du Congo, Léopoldville, Belgian Congo", *Books for Africa*, XXIV (1954), iii, 43-44.

26 Massaki himself translated his novel into French as *L'orphelin au coeur blessé* (Kinshasa, 1972). A Lingala and a Kituba versions have also been published.

27 Kituba is a widespread *lingua franca* derived from Kikongo. See Bernd Heine, *Status and Use of African Lingua Francas* (Munich, 1970), pp. 67-71.

28 For a closely argued exposé of this important linguistic problem, see Eyamba G. Bokamba, "Authenticity and the Choice of a National Language : The Case of Zaïre", *Présence Africaine*, 99/100 (1976), 104-142.

29 For background information, see René Lemarchand, *Rwanda and Burundi* (London, 1970). For a detailed survey of Rwanda writing, both in French and in the vernacular, see George Houdeau, *Panorama de la littérature rwandaise*, unpubl. diss. (Butare, 1979).

30 See G. van Bulck, *Les Recherches linguistiques au Congo belge*, p. 265; Marcel Walraet, *Les Sciences au Rwanda. Bibliographie (1894-1965)* (Brussels, 1966), pp. 80-85.

31 See especially Alexis Kagame, *La poésie dynastique au Rwanda* (Brussels, 1951) and *Introduction aux grands genres lyriques de l'ancien Rwanda* (Butare, 1969); André Coupez and Th. Kamanzi, *Récits historiques rwanda* (Tervuren, 1962), *Poésie dynastique rwanda* (Bujumbura, 1965) and *Littérature de cour au Rwanda* (Oxford, 1970).

32 See Gilles-Marius Dion, "Répertoire bibliographique de Monsieur l'Abbé Alexis Kagame (1938-1967)", *L'Informateur de l'Université Nationale du Rwanda*, II (1968), iv, 26-32. A short biographical notice can be found in J.M. Jadot, *Les écrivains africains du Congo belge et du Ruanda-Urundi* (Brussels, 1958), pp. 80-81.

33 See brief review by J. Gerson in *Africa*, XVII (1947), p. 148.

NOTES TO CHAPTER ELEVEN

1 Aubrey I. Richards, *The Multicultural States of East Africa* (Montreal and London, 1967) pp. 7-13. For general historical information, see Roland Oliver and Gervase Mathew (eds.), *History of East Africa* (Oxford, 1963) and Z.A. Marsh and G.W. Kingsnorth, *An Introduction to the History of East Africa (Cambridge, 1965)*. On the linguistic problem, see W. Whiteley, "The Changing Position of Swahili in West Africa", *Africa*, XXVI (1956), iv, 343-353.

2 Quoted in B. Struck, "Die Einheitssprache Deutsch-Ostafrikas", *Koloniale Rundschau*, 1921, 164-196.

3 Bernd Heine, *Status and Use of African Linguas Francas*, p. 92.

4 Robert Kilgour, *The Bible Throughout the World. A Survey of Scripture Translation* (London, 1939) pp. 42-43. For a detailed account of early Ganda writing, see R.A. Snoxall, "Ganda Literature", *African Studies* I (1942), 55-63.

5 Doke, "Scripture Translation into Bantu Languages", p. 94; C.H. Harford-Battersby, *Pilkington of Uganda* (London, 1898). It should be pointed out that in Buganda as in

Rwanda valuable linguistic work was done by Catholic White Fathers, such as L. Livinhac, whose *Essai de grammaire Ruganda* was published in Algiers in 1885.

6 Taban lo Liyong in his introduction to Ham Mukasa, *Sir Apolo Kagwa Discovers Britain* (London, 1975) p. vi.

7 Richards, *op. cit.*, p. 100.

8 On Ham Mukasa, see Taban's introduction mentioned above, Ernest Millar's introduction to *Uganda's Katikiro in England* (London, 1904), the biographical notice in Don Herdeck, *African Authors*, p. 262, and especially "The Story of Ham Mukasa, told by himself", in J.D. Mullins, *The Wonderful Story of Uganda* (London, 1904).

9 D.A. Low, *Buganda in Modern History* (Berkeley, 1971), p. 91.

10 Quoted in Wilfred Whiteley, *Swahili. The Rise of a National Language* (London, 1969), pp. 70-71.

11 Low, *op. cit.*, p. 184. Although the Catholic missions seem to have played only a minor part in the development of a vernacular literature, Catholics are very numerous in Uganda. On the eve of independence, they were claimed to be twice as numerous as the Protestants (see *Bilan du monde. Encyclopédie catholique du monde chrétien*, Tournai, Belgium, 1960, I, p. 575). As the leading Catholic layman of Kagwa's generation, and as a senior politician, Mugwanya's influence in this development was certainly far from negligible, even though it is usually on account of Kagwa's journey to England! Mugwanya played some part in Uganda party politics during the 1950s, and it is certainly revealing of his importance that, apart from the Kabaka's pamphlet and Musanje's little book mentioned below, his full-scale life history should have been written up in Joseph S. Kasirye's Ganda biography, *Stanislaus Mugwanya* (1965).

12 Stephen Neill, *A History of Christian Missions* (Harmondsworth, 1964), pp. 396-397.

13 Peter M. Gukiina, *Uganda : A Case Study in African Political Development* (Notre Dame, Indiana, 1972), p. 87.

14 Richards, *op. cit.*, pp. 40-45.

15 *Ibid.*, pp. 45-46.

16 See Charles Granston Richards, "The East African Literature Bureau", *Yearbook of Education* 1960, 536-539.

17 John Ndegwa, *Printing and Publishing in Kenya : An Outline of Development* (London, 1973), p. 15.

18 Okot's vernacular works are discussed in great detail in G.A. Heron, *The Poetry of Okot p'Bitek* (London, 1976).

19 Clement M. Doke, *Bantu: Modern Grammatical, Phonetical and Lexicographical Studies since 1860* (London, 1945), pp. 14-15.

20 *Ibid.*, p. 47.

21 William W. Neher and John C. Condon, "The Mass Media and Nation-Building in Kenya and Kenya and Tanzania," in David R. Smock and Kwamena Bentsi-Enchill (eds.), *The Search for National Integration in Africa* (New York, 1975), p. 269. See also Rosalynde Ainslie, *The Press in Africa : Communications Past and Present* (London, 1966).

22 John Hatch, *A History of Post-War Africa* (London, 1965), p. 331.

23 *Ibid., pp. 137-138.*

24 *Kenya Education Commission Report, Part 1* (Nairobi, 1965), para. 171, quoted in T.P. Gorman (ed.), *Language in Education in Eastern Africa* (Nairobi, 1970), p. 18.

25 A.M.K. Bagunywa, "The Teaching of Vernacular Languages in Primary Schools," in Gorman, *op. cit.*, pp. 25-29.

26 E. Gachukia, "The Teaching of Vernacular Languages in Kenya Primary Schools," in Gorman, *op. cit.*, pp. 18-24.

27 *Annual Report from East African Literature Bureau 1967-1968* (Dar es Salaam, Nairobi, Kampala, n.d.), p. 1.

28 Ali A. Mazuri, *The Political Sociology of the English Language : An African Perspective* (The Hague, 1975).

29 "An interview with Ngugi", *The Weekly Review*, 9 January, 1978, pp. 9-11.

30 "Ngugi Detained", *African Perspectives*, Feb.-Mar. 1978, pp. 14 and 35.

31 See Karugu Gitau, "The Play that was Banned", *Ibid.*, p. 13.

32 Fibi Munene, "The Last Word", *Daily Nation*, 14 Dec., 1977, p. 19.

33 *Nairobi Times*, 15 Jan, 1978, p. 1.

INDEX

INDEX

A